GW00992102

THE SACRED ROUTES OF UYGHUR HISTORY

THE SACRED ROUTES
OF UYGHUR HISTORY

Rian Thum

Harvard University Press

Cambridge, Massachusetts
London, England
2014

First Printing

Library of Congress Cataloging-in-Publication Data

Thum, Rian Richard.
The sacred routes of Uyghur history / Rian Thum.
pages cm
Includes bibliographical references and index.
ISBN 978-0-674-59855-3 (alkalne paper)   1. Uighur (Turkic people)—Historiography.
2. Uighur (Turkic people)—Travel.   3. Uighur (Turkic people)—Intellectual life.
4. Uighur (Turkic people)—Religion.   5. Manuscripts, Uighur—History.   6. Islam—China—
Takla Makan Desert Region—Manuscripts—History.   7. Pilgrims and pilgrimages—
China—Takla Makan Desert Region—History.   8. Sacred space—China—Takla Makan
Desert Region—History.   9. Takla Makan Desert Region (China)—History, Local.
10. Nationalism—China—Takla Makan Desert Region—History.   I. Title.
DS731.U4T48 2014
951'.60072—dc23   2014006244

CONTENTS

NOTE ON ORTHOGRAPHY

American Library Association—Library of Congress (ALA-LC) romanization systems are used for Persian, Uyghur, Russian, and Arabic. For the Turki dialect used in Altishahr before the development of the modern Uyghur alphabet, I have used the ALA-LC Persian transliteration system, with some vowel changes, mainly in words of Turkic origin. Pinyin is used for Chinese. Names and words with common English equivalents are written in the common English form that most closely matches the ALA-LC transliteration systems, for example, the prophet Muhammad and the Quran. The towns of Altishahr are given in the common English forms of the Turki/Uyghur names, for example, Kashgar instead of Kāshghar (Turki and Persian), Qăshqăr (Uyghur), or Kashi (Chinese). Non-English words that appear frequently in the text are italicized the first time but not thereafter, for example, tazkirah. The names of the personages discussed in the book have been written and pronounced differently in different periods. Because my transcriptions of these names from the original sources reflect such variations, the names of some personages appear with varying spellings.

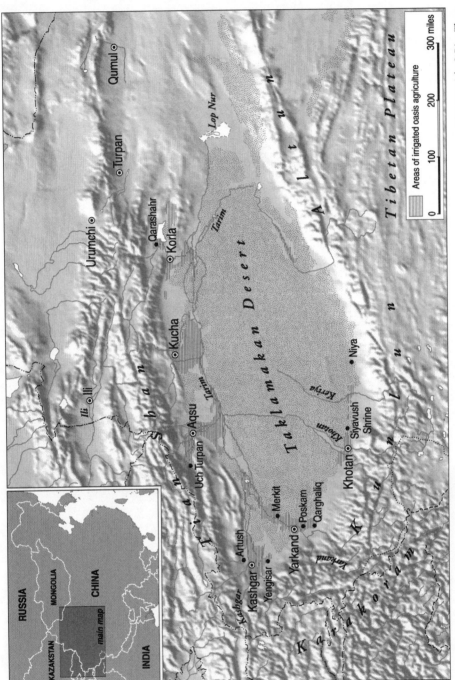

Map copyright © Rian Thum

INTRODUCTION

Like all historical works, this study is an attempt to link past and present, to make the cryptic realities of other times relevant, usable, and understandable today. In particular, it aims to tell the story of one community's imagination of the past as it changed over time. It is a biography of Uyghur history, the history created and learned by the oasis-dwelling Turkic Muslims of what is today far western China. I use the term "biography" figuratively, to emphasize the continuity and connectedness of Uyghur notions of the past across time, and because I want to imply that its story is less arcane than the word "historiography" would suggest. The story of Uyghur history making is a tale of conquests and rebellions, long journeys and moving rituals, oasis markets and desert shrines, foreigner saints, handwritten newspapers, friendships made, books loaned, censors duped. Because historical practice is an engagement with time, which itself exists in time, the story of histories past, the history of a history, is always at risk of sinking into a mire of abstraction. Moreover, the on-the-ground reality of history making, with its myriad associated practices, geographies, intellectual genealogies, and community dynamics, exposes the weaknesses of narrative explication. The central challenge in writing this study has been to make the biography of these accumulated embraces of the past, marching through time, seem as straightforward and natural as their reality deserves, without suppressing their complexity.

The "Uyghur history" that this study aims to understand is, in more precise terms, the Uyghur historical experience: the sum of those practices of learning and creating history that defined Uyghur interactions with the past. The focus is on history, not in the sense of those things that happened in the past, but rather, the habits and strategies by which people have engaged, consciously and intentionally, with what happened in the

1

past (or with what they believe happened in the past). There are many definitions of this kind of history to choose from, but most share an emphasis on the text.[1] A particularly compelling conception from Greg Dening calls history "the texted past for which we have a cultural poetic," the past "transformed into texts—texts written down, texts spoken, texts caught in the forms of material things."[2] My own research began as an attempt to understand the world of the Uyghur texted past but quickly expanded to an investigation of the whole range of human activities that supported and shaped that texted past, including practices such as book handling, shrine veneration, and travel. When we broaden our enquiry to include the means by which people experience history, the Uyghur example shows the text to be an essential element of historical practice, but only one among several.

Conceived in this broader fashion, the historical experience shares some of its territory with notions of memory, such as Halbwachs's "collective memory" or Assmann's "cultural memory."[3] In the many instances where the phenomena of history and memory overlap, I have taken history as my subject. Unlike memory—collective, cultural, or otherwise—history connotes a curiosity about the past on the part of either the producer or consumer. It tends to involve discovery in a way that memory does not.[4] Historical practice is a conscious, explicit effort to connect with the past, and its product exists outside its practitioners' minds. "Memory," on the other hand, connotes a mostly involuntary participation and a phenomenon rooted in the private realm of thought, even when those thoughts are held in common with others. The senses of curiosity, discovery, and effort were all quite immediately apparent in the attitudes toward history I encountered among Uyghurs. They are also present in the local historical works examined here, wherein the lost tombs of hero-saints are sought and found. Thus, while this book delimits history quite broadly in terms of the activities that constitute historical practice, it restricts "history" to intentional and active engagements with the past.

Names and Power, Past and Present

The nomenclature for the people and places involved in this study is both politically problematic and deeply entangled in the history of China's relationship with Inner Asia. And yet, this history cannot be discussed without reference to the peoples and places whose names are politically contentious. For this reason, an explanation of the terminological entanglements must unfold simultaneously with an introduction to the political and social upheaval of the last three centuries, the context in which this biography of Uyghur history proceeds. The place in question is that area of Central Asia, now controlled by China, in which Uyghurs and their ancestors have constituted the majority of the inhabitants. It is known among many Uyghurs as *Altishahr*, the Uyghur for "six cities." But the name *Altishahr* is not to be found on any map; it is a term used by people who are denied the political power to draw maps. The Uyghurs today live under Chinese rule, in a political system calibrated to strictly limit knowledge production and dissemination to ideas that support the status quo. In this environment, only the Chinese word, *Xinjiang*, and its Uyghur transliteration, *Shinjang*, are acceptable names for the region in official public discourse, while Uyghur terms such as *Altishahr* persist in everyday speech.

These tensions over geographic names are, in a basic sense, a product of conquest and colonization, though not of a simple us-versus-them dynamic. Indeed, the most powerful actors in the story of Altishahr's attachment to China were neither Chinese nor Uyghur. The initial incorporation of Altishahr into a China-based empire in 1759 was a historical accident, an unintended consequence of a transgenerational power struggle between the Manchus and the Dzungar Mongols. The Manchu ruler who brought a violent end to this feud was the Qianlong emperor, ruler of the Great Qing Empire, which encompassed Manchuria, Mongolia, China, and Tibet. From his capital in Beijing, Qianlong directed an enormous assault on the Dzungars, sending primarily Manchu and Mongol soldiers on a thousand-mile trek to the steppes beyond the western border of his empire. Qianlong's grandfather had subjugated the Dzungars before, and upon defeating the Dzungars in 1759, Qianlong took steps to ensure that they would never challenge Manchu supremacy in Inner Asia again. He ordered, and appears to have achieved, the complete extermination of the Dzungars. However, the Dzungars left behind a troublesome inheritance, one that continues to haunt its masters.

The Dzungar state that Qianlong annihilated was a different entity from the one his grandfather had humbled. Between the time of Qianlong's grandfather and Qianlong's own day, the Dzungars had extended their rule beyond the nomad-dominated steppes into the agricultural oases that ring the Taklamakan Desert to the south, namely, Altishahr. Some oasis elites saw the defeat of the Dzungars as an opportunity to throw off the extractive outsider rule of non-Muslims. Qianlong, however, was determined to take possession of everything that his vanquished Dzungar foes had owned, and so, although there is no hint that the emperor had previously held any interest in conquering the oases of Altishahr, he instructed his generals to enforce his new claim. The final battles between the indigenous Turkic Muslims and the Manchu invaders took place in 1759. Thus, Altishahr entered the China-based Qing Empire, where it was rather awkwardly attached to the steppe homeland of the now-extinct Dzungars, in an administrative unit called *Xinjiang,* "the new dominion." The territory was a huge drain on Qing resources, and in the following century, officials frequently advised their emperors to abandon it. But the emperors stood firm, and despite numerous Altishahri rebellions, some temporarily quite successful, the Qing were still in control over the region when the Republic of China replaced the old imperial system in 1912. Remarkably, despite the chaos of the Republican period, Altishahr remained under Chinese rule, with the exception of a brief moment of independence in 1933–1934, and, arguably, 1944–1949. Later, the Chinese Communist Party would strive, so far as was possible, to model the borders of its new People's Republic of China (PRC) after those of the Qing Empire. By this logic, Altishahr and Xinjiang would be transformed from dependencies of the Inner Asian Qing Empire to an integral part of the nation-state of China. The PRC's massive effort to "stretch the short, tight skin of the nation over the gigantic body of the empire," in the famous words of Benedict Anderson,[5] required a reimagination of Altishahr's history, in which Altishahr disappeared entirely into Xinjiang, the "new dominion." This geographical hybrid, an unnatural grafting of steppes and oasis-ringed desert, was itself reimagined as "the Northwest border region of our great motherland," (i.e., the nation-state of China), and given a new history.[6] The new history took previous interludes of China-based domination, in the Han and Tang, as evidence for a narrative that suggested the "new dominion" had always been a natural part of a monolithic, millennia-old Chinese nation.

Many of the current inhabitants of Altishahr, most of whom self-identify as Uyghurs, contest the official Chinese histories, and a large number of Uyghurs, probably a very strong majority, see Chinese rule over the region as illegitimate. The Chinese government's heavy-handed security policies prevent independent systematic opinion polling, but in a dozen years of regular visits to the region, I have rarely heard Uyghurs express support for PRC rule and frequently encountered aspirations for an independent Uyghur state. Such views are especially pervasive outside the regional capital of Urumchi, and, since the uprisings of 2009, increasingly mixed with ethnic animosity. It is unknown whether central government officials are aware of this situation or whether they believe their own claims that antistate ideas and acts among the Uyghurs are the product of a small group of troublemakers, fed on insidious foreign influences. Studies of Uyghur opinion by Chinese anthropologists and sociologists tend to be conducted in intimidating contexts by Chinese speakers using translators, an approach that yields rosy pictures of Uyghur attitudes. Meanwhile, acts of resistance, from the publication of underground literature to deadly knife attacks on police stations, continue throughout Altishahr and, more recently, in China proper. Like the Qing emperors before them, PRC officials have responded by clinging ever more tightly to a region that until recently produced relatively little in the way of natural resources, sending soldiers, settlers, and construction crews from China's interior in an attempt to pacify a largely resistant Uyghur population. In this historical and political context, geographical names have taken on an exaggerated significance.

Outside informal, spoken Uyghur discourse, *Altishahr* is not a commonly used term for the region examined in this book. It is also a term that held far more currency a century ago than it does today. As such, it is something of an archaism, but it is a strangely useful one, because it lacks strong political resonance.[7] The tangle of the last centuries' political struggles has left us without any other neutral term for this region, one of the world's important and cohesive cultural-geographical units. The full official name of the administrative unit that contains Altishahr is Xinjiang Uyghur Autonomous Region. However, the Chinese word *Xinjiang* is a symbol, for many Uyghurs, of illegitimate outsider domination. On the other end of the political spectrum, the mere mention of the term *Shărqi Türkistan* (Eastern Turkestan), a preferred term of Uyghur nationalists, is enough to draw accusations of separatism or even terrorism from Han Chinese. The Communist Party of China regards the term as an expression of nostalgia for the short-lived independent Islamic Republic of East Turkestan (1933–1934). Inside the region itself, the phrase *Eastern Turkestan* is one that must only be whispered. I hope that my use of the Uyghur term *Altishahr* will reflect Uyghur geographical understandings while eschewing political polemic, and perhaps avoid inviting either Uyghur nationalists or the primarily Han Chinese rulers of the region to dismiss this study for political reasons.

The term *Altishahr* has other merits too. It roughly fits the areas traditionally inhabited by the people who now call themselves Uyghurs, and thus the historical tradition under investigation here, while excluding the former Dzungar homelands of northern Xinjiang. Altishahr (alternative name, *Yettishahr*—"seven cities") was also the preferred term in many of the histories discussed here,[8] whereas *Eastern Turkestan* only entered the local textual tradition along with nationalist discourse in the 1930s. Because it is an indigenous term, *Altishahr* is also reflective of the ways people imagined the place in which they lived. The name *Altishahr* (six cities) is an eloquent hint at the geography of the region and at the relationship between the land and its inhabitants. There are many more than six cities in Altishahr, and no one has ever been able to establish common agreement on which of them are *the* six cities, but, as a description of connected points rather than continuous territory, the term reflects an imagination of the region as an archipelago of habitable oases on the edges of the enormous Taklamakan Desert. Finally, as a term that creates geographical connections across uninhabited space, *Altishahr* is particularly fitting. The story of Uyghur history is, among other things, an exploration of the ways that historical practices have drawn these cities together. The work of making and learning history involved activities particularly suited to that task, including regional pilgrimage and the literal binding together of local texts into larger composite books.

The Turkic-speaking, settled Muslim people of Altishahr have not been known as Uyghurs for very long. The first precursor to the current usage is probably to be found in the pen name of a reformist author who, beginning around 1911, styled himself Child of the Uyghur, claiming descent for his people from the great Turkic Buddhist civilization that built several powerful kingdoms in the ninth century.[9] It was many decades after Child of the Uyghur began writing that the name caught on among the rest of the settled Turkic speakers of Altishahr. In the meantime, people called themselves *Musulmān* (Muslim), or *yerlik* (local), or identified themselves by the name of their home oasis. To avoid anachronistically applying the name Uyghur to people who likely had never heard the term, and to circumvent the unwieldy phrase "settled, Turkic-speaking inhabitants of Altishahr," I have called the people in question "Altishahri" (people of Altishahr) whenever discussing the periods before the wide adoption of the term *Uyghur*. It must be remembered, however, that this term was not used by Altishahris themselves as an ethnonym, even though the geographic designation was common. It is thus a poor solution to the difficult question of how to name this group. However, *Altishahri*, if only partly reflective of indigenous terminology, at least has the benefit of avoiding the confusion that the indigenous terms *Muslim* or *Uyghur* would cause.

Such terminological difficulties remind us that history, despite its popular identification with the past, is at all times most relevant to the present. As both a practice and an imagination, history shapes communal and individual identities, enacts and provides justifications for political projects, and serves as a continually re-created general framework for understanding the present. Not only does Uyghur culture fit this pattern, but it can also be seen as an extreme expression of the significance of history in the present, inasmuch as historical practice is unusually prominent in Uyghur society. During fieldwork in Xinjiang, I found historical practice to be at once necessarily political and highly personal for most Uyghurs, both a popular pastime and a patriotic calling. It was something that everyone could and did engage in. The near ubiquity of daily historical engagement, represented most notably by the consumption of historical novels, historical debate and discussion in public places such as teahouses, and the private exchange of books, lends, in my view, the study of Uyghur concepts of history an absolute significance in addition to its comparative value. Concepts of history and the past vary wildly across different cultures, but the ramifications of this variation are rarely considered in depth. This study aims to understand how Uyghur history has functioned over the last three hundred years, and, to a lesser extent, how it differs from historical practices that have come to dominate China and the West. It argues that such an understanding is indispensible to any analysis of current Uyghur identity and the uncomfortable Uyghur relationship to the Chinese state. Moreover, it argues that the analysis of historical traditions in societies that have been considered "marginal" to the world's civilizational centers offers new insights into the nature of history as a practice common to all societies.

Overview of the Book

Although the story stretches from the seventeenth century to the twenty-first, its narrative begins from the perspective of historical practice as it existed in the first three decades of the twentieth century, tracing the roots of the system backward in time, and its transformation into new practices in the present. Those first decades of the twentieth century provide us with the valuable intersection of a vibrant manuscript tradition and a wealth of sources outside the tradition. Until at least the 1930s, the manuscript dominated the written world almost completely. Foreign visitors to Altishahr assembled large collections of manuscripts, providing us with rich cross-sections of the tradition. Only a tiny fraction of these manuscripts has yet been put to use by professional historians. As a body of texts and as individual works they are themselves important, but their value is further magnified by the testimonies of the outsiders who collected them and recorded their own observations regarding the ways manuscripts were used. Because the manuscript tradition is so recent, we also have a handful of insider descriptions preserved in a genre that only appeared after the manuscripts had given way to print: the memoir. In sum, Altishahr provides an unusually rich opportunity to understand how history was practiced in the world of the manuscript. Moreover, the Uyghur historical practices of the present can only be understood as they relate to this very recent dominance of manuscript technology.

This book thus begins on familiar historical ground by examining the written text in Altishahr, first looking at the stories and traditions preserved in written texts and then turning to habits of textual use and production. Chapter 1 offers an overview of the Altishahri (Uyghur) textual landscape as it stood at the beginning of the twentieth century, introducing Uyghur historical content that is critical for understanding the arguments that unfold in succeeding chapters. It demonstrates how the Altishahri material challenges common notions of textual indigeneity, leading a Uyghur man to cry over an apparently foreign hero. The chapter also serves as a foundation for the rest of the book by identifying a particular genre, called *tazkirah* (hereafter called tazkirah), as the primary textual vehicle of popular local history. The shaping of this new genre was necessary to make room for local heroes among the inherited foreign heroes, and the boundaries of the tazkirah were drawn along the lines of the social practices in which it was embedded. The tazkirah, Altishahr's predominant genre of local history, was intimately connected to the veneration of local saints, at whose tombs tazkirahs were read aloud to large audiences.

Chapter 2 examines the role of manuscript technology in shaping Altishahri views of the past, and at the same time prepares the way for our departure from the text as the central axis of history. A close look at the role of books in Altishahr suggests that the text was not a vessel of meaning but instead a fulcrum around which meaning turned. That is to say, texts functioned more as sites of debate than stores of content. The flexibilities of the manuscript tradition allowed for extensive reader participation in the creation of the text, and the new genre of local history was shaped through the practices of marginal notation, abbreviation, composite binding, labeling, and reader editing. The text is treated both as a physical object and in its social context, so that book production and book recitation are seen to be equal in significance to the content of the text, and as practices that participate in the continuous creation of the text's meaning. Manuscripts appear not so much as windows on a textual world, but as sites at which the community negotiated the meaning of the past. This raises the question of what else may have served as such an axis of Altishahr's shifting historical tradition, and the first answer proposed is the shrine.

Chapter 3 thus begins an exploration of place and the interaction of the text with place. It starts with an ethnographic description of historical recitations at shrines and traces continuities between pilgrimage practices in the present and those of the nineteenth and early twentieth centuries. The resulting picture of pilgrimage illustrates the authority of place inherited by texts during recitation, the sacred context of interactions with the past, and the experiential nature of historical practice in Altishahr. The spiritual presence of the saint and liminal character of the shrine also have implications for perceptions of time, which in turn reflect the oasis geography of the region.

Chapter 4 investigates the pilgrimage tradition as a mover of people, and argues that the deployment of origin tales along pilgrims' routes helped maintain a regional identity system before the arrival of nationalism. The chapter begins with an example of the originary content of the tazkirahs and then turns to the articulation of mobility, manuscripts, and graffiti, which knitted together a shared history for the Altishahris. Surviving shrine graffiti demonstrate that pilgrims crisscrossed Altishahr, binding the inhabitants of the various oases together through a network of travel and spreading local historical narratives (recited at the shrines) across the region. More importantly, this section considers the effects of the display of the graffito-records of travel, which advertised to pilgrims their connection to other oases. The geographical implications of collecting narratives through travel are reflected in the composite manuscripts that bind together multiple local histories, and demonstrate local weighting but region-wide coverage. It is argued that the shared view of the past supported by these phenomena constitutes a form of imagined community that is more complex and self-conscious than ethnicity but less homogenous than the nation. The last part of the chapter traces connections between this modular, local history and the patronage of the local rulers established under the Qing system of indirect rule, which bound Altishahr to China.

Chapter 5 examines the fate of the tazkirah tradition in the face of new worldviews and technologies, especially nationalism and printing. These forces, which had their own unique trajectories in Altishahr, undermined some of the basic pillars of tazkirah-related traditions, especially the flexibility of the manuscript and the oasis-based geographic arrangement of Altishahri identity. However, when we return to the content of Altishahri histories, we find that, in addition to text and place, personage was a major vector of historical meaning, one which has risen to new prominence in the print- and nationalism-dominated context of contemporary Uyghur historical practice. The histories attached to shrines were, of course, also linked to the personages buried in those shrines. As the practice of pilgrimage and the copying of manuscripts came under increasing government restriction in the second half of the twentieth century, the Altishahri historical tradition shifted to the world of print, and specifically, to the fictionalized historical biographical novel. When place and community-authored texts faded as fulcra of meaning, they were replaced by personage in the fictionalized biographies that came to dominate popular historical discourse. The idiosyncrasies of the hagiographical genre in its interaction with the shrine thus reemerged in the biographical novels of the last two decades, preserving particularly Uyghur approaches to the past in a new, local incarnation of nationalism.

Chapter 6 shows how the phenomena described in the earlier chapters functioned in their interaction. At the same time, it emphasizes the ragged edges of the system that has been sketched throughout the book, and the articulation of this system with other traditions of historical practice. The chapter follows the case of the saint called Afaq Khoja, perhaps the most written-about and well-known figure in Altishahr's history, arguing that, until now, the operation of Uyghur historical and religious traditions has been widely misunderstood. In the process, a final important element—the state—is integrated into our picture of Uyghur historical practice, for the story of Afaq begins with a saint becoming political ruler and ends with the Chinese state burning a novel about the saint. The story's twists and turns lay bare the profound effects of the manuscript and shrine on both Uyghur identity and Chinese attempts to assimilate the Uyghurs and provide a synoptic view of Uyghur history making as an alternative approach to understanding the past.

Intersections

This book focuses on traditions and interconnections within Altishahri society, and yet transregional connections will appear throughout. It tells the story of a regional society maintained in the context of such connections. For example, some wealthy Altishahri pilgrims made the long journey to Mecca for the *hajj,* sometimes spending many years abroad before returning home. Businessmen and caravaneers traveled to Kashmir and Ferghana. The Dzungars forcibly removed Altishahri farmers to the Yili valley. Small numbers of Chinese-speaking Muslim pilgrims visited Altishahri shrines, though linguistic barriers prevented them from participating in the historical tradition described here. Some well-off Altishahris held slaves who originated from Kashmir.[10] Invasions from Khoqand brought large numbers of people from the Ferghana Valley, including the descendents of refugees from Altishahr who had left during the Qing conquest. Merchants from Khoqand established permanent residences in Kashgar and took local wives. Europeans in Altishahr pursued varied goals, attempting to influence the state and even converting some Altishahris to Christianity. It was in spite of (and perhaps partly in reaction to) all these global connections that Altishahri society became self-consciously distinctive. The historical tradition described here created a sense of the local from global raw materials. While greater emphasis is placed on this sense of the local, it is important to emphasize that the society that cultivated this historical tradition was, of course, neither clearly bounded nor autonomous. Rather, it was a society with highly flexible and constantly active means for promoting a sense of boundedness in the face of an almost cosmopolitan connection to the rest of the world.

Altishahr's distinct local historical tradition, and thus its sense of boundedness, was built in large part from elements of the very cultures that it was defined against. Given the connections just described, it will be of no surprise that much of what looms large in the Altishahri tradition, and thus this book, has been common in other times and places, particularly within the Islamic world. Thus, the blending of Persian, Arabic, and Turkic historical traditions, the importance of shrines and local pilgrimage, the prominence of particular genres and poetic meters such as *masnavī* and *ghazal,* and the initial reluctance to abandon the manuscript for print, just to take a few obvious examples, can all be found in many cultures from Dehli to Istanbul. Pilgrimage, hagiography, and nationalism more generally find close parallels over a much larger swath of Eurasia. Few, if any, of the individual traditions and practices of Altishahri historical practice were unique, even if the sum of those shared parts was. This does not, of course, make these phenomena any less interesting in their Altishahri context. On the contrary, I hope that a careful analysis of the interaction of these shared elements in their particular Altishahri constellations, under conditions—geographical, political, and cultural—particular to the Altishahr of the nineteenth and twentieth centuries, will bring into relief new significances of practices that have been thoroughly studied in other contexts and perhaps even open new avenues of inquiry in well-trodden fields.

Readers already familiar with Uyghur history will want to know where this book fits among the works of scholarship on the Uyghurs, Xinjiang, and China. In the decades after the heyday of European exploration and espionage in Altishahr (ca. 1875–1938), quite little scholarship has been produced about the Uyghurs, and large parts of Altishahr's history have yet to receive even the most basic treatment. Therefore, very little of this book is an argument *against* any particular strain of Uyghur-focused scholarship. It is, instead, an argument *for* a particular understanding of phenomena that have until now been hidden or ignored. It is a historical exploration heavily influenced by the anthropological tradition of seeking ideas of global comparative value in the specifics of a single culture investigated deeply.

However, the trail of Uyghur historical practice does occasionally, almost haphazardly, cross territory covered by other scholars of the Uyghurs, and in some cases the results of my investigations raise challenges to their approaches. Two of these approaches stand out. One is Justin Rudelson's argument that exclusionary local oasis identities have acted as significant obstacles to large-scale identity formation. This approach is also linked to arguments that the settled Turki inhabitants of Altishahr simply had no ethnic or regional identity before the construction of Uyghur nationalism in the 1920s.[11] The notions of a shared history analyzed in the present book make such scenarios difficult to imagine. The origins of arguments against an earlier shared identity are understandable, insofar as nineteenth-century Altishahri identity maintenance bore little resemblance to forms of identity with which scholars are most familiar, for example, Benedict Anderson's nationalism or Barth's ethnicity. Indeed, I argue that the Altishahri identity represents an alternative type of imagined community to those described by Anderson or Barth: a relatively homogeneous regional identity nourished by manuscript technology and internal pilgrimage in an agrarian society. When we cleave to the Altishahri evidence and venture outside the limited catalog of identity forms that includes nation and ethnicity, the shape of a pre-Uyghur identity emerges in spite of our nation-dominated present. The Altishahri case suggests that many more alternative forms of imagined community are waiting to be described in other parts of the world.

The second strain of Uyghur scholarship that intersects this book is the body of work on recent Uyghur nationalism and resistance. Such work is extremely useful, but it sometimes flattens out Uyghur history and culture, shoehorning events of the last thirty years into frameworks that make the Uyghurs interchangeable with any other colonial subjects, rather than focusing on what is particular to the Uyghur case. Here my intervention is quite basic. Nationalism and resistance have limited explanatory value on their own; they can only be understood through their interaction with the idiosyncrasies of the individual cultural contexts in which they appear. My approach is to look beyond nationalism and resistance for deeper (chronologically and culturally) roots of Uyghur interaction with Chinese rule. I prefer to explain nationalism and resistance by older processes than to use nationalism and resistance as explanations. Despite these arguments, however, I hope that the reader will see such engagements with Western scholars as subordinate to my engagement with the Uyghur/Altishahri tradition and pay greater attention to arguments that, as of yet, await opponents: my analyses of Uyghur historical practice, linkages between time and geography, and the interface of mobility in the pilgrimage tradition with manuscript technology. In the later chapters, this book engages with questions of nationalism, identity, and even resistance, but it is not a book about nationalism, identity, or resistance.

If my challenges to Uyghur specialists are incidental, my interactions with Sinology are more deliberate. In the field of Chinese history, I hope that this work will show that exciting opportunities are to be found in the extraordinarily rich body of Uyghur and Turki sources, historical and otherwise. Because today's Uyghurs live within the borders of the People's Republic of China, they are too often conceived of first as Chinese subjects, whether as China's Islamic resistance, as examples of "Islam in China," or as a part of Chinese frontier studies. This book shows what happens when we start looking at Uyghur/Altishahri history through Uyghur/Altishahri perspectives: when Altishahr ceases to appear as a frontier or margin and begins to be seen as the center. I don't suggest that it is the only way to write the history of this region. Much extraordinary work has been done from the state's perspective,[12] some of it using Chinese sources alone. But I do think that history from the Altishahri perspective is a kind of history that needs to be done and hasn't been done enough.

This book also describes and analyzes numerous practices of popular Islam that have until now been poorly documented in print. Despite the significance of local shrine pilgrimage, the practice is often omitted or de-emphasized in characterizations of Islam among the Uyghurs.[13] Some of the limited work on shrines and pilgrimage has viewed such phenomena as a folk practice rather than an integral aspect of Islam in Altishahr. The texts that are central to the practice of pilgrimage, the hagiographical tazkirahs, are no longer accorded canonical status by historians and anthropologists, Uyghur and non-Uyghur alike. However, they were foundational texts that defined what it meant to be a Muslim for many generations of Altishahris into the middle of the twentieth century. To doubt the hagiographies was to become an infidel. These texts represent, in effect, a forgotten Islam. This forgotten Islam is papered over by our assumptions about what it means to be Sunni or Hanafi, assumptions based on a small group of texts read by a small segment of the elites. In the wider Islamic context, I'm not alone in trying to bring aspects of popular practice into our conceptions of Islam. Scholars are increasingly interested in how extratextual practices constituted Islam for people at all levels of society, for example, in Afzar Moin's *The Millennial Sovereign,* or Shahzad Bashir's *Sufi Bodies.*[14] But in the effort to counterbalance the old-fashioned and outsized emphasis on a small range of legalistic texts, it is important not to downplay the role of the written text itself. Nile Green's work on Indian Sufism, which I encountered rather late in the development of this project, provides an excellent example of the rewards that a focus on the relationship between written texts and popular practices can produce.[15] I share Green's conviction that the articulation of shrines, saints, and texts holds a special power to create sacred geographies and systems of belonging. Focusing on this articulation in the Altishahri case shows us that even in the manuscript tradition written texts can be both produced and consumed at all levels of society and uncovers an entirely new sacred canon, which defined Islam for many generations of Altishahris, even among highly educated elites.

Above all else, though, this is a book about history: what it is, how it is done, how it is shaped by technology and geography, and how it affects other realms of human activity, political, social, and subjective. Greg Dening once remarked that it is nearly impossible to say anything new about history. For those of us outside Uyghur culture, Altishahri historical practice, in its particular combination of approaches, is itself a new statement on history. A staggering amount of intellectual capital has been invested in the interrogation of elite Western historical practices, yielding discoveries that have changed the way we read, write, and think. Somewhat less attention has been paid to well-known societies such as China, Persia, and India. Those societies that have been viewed as marginal to "great civilizations" have inspired even less historiographical curiosity.[16] They represent a treasury of historical insight that has only begun to be tapped. In drawing from that rich resource, this book aims to contribute to a field that, if it had any real institutional form, might be called something like global comparative historiography. It argues that the Altishahri example, and for that matter any other understudied society's approach to the past, presents to the world a mode of history making that transforms our normative portrait of history as a universal human endeavor. Altishahr's is a history created by mass participation rather than experts, more akin to *Wikipedia* than to the *Histories* of Herodotus or the *Epic of Sundiata*; a history transmitted in sacred liminal places rather than royal courts, private studies, classrooms, monasteries, or museums; a history that ignores the crevasse that is supposed to exist between written and oral modes of historical practice; and a history that, in the mundane and sacred practicalities of its continued reproduction, knitted together a regional identity without the trappings of the nation. My goal is to make this system of historical practice, one that is alien to most readers, seem natural, and perhaps by doing so, make more familiar modes of historical practice seem alien.

1

THE HISTORICAL CANON

The past is an unimaginably vast resource, and no culture can colonize its expansive landscape completely. But in most societies certain parts of the past, shaped as history, become an "our history," the mediated past that matters to a certain group of people, at a certain time. The most eloquent and durable artifacts of such manipulations of the past are written texts. Although the pilgrimages, rituals, recitations, conversations, and oral traditions that comprised the larger part of historical practice in the Altishahr of a century ago are lost to us in their original evanescent forms—voice, gesture, travel—the written texts that were both by-products of and tools for these practices have survived in great numbers, presenting us with a remarkably rich picture of the content of history as it was cultivated in Altishahr. One goal of this book is to expand the focus of historiography beyond the written or memorized word to those impermanent forms of historical practice, but we cannot begin to understand Altishahri historical practice without some knowledge of the contents and forms of narratives that Altishahris deployed as they molded parts of the past into their own history. There is no greater source for this knowledge than the thousands of Altishahri manuscripts that are preserved in archives around the world, and so we begin by tracing out the constantly shifting historical canon as it was frozen in these artifacts. However, our indulgence in the world of the written narrative will be short-lived, for even as we focus our gaze on the text, we will find the analysis inevitably drawn outward to the social context that framed and even constituted history in Altishahr.

The phrase "our history" (Uygur: *bizning tarikhimiz* or simply *bizning tarikh*) was one I heard often in Altishahr, where it implied history pertinent to members of the Uyghur ethnic group, the descendants of the

Altishahris. In the context of the tensions between Uyghurs and their predominantly Han Chinese rulers, the phrase said as much about what history for the Uyghurs is not (i.e., the histories propagated by Han Chinese authors and institutions) as it did about what that history is. It was also a response to my own presence, as a foreign observer or participant. To my ears, the phrase also hinted at a suspicion that histories are culturally defined, that the salience of a certain historical discourse ends where the group who shared in the same systems of meaning ends.

There are many processes by which the selecting and shaping of the past into a group's "our history" occurs. In the Silk Road hub of Altishahr, where, like most places in the world, cultures continuously met, conquered, merged, and exchanged, many of the oldest historical texts may be attributed to a process of inheritance. The people who call themselves "Uyghur" today participate in a culture forged from Iranic, Semitic, Turkic, Mongolic, Indic, and Chinese influences, which contributed to the Uyghurs parts of their own "our history"s.[1] This process of inheritance, in which one people adopted the histories of others as their own, involved a winnowing at the points of both transmission and adoption. Written texts that existed in large numbers or were performed with great frequency in the transmitting culture had the greatest chance of being transported and of finding fertile ground in Altishahr. But not all texts that arrived in Altishahr flourished, for people had to find relevance in the foreign material. Many popular texts from Western Turkestan, for example, made it to Altishahr but were never fully embraced.[2] Yet despite the constraints on textual transmission from distant times and places, many foreign texts *were* adopted, to such an extent that more than half of the Altishahri manuscripts surviving today are copies of texts with foreign roots.

A millennium ago, when Buddhism, Zoroastrianism, Christianity, and Manichaeism in Altishahr began succumbing to the swords and sermons of Muslims, the region also started to inherit the heroes and villains of a wide Islamic world's vision of the past. From Indian roots came the fabulous tales of *Hazār Afsāne;* from a distant Greek memory, the story of Alexander the Great; from Persia, the *Shāhnāmah*'s account of great epic warriors; from the biblical tradition, tales of prophets; and from Arabia, chronicles of the Caliphs and star-crossed lovers. All of these depictions of the past would thrive in the manuscripts of Altishahr, where textual survival depended on copying, and copying was spurred by reader demand. For many Uyghurs today, each of these texts is fully and equally authentic, a source for the true events of their past. The heroes are no longer foreign; they have been domesticated and naturalized. Some of them, it turns out, were not entirely foreign to begin with.

By the end of the seventeenth century, however, new works from outside Altishahr ceased to be adopted. Virtually no manuscript works authored outside Altishahr after 1700, including Altishahri translations of such texts, are to be found in the archives of Altishahri manuscripts. At about the same time, local Altishahri authors began to produce their own written historical texts in increasing numbers. The emergence of locally authored histories, circulating side by side with older foreign texts, was critical to the formation of a historical tradition uniquely useful to Altishahris. The shape of this canon of historical literature is clearest in the period of about 1880–1930, during which many of the greatest surviving collections of Altishahri manuscripts were formed. This chapter presents an introduction to the texts that formed the foundations of the historical tradition as it was practiced in Altishahr during that period, beginning with inherited texts that can be traced deep into the past and far from Altishahr, and continuing with local texts produced in Altishahr itself. The boundary between inherited and local texts is of course not always clear. Inherited texts were often thoroughly reworked and appropriated, while many locally written texts display influences from distant cultures. Still, it seems useful to distinguish between the products of authors, both individual and communal, who shared symbols, geography, and language with their Altishahri readers, and those whose systems of meaning were less familiar in Altishahr.

Our survey begins with a tale that demonstrates the difficulties of distinguishing between inherited and local texts, and shows the complex means by which apparently foreign texts were domesticated. As a reminder that rich social contexts determined the meaning of each of the texts discussed below, this first stop in the Altishahri historical canon will be accessed by way of a live performance in a small and rarely visited oasis. The performance presents the curious case of a venerable Uyghur cleric crying over the death of a pre-Islamic Persian hero. It is an event that both sheds light on Altishahri notions of textual indigeneity, and provides a glimpse of the social contexts in which historical texts were delivered. While most of this book treats the historical tradition of Altishahr since 1700, analysis of the cleric's tale also serves as an introduction to the complex literary history of the region as it stretches back to pre-Islamic times. It illustrates a blending of foreign inheritance, deeply rooted—sometimes pre-Islamic—local traditions, and more recent Altishahri accretions and transformations, all of which shaped Altishahr's textual corpus, and in many cases, individual texts. And while it touches on Altishahr's deep past, this exemplary tale will also provide the reader with a taste of the Altishahri historical corpus as a living and lively tradition before we turn to the manuscripts that captured in physical form aspects of the tradition as it existed a century ago.

Cosmopolitan Inheritance: The Case of Siyāvush

Our exemplary historical narrative is the story of Siyāvush, a tale with a very complicated biography of its own, which, in its most famous version, reaches its tragic climax in the following verses:

> They will strike off this guiltless head of mine,
> And lay my diadem in my heart's blood.
> For me no bier, shroud, grave, or weeping people,
> But like a stranger I shall lie in dust,
> A trunk beheaded by the scimitar;[3]

Such were the words of the dying hero Siyāvush in Firdawsī's famous tenth-century rendition of the great epic of Iran, the *Shāhnāmah,* or *Book of Kings.* Seemingly endless ranks of heroes march through the verses of Firdawsī's epic, but for readers in Altishahr, Siyāvush holds a special place: among all the legendary champions of Iran, only this one is said to have made his home in Altishahr, in the city of Khotan. More importantly, Siyāvush died there, and in spite of the lament reproduced above, his grave has not been forgotten. To an outsider, Siyāvush may be no more "real" than Achilles, but to the pilgrims who weep at his grave, he is a martyr and a friend of God.

The memory of Siyāvush is remarkably tenacious, as has been demonstrated vividly over the last half century of trials. Until the last few decades, Siyāvush's grave lay on the main intercity road that strung together all the important southern oases, from Kashgar to Niya, in a single curving line. In those days, travelers between the neighboring towns of Khotan and Chira could visit the tomb along their way, and the shrine benefited from steady traffic.[4] Today, though, the old road has been replaced by a new asphalt highway that passes seventeen kilometers to the southwest. Like so many Islamic holy places, the grave of Siyāvush has also been the target of the Chinese Communist Party's varying efforts to control or eliminate Islamic practices. According to a neighbor of the shrine, the adjacent mosque was taken over to be used for Party business and the book that contained the story of Siyāvush was confiscated. Yet pilgrims still come to pray by the grave of Siyāvush, leaving cloth ribbons on the trees in record of their visits.

The pilgrims come to an oasis, Băsh Toghraq, that is no longer on the way to anywhere else, a patch of irrigated land about six kilometers across, hemmed in on all sides by the sands of the Taklamakan Desert. Those sands whip across the only road to the oasis, and in places bury it, before the road dives under the shelter of tall, thin poplars at the edge of town. Like most oases in Altishahr, Băsh Toghraq is watered by a stream carrying melted snows from the mountains that ring the Taklamakan Desert. Through a system of canals, this stream nourishes groves of walnut and apricot trees, grape vines, fields of wheat, and the rows of slender poplars that line the roads and channels. The shrine of Siyāvush sits in the center of this improbable patch of cultivation, forty kilometers into the desert from the foothills of the Karakorum Mountains.

When I arrived in Băsh Toghraq in 2005 from Khotan, I came in search of Siyāvush's shrine, and the taxi driver found it easily by shouting out questions to local residents from the car window.[5] I was enrolled at the provincial university studying the Uyghur language, and I was finding that my interest in local history led me again and again to the tombs of the saints. This was not just the product of my own investigative intuition. When I asked Uyghur friends, taxi drivers, and teahouse acquaintances about various historical events, the tombs of important personages were often mentioned as sources of knowledge. On this trip I was interested in seeing how a story quite hostile to the Turkic world had been adopted as a hagiography, for Siyāvush did not originally share the Turkic heritage of the Uyghurs who populate the land today.

In the various Persian renditions of the *Shāhnāmah,* the tale of Siyāvush goes something like this: Siyāvush is an Iranian hero, the son of the king, fighting against Iran's ancient enemy, Turan. He brings the enemy king, Afrāsiyāb, to his knees, and accepts Afrāsiyāb's surrender on terms quite favorable to Iran. But Siyāvush's father, the king of Iran, rejects the surrender in anger, determined to visit complete devastation on Turan. Despite the primordial enmity between his kingdom and Turan, the merciful Siyāvush is unwilling to carry out his father's bloodthirsty plans, and escapes to the refuge of his former enemy's court. There he is received as a son, and married to Afrāsiyāb's beautiful daughter. Afrāsiyāb grants the district of Khotan to Siyāvush, where the hero establishes the town of Siyāvushgird. Under the rule of Siyāvush, Khotan prospers, and the young king's power and happiness grow. But the alliance is doomed. Though Siyāvush remains loyal to his Turanian father-in-law, an evil vizier tricks both men into distrust of each other. The tale of Siyāvush reaches its climax when the evil vizier convinces Afrāsiyāb to send a Turanian army against Siyāvush, who is callously beheaded. Thus ends all movement toward rapprochement between Iran and Turan, which return to their roles as implacable enemies.

The Islamic manifestation of the Iranian epic cycle, most famously represented by Firdawsī's work, treated Turan as the land of the Turkic peoples, and many later Islamic authors perpetuated the identification of Turan with the Turkic world. It thus seemed surprising to me that Siyāvush, the Iranian hero, would find mourners among the Uyghurs, a Turkic-speaking people, in Altishahr. It was not that I expected the Uyghurs to hold any particular animosity toward Iran, but that I couldn't imagine how, in an age of nationalism, texts that cast the "Turks" in such negative light could remain sacred.

The driver parked his red taxi in the dust on the side of a country lane, and we stepped out in front of a low mosque, the most visible element of the shrine complex. A white-bearded old man was strolling down the lane, and I stopped him to ask about the tomb's occupant: "Who's buried at this shrine?"

"Let's sit in the shade and I'll tell you about it," he said. "I'm the shaykh of this shrine."[6] He led us toward a low grove, and without further introduction, talking as we walked, he began what would be a thirty-minute-long tale about Siyāvush, or, in the shaykh's version, Siyawushullah:[7] "The one called Siyawushullah, he was the son of the king of Kuwait City, the place now called Kuwait. He was the king's child, called Siyawushullah. His father was Kikawus. He was the king's son. . . . Now, Kikawus's son . . . Kikawus was king of Kuwait and Yettishahr [i.e., Altishahr].[8] Now, at that time, he had 400 wives, and from all the 400 wives, one gave birth to a son, and the others bore girls. At that time there was the guy who did that thing, there was that person, Rustam. Have you heard of Rustam?"

"Yes, I've heard of him," I answered. Rustam is perhaps the most famous of all the Iranian heroes, and in the *Shāhnāmah* he was charged with the education and upbringing of Siyāvush.

"Siyawushullah was the person who was raised under that, you know, Rustam. When Rustam had raised Siyawushullah to a grown man, he gave him to his father Kikawus, and after this, Kikawus, saying that he wanted to make his son a king, gave his son half the dominion, as king, giving it to him in his [Kikawus's] own time." The shaykh asked the driver if I could understand what he was saying. Story telling is, after all, an interactive performance, in which the narration is shaped in part by the audience.[9] With the driver's and my reassurances he continued. "Let me sit down and tell you. My foot hurts. It will be good if I sit in the shade." We all sat down on the dry earth. But for the buzzing of insects, the occasional child's cry in a distant orchard, and the hum of a passing motorcycle, it was a silent place.

"Kikawus was not a person in what is now this China. This Kikawus in Kuwait . . . took over the kingship of Iraq, Iran, India, Pakistan, Yet-tishahr. At that time there was no telephone. In order to talk, on account of not having telephones . . ." The shaykh continued, presenting a story quite similar in plot to the *Shāhnāmah* of Firdawsī, but the geographical and political implications had clearly changed. In those changes the problem of Turan and the Turks was resolved. "Turan means Bijin [Beijing/China]. At that time, in our language and in our books, Bijin was called Turan. Turan was above Kashgar. Above Kashgar it was called Turan in our old language, in books. So then, this Khotan was not a city. Before, it did not exist, Khotan. Before, the [only] city was Kashgar, the old city of Kashgar." Thus, the Turkic Uyghur identity of the shaykh and the pilgrims to this shrine could be associated not with Afrāsiyāb but with Siyāvush, whose father ruled Yettishahr, or Altishahr. The shame of the Turanian Afrāsiyāb's murderous deeds belonged to Beijing or China, not to all Turkic people.

Details of the plot diverged increasingly from the *Shāhnāmah* as events drew closer to Khotan. In the shaykh's tale, Siyāvush was not simply granted Khotan as his own appanage, but instead, was sent to the area in order to watch over a rest house for Afrāsiyāb's wives. After years guarding this place, Siyāvush built a great city for his own wife, and called it Wife's [Uyghur: *khotun*] City. Thus, the shaykh's story explained the origin of the city's name, Khotan. The shaykh asked the driver if he knew of a place called Mochang in the Lop oasis, where there was a certain school and an old carpet factory. The driver was familiar with the place. "There, before, was Ăplăpsiyăp's [i.e., Afrāsiyāb's] [wives'] rest house." This integration of the history with local geography, an act that bolstered both the authenticity of the tale and the significance of the place, was central to popular historical practice as it was undertaken at Altishahri shrines.

Here it serves as an illustration of the thoroughness with which inherited texts could be incorporated into the Altishahri world.

In the course of the tale, it became clear that the shaykh was drawing from a larger source. He would occasionally miss words and then go back to fill them in, giving the impression that his speech was partly memorized. At other times he would skip ahead. He often indicated that his tale was abbreviated, saying, "There were many words *(găp)*. I'll give the main meaning now. You don't have time, you don't have time. You won't know the reason, now, for Siyawushullah arriving and remaining here, if I don't tell you."

In those days, according to the shaykh, Afrāsiyāb, the king of Bijin, was a Buddhist. When his vizier stirred the king's suspicion of Siyāvush by reporting the construction of the great city of Khotun, Afrāsiyāb made a solemn vow before an idol that he would "dry out the liver and heart of Siyawushullah and eat them." As the shaykh's narrative approached the betrayal and murder of Siyāvush, his voice weakened. Siyāvush refused to fight Afrāsiyāb, who was, after all, his father-in-law. When Siyāvush was beheaded, his wife carried his body to the place of this shrine and buried him. She would pray there for the rest of her life. At this point, tears welled up in the shaykh's eyes, and his voice failed him completely. The shaykh gathered himself and resumed, his voice now stronger and more passionate, "The point of this story is not to say that Siyawushullah is in this place or that. Rather, *why* did this happen? How is it that this king came from Kuwait City and ended up staying here? If I didn't give this tale here, you wouldn't know!"

We were of course not the only people to hear the shaykh tell the story of Siyāvush, though surely, the telling was slightly different for each audience. The shaykh said that most people know nothing of the story, and so he tells it to each pilgrim who comes. "People have come from Kashgar; they have come from as far as Niya. When they come to pilgrimage Siyawushullah, if I don't tell the story of Siyawushullah, they don't know. So I tell the story." The shaykh was also proud that he had delivered the story to a television news reporter who had come, and that the story had appeared on television. He also noted his appearance in an important Uyghur book on shrines by the scholar, Rahile Davut.[10] The wide dissemination of the tale was a duty for the shaykh, the success of which could raise the status of the shrine he served.

The driver asked the shaykh if he had learned the story from an old book, and he confirmed that he had. "Yes. What I told is just part. In between there are many words, many words. It's been thirty-one years since I came here. My house is that one, over there. After making pilgrimage, let's go over to my house. There are apricots there."

History production and transmission in late nineteenth-century Altishahr was dependent on oral performances like the one just described, but it was, at the same time, closely bound up with the written text. As the shaykh at the Siyāvush shrine demonstrated, a written text can cast a long shadow, even when the book is inaccessible. The shaykh's performance shared many characteristics with the modes of historical transmission predominant in nineteenth- and early twentieth-century Altishahr, and one of these was a deep respect for the written word. The shaykh emphasized several times that his information came from books, tapping the written word as a source of authority. It was a strategy that resonated with the taxi driver, and it is one familiar to anyone educated in a literate society. More specifically, the shaykh cited "old books,"[11] which carries a multiple significance in Altishahr today. Old or ancient books are seen to come from a time when people were wiser. As a Uyghur traveling companion in the Khotan oasis once told me, "the ancient people were so intelligent!" Old books are also seen as more reliable, more "original." Manuscripts, which are still being produced in Altishahr, sometimes boast that they were copied from an "original text."[12] Moreover, an old text is also one that preceded the draconian system of censorship that has been in place under the People's Republic of China (PRC), and is untainted by the historical interventions of the current government.

The shaykh's transformation of a foreign written text into an orally performed local history helps us to appreciate the role of books authored outside Altishahr. The "old books" that circulated in Altishahr before the arrival of PRC rule were a diverse lot, and most of the manuscripts surviving today are local copies of works that were composed outside Altishahr.[13] The locally created texts that represent the remaining proportion are of the utmost importance for understanding Altishahri approaches to the past. However, before examining this local material, it is important to understand the "foreign" works that made up the bulk of the literary corpus consumed in the region up until 1949. These works helped establish the literary environment in which the local products were composed. Moreover, in the nineteenth and early twentieth centuries, these texts were not seen as foreign at all. The Siyāvush story as told by the Khotan shaykh is a powerful example of the seamlessness with which other cultures' texts about the past have been integrated into the Altishahri world.

The Siyāvush of the shaykh's tale, a Muslim betrayed by Buddhists, the first resident of Khotan, and a victim of Beijing/China, stirred strong emotions in the shaykh. The Persian Firdawsī may have had a powerful influence on the content of the tale, but, for the shaykh, this was a Uyghur story, even the story of a *Khotanliq* (a person from Khotan). Indeed, the shaykh expressed no awareness of the Persian contribution to the tale. For the shaykh, and for a small but widely dispersed segment of Altishahr's Uyghur population (the visitors to the shrine of Siyawushullah), the Siyāvush tale has become a part of "our history."

The story of the Siyāvush tale's wanderings through Central Asia, South Asia, and Iran, is unusually well documented. There is no space in this study for a full exposition, but the outlines will suggest the intricacies of Altishahr's literary inheritance. In fact, the oldest version of the Siyāvush tale has been traced to pre-Islamic Khotan itself, whence it traveled some two millennia ago to Gandhara in South Asia and was incorporated into the legend of Ashoka.[14] From there, the Siyāvush tale was absorbed into the Persian epic tradition, and eventually made its way back to Altishahr in the hands of the Turkic Muslims who conquered the region in the eleventh century. The presence of Firdawsi's *Shahnāmah* in Altishahr is documented by 1541.[15] Once the tale returned to Khotan, it may have circulated alongside other descendants of its ancient pre-Islamic ancestor, versions of the tale that focused on the founding of the city of Khotan, such as the one recorded in the seventh century by the Chinese monk Xuanzang after his visit to Khotan, or the rendering that was taken up into the Tibetan annals of Li-Yul, probably around the tenth century.[16] It is clear from shared terminology (e.g., *pahlavān*) and plot details that the shaykh's story is a descendant of the Persian *Shahnāmah*, but the differences also reveal, as we have seen, significant adaptation to the local context, perhaps even the influences of other, local, strains of the same tale. The city foundation tale remains an important genre in Uyghur literature, and the modern Uyghur oral examples of foundation tales share much in common with the shaykh's tale.[17] The transformation of Afrāsiyāb into a Buddhist also brought the tale into line with a local genre of holy war epics, described in more detail below, in which Muslims fought the Buddhists of Khotan. Finally, we should not forget that translation into the Turkic vernacular was also an important transformation.

The shaykh's tale is emblematic of processes by which histories were inherited and embraced in Altishahr. Many foreign texts were naturalized in Altishahr's textual world and underwent similar transformations.

Like the shaykh's tale, these diverse inherited histories must be understood not only as imported texts, but also as fully naturalized elements
of the Altishahri outlook on the past. Like most inherited texts, the
Siyāvush tale of the shaykh's performance was presented as a fully indigenous historical text. The importance of the Iranian *Shāhnāmah* to the
local history of the Khotan region is a warning that localness or indigeneity of texts should not always be judged by the origins of an original
author, even when, or perhaps especially when, we seek to understand a
particular group's "our history."

The shaykh's tale was also instructive in that it provided me an opportunity to receive a text in roughly the same way as it was delivered one
hundred years ago. The shaykh's promotion of Siyāvush's story is a rare
survivor from the time when history was transmitted in manuscript form,
and through institutions, like the shrine, that have been destroyed, abandoned, or restricted in the course of the twentieth century. Manuscripts
were formerly read out to audiences in a variety of social settings, among
them pilgrimages to the tombs of local saints. As we ate apricots in his
orchard, the Khotan shaykh told me he had lost his manuscript, but he
did his best to transmit the story contained in it and made sure that his
audience knew that the manuscript was at the root of his tale. This book
will argue that such intersections of manuscript technology with socially
and geographically embedded performances lie at the heart of Uyghur
notions of the past. However, the tale of Siyāvush is one of only a handful of traditions that have survived in such a dynamic and complete form.
Most of the central works of Altishahr's historical universe at the turn of
the twentieth century have been wrenched from the rich original contexts, like the shaykh's performance, in which they were originally transmitted. Many have been published in print, translated into modern Uyghur, edited, and given new social roles. Some are now hidden from the
Uyghur people, banned from dissemination. To access the widest spectrum of the manuscript world, it is necessary to turn to the archives.

The Archives and the Popular Canon

A large corpus of manuscripts, mostly produced within a few decades
before and after the turn of the twentieth century and distributed now
throughout the Northern Hemisphere, allows us to reconstruct the historical canon as it existed before the rupture of Communist Chinese
rule. Lithograph presses were not established in Altishahr until the

1890s, and even then, they were hardly successful. Less than two dozen copies of Altishahr's early printed works are preserved in archives today.[18] On the other hand, thousands of Altishahri manuscripts have survived the last century of upheavals, some now slowly disintegrating in the hands of antique-store owners and tourists, others waiting unread in closed archives, isolated by disinterest or paranoid bureaucracies. Over a thousand are carefully preserved in hospitable archives devoted to sharing their treasure with the world.

The flourishing of a manuscript tradition at such a late date in Altishahr coincided with phenomena that created a degree of preservation unseen in most of the rest of the world's manuscript traditions. First, the end of the nineteenth century saw an explosion of global travel by Europeans and Americans, including travel to Altishahr. Between 1873, the year of the first British Mission to Yarkand, and the expulsion of the Swedish Mission from Kashgar in 1934, hundreds of Westerners visited Altishahr, most commonly, government emissaries, big game hunters, adventurers, missionaries, and scholars.[19] Some brought back substantial collections of manuscripts, plucked from circulation in a living tradition. The manuscript tradition also survived to see the emergence of a state obsessed with monopolizing and archiving the textual world. When the People's Republic of China extended its control over the region in the 1950s, thousands of manuscripts, most of them only twenty to seventy years old at the time, were confiscated and preserved in state repositories.[20] Finally, the recentness of the manuscript tradition's heyday means that natural processes of deterioration have had little time to destroy those manuscripts that were not preserved by the PRC or European visitors. In the bazaars of major towns and in private homes throughout the region, hundreds or perhaps thousands more manuscripts are waiting to be read.[21] The combination of these three vehicles of preservation, European collectors, PRC confiscations, and private Uyghur ownership, constitutes an unparalleled global archive of a manuscript tradition. A survey of these surviving manuscripts provides a window on what people were reading and hearing about the past—a popular historical canon for Altishahr in its last age of manuscript history making.

Historians are often warned of the distortions of the archive, in particular the selectivity and meaningfulness of preservation. Nowhere is this danger clearer than in the reconstruction of a popular literary canon. I use the survival of manuscripts in the present as a clue to the popularity of works in the past, an endeavor that highlights the problematic nature of the archive. When absorbed in an individual text or investigating an event in the past, it takes willful contemplation not to forget the role of systematic preservation in forming our views of the past. But circumspection is more instinctive when writing the history of the histories themselves. As I grew more familiar with the manuscripts and manuscript catalogs of various archives, I came to recognize a great variation in the composition of the collections, suggesting hidden preferences and motives, many of which will never be known. Some, though, were apparent.

In the case of manuscripts collected by European visitors to Altishahr around the turn of the twentieth century, three problems were immediately obvious. First, there were some texts in which the European visitors had no interest, and these are underrepresented. For example, in his 1903 visit to Altishahr, the German Orientalist Martin Hartmann sought out, almost exclusively, texts written in Eastern Turki, despite the prevalence of Persian and Arabic works. Second, there are texts that caught the fancy of particular collectors, and these are overrepresented. Thus, the Russian consul at Kashgar brought back three copies of a European favorite, the *Tārīkh-i Rashīdī,* which had been well known in the West since its 1895 translation into English.[22] Finally, because collectors were interested in rare books and in obtaining representatives of as many different works as possible, diversity is strongly overrepresented. If one works only from the Martin Hartmann collection, for instance, one has the impression that no one text was any more important or popular than the next. With little duplication, it is impossible to gauge from the Hartmann collection whether some works were more widely disseminated than others.

Such problems are offset to some extent by the diversity of the archives preserving the manuscripts. What one collector ignored, another often pursued. A more effective counterbalance, though, is the existence of two large alternative systems of preservation in China. One of these is the semilegal book trade. During my visits to Altishahr, the sale of manuscripts was forbidden, not because they were considered antiquities (they weren't), but because they had not been approved by government censors. As of my last visit in 2013, the trade was an open secret, tolerated by police as long as it remained discreet. Manuscripts were usually sold in antique stores that relied on business from tourists, both Han Chinese and foreign. Most of the shopkeepers could not read their manuscripts, for even though the Eastern Turki literary language is extremely close to modern Uyghur, the texts' Persian-derived orthography is no longer taught. In all but one shop, I found that the owners exercised no selection whatsoever for content or language. Hospitable shopkeepers in Khotan, Yarkand, and Kashgar allowed me to peruse their manuscripts and create rough catalogs of their collections. This small, rough-and-ready catalog thus provided a degree of calibration or correction to the selectiveness of the European archives.

Chinese state collections also provide a check on the European collections. There is very little information about when or how their works were acquired. Government confiscations are one possibility. Informants I met at shrines frequently indicated that their manuscripts had been confiscated. Abundant rumors of book burnings have yet to be substantiated, but it is possible that some of the confiscated manuscripts were destroyed. Other informants believed that the confiscated texts were preserved in state-controlled museums or libraries. There were likely other means by which these archives acquired books, but until Chinese bureaucracies become more open about their own pasts, we will not know much about the sources of their collections. Although access to many of the state-controlled archives remains difficult or impossible, catalogs of their contents are available. Based on the catalogs, the composition of these collections seems to be quite similar to the corpus of books in trade, implying an indifferent or omnivorous acquisition process.

The data from the manuscript book trade and the state-controlled collections confirm the biases in the European archives suggested in their own compositions, and in the stories of their collectors. The underrepresentation of Arabic and Persian language materials is dramatic, as is the overrepresentation of diversity. Probably the greatest distortion in the European archives is the underrepresentation of devotional literature. Both the book trade and the state archives are full of prayer compilations, which are scarce in the European collections. Still, the European archives have the special advantage of being formed at a time when the manuscript tradition was flourishing and of remaining unchanged since. Hartmann's 1904 description of his collection still matches with his manuscripts preserved in the Staatsbibliotek in Berlin.[23] We can therefore rely on these collections to preserve works that may have been targeted by ruthless campaigns of book destruction and confiscation prosecuted under the rule of Sheng Shicai in the 1930s, and the PRC later on. There is no way to systematically account for all of the hidden selectivities that have changed the make-up of the manuscript corpus over the last 100 years, subtly distorting our view of the past. But taken as a whole, the entire assemblage, consisting of works preserved by foreign visitors, the Chinese government, and private owners in Altishahr, represents a compellingly diverse sampling of a flourishing manuscript tradition.

The archive and the selectivity of preservation do not only distort the written remains of the past. To reconstruct the popular canon from the archive is also to harness the meaningfulness of selective preservation. Preservation is a culturally significant act, a reflection of the values and worldviews of the people who took an interest in their history. The surviving manuscripts were not just histories worth keeping, they were histories worth copying, and nothing aided survival like abundance. A truly popular work could fall into anyone's hands: the Silk Road adventurer, the Swedish missionary, the Russian ambassador, the Chinese censor, or the Uyghur antique dealer. Many popular works ended up in all of their collections. In the characterization of the popular canon below, I have taken advantage of the varying strengths of the available archives, exploiting the European collections to understand the diversity of texts available and giving greater weight to the evidence from the Chinese archives and the Uyghur book trade for understanding the relative popularity of the various works that comprised the written corpus.

The Popular Canon: Inherited Histories

Not all imported tales underwent the extensive adaptation we have seen in the shaykh's version of the Siyāvush story. Imported texts display a range of transformations, from extensive re-working to rather faithful Turki translation, to abbreviation. From some large works, only excerpts were adopted. At the extreme of wholesale adoption, many Arabic and Persian works continued to be read mostly in their original language. Yet even these were fully incorporated into the Altishahri literary and historical worlds. We may take, for example, the Persian *Gulistān* of Sa'dī, a book of stories and poems that served as a basic textbook for young children in some *maktab* schools,[24] or the Arabic grammars and Quranic commentaries that were studied in the later stages of education in the *madrassas,* the colleges of Altishahr.[25] These texts were part of the core knowledge of an educated person and were consumed in their original language.

When it came to learning about the past, an activity that took place mostly outside of schools, Altishahris had access to many imported works, some of them heavily adapted and some in their original forms. Together with the locally produced texts that will be discussed below and the memorized unwritten texts that are lost to us today, these works formed "our history" for many Altishahris. A brief examination of the imported texts reveals that in the realm of universal or world history, the Altishahri corpus was comprised of works that were also common in Western Turkestan and Iran, and, for that matter, shared much in common with the Arabic-speaking world too. At the same time, the Altishahri corpus seems to have lacked many texts that were widely diffused in the rest of the Islamic world. While the Altishahri literary market adopted many important works, it also winnowed the texts into a smaller number of those that captured the attention of Altishahri readers.

There is one extensively copied text that was probably used in a greater variety of settings than any other: the Quran. The Quran, of course, contains an abundance of historical material, including stories of the Judeo-Christian prophets, Alexander the Great, and the prophet Muhammad. In the words of the sixteenth-century Altishahri writer, Mirza Haydar Dūghlāt, "a third of the reason for having such a 'book that can be touched only by the purified' [i.e., the Quran] is to inculcate the history of the ancients."[26] However, it is unlikely that the Quran had much influence on perceptions of the past among any but the most highly educated people. The Quran tended to be reproduced in the original Arabic, and, though many people memorized at least the most important suras, only a rare few ever learned precisely what these Arabic verses meant.[27] The most widely recited suras, chief among them the *fātiḥa* and *yāsīn*, have little or no description of past events. Thus, the Quran was a nearly omnipresent historical resource that was rarely tapped. Other works were relied upon to understand the past.

Among these, the most widely read genre with pre-Islamic historical content was probably the tradesman's *risālah,* a type of text that gives us a sense of how deeply embedded historical practice was in the lives of ordinary people. The *risālahs* are talismanic handbooks dedicated to particular trades and crafts, for which they are named. Common examples are the *risālahs* of farming, shepherding, blacksmithing, and shoemaking. These short texts prescribe the proper ritual actions (primarily prayers) performed during the daily work of a trade, for example, the appropriate Quranic verse to recite while shearing a sheep.[28] They also present the history of the trade's origin, in which God teaches the trade to its first master, most often an old-testament prophet such as Moses, along with a genealogy of famous masters. Such short histories focus on personages familiar throughout the Islamic world and do not touch upon Altishahr's local history. Each of these texts was probably most intimately linked to the practitioners of its specific trade, perhaps even the membership of a trade guild.[29] However, it is important to note that, at least in Altishahr, the *risālahs* often appear bound together in anthologies of up to ten different *risālahs,* suggesting that people who were not engaged in, say, blacksmithing, were also using the *risālah* of blacksmithing. Notwithstanding the anthologies, the texts themselves suggest that a practitioner of a trade had a particular duty to recite or at least carry the *risālah* of his occupation.[30] This would imply that huge numbers of ordinary craftsmen and even shepherds were familiar with these tiny histories of their crafts, and indeed, the implication is supported by the large numbers of *risālah* manuscripts that have survived. While some important European collectors had little regard for these humble books, leading to poor representation in Western archives, the large numbers available from antique and book dealers in Altishahr today show that the *risālahs* were among the most commonly produced manuscripts in the region.[31] The *risālahs* are elements of a wider shared tradition of popular literature that spanned both Persian- and Turkic-speaking Central Asia from the Caspian to Altishahr, including Afghanistan.[32] In fact, virtually all of the common inherited histories in Altishahr were read across this same Central Asian region, and many were read everywhere that Persian or Turkish was spoken.

Such was the case with two other prominent texts about the pre-Islamic past, Firdawsi's *Shāhnāmah* (and the related *Jamshīdnāmah*) and the *Qiṣaṣ al-Anbiyā'* of Rabghūzī. These two texts presented accounts of the pre-Islamic world so mutually divergent as to be in places contradictory, but the traditions were maintained simultaneously in Altishahr, just as they were in Iran. Both present the history of the world from the first man to the time of the prophet Muhammad, but while the *Shāhnāmah* follows the pre-Islamic kings of Iran, the *Qiṣaṣ al-Anbiyā' (Stories of the Prophets)* tells of the prophets of the Islamic tradition. While the *Shāhnāmah* was famous for its elegant verse, the *Qiṣaṣ al-Anbiyā'* garnered a large audience with entertaining and sometimes lurid prose accounts. In contrast to the *Shāhnāmah,* with its Iranian heroes, the *Qiṣaṣ al-Anbiyā',* which was descended from an Arabic work of the same name,[33] presented tales of Semitic prophets, including those from the biblical tradition, such as Joseph, Noah, and Jesus, as well as prophets more exclusively tied to Islam, such as Hud, Khidr, and Muhammad.[34]

Beyond offering views of the past from the Semitic and Iranian worlds with little overlap, the *Shāhnāmah* and *Qiṣaṣ al-Anbiyā'* presented two alternative models for chronology. Neither provides dates. Both, instead, mark time by the succession of their protagonists. In the *Shāhnāmah* the succession of dynasties, and within the dynasties, kings, proceeds without interruption through the entirety of the pre-Islamic past. The bad kings are discussed alongside the good, though they often receive less attention, and no king is too insignificant to record. To be sure, many kings known from other sources do not appear in the *Shāhnāmah,* but what is important is that the work presents itself as a complete record of the kings. The model of historical documentation provided by the *Shāhnāmah* is one that marks time continuously by the unbroken passage of rule from one king to the next. While the various works called *Qiṣaṣ al-Anbiyā'* from the Arabic, Persian, and Turkic traditions were probably never intended as universal histories by their original authors, the versions of these works read in Altishahr did provide an example of how to organize the past. In the *Qiṣaṣ al-Anbiyā'* time is again marked by the succession of personages, but here the progression is not continuous, nor does the work make any claim to cover all of the abstract time to which history is pinned in the European tradition. Only the prophets that matter are discussed, and while some succeed each other, the gaps are numerous. The accounts of selected prophets are oases of history in the vast wilderness of the unrecorded past. In the *Qiṣaṣ al-Anbiyā'* history is not an attempt to represent what happened in every place or every time; it is an embrace of those parts of the past that matter. The two chronological arrangements represented by the *Shāhnāmah* and the *Qiṣaṣ al-Anbiyā',* which will be referred to below as the "dynastic time" approach and the "oases of history" approach, were taken up by local Altishahri authors in their own historical texts, but before examining those local works, we turn to inherited texts about the Islamic past.

For the early Islamic past, biographies and long tales about individual Muslims of the first three generations, especially members of the prophet's family, were the most widely circulated texts.[35] Among these, biographies of the prophet Muhammad and stories of his grandsons, Hasan and Husayn, were copied in the largest numbers. Many of these works, such as the death books *(Wafātnāmah)* of Muhammad and of his daughter Fatima, were part of the larger Turco-Persian Central Asian body of popular literature.[36] Through episodic narratives in simple vernacular prose, they present the prophet and his descendants as great warrior-heroes with miraculous powers. Far more than the Quran or collections of *ḥadīth,* these texts, which were often recited for either private rituals or public entertainments, would have had the greatest influence on ordinary

Altishahris' understandings of Islam's founding generations. In this sense, uneducated Altishahris' engagement with early Islamic history was not much different from that of their peers elsewhere in the Turkic and Persian-speaking worlds. On the other hand, these popular tales of early Islam were often bound into the beginning of historical anthologies dominated by local histories, situating them at the roots Altishahr's local historical tradition discussed further below.

The texts discussed so far treat figures whose lives fit on a chronological scale of one sort or another, whether it was dynastic time, the succession of prophets, or the prophet Muhammad's family tree. All of these historical protagonists stood in a relatively clear chronological relationship to one another. Yet, there were many more works that described characters who lived in a past of uncertain depth, and whose relationships to each other were unclear and unmentioned. A bewildering variety of such stories circulated in written and memorized forms. Some appeared in collections, wherein they were labeled *ḥikāyat*. Many seem to have come from Persian originals.[37] Some are selections from the *1001 Nights* cycle.[38] Another important form was the love story, usually named after its protagonists, such as *Layla and Majnun* from the Arabic tradition, *Farhad and Shirin* from the Persian world, and *Gharip and Sanam* from the wider Turkic world. Both the *ḥikāyat* and the love stories presented readers with entertaining adventures set in the past of the greater Islamic world. They tended to reveal their foreignness within the text through the retention of place names indicating points far from Altishahr. The *1001 Nights* take place in Baghdad, Cairo, Damascus, and other cities of the Arab world. Stories in the *ḥikāyat* collections are set in places from Ferghana to Egypt. Layla and Majnun are from Arabia. Farhad and Shirin are oppressed by the Persian king, and Gharip and Sanam are born to the king and vizier of Diyarbekir in Anatolia. A smaller number of tales are completely unspecific, beginning, for example, "In the olden days there was a king."[39] Most of the *ḥikāyat* and the love stories involve kings in one way or another, and their main characters are often the children of kings. In addition to their entertainment value, many tales have a strong didactic element.

A related genre available in Altishahr around the turn of the twentieth century was the extended romance. Unlike the relatively brief *ḥikāyat*, the romance follows a single character, with occasional pauses for embedded tales, in a long adventure around the world. The most common of these was the prose *Iskandarnāmah,* or the Alexander romance. Like the Alexander romances that were so popular in medieval Europe, the *Iskandarnāmah*(s) that circulated in Altishahr can be traced back to the

Greek Alexander romance of the third century.[40] No scholar has yet traced precisely which of the several *Iskandarnāmahs* known from the Persian tradition spawned the Altishahri versions, but all of the Persian *Iskandarnāmahs* have roots in the Greek tradition. Because the *Iskandarnāmah* casts Alexander the Great as a Muslim who even makes a pilgrimage to the Kabaa, it is unlikely that the work was viewed by most readers as a treatment of the pre-Hijra past, though Alexander's appearance in the *Shāhnāmah* or his role in the Quran might have revealed his distant antiquity to a sophisticated reader.[41] The *Iskandarnāmah* was one of only a few examples of the Persian romance tradition that found readers in Altishahr, but it was a widely available one.

There was one other popular genre of imported works, which may have been viewed as history by some readers. This was advice literature, mainly represented by numerous copies of *Anwār-i Suhaylī* in Turki translation. The frame tale for this text describes a king in search of wisdom, and the wisdom he finds is in the form of dialogues between animals, most famously the two jackals, Kalīlah and Dimnah. The nature of the relationship between these stories and the past as it really happened was debated in the medieval Islamic world. Many highly educated authors viewed the tales as obviously false, but, in their discussions of the worth of such fables, they reveal that many ordinary readers did believe such events had occurred.[42] The talking jackals were, after all, hardly more surprising than some of the supernatural events in the stories of the prophets. Most of these debates played out long before and far away from Altishahr, but a manuscript in the Jarring collection reminds us that marvelous supernatural events were also taken quite seriously in the period under investigation here. In the margin of a nineteenth-century Altishahri copy of the *Iskandarnāmah,* a book full of the fantastic and the miraculous, someone wrote the following curse: "This is the *Iskandarnāmah*. Whoever should say it is a lie, his mouth shall be filled up with sheep droppings."[43] This kind of trust in the veracity of older works continues today. In 2007, when I asked a Uyghur friend in Khotan whether he believed that the story of Gharip and Sanam really happened, he was surprised by the question. The basic truth of the text was a matter of fact to him. He granted that perhaps some details had been distorted through the ages, but he was certain that the two lovers had really existed and had gone through all of the trials in the tale.

It is probably safe to assume that the talking jackals Kalīlah and Dimnah never existed in the flesh. We may even speculate that an original composer of the Kalīlah and Dimnah story invented the jackals and their tales out of whole cloth, that is, that the work is fiction. Probably many, if not most, of the *ḥikāyat* were, at one point, inventions as well. If such works later came to be viewed as accurate representations of the past, then how do they fit with the definition of history outlined in the Introduction, namely, that history is the past possessed in culturally different ways, the "texted past for which we have a cultural poetic"?[44] What do we do with a work created as fiction but received as history, a texted *invention* to which the cultural poetic imports a reflection of the past? There are at least two ways of dealing with the problem, both of which require that we take these works seriously as history. On the one hand, we may dismiss the problem by claiming that all narrative, by virtue of the attempt to make something recognizable as narrative, entails some conscious simulation of the past, even if it is in the service of invention. The other possibility is that the tradition in Altishahr demands a broadening of history's definition to embrace all works perceived as representing the past, even those that were originally intentional and undisguised inventions.

If not the *Anwār-i Suhaylī,* then certainly the *ḥikāyat* were commonly regarded as history in Altishahr around the turn of the century. A 1920 collection of *ḥikāyat* frames some of its tales as history *(tārīkh)* with phrases such as "according to the narrations *(riwāyat)* in the history *(tārīkh)* books."[45] The Turki word *tārīkh,* usually translated as "history," is the same designation that is applied to some of the most exacting and sober histories of Altishahri origins.[46] There is no other Eastern Turki term that indicates a closer relationship between a text and the past as it actually was. Thus, we may take *tārīkh* as a close equivalent of our "history," in the popular sense of trustworthy information about the past.

Putting aside questions of whether or precisely where the line between history and invention should be drawn, the manuscript corpus that survives today suggests that the texts described so far represented the majority of imported narrative about the past that was consumed in Altishahr. However, many other imported texts about the past were copied in Altishahr, even though they are only represented by a handful of copies, or none at all, in the archives today. Given the number and variety of collectors who were actively removing books from the living manuscript tradition in the late nineteenth and early twentieth centuries, such scarcity can only indicate that these works were not copied in significant numbers. The more popular texts described above were probably widely available either through public recitations or through the purchase, loan, or copying of the manuscripts themselves. Yet for every popular and widely produced title, there were many more rare titles that would have influenced a relatively small number of people. These included such famous works as the *Qabusnāmah,* an eleventh-century Iranian book of advice for rulers and Ṭabarī's *History of Prophets and Kings.*[47] Although such texts were less accessible, they would have made their mark. There was a market for books, and owners of rare titles charged fees for the right to make copies.[48] For those with the interest and the resources, rare books would have been an important source of knowledge about the past. In addition, the selective tendencies of the European archives mean that many rare Persian and Arabic texts have probably been lost. However, for most readers, such works compounded physical unavailability with linguistic inaccessibility, making them far less influential than the very popular Turki language works.

In many ways, the outline of imported texts described here is remarkable for its lacunae. If a scholar in nineteenth-century Altishahr wanted to know about events in Iran after the Islamic conquest, the Mongol conquest of Baghdad, or indeed any events outside Altishahr since the tenth century AD, he would have had little hope of finding relevant works. It may be that Altishahr's few famous libraries contained more works, which have not survived, but it is unclear how much access the average scholar, much less the ordinary person, was afforded. In any case, the main focus of this study is not the experience of the rare multilingual scholar, but the most widely held historical experience, the mediated past that influenced farmers, merchants, and craftsmen, in addition to the educated elite. The imported works described so far were part of this more broadly experienced historical tradition. They were read aloud in public and in private, in the marketplace and in homes, social settings that will be treated in more detail below.

The roots of most of the imported texts described above can be traced back over one millennium into the past. The *Qiṣaṣ al-Anbiyā'* has biblical roots. *Anwār-i Suhaylī* descends from the Sanskrit *Panchatantra,* and stories from the *1001 nights* arrived from ancient India via the Arab world. Just as with the shaykh's Siyāvush story, most of these works have been adapted to fit the needs of readers in Altishahr, some only through the process of translation, others through extensive editing. And like the Siyāvush tale, most made long and tortuous journeys to Altishahr. To tell the tales of all their travels and transformations would fill an entire book. By the time these texts reached Altishahr, they were hybrid works, bearing their own signs of age, traces of the hands of diverse peoples across many generations. They also placed Altishahris in multiple networks of shared textual traditions. Some works, such as the *risālahs,* were shared with Turco-Persian Central Asia, while others, such as the *Shāhnāmah,* connected Altishahris to the entire Persian-speaking world. The *Panchatantra,* ancestor of *Anwār-i Suhaylī,* continued to be read from Western Europe to Southeast Asia. Equally important was the Altishahri disinterest in certain other texts. Many of the works that were popular in Western Turkestan, such as Huwaydā's verse collection, *Rāḥat-i Dil,* never arrived in Altishahr, or, if they did, never found a readership.[49] The convergence of particular texts from the rest of Eurasia, along with the rejection or ignorance of others, was a part of the forging of Altishahri culture as it would come to exist in the nineteenth and twentieth centuries and comprised one half of a hybrid popular canon of historical literature. The other half was homegrown, the product of Turki speakers working in the towns and villages of Altishahr.

Homegrown History

Writing has been used for at least two millennia in Altishahr, but by the nineteenth and early twentieth centuries, virtually all of the early works were forgotten. Some of this was a result of the Islamization of Altishahr, which began with the eleventh-century Qarakhanid conquest and was more or less complete by the eighteenth century. Sacred histories of local gods, Buddhist sutras, rules for Manichaean priests, and Christian scripture, written in Khotanese, Sanskrit, Sogdian, Tocharian, and Chinese were of little interest to the later Muslims of Altishahr. As the case of Siyāvush demonstrated, some traces of these earlier texts survived in Islamicized forms, but, for the most part, these connections are untraceable today. Pre-Islamic Turkic traditions are somewhat more visible, as many of the Altishahri hagiographical texts described below have apparent roots in ancient Turkic epic traditions, but the unwritten nature of these lost textual ancestors hinders detailed analysis. Even early Muslim works were lost. Two of the works most celebrated by the Uyghurs today as indigenous masterpieces were unknown to their Altishahri ancestors. Yūsuf Khaṣṣ Ḥājib's book of royal wisdom, the *Qutadghu Bilig,* was presented to the ruler of Kashgar in 1069 or 1070 but is known only from manuscripts copied outside Altishahr.[50] The twelfth-century scholar Maḥmūd Kāshgharī is said to have spent his last days in Kashgar, but his now-famous encyclopedic dictionary, written in Baghdad, is also unknown in any Altishahri manuscript.[51] A local eleventh-century Arabic *History of Kashgar* is completely lost.[52] Jamāl Qarshī's fourteenth-century *Mulḥaqāt al-Ṣurāḥ,* composed in Kashgar, is known only from two Western Turkestani manuscripts, though the sixteenth-century Kashgarian author Mirza Haydar was also aware of the book.[53] In sum, the only local works from before the sixteenth century that survived in the local historical canon at the turn of the twentieth century were those that had been transformed beyond recognition by the encounter with Persian Islamic culture. The oldest texts to survive into the nineteenth- and twentieth-century canon in roughly their original forms were texts that grew out of the Persian literary tradition as it existed in the sixteenth century. At the same time, shades of pre-Islamic Turkic norms and aesthetics pervade those texts composed in Altishahr from the sixteenth century onward.

The oldest and most popular local Altishahri text to grow directly out of the Persian historiographical tradition was the very personal history composed by the cosmopolitan Kashgarian nobleman Mirza Haydar Dūghlāt in 1541.[54] Mirza Haydar had traveled widely under the tutelage of his more famous cousin, Babur, who went on to conquer India and found what would become the Mughal Empire. As he reveals in his own work, Mirza Haydar was much impressed by Babur's Turki memoirs and the great Central Asian historians of the Persian tradition. It was in dialogue with these works that Mirza Haydar wrote the *Tārīkh-i Rashīdī* from exile in Kashmir. He named the book after the king who had exiled him and killed most of his family, perhaps in the hope of inspiring reconciliation, and he wrote it in Persian. In the sixteenth century, Persian was the scholarly lingua franca throughout Central Asia, and so Mirza Haydar wrote in that language, though his mother tongue was Turki. His history is a fascinating and innovative mix of genres. Following the example of his cousin Babur, Mirza Haydar included extensive autobiographical material in his work. Unlike Babur, though, Mirza Haydar was not just documenting his own life. He wanted to preserve the memory of the dynasty that ruled Altishahr in his own time, the Moghul Khanate of Central Asia (not to be confused with the Mughals of India). He feared that "the history of the Moghul khaqans would disappear entirely from the pages of time."[55] In this way Mirza Haydar was participating in a Persian historiographical tradition, the dynastic history. This historical genre reflected the *Shāhnāmah*'s dynastic approach to time but took as its subject the fortunes of a single dynasty rather than the entirety of humankind's past. Persian dynastic histories were usually dedicated to a reigning king and recorded events from the first accession of his forefathers to power through to the dedicatee's own reign.[56]

The *Tārīkh-i Rashīdī* is the perfect point of transition between inherited and home-grown works, for much of the text consists of extracts from other Persian histories. Mirza Haydar was not convinced that he measured up to "the grave task of this history" and where another text had treated a topic well, he inserted a long excerpt.[57] These included other Central Asian dynastic histories such as Yazdī's *Ẓafarnāma*, a history of the first Timurid rulers, and Juvaynī's *Tārīkh-i Jahāngushāy*, a history of the Mongols from the rise of Genghis Khan to the author's time (1226–1283). Thus, the *Tārīkh-i Rashīdī* is another example of the reshaping of an imported text in ways that were relevant to readers in Altishahr. As was noted above, the imported texts that Mirza Haydar included did not survive in Altishahr in their original forms.

In the late seventeenth century two other authors followed Mirza Haydar's example and composed dynastic histories of their own. One work was an extension of the *Tārīkh-i Rashīdī*, picking up where Mirza Haydar had left off and continuing the narrative to the late seventeenth century.[58] The other, sometimes called in modern Uyghur the *Chinggiznamă*, was an original history of the khans of Altishahr and their ancestors, proceeding from Genghis Khan.[59] Neither of these works is represented well in the archives. The first is currently known from three manuscripts, and the other from four.[60] The *Tārīkh-i Rashīdī*, on the other hand, seems to have been somewhat popular. However, the archive is difficult to interpret in regard to the *Tārīkh-i Rashīdī*, because so many copies are concentrated in St. Petersburg, suggesting a strong collection bias. There are seven copies of the Turki translation in St. Petersburg, two in Tashkent, one in the Jarring collection, one in the British Museum, and one in Urumchi.[61] One Altishahri translator of the book complained that, despite his access to some of the region's best libraries, it took years to locate an intact copy of the work in the first half of the nineteenth century.[62] However, the fact that the Russian consul was able to locate three copies during his time in Kashgar would seem to support the hypothesis that the *Tārīkh-i Rashīdī* had some degree of popularity by the early twentieth century.[63] If we count Persian originals and Turki translations together, the number of surviving manuscripts climbs to over thirty, but it is important to remember that the Persian language was a barrier to popular consumption.[64] The predominance of Persian copies suggests that the work was particularly popular among highly educated readers. However we imagine the readership for these dynastic chronicles, it was eventually dwarfed by the rise of a new genre, the tazkirah, which, by the late nineteenth century, came to represent the core of the Altishahri textual historical tradition.

The Tazkirah

The tradition of writing dynastic history passed away with the last Muslim dynasty to rule Altishahr. The composition of the last dynastic history and the defeat of the last independent Muslim ruler both occurred in the late seventeenth century.[65] For the next seventy years the Dzungar Mongols ruled Altishahr as a dependency, and in 1759 the Qing took the region and began 150 years of indirect rule. During this period a new kind of historical work rose to prominence, a genre called the tazkirah. By the turn of the twentieth century, the tazkirah was by far the dominant brand of Altishahri history.[66] Tazkirahs comprise the great majority of the surviving historical manuscripts composed in Altishahr about Altishahr. Because of the great diversity among Altishahri tazkirahs, the genre is difficult to describe in a short phrase, and indeed, no one has yet examined carefully the breadth of these texts. There are many questions unanswered about this kind of book, not least among them being what exactly was a tazkirah? A close look at the works that comprised the genre reveals a surprising diversity of both form and content, a diversity that forces us to look outside of the text itself for explanations of the tazkirah as a category of historical text.

There were at least twenty-eight different works in the tazkirah category, and many of these are known from dozens of copies in the archives. As we will see, it is extremely difficult for cultural and chronological outsiders to define the tazkirah by its form or content, but the men who wrote out these manuscripts knew very well what a tazkirah was, for they wrote the word *tazkirah* at the head of certain works with remarkable consistency.[67] Authors of the region rarely concerned themselves to give titles to their works, and when they did, they embedded the title in the text. But, by the nineteenth century, the copyists who propagated the authors' works had taken up the habit of adding a title at the beginning of the text, allowing us to see which works they considered to be tazkirahs.[68] Frequently these scribes disagreed over the exact title of a work, and sometimes a single work can be found under half a dozen different titles.[69] But there are a certain number of works which, despite appearing under various names, are virtually always called tazkirah. In labeling these products, the copyists sometimes even used the term *tazkirah* in contradiction to the claims of the original authors. The first section of the biography of Sut Bibi is included under the *tazkirah* label in a copy that was kept at her tomb, despite the fact that it is described as a "lineage book" in the text.[70] What was this category, which was so clear that it brought the scribes together in agreement, even over the objections of the long-dead authors?

Before consulting our helpful scribes, however, it is important to note the antiquity of the term *tazkirah*, for the word was certainly not unique to Altishahr. The semantic range of the word *tazkirah*, which remains current in Arabic, Persian, and Turkic languages, is quite broad, but it will be treated here in its use as a literary term. Suffice it to say here that the word comes from an Arabic root with meanings of "memory" and "remembrance." Beginning in the thirteenth century, the term *tazkirah* appeared in the titles of Persian (and later Turkic) works that collected the sayings or writings of a selection of saints or poets alongside their biographies.[71] These early tazkirahs were a cross between anthology and biographical dictionary. Over time, and in the new contexts of the Persian and Turkic worlds, the genre evolved in several different directions, with the result that the meaning of the term at any time and place must be considered in light of its particular chronological and cultural contexts.[72] In most cases this is rather straightforward, as we find coherent groups of texts with enough shared formal characteristics to match the common understanding of genre. But when we look at the idea of the tazkirah in nineteenth- and early twentieth-century Altishahr, the definition of the term becomes more elusive, as a description of this local literature will show.

The tazkirah genre that was transmitted to Altishahr in its last major period of Islamization, the Sufi proselytizing of the sixteenth and seventeenth centuries, was clear enough: it was a hagiographical encyclopedia containing the biographies of dozens or hundreds of saints or poets, organized by generation, and composed by a single author. One such work may even have been composed in Altishahr during the sixteenth and seventeenth centuries, the *Tazkirah of the Uwaysīs*.[73] But, turning back to our nineteenth-twentieth century scribes, it is clear that this work, though still considered a tazkirah hundreds of years after its composition, had become the exception, rather than the rule, a lone artifact of a wider Islamic tazkirah tradition in a confusion of heterogeneous native tazkirahs, which, despite their wild formal variety, maintained an indisputable coherence among the local reading community.

The oldest of the works that eventually came to be regarded as tazkirahs were biographical accounts of the so-called Black Mountain Sufi masters. By the period under consideration here, the late nineteenth and early twentieth centuries, these works had for the most part faded into obscurity, but they provide important clues to the origins of Altishahr's popular biographical genres. These works sprang from the biographical traditions of the Khwajagan Sufis of Western Turkestan, works usually called *maqāmāt* or *manāqib*.[74] Under titles such as *Maqāmāt-i Khwājah Ahrār* and *Ẕiyā' al-Qulūb,* authors abandoned the biographical dictionary and focused on the miracles, deeds, and sayings, of a few Sufi masters from a single lineage, or even devoted an entire work to a single master.[75] This more focused, narrative approach would, together with the excerpting of chapters from the biographical dictionaries, come to dominate the realm of biography in Altishahr. And yet, while many of Altishahr's earliest tazkirahs emerged from this *maqāmāt/manāqib* generic tradition of Sufi biography, the great popular tazkirahs that dominated Altishahr's local historical literature at the turn of the twentieth century are often equally indebted to other genres such as the romance or epic, or they demonstrate mixed forms.

Oldest among Altishahr's indigenous tazkirahs with the focused, narrative approach was probably the *Tazkirah of Muhammad Sharīf,* written sometime between 1559 and 1724, and likely the earliest Altishahri tazkirah written in Turki.[76] The author of the work is unknown, and no title is given within the text. The name under which it is known today is simply the most common title attached to the text by later scribes, with the current appellation appearing as early as the beginning of the nineteenth century. The *Tazkirah of Muhammad Sharīf,* is, for the most part, the story of one man, thus breaking from the older Persian tazkirah format but remaining on the well-trodden path of Sufi *maqāmāt/manāqib* literature. A single, linear narrative follows Muhammad Sharīf, a Sufi shaykh also mentioned in other historical sources, from the age of four, when he lost his father, to his own death at the age of 95, and gives a short epilogue about Muhammad Sharīf's successor. Along the way, Muhammad Sharīf travels the world, prevails over dangers, discovers the tombs of saints, provides aid and protection to fellow Muslims, and takes the Moghul khan in Yarkand as a disciple.[77]

The author demonstrates a delight in far-flung adventures and exotic places that calls to mind the popular Persian romance tradition embodied in the tales of Alexander the Great and Amīr Ḥamzah. One illustrative episode even mentions Alexander by name, when the ship carrying

Muhammad Sharīf to Mecca is driven into "the whirlpool of the column of Iskandar." The ship languishes in the whirlpool for forty days, while the passengers fight off starvation and Muhammad Sharīf occupies himself with prayer and devotion. At length an old man[78] tells the pilgrims that if they climb the column of Iskandar and beat the drum that rests atop it, they will be released from the whirlpool. Raising his hands and calling out to his spiritual guide, Muhammad Sharīf closes his eyes and finds himself atop the column. After praying and worshipping again, he beats the drum, freeing not only his own ship, but also the bones and ships of all the sailors the whirlpool had swallowed over the centuries. But while the ship he rescued sails off toward Mecca, the hero remains stranded on the column. After ten days, he addresses a verse prayer *(munājāt)* of supplication to God, and immediately hears the approach of a horseman.[79] It is the first Muslim of Kashgar, the long-deceased saint-king, Sultan Satūq Bughrā-khān, who carries him safely to land. This is but one episode among many strung along the chronology of Muhammad Sharīf's career. As in the romance tradition, one mission leads to another while the towns and years pass by, and the hero's apparent end goal shifts continuously. But unlike Alexander or Amīr Ḥamzah, Muhammad Sharīf does not rely on his wits and bravery alone. Perhaps his greatest resource is a vast arsenal of prayer in various meters: prayers of supplication, glorification, mourning, and so on, some of which are presented in the text. Muhammad Sharīf also commands the loyalties of deceased saints who assist him in his missions, as in his deliverance from the column of Iskandar. Thus, it is the hero's relationship to God and his spiritual guides that drives the plot, while the narrative structure and setting often recall the romance tradition.

Another extremely popular work, the *Tazkirat al-Bughrā-khān* by Mullah Hājī,[80] relates the deeds of three successors of the same Sultan Satūq Bughrā-khān who appeared in the Muhammad Sharīf tazkirah. On Satuq's death, Hasan Bughrā-khān ascends the throne at Kashgar, and with the help of the princes ʿAlī Arslān-khān and Yūsuf Qādir-khān, carries out a grinding holy war against the Buddhists of Yarkand and Khotan. Though probably committed to writing not long after the *Tazkirah of Muhammad Sharīf*, the *Tazkirat al-Bughrā-khān* bears none of the former's resemblance to the romance tradition. Instead, the *Tazkirat al-Bughrā-khān* takes the form of an epic, and bears unmistakable hallmarks of origins in a tradition of memorized preservation and oral performance. The story consists of several long cycles of battle, martyrdom, mourning, and encomium. Within each of these cycles, the battle segment is further broken into day-long subcycles. Typically, the heroes awake, pray the morning prayer, announce their lineage, enter battle against the unbelievers *(kāfirlār)* reciting a poem, wage war with such grit that either blood flows like a river or infidel heads litter the plain like stones in the desert, retire to their resting places, partake of food, recite the Quran, and pass the night in devotional ecstasy. The next day the same series of actions ensues, occasionally punctuated by a vaguely described stratagem of one side or the other. The repetitive battles are resolved at several points by the martyrdom of a Muslim hero, usually through the Buddhist enemy's trickery or treachery. In response to the hero's death, the sky blackens, the earth shakes, and the Muslims lose consciousness in their grief. A shrine is established by the surviving heroes. Of the three main characters, only Yūsuf Qādir-khān survives to the end of the work, while his cousin Maryam, uncle Husayn Bughrā-khān, and several generals also drink "the nectar of martyrdom" in turn.[81] All are given shrines, and verse encomia follow the deaths of the two main martyrs. Throughout the work, narrative structures, metaphors, and similes are repeated—often word for word—in formulae typical of the oral epic. The prominence of death and mourning suggests that this particular form of epic developed out of the Turkic popular genre of "lamentations-elegies" which was widespread in Central Asia from pre-Islamic times.[82] Thus, in the *Tazkirat al-Bughrā-khān* we see the theme of holy war overlaid on the earlier genre to create an Islamic epic.

The *Tazkirat al-Bughrā-khān* is just one example of the holy war literature already mentioned in connection to the shaykh's tale of Siyāvush. There are several other tazkirahs that are largely similar in form and content to the *Tazkirat al-Bughrā-khān*. The popular *Tazkirah of the Four Sacrificed Imams* bears so many similarities that it must have emerged from the same time period. Others, such as the *Tazkirah of Hazrat Begim,* the *Tazkirah of Imam Ja'far Tayaranī,* and the *Tazkirah of Muhammad Ghazālī* may be later imitations.[83] Some of these works clearly emerge from the oral epic tradition, while others seem to owe more to the kind of prose storytelling tradition that is behind the *hikayāt*.

The *Tazkirah of the Seven Muhammads* (written ca. 1690 to the mid-eighteenth century),[84] was also very popular around the turn of the twentieth century, and bears little resemblance to familiar genres of the Islamic world and elsewhere. The first half of this story tells of seven "Muhammads"[85] who were sent from heaven to cure the prophet Muhammad's daughter of an illness. After curing her, the seven Muhammads wander the earth helping Muslims and seeking their own (final) resting place. Eventually they find this place in Yarkand, and one day lie down in their own graves to die. Throughout the text, these seven saints are treated almost as a single character; without exception, they act and speak in unison. The second half of the story details the discovery of their tomb over seven hundred years later by a Sufi wanderer, Shāh Ṭālib, and relates his struggle with the Khan of Yarkand to prove his and the tomb's legitimacy. In the end he prevails through a display of miraculous powers but leaves for Western Turkestan in disgust. The prose is basic and terse, and the shift between the tale of the seven Muhammads and the story of Shāh Ṭālib is abrupt, with only the grave to tie the two halves together. The result is that the book acts as a history of the shrine more than the story of any one character or group of characters.

Fragments of the older Central Asian version of Sufi biography also survived into the twentieth century and were labeled *tazkirah*. Chapters were selected from the above-mentioned *Tazkirah of the Uwaysīs,* a work in the form of a biographical dictionary, and propagated as individual texts. The two most popular choices were the biographies of Sultan Satūq Bughrā-khān and his teacher, Abū al-Naṣr Sāmānī. Several chapters surrounding these two biographies were frequently excerpted as well. This excerpting allowed the earlier tazkirah tradition to remain relevant while adapting the text to the later predilection for tazkirahs with a single narrative, as opposed to the dictionary format.

Even at the sentence level the tazkirahs display a remarkable variation, represented most notably by the presence of several verse tazkirahs among the more numerous prose works. During the eighteenth century at least four tazkirahs were reworked in verse, and further tazkirahs were versified in the nineteenth century. Poetry probably accounts for the greatest diversity of indigenous, original, written, textual composition in Altishahr from the seventeenth to the twentieth centuries. As authors sought subjects for versification, the popular prose tazkirahs were obvious candidates. One author claimed that his verse tazkirah was not simply intended to serve as a proving ground for his poetic skills. Abū al-Qāsīm, versifier of a work he called *Ūlūgh Tazkirah-'i Bughrā-khān (Great Tazkirah of the Bughrā-khāns),* hoped that versification would make the tazkirah more palatable for ordinary people.[86]

The body of works labeled *tazkirah* thus included prose and poetry, romance and epic, monographs and encyclopedias, biography and genealogy. Given such diversity in form and subject, it is clear that none of the well-described genre categories of either Western or Islamic literary studies can accommodate all of the popularly copied tazkirahs of Altishahr. Biography, the account of a life, is perhaps the most prominent contender, but presents several important problems. Except for Muhammad Sharīf's tazkirah, none of the works described here aim to document even the greater part of the life or career of their subjects. A large number of tazkirahs focus only on one short period of the subject's life, usually leading to his or her death.[87] Secondly, in contrast to biography's concern with the individual, many tazkirahs treat multiple, inextricably intertwined heroes. The *Tazkirat al-Bughrā-khān,* for example, focuses equally on the three khans who interact and work together, giving us the story of a family and king's court. In the *Tazkirah of the Seven Muhammads,* half of the work is devoted to the seven Muhammads, who speak and act in unison, and half to the Sufi master Shāh Ṭālib, who discovered their graves. This is not to mention a lack of interest in explaining the character of the protagonists and a host of formal contrasts to biography as it is known in other literary traditions.

The broadest definitions of "history" might cover all of these works, but those definitions would then include many works that were never considered tazkirahs, such as the *Tārīkh-i Rashīdī.*[88] "Hagiography," if stripped of all formal implications (including its association with biography), may be the closest fit, because the term implies any writing designed to glorify a holy person. It can indeed be said that the main characters in all of the tazkirahs were considered holy and probably always *"awliya,"* the "friends of God," namely, saints of the Islamic tradition. Yet by stripping "hagiography" of both formal significance and content requirements (aside from the presence of saints), we render the term quite useless. In any case, there were several popular works in Altishahr at the turn of the twentieth century that documented the lives of holy people but were not considered tazkirahs, among them the *Death Book of Muhammad,* the stories of Husayn and Hasan, and the biography of the Sufi Shāh Mashrab.

Of course, the matching of outside literary categories and indigenous Altishahri literary categories is not only doomed to failure, but if it were achieved, would likely obscure more than it revealed. The real opportunity presented by this body of texts is the chance to discover something new in the Altishahri understanding of the tazkirah genre. Even abandoning outside categories and letting the texts speak for themselves presents a challenge, as the texts of the tazkirahs have very little in common.

They are all about the past, they all treat human protagonists, they all describe the deaths of those protagonists, and they all deal with people who died in Altishahr. Yet these few similarities are also found in important works that are never called tazkirahs, such as the *Tārīkh-i Rashīdī,* the *Chinggiznāmah,* and the *Tārīkh-i Ḥamīdī.*

Surely, such a small number of shared characteristics would be insufficient to support a consistent literary category. Yet the word *tazkirah* was both applied consistently to the titles of certain works and used within texts to describe other works. Authors discuss the tazkirah as a type of literary work from at least the early nineteenth century, when Mullah Hājjī, in his *Tazkirat al-Bughrā-khān,* wrote of "gathering the true stories from the tazkirahs."[89] The cohesion of the tazkirah category is further demonstrated by common Altishahri habit of binding together many tazkirahs into one manuscript volume, a practice discussed in more detail later.[90] It is clear that the works labeled *tazkirah* were either seen to belong together or expected to be used together.

Indeed, it is in the *uses* to which the tazkirahs were put that we find much stronger grounds for associating these works. In any society suffused with the written word, but particularly in manuscript traditions, reading practices vary along the lines of genre and social context, and the tazkirahs in Altishahr were no exception. Our picture of the practical use context for these books is far from complete, but there are many scattered clues, and they suggest a strong association between the tazkirah and the local shrines that drew pilgrims from near and far corners of Altishahr. From the records of early European explorers we know that the tazkirahs were recited at shrines during pilgrimage festivals. Swedish Turcologist Gunnar Jarring tells of tens of thousands of pilgrims gathering at the grave of 'Alī Arslān-khān and listening to the *Tazkirat al-Bughrā-khān.*[91] In their search for copies of the tazkirahs, some explorers even went straight to the shrines and bought them from the shrines' caretakers.[92] It seems that every major shrine had a copy of the tazkirah that described the death of its occupant. A look at the heroes of the tazkirahs reveals that, with few exceptions, every major tazkirah personality had a shrine in Altishahr.[93]

Many tazkirahs also contain instructions on how to worship at the shrines. Sometimes, as in the case of the *Tazkirat al-Bughrā-khān,* the instructions are implied in the example of the heroes. We learn from watching Hasan Bughrā-khān's sons worship at his shrine how to do it ourselves. In other cases, the reader's worship is addressed more directly, in a combination of blessings and instructions. Thus, one tazkirah says of its shrine, "whoever meets difficulties and comes to this holy tomb and makes a request will achieve his/her wish" before describing the ritual activities of a contemporary who survived the saint's death: "He came each month and made sacrifice and made the pots boil and read the Quran."[94] The tazkirah filled several functions, all related to the shrine and the power of the saint: pilgrimage instructions, talismanic blessings, ritual liturgy, and explanation of origins. It is not surprising, then, to find clues of a strong conceptual link, even a perceived equivalence, between the tazkirah and the shrine. Gunnar Jarring reported that when he visited the region in the late 1920s, the *Tazkirat al-Bughrā-khān* was known among the population as the Ordam Padishah tazkirah.[95] Ordam is the name of the shrine at which a central character in the tazkirah is thought to be buried, and the place where the tazkirah was read during the annual pilgrimage festival.

In light of this association between the shrines and the tazkirahs, we can bolster the negligible literary similarities between the tazkirahs with important functional ties, accounting for nearly all of the works labeled as such by copyists, and excluding those works not labeled as such. The tazkirah was the book that was read at its hero's or heroes' pilgrimage festival, a manual for shrine veneration, and an account of the origin of the shrine. It was at once a shrine's handbook and its liturgy. Viewed in this way, the extreme formal diversity of the tazkirahs seems less unsettling. Many of these works were originally authored with different purposes in mind, but taken up later by pilgrims and shrine caretakers to fulfill the tazkirah's social role. In this sense, several works actually changed genres from whatever they were intended to be to the shrine-book tazkirah category of the turn of the century. The copyists and readers cemented this change not only in their title labels but through the addition of postscripts and marginalia that tell the reader how to use the book, with messages like "If the common people have it read aloud [they will accrue] the fullest merit."[96] The appearance of this kind of notation in, say, an epic, marked its final transition to a new social context, divorced from the bard, relabeled as *tazkirah,* fitted with talismanic marginalia, capped with a postscript blessing, bound together in volumes with other tazkirahs, and preserved at the shrine. When old works could not be found for a shrine, new ones were created. In either case, it was the interaction between the text, the shrine, and the saints' devotees that set the boundaries of the tazkirah genre. We thus have a literary category defined almost exclusively by its social function, and in many cases liberated from the designs of the original authors.

All of this is somewhat hard for us living in the world of print to imagine. For us, books are given titles, and they usually keep them. A copy of a printed work does not engender further copies from its text, so our penciled notes or highlighting are lost to other readers, whereas in the manuscript tradition those notes were sometimes kept in further copies. The biggest difference, though, was the strong variation of reading practices across genre and social context. In the print world, our cheap and portable texts are usually read silently. While we discuss our reading, the act itself is usually a solitary experience. In contrast, reading in the manuscript tradition was nearly always done aloud. With the cost of books high and literacy limited (though not rare), the number of people who had heard a book may have surpassed the number who had read it with their own eyes. Traveling scholars gave readings from works of exegesis or law at mosques after the early prayer. Romances, folktales, and epics were read out at a barbershop. The tazkirahs were read aloud at the shrines. Private reading was done aloud as well. Such is still the case in parts of Altishahr, where one sometimes sees people reading aloud to themselves, and often others gather to listen. In this environment, different types of books were associated with specific places and events. It is not so startling, then, that literary categories should be built around the social and even geographic contexts of the works. This functional categorization, in addition to resolving our problem of the tazkirah, also suggests that many people of early twentieth-century Altishahr saw literature quite differently than we do today. Literature was judged not only on what it said but what it did.

Taken together, the tazkirahs made up the written history of Altishahr for its Turki inhabitants. Some of the tazkirahs had roots in the sixteenth century, or even earlier, but just as the imported works were consumed without regard to place of origin, the local works were read without regard to the time of their composition. None of the popular tazkirahs bear dates of composition, nor do they make explicit reference to the influences that shaped them: oral epics, Persian romance, Central Asian verse forms. Excerpts from the *Tazkirah of the Uwaysīs* don't even include the word *Uwaysī*. Once bound together in a composite manuscript, all of these works appeared as a smooth, comprehensive view of the past. This is not to say that the tazkirah corpus covers all time periods. On the contrary, it is assembled in the spirit of the "oases of history" approach represented by the popular *Qiṣaṣ al-Anbiyā'*. But the tazkirahs are geographically comprehensive. They tell the stories of the most important men and women of each major oasis in Altishahr.

In terms of content, the divide between the tazkirahs and the inherited histories was a sharp one. With few exceptions,[97] histories written in Altishahr focused on events that occurred in Altishahr. The rest of the world was covered by popular inherited histories, which, aside from rare exceptions such as the tale of Siyāvush, did not treat the past of Altishahr. However, it is important to note that this divide is only visible from outside the tradition, as both the tazkirahs and the inherited histories tended to circulate in manuscripts that did not include the names of authors. For the most part, all of Altishahr's historical texts would have appeared equally local in origin, at least to the majority of consumers, who would have lacked the education necessary to recognize, say, Navā'ī Alexander romance as the work of a poet from Khorasan. Together, the local and inherited texts comprised what must have appeared to be a comprehensive and impossibly vast view of the past that mattered to the people of Altishahr.

A search for Altishahr's "our history" inevitably leads away from the text as an abstract sequence of words by two routes. On the one hand, casual inquiries among Uyghurs today elicit talk of the tombs as sites that yield answers to questions about the past, tombs that are haunted by ghosts of the "old books." On the other hand, a survey of surviving manuscripts turns up the tazkirah as the most popular genre of local history, a genre that can only be understood by its social function, and by its connection to place, in particular the saint's tomb. Both insights invite us to reexamine the manuscripts that have supplied our sketch of the Altishahri historical canon. They remind us that books are not clear windows on an independent textual world but, rather, physical objects that are created and used in culturally specific ways. The practices and technologies particular to the manuscript book as it was deployed in Altishahri culture were integral to the apparently seamless integration of local and inherited texts in Altishahr's historical tradition. These practices of book use and book creation placed the meaning of texts in the hands of a wide community.

2

MANUSCRIPT TECHNOLOGY

Our access to the stories, themes, and genres that dominated Altishahri understandings of the past a century ago is obviously heavily dependent on the manuscripts that have survived. However, these manuscripts reveal a great deal more about Altishahri history than simply what kinds of narratives were told about the past. They also tell us how those narratives were delivered and received, what was the source of authority in representation of the past, who controlled the popular images of the past, and how technologies of writing articulated with Altishahri traditions. A close look at the manuscript as a physical object, one that was created and then used in culturally specific ways, can begin to expand our understanding of Altishahri historical practice beyond the realm of the text, while at the same time deepening our knowledge of the very important place of the text in Altishahr's historical traditions. We begin with a short exemplary tale about the motives and goals of an Altishahri author, Abū al-Qāsim, who wrote the *Ūlūgh Tazkirah-'i Bughrā-khān* (*Great Tazkirah of the Bughrā-khān*[s]). Abū al-Qāsim's book was certainly not the most important historical text of the nineteenth century, but the story of his authorial venture is an excellent illustration of the curious role of the book in Altishahr, and the ways that habits of book use shaped both the texts themselves and the nature of Altishahri historical practice.

Sometime in the 1820s, a scholar by the name of Abū al-Qāsim was, according to his own words, visited by the long-dead saint, Sultan Satūq Bughrā-khān, a tenth-century prince of Kashgar. Satūq Bughrā-khān had, against the wishes of his uncle, and at great personal peril, become the first person to accept Islam in Altishahr.[1] Nine centuries later, Abū al-Qāsim recognized this royal visitor from a great tazkirah (now lost), a Persian work that Abū al-Qāsim and other scholarly men had read. If

Abū al-Qāsim's experience was anything like the other recorded visits of the sultan from the other world, it probably took him a moment to recognize that he was speaking to perhaps the holiest figure in Altishahri Islam, after Muhammad and God himself. Sultan Satūq Bughrā-khān came with a command, that Abū al-Qāsim should rewrite the *Great Tazkirah*, a book focused not so much on the sultan himself, but on his children and grandchildren, the Bughrā-khāns, who, by force of arms and at the cost of their own lives, spread Islam from the sultan's capital in Kashgar all the way to the great Buddhist kingdom of Khotan. Abū al-Qāsim was to recast the tazkirah in Turki and shape its prose into verse, for there were problems with the Persian tazkirah, not so much in the original text, which had been passed down faithfully, but in the ways the text was used. As Abū al-Qāsim described in his new work, there was some controversy over the contents of the original tazkirah. At the shrines where the sultan's descendants had fallen in battle, the tazkirahs were preserved, and the shaykhs, caretakers of these holy places, read them out. The common people, though, many of whom made regular pilgrimages to the shrines, could not understand Persian, and, according to Abū al-Qāsim, the shaykhs took advantage of this, adding improper content to the stories in the tazkirah, deriding anyone who questioned them.

The solution that Abū al-Qāsim undertook for the holy sultan speaks eloquently of the role of the written text in Altishahr. Rather than simply provide a silent, authoritative translation to stand against the manipulations of the shaykhs, he endeavored, instead, to produce a verse adaptation that could be read aloud in place of the Persian tazkirah, and to make it both understandable and interesting. To the latter end, he compressed the tazkirah, substituting, in his own words, "one line for a thousand," so that the people who heard it would not lose interest. If he kept it short, he noted, they could hear it from beginning to end. In the process, he, of course, recast the tazkirah from his own perspective. He was, in effect, countering the "inappropriate" accretions of the shaykhs with accretions of his own.

Both the problem of the shaykhs' additions and the manner in which Abū al-Qāsim defended the sultan's legacy highlight the inability of the written text to stand alone in Altishahri culture—the embeddedness of the book in social relations. Although Abū al-Qāsim emphasized that the Persian language was a barrier to people's understanding of the text, the shaykhs could have done just as much "adding inappropriate words" if they were reading out a Turki book. As we will see, in the Altishahri tradition, historical texts were expected to be the products of authoritative transmission from either the past or supernatural beings, not the results of an author's investigation or interpretation. However, recitations, the dominant mode of textual dissemination in Altishahr, took the text out of the hands of both author and transmitters. The deployment of books in recitations entailed mediation, and even if the mediators did not think that they were adding meaning in the process, someone else certainly could.

As in so many of the manuscript cultures that have come and gone around the world, books were expected to be heard as much as seen, and in the case of Abū al-Qāsim's work, we see the author's thought process as he considers the attention span of a listening audience and the time limits on a live reading. Abū al-Qāsim took for granted the purity of the Persian tazkirah to which the shaykhs and he both had access. Yet its meaning and transmission were in the hands of a broader community. Abū al-Qāsim was not interested in preserving the truth of the Persian tazkirah with a careful translation but in reshaping that truth in a way that maintained its relevance for a wide audience. He wanted to reduce the mediation that stood between the common people and the tazkirah, but he did not think to eliminate it. The text would always be read out. There would always be an expert involved. Rather than purify the text, he aimed to broaden participation, to break the shaykhs' monopoly on mediation. In the process, he opened the text to new mediators too, the reciters who would spread his tazkirah to the world. Yet this did not undermine the significance of that true, transmitted original. Abū al-Qāsim cited it again and again as he composed his new versified tazkirah. While Abū al-Qāsim's new text presented a refreshed tradition of the Bughrā-khāns' lives, the concept of the ideal original remained present as a site of negotiation, the fulcrum around which competing narratives of the Bughrā-khāns' past turned.

Although Abū al-Qāsim hoped to bring about a wider and clearer understanding of the sultan's *Great Tazkirah* through his versification, he could not rely on his own poetic skills alone. In any manuscript tradition, the author shared control over the message with other members of his community. Abū al-Qāsim's own work would be recited too, and he could not prevent his unknown reciters from "adding inappropriate words." More crucial, at least in this case, was the cooperation of the scribes and reader-copyists. Here Abū al-Qāsim failed. His work never really caught on, and despite his rhetorical care and supernatural inspiration, Abū al-Qāsim's tazkirah just didn't get copied much, though it commanded enough interest to survive into the twenty-first century in three copies. If Abū al-Qāsim's tazkirah had caught on, he would have surrendered control on other fronts. In the other popular tazkirahs, the saints' titles were changed, errors crept in, lines deemed uninteresting were cut out, and verses were added. At least Abū al-Qāsim's work did better than the original Persian tazkirah, which, if it ever existed in a form like that described by Abū al-Qāsim, is now lost. Perhaps the rise of the vernacular, Turki, and the fading of Persian left few people to take an interest in copying it. As for the shaykhs' improper modifications, we cannot know how often they were retold in the informal storytelling that took place at shrines, or whether they influenced another recaster of the Bughrā-khāns' tales. All of these voices, the shaykhs', Abū al-Qāsim's, and the Persian original's, were eventually eclipsed by another text on the same subject, which grew to be one of the most popular works of Altishahri history, Mullah Ḥājī's *Tazkirat al-Bughrā-khān,* expressing Mullah Ḥājī's own synthesis of the traditions circulating in shrines and manuscripts, and accumulating in its pages, through extremely wide copying and the notations of readers and owners, the influences of hundreds of other devotees of the saints.[2]

As the story of Abū al-Qāsim's tazkirah suggests, the Altishahri embrace of the past was not limited to the creation and use of written texts. In fact, only a small portion of the population experienced the written text without mediation. For most, the written text was conveyed by a reciter, and secondhand retellings, like the shaykh's tale at the shrine of Siyāvush, were common. Other texts remained in the oral world, never recorded in writing. Yet Abū al-Qāsim's project also reflects a trend of increasing book production and availability, which followed the rise of the vernacular in the seventeenth century and reached a crescendo in the early twentieth century. By the 1800s, the growing numbers of books in Altishahr held a special place in historical practice, in part because writing was venerated as a source of both supernatural power and truthful authority. Storytellers reassured their audiences that their tales came from books, and the mere possession of books promised blessings for the owner. For the scholar trying to reconstruct the historical experience in the Altishahr of one hundred years ago, the written texts stand out as the only insider's records of the both the historical canon and the means by which that material was created, reshaped, disseminated, and used. Such clues in turn reveal that the book was but one locus among many of historical meaning.

Books themselves were important as fulcra of historical meaning, but they were merely one component of larger processes. Wherever books have been used, they have been more than transparent windows on an independent textual world.[3] Books have physical lives of their own, and attention to this dimension is especially rewarding in the case of Altishahr, where those physical lives strongly influenced the ways the past was embraced. Books were both tools for and byproducts of the creation and maintenance of historical meaning, rather than vessels storing the contents of history. The ways they were handled reveal a historical experience open to wide participation, an experience in which the author's role was surprisingly small. The Altishahri traditions of authorship and book production created the appearance of immutable texts transmitted from an authoritative past, while at the same time allowing a great deal of flexibility in their contents, flexibility in which other authors, copyists, and even ordinary readers of manuscripts participated, recording their own reading experiences in the margins, correcting errors, designing anthologies, abbreviating texts, adding titles, and even composing epilogues. Nonliterate people could hear recitations and reshape texts in the retelling. Literate people could reshape the written text itself. Indeed, the written tradition was so open to intervention that much of Altishahr's manuscript corpus can be considered the product of community, rather than individual, authorship.

These phenomena, many of which have their own individual parallels in other manuscript traditions around the world, need to be considered not just for their evidentiary value in regard to book use and production, but in their sum total, as a constellation of practices that shaped the experience of history in Altishahr. The communal nature of reading and writing in Altishahr created strong connections between genre and social context, thus shaping notions of history along the contours of community gatherings. The physical presence of the book also brought about what might be called the inlibration or bookification of knowledge about the past, as texts became physical and countable units, creating new relationships to space and place, new relationships between texts, and new forms of textual authority, guaranteed by the visible imprint of community transmission in owned books.

Written and Unwritten

It is important to emphasize that a good deal of now-lost, unwritten narrative material circulated alongside, and interacted with, the manuscripts that have been passed down to the present. At the same time, the manuscripts captured in their pages much material that had previously circulated in unwritten forms, namely, what is usually called the *oral tradition*.[4] It is difficult to get a clear picture of this body of texts as it stood before the arrival of PRC rule in 1949, but the clues that remain suggest a close relationship between the popular written texts and those narratives that were recited from memory and/or improvised. In her study on the relationship between "the written and the spoken" in the Altishahri context, Ildikó Bellér-Hann notes that the two "existed alongside each other, in a complementary and symbiotic relationship. Oral performances were closely connected to the written mode and a constantly shifting, two-way traffic between the oral and the written domains could be observed."[5] In the realm of Altishahri history, the intertwining of unwritten and written was most visible in the activity of storytellers and epic singers (*ghazalchī* or *dastānchī*), both of whom tended to recite materials from written sources of Persian origin.[6] For the French scholar Grenard, who endeavored to collect specimens of a purely unwritten literature during his 1891–1895 expedition to Altishahr, this was a nuisance. He noted with some disappointment that, "For the popular tales one can make the same observation as for the songs, namely, that they are generally borrowed from books that circulate in all Turkestan and which are in general translated from Persian."[7]

Unfortunately, for the few decades before and after the turn of the twentieth century, we have few records of performances of unwritten texts with local origins. Nor are there recorded oral performances of unwritten texts treating local history. Some such performances are undoubtedly partially preserved in the Altishahri written histories that have come down to us, though it is never clear to what extent. Those histories that never made their way into the written realm are largely lost to us today. Uyghur scholars and musicians have recently collected and recorded unwritten material from modern informants, but such tales are relatively few in number, especially when it comes to works of a local historical nature, and the methods of documentation make them difficult to use.[8] Grenard himself pursued such material in person, and found little success. "Work becomes singularly complicated if one endeavors to collect only the oral songs or tales particular to a given district; and finally, after long and tiresome research, one is convinced there is very little to be accomplished on this front."[9] Perhaps Grenard would have been less frustrated had he expanded his concept of "oral" tradition. We have seen that popular local history, was, by and large, contained in the tazkirah tradition. Internal evidence from some tazkirahs strongly suggests sources in purely unwritten tradition, and several unwritten tales about shrines and saints have been recorded in recent fieldwork.[10] No detailed description of shrine- or saint-related oral performances is known from before 1949, though there is ample evidence that such performances occurred, as will be demonstrated below. It is not unlikely that some of the tazkirahs were essentially transcripts of material that previously circulated in unwritten forms. Works in the epic tradition, such as the *Tazkirah of the Four Sacrificed Imams* and sections of Mullah Ḥājī's *Tazkirat al-Bughrā-khān* are likely candidates. Since all context for the unwritten predecessors of these works has been lost, it is difficult to assess the role of such material in Altishahr's local historical tradition. However, it is probably safe to say that those shrines that did not have associated written tazkirahs did have associated unwritten narratives, as they do today, remembered and disseminated orally by their shaykhs. Shrines that did have written tazkirahs probably also attracted parallel and alternative unwritten narratives alongside the written work.[11] Dawut has documented many shrines to which several, sometimes contradictory, tales are attached today.[12] We can also know, in part because the written source of many oral performances is well documented,[13] that oral retellings extended the range of written works far beyond the immediate presence of manuscripts.

The Altishahri manuscript tradition adds to a wide body of evidence worldwide that a simple distinction between oral and written textual transmission is often quite problematic, especially in manuscript cultures.[14] Most manuscript traditions, including the Altishahri tradition, have typically involved written preservation of the text, visual access by the reader, oral transmission by the reader, and aural reception by an audience and/or the reader. The constellations of practices that constitute the idealized "oral" and "written" types of transmission each include some, but not all, of these elements of a typical manuscript tradition. This has led many scholars to speak of "mixing" or "interaction" of oral and written elements.[15] According to this approach, the term "manuscript tradition," as it is used here, would be considered a mixed written-oral set of technologies and conventions. The Altishahri tradition of memorized and orally performed narrative in the nineteenth and twentieth centuries could not have existed in the form it did without the manuscript, and vice versa. Not only did most orally performed material derive from written texts, but most uses of written texts were, in fact, oral performances. Most of this chapter, however, will abandon the conception of the manuscript tradition as a "mixed" oral and written tradition, considering the manuscript tradition on its own terms and describing transmission, preservation, and reception separately. Given that much, if not most, nonmodern written transmission throughout the world has relied heavily on oral recitation, it would be a mistake to consider recitation an element of an entire cultural complex called *orality*. This kind of distortion, which I hope to avoid by abandoning the oral-written binary, is caused by the specificity of our concepts of oral tradition and the written tradition, which are based, respectively, on an idealized pure oral tradition and the hypertextuality of the print world that prevailed when scholarly analyses of orality and literacy emerged in the twentieth century.

By describing the manuscript tradition on its own terms, I also hope to open up the view of historiography in Altishahr to its social dimensions. This requires denying the written texts studied here the rigid authority that they laid claim to themselves. As the popular historical tales passed in and out of memorized and written modes, certain moments in their development were captured in manuscripts, which now represent the physical traces of a larger process. It is important to view the manuscripts not as definitive texts (although there was a mechanism for presenting them as authoritative in their own contexts) but as artifacts of a complex of historical practices that involved reading, writing, ownership, display, memorization, remembering, recitation, and listening.

The Rise of Book Access and Reading

Reading has played a wide range of roles in manuscript traditions worldwide, from cultures where manuscripts were restricted to elites and reading was largely private to more public traditions in which readers and listeners of all stations had access to written texts. Within this range, Altishahr's late nineteenth- and early twentieth-century manuscript tradition seems to rest at the extreme of popular access. Between the seventeenth and early twentieth centuries Altishahr saw an expansion of both vernacular usage and manuscript production. The eighteenth century is particularly notable for the rise of the vernacular, while the nineteenth and early twentieth centuries are notable for what appears to be an increase in the production of manuscripts. Here the implications of this vernacular written tradition for history in particular are considered, but the wider ramifications are worth a study of their own. The scale of change in book production may be similar to that seen in late medieval and Renaissance Italy, a shift that Daniel Hobbins called "as revolutionary as print itself."[16]

Even before an expansion in book numbers at the end of the nineteenth century, the manuscript tradition in Altishahr became an integral part of popular culture. This phenomenon was enabled by the rise of the vernacular, a phenomenon often associated in other parts of the world with print. In Altishahr, the creation of original and translated texts in the local language began in the late seventeenth century, and by the late nineteenth century, vernacular manuscripts approached the Persian and Arabic manuscripts in number. Beginning in the eighteenth century, translation of Persian and Arabic literature into Eastern Turki came to represent a major part of local literary activity. The prolific eighteenth-century author, Muhammad Ṣādiq Kāshgharī, for example, translated Mirza Haydar's *Tārīkh-i Rashīdī* into Eastern Turki and possibly also Ṭabarī's *History*.[17] At the same time, only one local text that I am aware of was authored in Persian or Arabic after the eighteenth century.[18] The availability of vernacular books, combined with the vernacular education described below, allowed for broad popular participation in the textual world. Learning about the past was a popular pursuit, absent from the highest educational institutions but encountered at the sites of everyday life, both mundane and sacred, such as the barbershop, the cobbler's shop, or the shrine.

The number of books surviving from the late nineteenth and early twentieth centuries is quite large, suggesting that books touched the lives of many, if not most, Altishahris. From that period, the manuscripts on all subjects, in Turki, Persian, and Arabic, number over 2,000 in the archives of Urumchi alone,[19] while many more remain in private hands, were taken further from Altishahr than Urumchi,[20] or were lost. When compared to the small population of Altishahr, estimated variously between 800,000 and 2.5 million around the turn of the twentieth century,[21] even the most conservative calculations would suggest that contact with books was a possibility for a significant part of the population. Anecdotal evidence suggests that these calculations would vastly underrepresent the availability of books.[22] The public book recitations described below, at mosques, private homes, shops, and shrines, gave anyone who lived in or visited a town access to books. More importantly, education at private elementary schools, or *maktabs*, was pervasive, and books seem to have been used in some numbers at those schools.[23]

The large readership implied by extensive book production was supported by Altishahr's numerous and well-attended community schools, in which the teaching of reading skills was the main activity. The education system in Altishahr has been described in some detail in other studies, so it will suffice to provide a general sketch here, and to add a few details that shed light on the prevalence of reading in the region.[24] The maktab was a pervasive, though certainly not universal, feature of life. Many maktabs were established by local communities, while others were private initiatives of educated men, mullahs, who received fees and gifts from the students in exchange for classroom instruction. Some maktabs were attached to shrines or mosques, and presumably benefited in some way from those institutions' endowments. The prevalence of these schools was great enough that when Ya'qub Beg ruled Altishahr (1865–1877) his morality police enforced children's attendance.[25]

It is extremely difficult to get an accurate picture of literacy rates achieved through these schools, and literacy itself is a problematic concept. Most European observers reported that maktab education was widespread but often ineffective in promoting literacy. However, as Brian Street points out, it is important to recognize multiple forms of literacy that are not "autonomous" but, rather, socially embedded practices "mixing" oral and written skills.[26] Even if what Street calls "maktab literacy" did not fulfill nineteenth-century European expectations of "literacy," which imagined both the reading of texts in all genres and the skill of writing as integral to "literacy," a local version of "maktab literacy" may have suited Altishahri textual practices quite well.[27]

The important question for this study is which part of the population was enabled by maktab literacy to access popular written texts without the assistance of a more educated reciter? That question is, unfortunately, difficult to answer with any certainty. The only explicit record of literacy trends in Altishahr are European sources, which tend to mix judgments on the effectiveness and prevalence of education in the region. The observations of archaeologist Aurel Stein, who spent several years traveling to the remotest parts of the region, illustrate the mixed signals that prevail in the European sources. Stein noted that "The amount of knowledge imparted by the schools attached to many mosques and Ziarats [i.e., shrines] is, indeed, very limited," but also wrote, "I was more than once surprised to find even in most unlikely places, and among people of the humblest calling, individuals who had learned to read and write Turki." As an example, Stein described how he found "that a considerable proportion of the children of the shepherd families which wander with their flocks in the lonely jungles along the Keriya river had been at school for varying periods at the Ziarat [shrine] of Burhanuddin Padshahim or in Keriya town. Yet the appearance and conditions of life of these people might at first sight be easily mistaken by a traveler for those of semi-savages."[28] Whatever the overall prevalence of reading skills was, the ability to read at least some kinds of texts seems to have been rather widely spread geographically, present in even the most remote locations in addition to urban areas. A high rate of literacy was, of course, not pivotal to the operation of the manuscript tradition due to the ubiquity of aural reception. However, a wide geographical distribution of literacy was important for providing the necessary reciters and copyists of texts.

The Altishahri educational system shared much with the better-documented system in Western Turkestan, right down to the formula a father spoke when delivering his son to the teacher on the first day of school, "the meat is yours, but the bones are ours."[29] However, it seems that in Altishahr there may have been a greater emphasis on vernacular education, a trend with important implications for literacy and the manuscript tradition in Altishahr. Though students learned to recite Arabic passages from the Quran, they also studied works in Persian and their native Eastern Turki. The playwright and short story writer Zunun Qadir (1912–1989), provides what is probably the most detailed first-hand description of Altishahri maktab education in his memoirs.[30] His experience began with a short book he called "Shărti Iman," probably the same work as Sharā'it al-Imān, which is known from eight copies in an Urumchi archive[31] and still circulated in Altishahr in manuscripts in the first decade of the twenty-first century. It is a short Turki-language primer on the fundamentals of Islamic faith as practiced in Altishahr. The second text that Qadir used was the Haftyak, a collection of shorter verses from the Quran, which was also widely used in maktab education in Western Turkestan.[32] After that, Qadir studied the Turki verses of Sufi Allah Yār. As in Western Turkestan, the method of study was rote memorization, which did not require functional literacy, and many students must have left the maktab largely unable to read. However, the prominent role of vernacular texts made the acquisition of literacy much more likely, and Qadir's descriptions suggest that he and other students in his maktab did, in fact, learn to read. This may be contrasted to the experience of Sadriddin Ayni in late nineteenth-century Bukhara, who recollected that when he left the maktab, he still could not read. His educational experience had mostly consisted of memorizing text in a language he could not understand, Arabic.[33]

Another memoir, by Abdurishit Khojăhmăt, largely confirms Qadir's picture of Altishahri education, both in the nature of texts taught and the implications for literacy. Khojăhmăt described a traditional maktab in the town of Qarghaliq (near Kashgar) during the period of 1926–1936. Of the books taught in the schools he lists first a *qa'idă* and second the *Haftyak,* a curriculum that very much resembles that at Zonun Qadir's school. The work he calls *qa'idă* was most likely a statement on foundational Islamic dogma, perhaps the *'Aqā'id* of Nasafi or a catechism like the *Sharā'it al-Imān* the Qadir studied.[34] The other listed works are the Quran, a *"Pătnamă" (Fathnāmah? Pandnāmah?),* a work by Navā'ī, and a work by Khoja Hafiz. Unfortunately, it is unclear from Khojăhmăt's memoir whether the *"Pătnamă"* and the Navā'ī verses studied were in Persian or Turki. Khojăhmăt does imply that students left the school with the ability to read, and, in fact, describes the process of learning to sound out words written in the Arabic script. He is very clear, however, that students were usually not taught to write, and that the skill of writing was only learned by those who continued their education beyond the maktab.[35] It is an important reminder that, in the world of the manuscript, reading and writing were often seen as two entirely separate skills. Like Qadir's memoirs, Khojăhmăt's description suggests that reading, if not writing, was a widespread skill. Further confirmation of effective maktab education in the vernacular reading skills is to be found in Gunnar Jarring's 1935 interviews with Maqsud Hadji, who described maktab education in detail.[36]

Madrassas, the local institutions of higher learning, played a less prominent role in popular education. There were few students and resources were scarce, because the madrassas were, after the 1870s, extremely underfunded. The salaries and stipends of teachers and students provided only the barest level of subsistence, and the endowments did not provide for libraries. In fact, according to Hartmann, there were no publicly accessible collections of books in Yarkand or Kashgar at all.[37] The madrassa curriculum varied between teachers, but the focus was in four areas: Arabic grammar, dogma, formal logic, and Quranic exegesis. History was absent from the curriculum, as was vernacular literature.[38]

The nature of reading in the Altishahri tradition meant that the extensive maktab education system was unnecessary for an interaction with the written word. Reading was, by default, vocalized. While there are hints of this throughout the literature, it is nowhere clearer than in Muhammad 'Alī Damolla's essay on reading, written for Gosta Raquette.[39]

Muhammad ʿAlī lists several rules for reading, the last of which make clear the vocalized nature of reading: The reader should not hold the text to close to the eyes while reading. Nor should the reader move his head while reading. One should not slur words together. After finishing each word, the reader should draw a breath and say the next. And one should not half-pronounce words. Finally, one must read with care. The vocalized reading described by Muhammad ʿAlī is hardly surprising when compared to other cultures. It is well known that not only was reading a vocal activity in other parts of the Islamic world, but such a tendency was common among manuscript cultures everywhere.[40]

The terminology for *reading* in Eastern Turki reflects the importance of aural reception in the manuscript tradition. The range of meaning conveyed by the English word *reading* does not match precisely any one term in Eastern Turki. Written texts were consumed in two different activities, *oqup eshitmäk* and *köröp oqumaq,* literally "to listen while reciting" and "to recite while looking." Both compounds are based on the verb *oqumaq,* which has a basic sense of "to recite." The activity to which *oqumaq* refers does not necessarily require the immediate presence of a written text. Thus, for example, performing the daily prayers *(namaz)* is rendered *namaz oqumaq.* The word can also convey singing, solitary reading, or study, but in the manuscripts it was rarely used outside compound forms. *Köröp oqumaq* was closest to the usual sense of reading in English, the idea of following and comprehending the text of a book for oneself, though it still included the pronouncing of the words. *Oqup eshitmäk* indicated hearing the recitation of a book. *Köröp oqumaq* required some degree of literacy, and *oqup eshitmäk* required the assistance of someone literate.

The vocal nature of reading helped to disseminate texts, as it could lead to spontaneous group listenings, turning *köröp oqumaq* into *oqup eshitmäk.* I witnessed one such spontaneous audience in the Altunluq cemetery in Yarkand, where I found a man reading aloud the *Qiṣaṣ al-Anbiyāʾ* to two rapt listeners. I assumed that all three had arrived together, but when the call to prayer rang out, the reader put his book in the grain sack he carried with him and left for the mosque. The other two men headed off in different directions. When I passed back through the graveyard an hour later, I saw the same man reading alone and aloud. Presumably, the earlier audience had been passersby who stopped to listen spontaneously. Reading remains a very public act in parts of Altishahr, giving a glimpse of the surprising connections and transmissions that were possible in the manuscript tradition. While book circulation was deeply embedded in social networks, book recitation could transmit knowledge more broadly, to strangers assembled by a chance encounter.

Authorship

Altishahri conceptions of authorship reveal much about the social contingency of manuscripts in Altishahri historical practice, presenting the ideal historical text as an artifact of transmission from a deep and authoritative past while simultaneously opening the text to interventions by succeeding generations. Above all else, authors present themselves in the prefaces to their works as insignificant conduits of authoritative text rather than creative forces. In fact, the purpose of the preface appears to be precisely the establishment of this authorial identity, along with the formulaic praise of God and holy figures. Fittingly, given the convention of authorial insignificance, most authors did not even take credit for their labors, but where they did, they often followed the Perso-Arabic tradition of introducing their work with self-effacing remarks. Thus Mirza Haydar wrote his history "despite . . . lack of talent," and felt he was "not capable even of making an introduction and beginning to the book with a praise of God and the Prophet."[41] Mullah Ḥājī called himself "I, of little ability" and the anonymous author of the *Tazkirah of the Companions of the Cave* called himself "poorest of the poor and most insignificant of the insignificant."[42] Such statements were conventional expressions of modesty, present in works of all kinds, but in historical texts, they reinforced the idea that the author was a minor figure in the creation of historical meaning, a conduit for messages from more authoritative sources.

In order to demonstrate a work's roots in tradition, source documentation of one kind or another appears at the beginning of almost every history produced in Altishahr. Thus, in the *Tazkirat al-Bughrā-khān,* Mullah Ḥājī writes that he "collected the true narrations from the *History of Hasan Bughrā-khān* and other tazkirahs."[43] The author of the *Tazkirah of the Companions of the Cave* names by title seven books from which he collected notices on his subject.[44] Most authors, however, gave only unspecific nods to the convention of source documentation. The most common formula was, "the narrators-transmitters relate such a tradition that . . ." or some variation thereof.[45] A few works omit the source documentation altogether,[46] but these constitute a small minority.

Authors were careful to connect their texts to tradition, but this duty to transmit rather than create did not prevent them from writing texts that had never been written or spoken before. Revelation, namely, transmission from the supernatural realm, provided a valid alternative to the transmission of human tradition. Mirza Haydar, citing an acquaintance as a trustworthy source for the identity of a certain shrine's saint, wrote, "I do not remember whether he had seen this in a book or knew it by revelation [*kashf*]."[47] Either method was acceptable. Some authors describe in their introductions how they wrote their works at the behest of long-dead saints, who appeared in dreams or in waking visions and narrated their own life stories. So it was in the *Taẕkirah-i Uvaysīya*, the biographical compendium that straddles the traditions of Altishahr and Western Turkestan. In this work the author, most likely Aḥmad b. Saʿd al-Dīn al-Uzghanī al-Namanghānī (hereafter Uzghanī), writes that from the other world the deceased saints dictated to him, and that,

> Pen came to hand and paper was produced, and whatever came from the bounteous world to the exuberant heart, was fixed in the heart. From the heart it arrived to the tongue, and the tongue pronounced. And from the tongue it came to the hand, and from hand to pen directly, and the hand wrote and it arrived complete.[48]

Here the author is almost entirely removed from the process of writing. The text itself does the acting, moving through the author to the paper. The author's participation is credited to his tongue and hand, acting independently in aid of the text from the "bounteous world." Revelation was itself a kind of transmission. Uzghanī's depiction of the writing process also reveals a striking devotion to the spoken word. It is well known that elsewhere in the medieval Islamic world, the composition and publication of books involved important oral/aural components. For example, book publication in the medieval Arabic tradition consisted of an author dictating his work in public to interested scholars, and subsequent copies of the works were approved through recitation, often public, in the presence of the author or an authorized transmitter.[49] Uzghanī's description suggests a central role for the spoken word even in more private acts of composition (transmission) by presenting writing as the act of dictating to his own hand. His description of the dictation is perhaps a literary conceit, but it expresses very clearly the common notion of writing as the spoken word embodied. Writing for Uzghanī was not an expression of thought, but a representation of speech. In light of the current widespread practice in Altishahr of solitary reading aloud (and not just for sacred texts), we must also entertain the possibly that Uzghanī not only conceived of writing as dictation but actually pronounced his book as he wrote it.

Uzghanī went on to write that he made no change to the words he received, except that he put them in writing. Thus, the *Tazkirah-i Uvaysīya* is a work with no known or professed written forerunner[50] and no acknowledged source in the unwritten tradition, but its author presents his work as an act of pure transmission. According to Uzghanī's description of the writing process quoted above, he was more scribe than author. The presentation of the work as a transmission from dead saints was enabled by the widespread Central Asian belief that one could communicate with such saints by concentrating on their spirits, and that saints sometimes visited people for their own purposes, often while a believer was engaged in acts of devotion such as extended prayer or pilgrimage. Uzghanī defined the term *Uvaysī* as a person who received spiritual guidance from a prophet or saint.[51] Such communication with deceased saints was a common idea in Altishahr from at least the sixteenth century, though it was not always labeled with the Uvaysī term. For example, the tazkirah of the sixteenth-century saint, Khvājah Muhammad Sharīf, relates how he located Sultan Satūq Bughrā-khān's tomb with the aid of the saint himself. We have seen above that Abū al-Qāsim, in his *Ūlūgh Tazkirah-i Bughrā-khān,* states that Sultan Satūq Bughrā-khān came to him one night and commanded him to write a versification of a Persian *Tazkirah-i Bughrā-khān.*[52] Today in Altishahr, many Uyghurs still maintain communication with deceased saints not just through prayer but through dreams. After I had visited a particular shrine several times over a six-month period, a man who had often seen me there asked me if the saint had appeared in my dreams, and was quite surprised when I said that he hadn't.

Not all authors cited interactions with the saints to justify their work. Mullah Ḥājī says that he wrote at the command of "the capable one," probably referring to God but perhaps a reference to a patron.[53] When an author could not claim any holy inspiration, he might compensate with a long description of the reasons for writing his work, almost as though he needed an explanation for writing at his own behest. Thus Mirza Haydar wrote that "my audacity in this important task is based on necessity, for if I were not so bold, the history of the Moghul khaqans would disappear entirely from the pages of time."[54] Mullah Mūsá Sayrāmī, whose *Tarīkh-i Ḥamīdī* never gained wide popular readership, cited the urging of his friends, extensively quoting their pleas that he might record the history of Altishahr's dozen years of independence under the Khoqandi military officer Ya'qub Beg (1865–1877).[55] Through his friends' exhortations, Sayrāmī presented arguments in support of his endeavor, chief among them the fear that important events might be forgotten. In the midst of this justification, Sayrāmī cites Mirza Haydar as an example of the merit of recording the past, implicitly acknowledging his debt to the earlier author, not only in the method of compiling his history but also in the underlying concept. It is probably not a coincidence that Sayrāmī and Mirza Haydar, who stand out for writing without a claim to divine inspiration, composed perhaps the most extensive apologies for the act of writing to appear in the Altishahri historical tradition. It is also significant that they aimed to document events in living memory, and wrote works in the less ritualized dynastic chronicle tradition rather than the tazkirah tradition.

The source documentations and declarations of motive common to Altishahri historical works are connected to much older conventions of book writing inherited from Arabic traditions, and transmitted to Altishahr by way of Islamic Persian books. Like most medieval Arabic books, Altishahri works began with the *bismillah,* the phrase, "in the name of Allah, the Beneficent, the Merciful" after which usually came a short encomium of God and the prophet Muhammad, and sometimes other holy figures such as the Companions or the Four Rightly Guided Caliphs. As in the Arabic tradition, the introductory praise is often separated from the rest of the introduction or the body of the work by the phrase *ammā ba'ad* meaning, roughly, "and thus" or "after these premises." Most texts ended with a concluding phrase such as "and [only] God knows" and the word *tamām* (finished). The concluding conventions, however, tended to be at the mercy of the copyist rather than the author, for they came after the copyist's colophon.

Though Arabic book traditions lay at the root of Altishahr's standards of book composition, those traditions usually persisted in only the most schematic form. Compared to the bulk of Altishahri historical writing, the specific examples cited so far contain unusually rich introductory material. In the greater part of the Altishahri historical tradition, and especially in the popular tazkirahs, the Arabic conventions were pared down to their barest essentials, though it is not always clear whether this is a result of the author's intentions or the copyists' abbreviations. Thus, for example, one copy of the *Tazkirah of the Four Sacrificed Imams* begins, "In the name of Allah, the Merciful the Beneficent. *Amma,* the narrators of tales *(akhbār)* and reporters of traditions say that . . . ," and from there launches directly into the narrative.[56] When everything else was shed, claims of a connection to tradition remained.

The traditional authors' introductions give few clues about the process of writing itself, but from one Altishahri author we have a more immediate kind of evidence, the autograph. Mullah Mūsá Sayrāmī, in writing his history of the Ya'qub Beg period, made several copies of his work in his own hand. In these we see a process of frequent revision, ranging from the rephrasing of certain passages to the addition of entire chapters.[57] Sayrāmī completed the earliest known version of his history, *Tārīkh-i Amniyya,* in 1903–1904.[58] Another manuscript of the same work, also thought to be an autograph, was completed in 1907–1908.[59] Sayrāmī continued to revise the work, and completed another autograph in 1911.[60] In the latest version, Sayrāmī even changed the title of the work from *Tārīkh-i Amniyya* to *Tārīkh-i Ḥamīdī.* Sayrāmī's history does not appear to have been a very popular work, but at least four manuscript copies were produced by people other than the author, including a copy of the earlier *Tārīkh-i Amniyya* that was made after Sayrāmī had finished the *Tārīkh-i Ḥamīdī* version.[61] The fact that copies were made from various versions produced by the author himself demonstrates that, at least in Sayrāmī's case, authors could make several stages of composition and revision available for copying, rather than holding them back until a "final" version was completed or dictating a single "final" work. Such continual authorial revision and publication, which has been called *serial composition* in the case of seventeenth-century England, resulted in great differences between manuscript copies, copies which themselves bore no explicit internal signs that there were alternate versions in existence.[62]

Community Authorship

The focus so far on the individual author is important for understanding notions of textual authority and flexibility in Altishahr, but it would be misleading to leave the question of authorship there. When an individual author wrote out the formulaic final words, "and God knows" or "finished," with his reed pen and homemade ink, he presented to the world a text with claims to completeness, and to transmitted or revelatory authenticity. However, the popular texts that circulated widely in Altishahr were not the products of their original authors alone. They were, in a very literal way, also creations of copyists, readers, reciters, binders, and owners. All of these people left marks on the work. Together, these influences reshaped popular texts in such significant ways that their interaction is perhaps best understood as community, rather than individual, authorship.[63]

Altishahr's popular manuscripts exhibit an extreme form of what has been called *textual drift* in regard to the manuscript tradition in Europe,[64] parallel to the *mouvance* of the oral tradition.[65] As has been demonstrated for several traditions, the metamorphosis of texts in the process of copying is not a necessary characteristic of the manuscript tradition, any more so than oral/memory-based traditions can be said to be incapable of accurately transmitting texts. In the millennium-plus that has elapsed since the Quran was standardized, for example, only the most minor variations have appeared among manuscript copies. Another example of precision in manuscript transmission is cited by Tony Stewart, who describes an Indian text for which "a critical edition . . . would make no sense, because copies are virtually identical."[66] If these examples represent one extreme of the accuracy of manuscript transmission over time, the case of Altishahri popular literature marks the other. It is often a challenge to find a single identical sentence shared between two manuscripts of the same text. Narrative content often diverges substantially, and texts can be highly abbreviated or expanded with new material.

This is not to say that extreme textual drift was either representative of the entire Altishahri tradition or unique to Altishahr. While variants among popular texts were numerous, contemporaneous local manuscripts of the Quran showed very few variations and often none at all.[67] And there are parallels to Altishahr's textual drift in other times and places. Similar cases can be found in the ancient Near East, for example,[68] and in the popular literature of Persian- and Arabic-speaking parts of the Islamic world.[69] Perhaps there is advantage in seeing these traditions too as products of community authorship. Here though, it is particularly useful to frame Altishahri textual production as community authorship, because it helps to explain how a new canon of sacred historical texts was transformed to meet the needs of the community while maintaining a sense of pure transmission from the deep past. Moreover, by expanding the ranks of those considered "authors," Altishahr's tradition demonstrates that the

continued composition of history, in the limited sense of creating or transforming written texts, can be an important component of ordinary popular historical practice, as opposed to seeing authorship as the privilege of
an elite few shapers of the historical landscape.

Reframing extreme textual drift as community authorship also reminds us that the meaning of the Altishahri text was inextricable from
the social practices in which it was embedded, constantly reimagined as
simultaneously a transmission from the deep past and a part of the lived
present. Over time, the marks of social practices accumulated and reshaped the significance of the text. This made the written text increasingly rich after the moment of first recording, during the long periods
when it was still seen as part of the present and continuously reworked.
One of the social practices that reshaped the text was copying, the act
on which the survival and dissemination of the core text depended. As
we have seen, most of the works that comprised the popular historical
canon were the products of earlier ages. Few, if any, manuscript specimens survived from the times when these works were composed. It was
the copyist who recreated such works for successive generations.

The important role of the copyist was not lost on authors participating in Altishahr's manuscript tradition. Taken at face value, the authors'
claims to pure transmission might suggest that their texts were rigid and
firmly fixed, that alterations or alternate versions might be a betrayal
of the venerable sources that spoke through the author. However, despite
the authors' concern for transmitting tradition without interference, they
did not consider their own texts inviolable finalities. Just as the emphasis
on transmission did not prevent unprecedented texts from appearing,
attitudes toward reading and copying allowed for consumers to reshape
the text. We have seen that at least one author issued multiple versions of
his historical writing as he refined it over the years. Authors also expected readers and copyists to participate in the continued creation of the
text as it was reproduced and transmitted across generations, with the
implication that transmission, while facilitated by authors, was ultimately in the hands of the wider community.

One form of this consumer participation was the habit of writing continuations of older historical works, a phenomenon common to many
parts of the Islamic world. In this tradition, one author simply picked up
the narrative where another had left off, extending a history down to his
own time. The best example from the Altishahri context is Churās's
Tārīkh of ca. 1690, which not only continues Mirza Haydar's *Tārīkh-i*

Rashīdī but even reproduces large sections of the earlier work as the first half of the text. Mirza Haydar's work itself was to some extent a continuation of two earlier histories from Western Turkestan, the *Jami' al-Tavārīkh* and the *Tārīkh-i Jahāngushāy,* large stretches of which were incorporated wholesale into Mirza Haydar's work.[70] The act of writing historical continuations was somewhat rare, as was any kind of large-scale original writing, but the products of this tradition, such as Mirza Haydar's *Tārīkh-i Rashīdī,* were disseminated widely enough among elites to bring the practice into the consciousness of educated readers.[71]

More striking are requests from the authors themselves for the reader's participation as coauthor. A handful of works include a call to the reader to amend the shortcomings of the book. One of these is the *Tazkirah of the Companions of the Cave,* whose author writes, "I request men of learning that, if there should be any mistakes and faults in this *tazkīr* [*sic*], they should amend them with a kind postscript and bring them into shape."[72] Even if we read such requests as formulaic expressions of authorial humility, they express a sense of flexibility in the written text and a remarkable comfort with the idea of textual alteration. Certainly, the surviving manuscripts testify to a great deal of alteration. Such requests for "emendation" are, of course, unthinkable in the world of print, where a single corrected text is dwarfed by centralized mass production, but manuscript publication's process of slow, yet potentially exponential, growth made reader interventions meaningful. One amended copy could give birth to further copies bearing the same corrections, and those to even more. The author ceded control of the text, and the readers gained a voice in a larger textual conversation.

But what was the actual process of the alteration of a text, as it is implied in the *Tazkirah of the Companions of the Cave?* When we closely examine the details of the act of correction, we are faced with a mystery. In light of the *Companions* author's request, it is surprising to find that the margins of most manuscripts lack significant corrections or alterations. If we approach the role of reader participation from the assumptions of our own print culture, we turn our attention to the readers of finished texts, and indeed, such readers undertook the role of editor with some frequency, though not to the extent that the *Companions* author implied. Identifying the comments of a reader of a finished text by a difference of handwriting, we find that corrections are few and rather minor, usually alterations of orthography and occasionally rising to the level of insertions of omitted words.[73] A copy of the *Tazkirah of the Four*

Sacrificed Imams, for example, exhibits a reader's verb conjugation correction from the respectful to the familiar form for the subject "God."[74] Other manuscripts have insertions where the copyist omitted a saint's titles, such as "His Holiness."[75] Such small additions by readers of finished texts hardly fulfill the potential suggested in the author's call for help.

Yet the tremendous variation among texts represented in the surviving manuscripts suggests a much greater degree of change than such minor corrections can account for. The *Tazkirah of the Companions of the Cave* was not copied widely enough to provide a sufficient sample size, but if we examine a more popular work, such as the *Tazkirah of Muhammad Sharīf,* we find so many different versions that it is impossible to establish an authoritative text. Nor can we properly consider the various manuscripts as different works, because all of them share large sections of text similar enough to suggest a single origin. There was, hypothetically, an earliest written text (or several early texts, later combined), set down at some point in the late sixteenth or early seventeenth century,[76] but by the time the work reached its greatest popularity in the early 1900s, such a first text would have been drowned out by the multitude of later, transformed copies, if it even survived. The low frequency and minor character of readers' marginal corrections will simply not explain the variety in the *Tazkirah of Muhammad Sharīf.*

The solution lies not with the reader of the finished text so much as the copyist or copyist-reader. With so few corrections attributable to post-production readers, it is only the copyist who can account for the vast diversity among manuscripts of the same titles. Here still, significant expansions of the narrative content of the text, such as suggested by the *Companions* author's "kind postscript" do not seem to have appeared very often, though such additions did occur from time to time. Rather, the most common and dramatic alteration to the content of the text was abbreviation. A text may have lines omitted throughout, or large sections excised, or even begin an unusually full rendition and, halfway through, skip abruptly to the concluding page.[77] One incentive for such abbreviations was economy of time or money. For those able to read but not write, copying required the paid services of a professional scribe, or *kātib,* and even skilled writers willing and able to make their own copies needed to borrow the book from someone. Either case presented pressures to reduce copying time. At the same time, abbreviation was an expressive and meaningful act. The copyists' choices of what to abbreviate provide an interesting window into what was considered significant in these texts, information which will be touched upon again later. Here though, it is important to note that virtually all of the popular manuscripts circulating in Altishahr in the early 1900s were abbreviated to a greater or lesser extent, effecting a distillation of meaning into the most potent and relevant aspects.

If there were few major historical or factual additions to the text, there were still many "corrections" undertaken by the copyist, though they are often difficult to distinguish from errors, misreadings, or differences of taste. Some are clearly based in the vagaries of handwritten script. Did Muhammad Sharīf see "a fifteen-hundred horse caravan" or "fifteen hundred fifty caravans?" Here the similar-looking words "horse" *(ātligh)* and "fifty" *(iyligh)* are exchanged.[78] Also common are changes of word choice, with different synonyms appearing at the same point in different manuscripts. Copyists seemed to have exercised personal judgment when deciding on exactly how to name saints, as in "Muhammad Sharīf Khvājam" or "Haẓrat Buzurgvār" or "Haẓrat Khvājah Buzurgvār" in three versions of the *Tazkirah of Muhammad Sharīf*.[79]

The accumulated copyists' alterations and abbreviations had the potential to turn a text into garbled nonsense. In the case of the hagiographies, the majority of manuscripts maintained a reasonable level of grammatical and orthographic consistency, but the trade manuals, which were more talismanic, often display a level of textual corruption that brings them to the brink of unreadability.[80] Members of trade guilds memorized their relevant manuals as part of their apprenticeship, and it may be that such works were occasionally even copied out from memory. Memorization is important because it suggests that such texts had a formulaic and ritual value. Like the other text that was memorized by most Altishahri men, the Quran (or more precisely, small selections from the Quran), full understanding of the text's meaning was secondary to the ability to recite the text, and, in the absence of that ability, the carrying of the text for its talismanic value. People were comfortable memorizing and hearing texts in other, unintelligible languages (especially the Arabic of the Quran, but also the Persian of the *Gulistan*), so it is not surprising that they should accept unintelligible texts in their own language. However, it should be emphasized that this sort of garbled product was largely limited to those texts, like the trade manuals, that were primarily valued as talismanic or memorized texts.

There are some cases of substantial additions to texts, and though they are exceptional, they are worth examining. In rare cases extensive narrative material was added to manuscripts. One such case is a manuscript of the tazkirah of Afaq Khoja (Prov. 369), which includes the story of a young Afaq causing the death of children who mock him. This tale is absent not only from all other Turki manuscripts of the Afaq tazkirah that I have examined, but also from the Persian work from which the popular Turki tazkirah was likely adapted.[81] While we can only speculate as to the origin of this apparent interpolation, the intervention of a tale that circulated orally seems likely. Another dramatic example can be found in a manuscript in the British Museum collection, which contains an addition so large as to essentially constitute separate work.[82] Someone copied two sections concerning the saints buried at the shrine of Kohmarim (near Khotan) from the *Tazkirah-i Uvaysīya,* and appended an additional tale, describing the interaction of another saint with the same shrine, subsequent to the first two saints' deaths. The resulting composite text could be considered an independent work, in the Perso-Arabic tradition of extending histories mentioned above. At the same time, it represents the potential within manuscript tradition for community creation of historical and/or sacred texts. Until other copies become accessible, it will be impossible to know if this work was a singular event or if the author of the continuation succeeded in creating a new tazkirah for the Kohmarim shrine with popular acceptance.[83]

The most common major intervention is the copyist's colophon, often recording the date of copying, and sometimes the place or the copyist's name. Occasionally, a copyist would append to a tazkirah additional praise of one of the saints treated therein, or blessings on the reader of the book. Other copyists appended what appear to be their own verses to manuscripts, often connected to the subject matter of the core text. Consumers reading texts after copying added many other types of information. These additions are treated below, in the subsection on reader-writers.

We have seen above that only the copyist's role can account for the corrections and variations, which are not only called for in the texts themselves but demonstrated in the surviving copies. But who were these copyists? It is not always easy to separate the producers and the readers of books. The act of producing a manuscript through copying was also an act of reading, so that a professional scribe was by default a rather widely read individual. Furthermore, the work of copying was not undertaken by professional scribes alone but also by consumers themselves.

The creative power of the monastic scribe in Europe, especially as a perpetually modernizing force, is well known.[84] In Altishahr, the modernizing force of the scribe shaped texts to meet the rising interest in shrines and local history. Unlike medieval European scribes, though, the scribes of Altishahr were not concentrated in monasteries or universities, and the practice of copying was not limited to a handful of specialists. Nor was copying regulated by the tradition of *samā'āt* that held sway in the medieval Arabic world, wherein copies were checked through recitation in the presence of the author or an authorized transmitter, and unauthorized copies were scorned.[85] There was no parallel to the *peciarii* of later medieval Europe, who examined texts offered for sale or loan and fined those responsible for incorrect work.[86] In Altishahr, the production of books was a far more casual affair. Some people did make a profession of writing, and these sat in long rows at the bazaars, waiting for customers.[87] However, manuscripts could be copied by any literate consumer. A manuscript in the Jarring collection, for example, was copied by a certain Sulaymān Akhūnd, who identifies himself as a professional storyteller.[88] This feature of Altishahri book culture was shared to a large degree with the broader Central Asian Islamic book culture of the time, in which, for example, tradesmen such as blacksmiths and cobblers copied their own trade manuals.[89] For Altishahr's popular history, such broad participation in book production was important because it interacted with an openness to textual intervention to reshape texts continuously in the process of community authorship.

Democratic Production

The prevalence of amateur copying can be traced in part to the dynamics of book acquisition. Manuscripts could be legitimately obtained in several ways: copying for one's own use, commissioned copying, borrowing, and the purchase of a used book. In order to understand the role of the copyists (both amateur and professional) in making manuscripts available to readers, it is useful to compare copying to the market for used books, because the nature of the book trade made self-copying and commissioned copying into dominant mechanisms of manuscript acquisition. Both new copying and used manuscript purchases required social connections. Copyists in the bazaars produced books to order, yet they required an original, and some texts were not readily available for copying. One could borrow a book from a friend for copying, but acquiring a specific work could prove difficult or expensive. As was mentioned above, owners of rare works charged fees for the right to copy them.[90] Social networks were also important in the purchase of used books, for there was no open, depersonalized book market of any significance. European visitors noted that booksellers in Altishahr's bazaars offered a limited selection of manuscripts, if any. Bellew, who visited Yarkand in 1873–1874, found bookshops in the bazaar stocked with Turki manuscripts on "religious subjects," along with lithographs in Persian from India, but noted a lack of "historical records of the country, or native literature in poetry or prose."[91] During the same period, Kuropatkin reported that he had seen no bookstores at all "after going through the greater part of the country."[92] When he first arrived in Kashgar in 1929, Gunnar Jarring observed that only lithographs imported from Central Asia were available for sale in the Kashgar bazaar, lamenting that no manuscripts or local works of any kind were to be seen. Both Bellew's and Jarring's observations are startling in light of the composition of archives of Altishahri books, in which manuscripts far outnumber foreign lithographs, and local works are numerous. Jarring seems to have suspected that the booksellers did stock manuscripts in some hidden place, but that they were unwilling to sell them to him because he was a foreign nonbeliever. Without the appropriate social connection, he was unable to purchase any manuscripts. Yet we know that used manuscripts, including works of local origin, were sold, for in a few manuscripts such transactions are recorded on endpapers or margins with prices.[93] If Jarring was correct that, at the time of his visit, manuscripts were not offered publicly in the markets, then such transactions must have been facilitated through networks of friends and acquaintances. Jarring was eventually able to tap into this system by establishing a relationship with a peddler of jewelry and curios, who agreed to seek out and sell to Jarring large numbers of manuscripts.

A similarly restricted manuscript market persists today, partly because manuscript sale is prohibited under Chinese Communist Party rule but also because of the labor involved in producing manuscripts, and the personal connection that copyist-owners develop with their handiwork. The situation was explained to me by a bookseller who frequently made the rounds of the countryside in search of manuscripts. He reported that most contemporary manuscripts are owned by their copyists, and that the amount of time required to produce a book is so great it prevents the establishment of a significant market in manuscripts. Due to the enormous investment of time, copyist-owners will only sell their products at prices far higher than printed works, and few customers are willing or able to pay such prices.[94] According to the book dealer I spoke with, most of the manuscripts that reach the market today come from the heirs of copyist-owners who have died.

To produce one's own manuscript required money as well as time. The major material expense in book production was paper. Paper was not cheap, but, thanks to a healthy indigenous papermaking industry, it was not entirely out of reach of ordinary people either. Paper was produced from mulberry trees, especially in the oases of Khotan and Guma.[95] While such paper was inferior to the products of Western Turkestan (Khoqandi paper was particularly prized),[96] the local paper was sufficiently smooth and regular for book production. Yet even the inferior local paper represented the most substantial expense of book production. As of 1906–1908, the cost of sufficient local paper for a medium format (octavo-size) book of average length (156 folios) was about 10–20 copper coins *(pul)*, the equivalent of one to two days of unskilled labor or the approximate price of a hen.[97] Of course, many popular works were much smaller in format or length, especially prayer compilations and trade manuals, which, due to their small page sizes, could get four times as many folios from a sheet. Such books required as little as one or two *pul* worth of paper. On the whole, we may say that paper, though not unobtainable, represented a moderate to considerable expense, especially for the kind of larger manuscripts that contained historical writing. At the same time, the presence of a local paper industry, which kept the main raw material for books widely available, may have been a strong encouragement to the flourishing of manuscript culture in Altishahr.[98]

However, if paper was a moderate expense, completed books were far more costly. The four manuscripts I have located in which an Altishahri owner recorded the price paid fetched between 40 (for a 67-folio manuscript consisting of two tazkirahs) and 3,200 *pul* (for a 272-folio copy of the romance of Abu Muslim), with an average price of 1,185 *pul*. It is of course possible that some of these notes overstate prices paid in order to influence potential buyers, but they are, on the whole, in line with the prices paid by Swedish manuscript collectors, who documented the cost of many of their manuscripts in the 1920s–1930s. Gunnar Jarring's average expenditure for a manuscript was 616 *pul,* while the missionary Gustaf Ahlbert paid an average of 1,727 *pul.*[99] Although some bargains could be found, as in the 40-*pul* tazkirah compilation mentioned above, the typical book price was prohibitive. Even Jarring's average, which is lower than the average documented transaction involving only Altishahris, is a high price relative to labor (equaling 62 days of unskilled labor wages) and goods (41 hens).

Although completed books were extremely expensive items, new manuscripts were far more attainable for those who could produce their own copies. At the turn of the twentieth century, print alternatives were few, and manuscripts were items of such great value that we might expect them to be seen as luxuries. But unlike many luxuries, they could be produced by their users, and virtually all of these users were connected to an agricultural cycle that provided long stretches of leisure time. The average mullah might not be able to purchase or commission a manuscript but would likely find himself with sufficient time to produce his own over the winter, provided he could acquire paper. Given the limited and prohibitively expensive nature of the used-book market, it is likely that many of the manuscripts surviving today were copied by their owners or commissioned from professional copyists. The diversity of writing skills brought to bear in this system of consumer copying is immediately visible in the execution of calligraphy in surviving books, ranging from delicate to nearly illegible.

Today most of the works copied in manuscript form are texts that have not been published by the print industry, which is strictly controlled by the Chinese government. Common manuscripts produced in the last twenty to thirty years include collections of prayers, faith manuals that used to be the staple of maktab education, and tazkirahs. This suggests that some Uyghur readers are taking advantage of the previously dominant manuscript technology to circumvent government control of the publishing industry and reproduce books that are proscribed by the authorities. This is, of course, a role that manuscripts have filled in numerous cultures, from Renaissance literature during the emergence of print to the *samizdat* publications of the Soviet Union.[100] However, the avoidance of the censors, while certainly an important factor, does not entirely explain the persistence of the manuscript in Altishahr today, for at least one recent manuscript was copied from an out-of-print work from a state-controlled press.[101] In that case, scarcity may have provided the motivation for manuscript reproduction.

My efforts to learn about today's manuscript copying met with little success, due to the secretive nature of the activity, and informants' shyness about their own writing skills. Twice friends agreed to teach me how to copy a manuscript but postponed the lessons repeatedly. On only one occasion did I witness the copying of a manuscript. On a Friday, just after the noon prayer had ended, a man squatted on a dusty path, leaning against a mud-brick wall in the graveyard behind a mosque and in front of a saint's shrine. While the worshipers dispersed, he crouched alone in the graveyard, holding two books in his hands, hurriedly copying from one to the other, about six words at a time, reading them under his breath before copying each group. The man declined to be interviewed but did not object to me observing his work. I saw that he was copying incantations against "oppressive enemies," which prescribed a series of prayers and precise numbers of repetitions of suras from the Quran. The spell was one of dozens of small texts that comprised the manuscript, which he appeared to be copying in full. To judge from Gunnar Jarring's experience in 1929–1930, books of incantations were rare even before the arrival of the Chinese Communist Party.[102] Certainly, today, they are not to be had from any of the official presses, which are restricted to publications that reflect the official Islam of the Chinese state. Yet while the state has prevented print publication of a genre that was already considered somewhat sensitive, the tools of manuscript reproduction have become more efficient. The advent of the ballpoint pen and cheap, smooth paper that needs no preparation has clearly made such copying quicker and easier. A century ago copyists would cut their own reed pen, mix their own ink from lamp black, acquire paper that received the ink without excessive bleeding, and use a special quire holder to keep the paper in place.[103] By contrast, the man in the graveyard was able to copy his presumably borrowed book in less than ideal surroundings and apparently under some time pressure (exacerbated by my own presence). This makes today's updated manuscript technology ideally suited for the propagation of underground literature, especially considering the alternative of photocopying, which many Uyghurs believe to be monitored by government authorities.

Such use of manuscripts highlights one of the major characteristics that this technology has always possessed. The wide distribution of a work in manuscript form is dependent on the combined activities of a large number of strangers, and the survival of a work is much more likely when these activities continue over several centuries. The material barriers to participation are small, at least in comparison to printing, though some form of literacy is required, and literacy can be a rather expensive skill to acquire. A manuscript author does not need state approval to publish a work, and it is extremely difficult for a state to eliminate works that it finds threatening, especially if those works have a large and enthusiastic readership. Manuscript technology does not rely on a concentration of capital. Whereas marketplaces are central to print distribution, social networks often guide the spread of texts in the manuscript tradition.

One remarkable aspect of manuscript culture as it developed in Altishahr is the near absence of the state, and even the wealthy, as significant publishing forces.[104] Whereas patronage and/or institutional support have loomed large in most manuscript traditions, in Altishahr, the manuscript seems to have multiplied on account of consumer demand, in a process somewhat similar to the "user publication" described for the manuscript tradition of seventeenth-century England.[105] This is not to say the people in positions of power did not have any role at all. In the case of the tazkirah, for example, demand was stoked by the role of the shrine and the shaykhs' promotion of their shrines. However, Altishahr's manuscript tradition was marked by the absence of powerful book-promoting institutions to parallel the wealthy nobles of Renaissance Italy, monasteries and universities in medieval Europe, and the royal patrons of the wider Islamic world and India,[106] to take just a few examples.

The act of copying provided the only reliable guarantee of a work's long-term survival: large numbers. That such a valuable power was spread so evenly among the educated populace made Altishahr's manuscript tradition more democratic than the technologies that preceded and succeeded it. Throughout the ancient world, before wide reproduction and distribution of books, monumental inscriptions were the most reliable way to preserve a written text, and these inscriptions fell, of course, under the purview of the most powerful. Print technology shares some of this monumentality, for the copies of a printed work usually emanate from a centralized source, supported by extensive capital. In Altishahr's manuscript tradition, on the other hand, survival was guaranteed only by the readers. Those readers, especially copyist-readers, had their own say in the form of the text they produced, changing it to fit the needs of their presents. Manuscripts were works that survived by adaptation in a system of diffuse production.

Reader Writers

In some senses, the production of books was the least significant part of the manuscript tradition. The relatively short period of production was often overshadowed by a long life of use. As in many times and places where the manuscript was predominant, reading in Altishahr's manuscript tradition was a social act, involving performances public and private, and depending on the borrowing, storage, and trade of books. And, as in other manuscript traditions, those aspects of use often left marks in the form of marginalia and other readers' marks.

An overwhelming proportion of readers' marks speak to the sacredness of writing in the Altishahri tradition. This was partly an Islamic inheritance, for writing, the book, and language, particularly the Arabic language, have held a special connection to the true faith in most expressions of Islam. Even if Altishahris did not use the language of the Quran, they at least used the script of the Quran—the Arabic alphabet—with a few minor modifications. The production of this script was viewed as a meritorious act, even when copying nonsacred texts. Thus, one marginal comment in a collection of *ḥikāyat* reads, "Whoever should copy this book does a good deed."[107] Reading and listening to readings were also regarded as meritorious. As a reader noted in a margin of a tazkirah compilation, "Great merit" will accrue to "the common folk who have this book read out and listen to it."[108] People who read works themselves let others know about it. Readers often commemorated their participation in the text with short inscriptions in the margins or endpapers of a book, such as "I, Ẓiyā' al-Dīn Qārī read this book."[109]

Through such notations, readers not only recorded a praiseworthy act but also marked their place among the heroes of the histories they were reading. And they not did limit their textual contributions to commemorations of reading. Rarely, they left notes in margins detailing their personal knowledge of the material. One reader recorded in the margins of a tazkirah that he had seen the sands at which the imam Mahdi had appeared, as related in the *Tazkirah of the Four Sacrificed Imams*.[110] Empty endpapers could be filled with almost any kind of information. Gunnar Jarring purchased a manuscript in which a reader had recorded the birth of conjoined twins, who were taken from their village to Kashgar for all to see. In the last pages of a manuscript, blessings on readers are common, as are verses in praise of the saints, or prayers.

Scholars have often noted the importance of marginalia in manuscript traditions[111] and exploited these marks for their evidentiary value. Studies focused narrowly on readers' marks have tended to ask how books were used or investigated the motives of the writer of marginalia.[112] However, marginalia were not simply read by their creators and then ignored until they caught the attention of today's literary critics and historians. It is important that we also consider the subjective effects of marginalia on subsequent readers.[113] The sacredness of reading and writing was not just *documented* in marginalia; it was *perpetuated* for subsequent readers by those marginal notes, which trained future readers about the norms and meanings of reading. Marginalia and ownership inscriptions also shaped perceptions of a shared readership. Readers' marks are an aspect of community authorship that was widespread in manuscript worlds but has not been considered as a form of authorship, despite a general awareness of the frequency with which books have changed hands. If we accept that the book does not consist only of the central column(s) of text, that marginalia contribute to the meaning of the book and the subjective experience of reading, then we must admit readers into the broad community of authors that shaped Altishahr's textual tradition.

Contextually Bound Reading

The participatory approach encouraged by Altishahr's manuscript tradition eliminated what Ricoeur called "the semantic autonomy of the text"[114] and allowed the reader to participate in the continuous production and reshaping of history. The widely dispersed powers of manuscript creation and the participation of ordinary readers combined with a close integration of text and social interactions to such an extent that it is impossible to consider writing as "context-free" language, even in comparison to oral tradition.[115] At the manuscript level, this participation would have been limited to those who could write, but, as we shall see later in the examination of shrine graffiti, the phenomenon has extended in some way even to nonliterate pilgrims. More importantly, the predominance of oral recitation as a means of deploying written texts situated writing in rich social contexts, which both influenced the reception of the text and turned back upon the physical text to reshape it.

Different genres of writing became associated with specific social settings through public readings. Zunun Qadir described several types of reading that otherwise seem to have escaped the historical record. Qadir's descriptions of incidents from his youth in Tarbaghatay and Ghulja add valuable detail to our picture of the Altishahri reading culture from the 1910s through the early 1930s.[116] His records of public readings at the mosque, a barbershop, and a cobbler's shop, demonstrate that the public recitation at the heart of Altishahr's manuscript tradition closely intertwined social context and genre. They also show that nonliterate Altishahris could be avid consumers of books.

According to Qadir, many mosques hosted what he called a *"kitab-khanliq,"* or a book reading, every day after the predawn prayer. Apprentice mullahs would read out texts in Arabic and Persian, and teaching mullahs would provide the audience with translation and interpretation. Famous scholars could draw audiences of "countless" people, and Qadir's father kept tabs on who would be holding readings in which mosques, sometimes traveling great distances to see well-known scholars.[117] Qadir described his first visit to a book reading at a mosque, during which he heard the *Ṣaḥīḥ* of Bukhārī, a hadith collection. The apprentice reader knelt in front of the master scholar, who would interject after every few sentences in order to provide a translation and explication. This kind of gathering provided nonliterate listeners, such as Qadir's father, a chance to access major works of Islamic scholarship. Due in part to his father's regular attendance of *kitabkhanliqs,* Qadir considered his father a "mullah of the ear." This term implied that, although his father's non-literacy prevented him from using the title "mullah," he had achieved a comparable level of education through his enthusiastic attendance at public readings.[118]

Qadir himself frequently read out books to listeners at a certain barbershop. The barber was unable to read but nevertheless owned a substantial collection of manuscripts, which he kept in a wooden box. He was also, in Qadir's words, "a lover of books and a mullah of the ear."[119] All of the texts in the barber's books were of foreign origin (though this foreignness was invisible from within the tradition), from the epic, romance, and *ḥikāyat* traditions. Most of these books were known in Altishahr through Turki translations. They included *Jamshīdnāmah* and "*Rustemi Dastan*" (both from the Iranian epic cycle), "*Aba Muslim,*"[120] *Qahrimān Qātil* (a Turkic epic), Amīr Khusraw's *Chahār Darvīsh* (the Indian Sufi's famous group of stories in the *ḥikāyat* tradition), the *Thousand and One Nights, Totīnāmah* (a Persian translation of Sanskrit tales in the *ḥikāyat* tradition, in this context presumably a Turki translation thereof), a sensationalized biography of Ibn Sina, and a work called "*Shahi Maran.*"[121] Qadir categorized all of these books as "*jangnāmahs* and mythological stories."[122] Both literate listeners who could not obtain their own books and those who could not themselves read came to hear Qadir's readings. In the evenings he would often retell the stories from memory at a cobbler's shop, returning them to the oral realm.

Qadir was participating in a larger tradition of performing similar tales in public market areas. Though they probably usually worked from memory, professional itinerant storytellers recited tales to large crowds on bazaar days, taking most of their materials from Turki translations of Persian books, and in some cases reading directly from books.[123] Grenard provided a list of storytellers' staples, a canon that overlaps significantly with Qadir's barbershop repertoire: *Shāhnāmah, Iskandarnāmah,*

'Alīname, Kitāb-i Lataif, Shah Tuti (=*Totīnāmah?*), *Chahār Darvīsh, Bakhtiyarnāmah, Farhād va Shīrīn,* [*Amīr*] *Ḥamzah,* and *Dil Arām.*[124] While most of the titles differ from the barber's library, the type of material is very much the same, namely, Persian epics, Persian romances, *ḥikāyats,* and Persian love stories, the components of Qadir's "*jangnāmahs* and mythological stories" category. Similar texts were read at male social gatherings called *mashrab.*[125]

A more sacred kind of public reading occurred at shrines. Several sources mention the telling of tazkirahs, though it is not always clear whether the texts were summarized, recited from memory, or read directly from books. The earliest clear evidence of such practices may be several distichs in the book *Ūlūgh Tazkirah-'i Bughrā-khān* of Abū al-Qāsim, completed in 1829–1830:

> At the shrines the tazkirahs are many,
> In words the great tazkirah is wealthy,
> The great shaykhs read out the tazkirah together,
> Adding to it words improper.[126]

Abū al-Qāsim goes on to say that that the Persian prose of the original tazkirah made it hard for the regular people to understand, and

> Thus, the story, in Turki verse was unfurled
> That all of may hear it, these people of the world.[127]

Throughout Abū al-Qāsim's introduction, his concern for the uneducated is clear. Although he cites the command of Sultan Satūq Bughrā-khān as the main reason for writing the work, he also mentions many times that his translation will make it more accessible to ordinary people, who could not understand Persian. He further explains that because he has versified and condensed the tazkirah, people will not tire of listening to it but will hear the story from beginning to end. Taken as a whole, the introduction suggests that Abū al-Qāsim was dismayed by the shaykhs' control of the saint's history, that a Persian version was recited at the shrines, and that Abū al-Qāsim aimed his tazkirah primarily at a listening audience.

There is also evidence for tazkirah readings from a European observer. Gunnar Jarring reported that pilgrims to the Ordam Padshah system of shrines, near Yangihissar, recited long passages from "the tazkirah."[128] Jarring also recorded that at Artush he visited the tomb of Sultan Satūq Bughrā-khān, where the shaykh "lectured about all of Satuq Bughra

Khan's good deeds and he described his life, according to the biography, tazkirah, which I had looked into previously."[129] It seems that informal presentations of the tazkirah material could happen without immediate reference to a book. The Uyghur playwright and novelist Săypidin Ăzizi, recounting his childhood in 1920s Artush, reported that when he and his friends went to play at the tomb of Sultan Satūq Bughrā-khān, the elders and shaykhs would tell him stories about the saint.[130] The stories referred to by Ăzizi and Jarring reflect the parallel circulation of unwritten narratives at the shrines. Jarring's observation in particular confirms that this material was very close to the written tazkirah. At the same time, an unwritten tradition of unknown age recorded in the 1990s suggests that tales with material unknown in the written tazkirahs were also available in unwritten form.[131] The shrines were thus a meeting and mixing point for unwritten and written histories of the saints.

It is also clear that tazkirahs were kept at shrines. Martin Hartmann acquired his copy of the *Tazkirah of Sut Bībī Pādshāhim* from the shaykh at the Sut Bībī shrine, in the suburbs of Yarkand. It was one of two copies the shaykh kept.[132] Bellew, leader of the British expedition to Altishahr in 1873–1874, after complaining about the lack of local manuscripts in the market, reported that historical works were all hidden away in shrines.[133] Explorer and future president of Finland, C. G. E. Mannerheim, purchased from "the mullah" at the shrine of Imam Mūsá Kāẓim, near Khotan, the imam's tazkirah. Interestingly, the shaykhs also seem to have maintained tazkirahs connected to shrines other than those they guarded.[134] Like most texts, Mannerheim's shrine copy of Imam Mūsá Kāẓim's tazkirah was bound together with tazkirahs of other saints, many from the same area, including the *Four Sacrificed Imams* and *Imam Ja'far Ṣādiq*.[135]

The colophons of three other manuscripts show that tazkirahs were also produced at the shrines.[136] A manuscript now in Berkeley's Bancroft library bears an unusually detailed colophon, in which the copyist reports that he worked for twelve days and nights at the tomb of Imam Ja'far Ṣādiq to complete the book for a certain Aḥmad Khwājah Ishān. This not only speaks to the creation of the copy in question, but also to the presence of the tazkirah from which it was copied at the shrine. Whether the model copy was one in the possession of shrine staff, such as a shaykh, or a copy brought to the shrine by a pilgrim is impossible to know with absolute certainty. However, the length of time necessary for copying and the numerous documentations of tazkirahs' presence at shrines certainly suggests that the Bancroft manuscript was copied from a tazkirah kept at the shrine or in the possession of its shaykhs. Whatever the source of the "original" may have been, it's important that the colophon documents the presence of two copies of the Imam Ja'far Ṣādiq tazkirah at his shrine on the day that the copyist finished his work. It is also significant that the copyist thought the book's creation at the shrine, the ultimate source of historical authority, was worth recording.

Today, shrine activities are carefully regulated by the Chinese government. Not only have the tazkirahs been removed from the shrines but textual performances are discouraged or forbidden. However, the information in the tazkirahs has not been forgotten and continues to be delivered in informal ways to small audiences, similar to the practices described by Jarring and Ăzizi at Artush. On the whole, the practice of reading, reciting, or retelling the tazkirahs has been rather successfully suppressed by government policies. In the most comprehensive survey of contemporary shrine culture to date, Uyghur anthropologist Rahile Dawut, does not record the practice anywhere.[137] At the same time, the biographies of the saints are still known to many shaykhs, and based on conversations with them at their shrines, Dawut has recorded much of the shaykhs' knowledge in her book. Where corresponding tazkirahs are known, they usually match closely the shaykh's tales that Dawut recorded. In fact, though she does not note it, Dawut's research activity itself, and the participation of the shaykhs, was an enactment of the tazkirah tradition at the shrines, wherein Dawut, in the place of a pilgrim, received the tale of the shrine from the shaykhs.

The special associations between certain genres and social contexts did not preclude the use of the genres in other contexts. As was noted earlier, there are many copies of the popular tazkirahs—more than could have been usefully kept at one shrine, or even a handful of shrines. Judging from copyists' notes and manuscript find locations, the tazkirahs were spread over a wide geographic area. Swedish explorer Sven Hedin wrote that during his trip down the Tarim River, his guide, "the mullah," entertained the boatmen with readings from two books about "the travels of the earliest Muhammadan missionaries in Altishahr."[138] Assuming that Hedin understood the readings correctly, it may fairly be concluded that these works were tazkirahs, for only the tazkirahs contain such tales.

Though the link between certain performative contexts and genres was not exclusive, it is still clear that contextual links lent important associations to written texts. We have already seen, for example, that the *Tazkirat al-Bughrā-khān* was known popularly as the Ordam Padshah tazkirah, identifying the text with the place at which it was recited, namely, the shrine called Ordam Padshah. The tazkirah or hagiography was that piece of the past that belonged to its shrine. The romance and *jangnāmah* was connected to the marketplace. A specialized association between genre, place, and event mediated the meaning and authenticity of these texts.

Authority and Inlibration of Knowledge in the Manuscript Tradition

Once a "transmitted" text was given physical form in a book, the text gained an ontological autonomy, despite the fact that community authorship avoided the formation of any true semantic autonomy. The "bookification" or inlibration of knowledge made the text countable and imaginable as something that had its own independent existence. It also created an idealized text as a site of authority. Despite the coexistence of numerous divergent versions of any text, each physical book was treated as an authoritative instantiation of the ideal text, and that ideal text was authoritative in part because of its book form, for the book and writing were by nature sacred, even talismanic.

Inlibration was particularly important for the articulation of historical knowledge in space. The saints who were the protagonists of Altishahri history were connected to places through the shrine. The inlibration of their biographies allowed not just the saint but also a particular history of the saint to attach to place. The notion of location is, of course, generally tied to physical existence, and so the transformation of text into object by inscription in a book aided in the connection to place. The tazkirah was kept at the shrine, as Abū al-Qāsim was careful to point out. Rather than being knowledge in the minds of experts, it became an independent existence, one to which a pilgrimage could be made. At the same time, the mobility of books had effects, such as the spread of shared imaginations of the past.

To the reader in the modern print tradition, the authority of the community-authored book is counterintuitive, because such a work lacks so many of the printed work's sources of authority. Part of the authority of the printed work comes from that fact that I myself, unlike the consumer-copyist of the manuscript tradition, cannot produce a book. A product greater than the efforts of one individual, one that grows out of the collaboration of several experts (writer, designer, editor, copyeditor, machinist, engineer, printer) is surely more worthy of serious attention. Furthermore, as a result of this corporate and mechanical production, in the printed book the perfect regularity of the letters, spacing, and layout promotes a sense of precision that can easily be understood as authority. The method of production is apparent in the text itself, reassuring the reader that each copy of the book is identical and thus accurate and authoritative.

It is difficult to access Altishahri ideas about textual authority. Marginalia give a general sense that every written book was considered authoritative, but there are no clues as to how, specifically, this authority was maintained. However, it is plausible that the mechanism of community authorship, despite its creation of highly varied texts, lent those texts an aura of trustworthiness. The community-authored manuscript shares with print a claim to a corporate or community voice, not through rigidity and perfection but through alterations, additions, and errors. The alterations and errors of a manuscript accumulate over time, across several or even many copyists. As artifacts of a wider community authorship, they produce a sense of ancient authorship. In some cases, they even produce impenetrable nonsense that will be dutifully recited by the faithful. It is conceivable that the accumulated awkwardness or impenetrability became a mark of authority inherited from some other time or place, not attributable to a single person (for who would intentionally interpolate nonsense?), just as the archaic language of the King James Bible gives it authority today. As in the print case, there often remained some basic sense of individual authorship, but the author's voice was merged into a corporate network. This network was, unlike in the print tradition, temporally deep in ways that were obvious to the reader. In such a work, then, the voice in the text comes not just from nowhere, but also from no time. It is a product of a diachronic community effort, a project so large that it might even appear as a reflection of the divine. The sacred authority of the manuscript can only be enhanced by its transcendence of the personal and the individual, its incorporation of the incomprehensible, namely, byproducts of the complexities and chance of a larger system of community authorship.

Ownership

One of the great differences between unwritten and written forms of communication is that the latter can be owned. People in Altishahr often

ascribed great importance to the ownership of a text, because of its talismanic virtues. This applies especially to the tazkirahs, trade manuals, and
prayer compilations, some of which, after blessing readers of the books,
bless those who do not read but simply carry the book.[139] Everyday carrying was easy when it came to the trade manuals, which were often no
bigger than a deck of playing cards. Books traveled long distances, and
were shared among people from various towns. An example of such inter-
oasis sharing is recorded in a copy of Navā'ī poetry. A man from Yarkand
wrote that he read the book, which belonged to a man from the town of
Guma, at a *sarāy* (inn) in Kashgar.[140] Another borrowing is documented
in a copy of the *Jam'i al-Ḥikāyat,* where a note records that Mehmān
Khālipatim of Ghandjī village near Qarghaliq borrowed the book from
Sharīf Akhund of Chahār Bāgh.[141] Perhaps because of the frequency of
lending, owners were careful to mark their books, sometimes with a simple "this is Turdi Akhon's book" and sometimes with the common curse:
"This is Aḥmad Akhūnd Khoja Hafiz. If someone says that it is not so, his
mouth will dry up."[142] Records of ownership did more than prevent theft.
Like the documentations of reading, they record the owner's connection
to the history of Altishahr. In a tradition in which book owners were
blessed, and both reading and owning were carefully documented, ownership itself was a part of the entexting of the past.

The binding of books in Altishahr merits careful consideration, because
multiple works were often bound together in composite manuscripts that
we might call anthologies. This raises the questions of who carried out the
selection process for these anthologies, whether the works were brought
together and copied at the same time, and whether whole anthologies
were copied or composed anew. Unfortunately, no one seems to have
written a description of the book-making process. While Muhammad 'Alī
Damolla described the process of writing, he did not reveal whether his
ideal writer was writing on single pages, quires, or a prepared codex of
blank pages. However, the surviving manuscripts themselves provide
many clues, and suggest a wide variety of methods and traditions, exactly
what we might expect from a tradition of book-making open to amateurs
as well as professionals.

If binding after copying were a universal practice, we would expect
the manuscripts we see today to have precisely the number of pages required for the works in the manuscript, plus a few protective flyleaves.
Manuscripts of this sort are indeed numerous, but examples also exist
with numerous blank pages at the end, suggesting an owner was pre-

pared to add to his or her anthology. An examination of manuscript quires, the groups of paper sheets folded together before sewing into a complete book, provides a few more clues. In nineteenth- and early twentieth-century Altishahri manuscripts a quire is most commonly composed of four sheets folded in half together to create eight folia, or sixteen pages. Some manuscripts have irregular quires at the beginning and end of their constituent works, with a greater or lesser number of sheets used to ensure that a single text begins at the first page of a quire and ends at the last page of a quire.[143] This is consistent with a slow accumulation of works, as a copyist-owner conserves paper, avoiding blank pages and only adding sheets when a new work is to be added. If the anthology were copied all at once, there would be no need to cut short or lengthen a quire at the end of a work, as the next work could be immediately begun on the remaining pages.[144] The text could be protected in an unattached leather cover before reaching some stage of completeness that inspired a more elaborate binding. Other manuscripts have regular quire sizes throughout, and the various texts within the book end and begin without regard to the quires.[145] This suggests that either the entire anthology was written out at once before binding, or that the works were copied into a book of blank pages. Thus, it seems that both planned volumes and volumes created through accumulation over the years existed. The latter included a compilation of prayers and spells from the Jarring collection that records eight different dates spanning twenty-one years from 1902 to 1923, and uses three different kinds of paper.[146] In such cases it is not always easy to tell whether sections were spliced together or new pages were added and then filled with additional material. What we can say with some certainty is that the books were produced in a variety of ways, probably including splicing, rebinding, copying to plan before binding, and copying into prebound books, lending further flexibility to the traditions of book production.

Composite manuscripts or anthologies represent a significant portion of Altishahri manuscripts.[147] Often, the works bound together in a single volume are of the same genre. Such was the case especially for trade manuals, books of prayers and incantations, and tazkirahs. Thus the tazkirah, after having developed over centuries into a monographic form (as opposed to the earlier biographical dictionary) was bound back together with other tazkirahs in the process of copying, creating a personalized anthology, arranged by the scribe or reader-copyist rather than the author. These personal anthologies provide clues as to what kinds of works were seen to belong together, or were used in the same context. The anthologies are snapshots of individual literary interests, acting as small, portable libraries.

The works that made up such copyist anthologies tended to retain markers of their continued status as independent texts. The introductory praise and source documentation were kept intact, and in many manuscripts the *bismillah* was repeated at the beginning of each individual work. In some cases, though, works combined in a composite manuscript were stripped of their introductory materials and run together, causing them to appear as a single, unified text, despite their varied sources.[148] The opposite phenomenon occurred as well. Certain chapters from the biographical dictionary, *Taẕkirah-i Uvaysīya*, were often copied and bound together with monographic tazkirahs. In one manuscript, a copyist has stripped the chapter numbers and given the chapters separate titles, thus presenting elements of a single work as separate works.[149]

The practices of combining works under a single cover gave the copyist and binder the opportunity to make many works out of one, or to make one out of many. Groupings of works carried meaning. Not only were works of the same kind, such as trade manuals or tazkirahs, put together, but their ordering was significant too. In the tazkirah anthologies, saints usually are grouped by geography, with Yarkand saints near Yarkand saints, for example. Those collections that included stories of the prophet Muhammad or Hasan and Husayn placed such works at the beginning, perhaps reflecting a chronological arrangement. The grouping of works made sense of histories, and brought individual monographs together to form a more comprehensive view of the local past. Interestingly, this more comprehensive view of the past was entirely in the control of those who decided which works would be bound together, not the authors. As the designers of anthologies arranged the texts that were the premade building blocks of local history, they created competing pictures of the region's past that circulated side by side. As will be explored later, these visions often had a geographical dimension, as anthologies were designed to emphasize hometown saints.

Altishahr's textual world, and thus, historical practice, was highly communal. Rarely, if ever, could the act of reading be considered a simple communication between author and reader. The central text was the joint product of the author(s) and the copyists, and it was enriched by the notations of the owner, and even borrowers. Often, the history of the book's reading and ownership appeared alongside the core text, and reading itself tended to involve more than one person. In lending and copying, books moved along the lines of personal relationships.

The written text was an important link between individuals and the past, though in the vast majority of cases it was necessarily highly mediated by qualified readers, such as professional storytellers or shrine shaykhs. Related unwritten tales circulated around the texts and always had the potential to intervene in the textual world at the point of copying or composition. In this environment, the existence of the text was perhaps as important as its contents, just as the existence of the shrine was as important as its architectural or geographic form. The mere knowledge of a text's existence, along with the references to such a text (as in Abū al-Qāsīm's introduction), served as a locus of historical meaning, a phenomenon that called out for interpretation and legitimated historical practice through the popularly recognized authority, sacredness, and magical power of the book.

The book-related practices, in their interface, undermined the author's monopoly on creativity, and put the meaning of the book in the hands of a large community. At no single moment did any one of these practices permit an individual to dramatically alter the work's significance, but over time, the interaction of such practices brought major changes to the form, content, and context of texts, at times carrying them far from the intentions of their first authors. The powers of authorship could be distributed widely, and yet, the manuscripts preserved their claims to authenticity, eschewing notions of authorial creativity in favor of images of transmission. Thus, the manuscript tradition supported a strange and powerful contradiction. Texts were extremely flexible, able to change dramatically over time to reflect the changing needs of the community of readers. At the same time, they were seen, despite this plasticity, as immutable, accurately transmitted, and supremely authoritative encapsulations of knowledge from the past.[150] This combination of actual flexibility with imagined rigidity permitted the community of Altishahri readers and writers to shape a new genre that was uniquely suited to their historical needs, and yet to see in that genre, the tazkirah, an unquestioned and ancient sacred authority. It allowed new texts to enter a sacred canon, to become a part of the core Islamic (and historical) texts of Altishahr, without anyone making a heretical claim to originality or prophecy.

As was noted earlier, the potential for community authorship manifested itself dramatically in the tazkirah tradition, which demonstrates powerfully the potential cumulative effects of manuscript phenomena and Altishahri book-related practices. Having examined the flexibilities of the manuscript tradition, we can now understand the mechanisms by which the late Altishahri tazkirah genre took shape in more detail. The popular tazkirahs became a genre by many mechanisms, but rarely by authorial composition. It was despite a wild variation in form and content that the consumers of histories shaped a genre and a canon under the term *tazkirah*. In the copying, phrases and sections less relevant to shrine culture were eliminated through the meaningful act of abbreviation. The saint's name was changed to a form suitable to the copyist's taste. More importantly, the copyist often signaled the work's function and its relationship to other works by designating it as a "tazkirah" at beginning of the first page. The designers of anthologies (whether copyist-readers or copyists' customers), strengthened the associations between works by collecting them from varied sources and binding them under one cover. In rare cases, copyists even melded the various parts of an anthology into a single, continuous text. Readers wrote themselves into the history of a saint's veneration by documenting their reading in the margins and endpapers. After all, many tazkirahs were as much histories of the shrine and the saint's veneration as they were biographies of the saint. Cultural practices not necessarily connected to manuscript technology played a role too. Pilgrims and shaykhs continually reinforced the tazkirahs' connections to the shrines by reciting them there. Archiving served the same function, as the books containing tazkirahs were kept at shrines. At the shrine of Muhammad Sharīf, a patron inscribed a summary of the relevant tazkirah on the wall of the saint's tomb.[151] In such ways, the apparently minor flexibilities inherent in manuscript technology interacted with culturally specific approaches to book use to significantly alter the meaning of a text in a process of community authorship.

The clues left in Altishahr's manuscripts emphasize that the written text is but one artifact of historical practice. In the manuscript form, a written text speaks eloquently of the development of the past-in-the-present, an "our history," over time, because it was continuously reshaped by the vast world of social practice, not just the selective preservation of the archive. But, despite this eloquence, the manuscript was still, in its own time, only one fulcrum of meaning among several. The term *historiography* embraces a host of endeavors, but in the literal sense of the word's components, entails a focus on the written text, which threatens to limit our understanding of histories past. Much historiography posits the written text as its end. The historiographer, in tracing those factors that contributed to the creation of the written text, works to understand the written text itself. In contrast, my goal in this study is to take the historical experience as historiography's end, letting the written text become a clue to what is usually treated as context. From this point of view, wherein the context, namely, the larger social process of historical meaning's maintenance and development, is the object of inquiry, we might even call the written text "con-praxis," subordinating the text to the speech, travel, performance, and place creation that constituted so much of Altishahri historical practice. If the physical, written text was only one element of the manuscript tradition, the manuscript tradition, in turn, was part of a larger constellation of phenomena that created and recreated historical meaning around the fulcra of texts, places, and personages.

3

THE SHRINE

As we have seen, the texts of Altishahr's local history, both unwritten and written, were most powerfully deployed in the rich settings of saints' tombs. Like the manuscript, the shrine in Altishahr was a fulcrum of historical meaning, in the sense that texts about the past were attracted to the shrine, circulated there, and, as the case of Abū al-Qāsīm demonstrated, disputed there. At the same time, these fulcra, around which continually transforming texts turned, were themselves manifestations of the past. Put another way, the shrines were both the context of historical practice and the very stuff of history. This means that a deeper understanding of Altishahri and Uyghur local history cannot be achieved without an analysis of the shrine's place in that tradition: the role of these sites in both daily life and special festivals, the understandings of the shrines reflected and disseminated in tazkirahs, the forms of the shrines themselves, and the relationship between the shrines and Altishahr's geography. What, for example, does it mean to remove your shoes at the point of historical learning? How is the shrine's relationship to an archipelago of oases, concentrations of meaningful places in the vast empty space of the desert, reflected in notions of the past and of historical personage? What are the practical consequences of learning history at gatherings of strangers from distant places? The answers to these kinds of questions begin to shed light on the effects of tying historical practice firmly to particular points on the landscape. Shrines provided pilgrims a physical and geographical link to the past, which further drew history into the realm of personal experience, much like the museums and monuments of certain other societies. Altishahri conceptions of place and of the shrine lent local history a glow of sacred authenticity and connected the texted past to points on the landscape regarded both as blessed emanations of the past and as important sites in daily ritual life. The connection of local history to the shrine also performed a more mundane and practical function. Through the institution of pilgrimage, the shrine attracted large gatherings of people from diverse walks of life, facilitating the creation of a shared view of the past through tazkirah recitations.

The Shrine as Local Institution

History readings that took place during pilgrimages were only one small part of the shrine's role in the community. Long-distance pilgrimages to famous shrines were common, but the shrine was also a local neighborhood institution throughout Altishahr. The pilgrims who made the journey to a distant, famous shrine left from hometowns with shrines of their own. Even the smallest villages had holy graves at which the suffering prayed for God's favor, and around these sacred tombs the villages buried their deceased. In some places, the local neighborhood mosque was also attached to a shrine, as at the Muhammad Sharīf shrine in Yarkand, thus ensuring daily visits from the surrounding community. Major shrines located in towns or villages with weekly markets were further connected to the oasis-wide community through trade patterns, which created the opportunity to combine pilgrimage and market activities in journeys less formal than the annual pilgrimage festivals. This chapter traces the integration of the shrine with the local and oasis communities and then demonstrates the ramifications of this integration for historical practice by describing the contemporary situation at two shrines on Altishahr's Southern Silk Road, based on my visits from 2004 to 2009: the tomb of the Seven Muhammads (*Haft Muḥammadān* or *Chiltän*) in Yarkand and the shrine of Imam Shākir just outside the Khotan oasis.[1]

The tomb of the Seven Muhammads lies in the midst of Yarkand's central cemetery, near the tombs of the khans of the Yarkand Moghul Khanate (1514–1678) and the leaders of the Black Mountain Naqshbandi Sufi order. However, most of the graves in the cemetery belong to ordinary people. When I visited on weekdays, I noticed that the majority of visitors to the cemetery were those who came to tend their relatives' graves. They would tidy up the low adobe memorials with a broom and a bucket of water, irrigate nearby plants, and perhaps scatter grain to attract birds to the grave. Most said a silent personal prayer *(du'a),* and some read a sura from the Quran, usually the *Fātiha* (1) or *Yāsīn* (36), for the benefit of the deceased. A few people would approach the tomb of the Seven Muhammads with a silent prayer for personal assistance. Beggars lined the dusty, poplar-shaded path to the saints' tomb, providing pilgrims with the opportunity to perform pious charity. The cemetery was a quiet place, and visitors navigated the paths between the graves with care. Occasionally, someone would take a shortcut through the graveyard on some other business and mutter a prayer for the dead under his or her breath. Some told me that they could sense the presence of the spirits who wandered the cemetery, or even that they feared them.

Wednesdays and Thursdays, traditional days for the tending of graves, brought larger numbers of visitors. A few shaykhs stood ready at the shrine to offer prayers for the local residents who stopped by after a visit to their parents' grave. However, it was on Sunday that the cemetery really livened up. On this day Yarkand held its weekly market, attracting buyers and sellers from towns and villages throughout the Yarkand oasis, and even some from more distant locations such as Kashgar and Khotan. On market day the shaykhs who maintained the Seven Muhammads tomb would open the doors to the inner shrine and welcome a steady stream of pilgrims. After passing the rows of beggars, the pilgrims would enter the shrine complex, rebuilt in 1872–1873 on the site of an older shrine,[2] pass through a vestibule, and emerge in a mosque of traditional Central Asian style, wrapped around an open courtyard. At the opposite end of this courtyard was a platform on which several shaykhs would sit. The pilgrims would approach and offer a donation, either in the form of food, such as a piece of bread or a live goose, or money. Odd amounts were preferred, for the avoidance of even numbers, or "pairs," as they were known, recalled the unity of God. The shaykhs would pray together on behalf of the pilgrims, who then proceeded across another courtyard toward the building that houses the graves of the Seven Muhammads. Many pilgrims would then offer a prayer while facing the back or side wall of the tomb. During these private, personal prayers, usually silently mouthed or spoken in very quiet voice, some pilgrims wept. This weeping was a conventional form of devotion, wherein the pilgrims expressed their sadness over the passing of the saint from this world. At the same time, it was sometimes also an expression of grief over a difficult personal situation, such as infertility, for which the visitor was requesting the saint's aid.

The final stop on the pilgrimage was the doorway of the saints' tomb. Another shaykh would sit in the doorway and collect another donation in exchange for another prayer. If the pilgrims had a particular difficulty or illness they wanted eased, they might tell the shaykh of the trouble. Some pilgrims requested to enter the building and inspect the graves, and usually they were permitted to do so. The people who came to the shrine on Sundays represented a small proportion of the throngs that attended the market, but they kept the shaykhs (usually about six older men) busy, and lines occasionally formed. For most of these pilgrims, the shrine was a familiar place, one they visited whenever they came to Yarkand's market, though new visitors could sometimes be recognized by their unfamiliarity with the normal procedures. If they brought their children, pilgrims might explain to them in a whisper the proper conduct in the shrine or the names of the saints buried there. Such visits, joined as they were with the important economic activity of the market, lacked the concentrated, extended devotional character of the activities during the major pilgrimage festivals. Interactions with the shaykhs were brief, and the typical visitor completed the circuit of the shrine within about fifteen minutes. The power of the prayers sought by these pilgrims stemmed, in the most "orthodox" interpretations, from the piety of the shaykhs and the closeness of the entombed saints to God. Both figures acted as intercessors. In more popular interpretations, the saints themselves retained supernatural powers, which they wielded from the spirit world. In either case, acts of devotion at the shrine gained solemnity from the sacred setting. The earth was made holy by the presence of the saints. The interior of the tomb was embellished with a forest of prayer flags and the enormous horns of wild Marco Polo sheep, brought as offerings by previous pilgrims. Such offerings demonstrated the great number of other pilgrims with whom the visitors shared their experience, and made the sacred status of the place immediately visible.

It is hard to say exactly what pilgrims made of my own presence at the shrine. I visited several dozen times between 2004 and 2009[3] and, as a nonbeliever, I always feared disrupting or profaning the activities there, despite the shaykhs' assurances. Pilgrims would occasionally ask if I was a Muslim, and when I told them I was not, they would ask why I came. My usual answers, that I was investigating Uyghur history or Uyghur culture, seemed to be satisfactory. From time to time someone would try to convert me, often by describing hell and warning me that it was the final destination of non-Muslims. In my earlier trips, I observed the shrine from the perspective of the pilgrim, making the circuit and leaving the main structure, sometimes lingering outside with the beggars, other times exploring the large graveyard that surrounds the central shrine. As I got to know the shaykhs, and once they decided I was a "good person," I began to spend more time inside the shrine, chatting with the shaykhs while the steady trickle of pilgrims flowed through. Eventually, my presence became unremarkable, and even pilgrim strangers, taking their cue from the shaykhs, began to treat me as an ordinary participant. From my earliest visits, everyone, from beggar to shaykh, seemed happy that an outsider should take interest in their sacred place, and extended great hospitality to me, for which I am extremely grateful.

Probably the largest annual gathering of pilgrims at the Seven Muhammads tomb took place during the holiday of Barat, known more popularly in Yarkand simply as *Tünäk* (the Vigil). On the twelfth, thirteenth, and fourteenth of the Islamic month of Sha'ban, Muslims visited tombs to pray for the intercession of the dead and keep vigils all night, praying the rosary alone or in groups, and reciting the Quran. The Seven Muhammads tomb was the most popular shrine in Yarkand for Barat devotions. The same circuit of donations and prayers that took place on market days played out on a grander scale, especially in the hours just after sunset, when thousands of pilgrims, both from Yarkand and from distant towns, streamed through the shrine complex in the dark. An additional door, which remained locked during the rest of the year, was opened to allow for more traffic.

I participated in the Barat vigil in 2007 and again in 2009. Despite the flashlights and candles people carried, the immense graveyard was dark, and the muttering and melodic chanting of Quranic verses floated from unseen corners. At the shrine itself, the shaykhs sat behind enormous piles of donated bread, and the beggars brought bags to carry home the expected Barat bounty. For shaykhs and beggars, Barat is a time of plenty, and both groups alloyed their respectful piety with joy. With the collusion of children, who were excited to be out so late and to eat the special fried bread prepared as offerings, the celebratory mood rubbed off on the adult pilgrims. Despite the dark and the quiet, the sound of so many unseen footsteps created excitement, and laughter interrupted the hushed proceedings from time to time. Crowds formed at the door to the inner tomb, and the shaykhs began to offer their prayers and recitations for groups of pilgrims rather than individuals. A bright yellow light bulb hung from its wiring above the shaykhs, who sat on thick felt mats amid the piles of bread, alternately counting their money and offering prayers. Late into the night, women and men sat in separate circles within the open-air mosque, repeating sacred formulae for hours on end to gain merit, passing thousands of small polished stones from hand to hand to keep count of the group's combined repetitions. Some pilgrims circum-ambulated the complex; others wept for the saints or for members of their own families at the walls of the inner shrine.

Barat is not a pilgrimage festival dedicated to the Seven Muhammads. It is a holiday observed in various ways in different parts of Altishahr, focused on pleasing the souls of the dead and gaining their intercession. In much of Altishahr, the practice has died away, but the Seven Muham-mads shrine still saw more than 1,000 pilgrims on the second day of Barat celebrations in 2007. The shaykhs told that, during Barat, angels carry out an accounting of Muslims' deeds throughout the previous year. As-sisting the spirits of the dead, whether by repeating prayers in their name or by nourishing them with the scent of food, both gained the worship-per merit to atone for the sins of the previous year and earned the inter-cession of the spirits. Few spirits were considered more powerful or nearer to God than the spirits of the Seven Muhammads. Thus, even those who did not have relatives buried in this graveyard would come to visit the saints' tomb.

Though the Barat observances differ from the pilgrimage festivals, the assemblage of so many visitors at the tombs inevitably encouraged some of the practices associated with the festivals. During the 2007 Barat, for example, a singer-storyteller arrived with his *rabap* (a stringed instru-ment) to play for donations, but was quickly chased away, perhaps for fear of drawing unwanted attention from the police, whose interference was feared each year. Later in the evening, a shaykh gave a long speech about the history of the Seven Muhammads, prompted by visitors from Urumchi who had asked about the saints' identity. At the time of my vis-its, the Seven Muhammads shrine did not seem to have its own desig-nated pilgrimage festival, and the shaykhs took advantage of major holi-days, namely Barat and the Feast of the Sacrifice *(Qurban Heyt)* to perform their traditional roles as temporary community leaders and arbiters of the past.

The shrine of Imam Shākir, in the desert near the Khotan oasis, pro-vides an example of a very different connection between shrine and com-munity. The Imam Shākir shrine marks the place where a leader of the armies that spread Islam to Khotan was martyred, as recounted in the *Tazkirah of the Four Sacrificed Imams*. Local government authorities shut down all religious activities at this shrine in the spring of 2009, and as of August 2009, the interdiction was still preventing pilgrims from arriving. Before that time, however, the shrine received a regular flow of pilgrims. The shrine is located some eight kilometers from the nearest cultivation, thirteen kilometers from the nearest village, and is accessible only by sandy desert tracks solid enough for a donkey cart or motorcycle but not for a car. Not surprisingly, inhabitants of the nearby villages did not bring their dead to this remote location, so there are no graves of ordinary Muslims here, only the tombs of the saint and his associates. Travel over the desert is difficult, and even those wealthy enough to arrive by motorcycle had to push their vehicles through the particularly soft patches. Daily worship was thus impractical, and even before the government closure, the shrine was empty for most of the week. On Thursdays, however, a small community of twenty to eighty regular worshippers arrived.

In the hour or two before the midday prayer, pilgrims would gather behind the shaykh on the dunes, kneeling in the sand and facing eastward toward the tomb of the martyred saint Imam Shākir. There the shaykh and others took turns reciting Quranic passages and Uyghur-language *hükmät,* songs comprised of verses from Central Asian Sufi poets such as Yasavi, or versified narratives about early Islamic figures such as the prophet Muhammad's daughter Fatima.[4] After these recitations, members of the congregation would request prayers, and the shaykh would comply. Everyone said, "Amin," in unison. After prayer at the main tomb, the group would rise and proceed to another grave, where further recitations and prayers were performed for another fifteen minutes. After this, the group would move to a third tomb, time, weather, and interest permitting. Once prayers at the saints' tombs were completed, people would gather in a special hall for the silent repetition of Quranic verses, all the while monitoring the group's progress with buckets of smooth counting stones. After performing the midday prayer, the pilgrims assembled for *dhikr,* the remembrance of God. In this case, *dhikr* took the form of rhythmic chanting of the syllable "hum," while a shaykh or a member of the congregation sang a *hükmät.* As the rhythm gradually increased in speed, some people would stand up and begin to step in time, turning about, and occasionally bumping into each other. Eventually, all of the participants rose to their feet, and those who did not join the dancing wagged their upper bodies from side to side. After ten minutes or so of energetic chanting and dancing, rising to a disorienting and frenetic crescendo, the shaykh would loudly call out an end to the cycle. If someone collapsed in ecstasy or exhaustion, the shaykh would call the end of the cycle at that moment. In response to the shaykh's call, everyone would sit again, and someone else would begin a new *hükmăt* or *munajăt* (a verse of supplication), starting the cycle all over again.

The leadership of each cycle shifted among members of the congregation in improvised rotation. As a cycle drew to a close, everyone would look around to see if someone was volunteering to lead. Sometimes someone would nudge his or her neighbor, or even prod someone verbally to take over. The leadership drifted between men and women, old and young, with apparently little regard for social status. Some people had come prepared with pocket-sized notebooks in which the words of *hükmăt*s and *munajăt*s were written. In the midst of each cycle were further opportunities to request a prayer from the group, either for oneself, for one's family, or for someone else in the congregation. Through such prayers, people were able to express to a wide community their own hardships or to show their concern for others' hardships in direct ways that were not always permissible during normal social situations. The tightness and regular attendance of this *dhikr* community was revealed in one instance when a man referred to several people who had joined for the first time, and for whom he had requested a prayer, as "guests from Khotan." Some cycles included periods of intense lamentation, during which the congregation wailed loudly. The *dhikr* would continue for as many as four hours or as few as two. On one occasion, a visiting shaykh gave a short sermon after the *dhikr,* instructing the community on the meaning of the Sufi way *(tariqat).* As evening approached, the women often prepared a communal meal of *polo* (pilaf) from ingredients brought by the pilgrims. Finally, the worshippers would pray the evening prayer, and begin the long journey home, by donkey cart and motorcycle. On one of my visits, several participants shared with me a ride back to town on a three-wheeled motor cart, and we continued singing and chanting *hükmăt* for the whole trip home.

Nearly all of the pilgrims who participated in the weekly *dhikr* at Imam Shākir were from the same town. They were fined heavily by the police when their practice was eventually banned as the "social crime" of "cross-village worship."[5] Before this interruption, however, the shrine provided them a safe and sanctified place to perform their devotions. Local authorities often discourage *dhikr* because it does not fit with the official version of Islam recognized by the Chinese state, and so the remote, private location of the shrine was surely attractive for the relative freedom it provided. But the pilgrims' attention to the tombs themselves demonstrates that the sanctity of the martyrs' graves was also significant. While praying before the tomb, shoes were removed. Although the standard five-times-daily prayer *(namaz)* is always performed facing westward, toward Mecca, the personal prayers *(du'a)*, Quran recitations, and *hükmăt*, were performed facing the Tomb of Imam Shākir, with the pilgrims' backs toward Mecca. Thus, the shrine, like most in Altishahr, possessed a sanctity that an ordinary home, or even a mosque, could not provide. The shrine was therefore the ideal location for a *khaniqa,* or prayer hall, providing a single community with a sacred space for the remembrance of God, and this became the primary role of the shrine.

However, as at the Seven Muhammads tomb in Yarkand, the shrine took on a different significance when pilgrims from outside the usual community arrived. On a Thursday near the end of Ramadan, in 2007, I arrived at the shrine before the noon prayer and encountered four young men I had not met in previous visits. The shaykh was just beginning to give them a tour of the shrine. He introduced me to the newcomers and invited me to join the tour. We climbed the sand dunes behind the *khaniqa* toward the tombs of Imam Shākir and his soldiers. At the first and most important grave, we all knelt in the sand. One of the pilgrims recited a sura of the Quran from memory (and at lightning speed), and then everyone undertook a silent prayer. Next, the shaykh invited us to come nearer the tomb and inspect the cradle-like wooden structure that served as a grave marker. He gave a brief history of the martyrdom of the imam and his army, partly corresponding to the tale in the *Tazkirah of the Four Sacrificed Imams* but also embellished with details about the tomb itself, such as the claim that a particular beam in the tomb marker extended very deep into the earth. I was surprised to see that the pilgrims did not follow the example of the shaykh and remove their shoes before approaching the tomb. Between the explanations made at various tombs, the shaykh offered short prayers for the pilgrims. At the end of the circuit, everyone offered another silent prayer, this time standing, and we returned to the *khaniqa.* The pilgrims each gave one yuan ($0.12) to the shaykh, who prayed for them once more, and they invited me to join them on their way to another shrine. I hopped on a motorcycle and we were off for a tour of the shrines of the Khotan oasis.

As we walked, pushed, and rode across stone, dust, and sand wastes, we introduced ourselves, and my companions told me about their trip. They were farmers with some free time, and had decided to spend the day visiting as many shrines of the Khotan oasis as possible, starting with Imam Shākir. They introduced themselves to me and to everyone we met that day as coming "from Kichik Eriq, near the shrine of Kohmarim."[6] I was surprised that people from the other end of the Khotan oasis had heard of the Imam Shākir shrine, because, aside from the people I met at the shrine itself, I had never encountered anyone who had heard of the place. It was only with the aid of Aurel Stein's 1904 maps, drawn when the shrine was an important stop on the old Khotan-Kashgar road, that I had found the place myself. The man who led the group answered that he had heard of the shrine from stories (riwayātlăr) and had only found the shrine after several attempts. I was happy to be in the company of so knowledgeable and adventurous a guide.

The view from these pilgrims' perspective was quite different from what I had experienced spending long days at shrines, sitting with the shaykhs, watching visitors pass through, or learning dhikr at more remote tombs. From the point of view of the shrine, the daily or weekly activities of the local community were most prominent: the grave tending, or the dhikr, or the intimate pleas for help from a familiar shaykh. The saint was always there as a powerful unseen force, but he or she was rarely, if ever, audibly mentioned by name. From the back of the motorcycle, however, the shrines became monuments. The saints, their names, and their stories emerged into the foreground.

After learning about the martyrdom of Imam Shākir, we traveled to the grave of a saint known popularly as the Only Son (yalghuz oghul). On the way, we stopped at the shrine of the Only Son's mother, and found no shaykhs or pilgrims there, though the traces of people's devotion—flags and prayer-counting stones—were present. We moved on to the shrine of the Only Son himself, a few hundred meters away. Here again, the shaykh appeared quickly and introduced the shrine. He told not only of the Only Son's disappearance after he went to fight the unbelievers, but of his relation to the other saints in the Khotan area, saying that the Only Son was the ancestor of Khotan's twelve imams.[7] The shaykh reluctantly accepted a donation from the pilgrims and offered a prayer under his breath. From the muttered prayer I caught one line, "May their enemies not find success. . . ." Inside the shrine, the pilgrims asked a local worshipper about the saint, and she provided a name for the Only Son: Muhămmăt Hănipă Dăvrănim. After brief prayers, we headed for the next shrine, the tomb of Imam Ăskăr.[8]

However, a flat tire interrupted our plans. A kind stranger took us into his home and helped our leader to repair the tire. While the rest of us waited, I studied index cards with Uyghur words written on them, which I carried in my pocket to improve my vocabulary. One of my companions grabbed a card and wrote on its back a short verse:

Should I not go to the shrine,
The shrine will not come to me.

He showed it to his friends, and we all laughed together at the absurd idea of the shrine making a pilgrimage to the pilgrim. The sun was setting, and there was no time to travel to the last shrine, so we headed back to the nearest town in the now-cold dusk. There, after a shared meal of meat pies around the warmth of a baker's oven, we parted ways.

The Yarkand and Khotan shrines described here illustrate some of the many roles that shrines can play in Altishahri culture. For their local communities, the shrines were sources of supernatural assistance, sites of regular care for the dead, or sacred sites at which to perform devotions associated with *dhikr* or with religious holidays. In this context it was the sacred and liminal nature of the shrine, situated at the boundary of the physical and spirit worlds (*'ālam-i fānī* and *'ālam-i arvāḥ*), that appeared most salient.[9] However, when pilgrims from outside the community arrived, the shrine's connection to the past and the character of the saint became central. The hallowed setting and supernatural force of the shrine remained important, lending a sacred authenticity to the historical texts summarized or recited, but the saints' own stories, perhaps mere background for the local worshippers, became an integral part of the practice of pilgrimage for both the outsiders and the shaykhs who welcomed them. The act of leaving the home shrine changed the pilgrim's identity, transforming him or her into a welcome stranger who needed to be taught the history of the saint. The historical potential of the shrine was activated by pilgrimage.

Shrine Continuities

Though the distinction between local and stranger pilgrims is absent from the historical record, many other elements of the shrine roles described so far have also been noted in historical records of the nineteenth and early twentieth centuries. The association of ordinary graves with shrines is securely documented both in foreign travelers' memoirs[10] and in photographs.[11] The most frequently mentioned accumulation of graves around the tomb of a saint is the cemetery stretching two kilometers from the Afaq Khoja shrine to the outskirts of Kashgar, dubbed the "Via Appia of Kashgar" by Stein in 1904.[12] Normally, however, the ordinary tombs and the mundane, day-to-day tending they received went unmentioned in both indigenous and foreign sources. Working from modern analogues, though, Ildikó Beller-Hann has interpreted the French explorer Fernand Grenard's comment that children were valued for their ability to "carry out the rites of domestic religion for the benefit of the parents in the other world," as a reference to prayer at the graves of the parents.[13] Forsyth noted in 1878 that the tombs near the Afaq Khoja shrine were "neatly kept," no doubt by the relatives of the deceased.[14] Given the widespread and longstanding currency of this practice throughout the Islamic world, it is safe to conclude that it was as common a century ago as it is today, if not more so.

The connection between trade patterns and shrine worship suffers similarly from inattention in many sources. The seven-day weekly market cycle itself did get frequent mention from European travelers, if often only by accident.[15] In the case of the traveler Schomberg, it was frustration at closed shops during the rest of the week that led him to mention Khotan's weekly cycle.[16] Yet European travelers did not take an interest in the weekly cycle of activities at shrines. Fortunately, we have a rich description of the weekly festivals at the shrines in Yarkand, penned by the Yarkandi poet Zalīlī in the first half of the eighteenth century. Zalīlī describes crowds arriving in Yarkand on Thursday and Friday, timing that aligns with what we know about Yarkand's market day (Thursday) as it stood before PRC rule. About the shrine of the Seven Muhammads he wrote:

> The people of pilgrimage come in for prayer,
> Each week for a marvelous festival here . . .
>
> The environs of the tomb are of silver,
> The cemetery is illuminated by its graces.
> All being gathered, near and far,
> On Friday and Thursday they bring lamps.
> Halls of remembrance are all around,
> The flags of the tomb are a parasol for the crowds.
> [Its] graces and victories are not few,
> Whoever does not make pilgrimage, his life is in vain.

Zalīlī also records the activities at Yarkand's other major tomb, the shrine of Muhammad Sharīf:

A high dome and a *khaniqa* too,
Therein all travelers find peace.
That is, there all who are hungry feast,
Those who are naked are clothed.
On Friday and Thursday day and night,
Myriad people come and make pilgrimage.[17]

Several differences are notable between the Yarkand of today and Zalīlī's descriptions. First, it is clear that the popularity of the Muhammad Sharīf shrine waned significantly at some point after Zalīlī's time. Today, while the shrine of the Seven Muhammads buzzes with activity, the Muhammad Sharīf shrine remains mostly quiet, even on market days. The provision of food and clothing to the poor continues at the Seven Muhammads shrine, through the donations of pilgrims. However, it is likely that in Zalīlī's time, when the shrines held large and profitable properties in *waqf* endowments, the shrines themselves were able to provide more significant aid to the poor. The day on which the market is held is also different. The change to Sunday seems to have been relatively recent. In the late nineteenth century, Yarkand's weekly market was still held on Thursday, and the crowds that arrived from distant villages swelled the population by an estimated 9,000 individuals.[18] Thus, it seems likely that connection between weekly market days and shrine pilgrimage is a longstanding one, and that the Seven Muhammads' tomb has been a lively place for several centuries. The popularity of the shrine can be traced back even further, as Mirza Haydar, writing in 1546, singled out the shrine of the Seven Muhammads above all others in Yarkand as "the one the people believe in."[19]

Diverse forms of Barat observances at shrines throughout Altishahr were recorded by several indigenous and European observers. These notices have been thoroughly studied by Ildikó Bellér-Hann, but here it may be of some interest to note the similarities and differences between the practices observed in contemporary Yarkand and those preserved in the historical record.[20] The richest indigenous account, composed in Kashgar around 1905–1910, accords very well with the activities I witnessed at the Seven Muhammads shrine. According to this account, on the Barat night, people would go to shrines and cemeteries "and bring *qoymaq* breads to the graveyard, and having someone read suras from the Quran they give [the breads] to him. Everyone goes to the graves of their parents and friends to read verses from the Quran for the dead, and pray for forgiveness."[21] People then returned home and kept the vigil there, a practice that informants in Yarkand attested to as well. The author also records some practices that have been lost, namely the circulation of young people reciting Quranic passages in the streets, and the playing of music in homes. Informants in Yarkand expressed surprise at the idea of playing music, and one even implied it might be sacrilegious. Another element that has mostly disappeared is the strict gender separation recorded by the French explorer Grenard, who reported that, as a general Altishahri practice, it was only the women who brought the ceremonial bread and kept the all-night vigil.[22] With this important exception, however, the practices at the shrine, as opposed to those in private homes and public streets, remain largely unchanged.

The *dhikr* and saint veneration I witnessed at Imam Shākir are also attested in historical accounts, though not for the Imam Shākir shrine itself. In fact, the development of the Imam Shākir shrine's current role as a remote sacred space for restricted religious activities is the result of a major transformation. A century ago the main Yarkand-Khotan road passed through the Imam Shākir shrine area, where all Muslims were obliged to dismount and approach on foot.[23] The place was famous for its flocks of pigeons, said to be descendants of two doves that emerged from the fallen martyr's heart. The sacred birds were sheltered in small houses around the shrine and fed by pilgrims. In this roadside manifestation, the shrine was primarily engaged in receiving pilgrims from distant places. Probably the shaykh would have told the tale of Imam Shākir frequently, as he did when Aurel Stein visited in 1902, and Ella Sykes in 1915. However, the Chinese government built a new road that bypassed the shrine six kilometers to the south, and thus, in the last decades, the shrine has taken on a far more local character.[24] A site that was once very difficult to avoid became difficult to find. Still, the local community *dhikr* and saint veneration performed there in 2007–2008 would not have been unusual at other shrines of Altishahr a century ago, even though, at that time, Imam Shākir itself was still a popular roadside attraction. *Dhikr* was not always regarded with such suspicion as it is now. At the beginning of the twentieth century, *khaniqa* activities were common in both rural and urban areas.[25] *Khaniqas* were attached to many shrines, not only those which marked the tombs of Sufi masters, and their foundation is often recorded in the tazkirahs.[26] Accounts from the turn of the twentieth century record the same kind of *dhikr* as occurs in Altishahr today, with rhythmic chanting, singing, swaying, and dancing.[27]

Scattered references attest to the continuous arrival of pilgrims from more distant oases throughout the year, even outside the pilgrimage festivals and weekly market-related gatherings. Gunnar Jarring, for example, visited the great Ordam Padshah desert shrine in the 1920s during its off-season and encountered pilgrims along the way.[28] One factor contributing to the continuous flow of long-distance pilgrims was the tradition of the extended pilgrimage. The poet Zalīlī, for example, embarked on a fourteen-year journey as a mendicant, documenting his journey from one shrine to the next in his *Safarnāmah*.[29] This kind of pilgrimage was supported by numerous travelers' inns *(langars)*, which drew their funding from charitable endowments *(waqfs)*, and admitted poor pilgrims. Shrine graffiti also confirm that pilgrims visited shrines on all days and at all times of the year. The informal narration of tazkirah-based stories, as I witnessed both at the Seven Muhammads shrine and the Imam Shākir shrine, appears in two sources for the 1920s, one of which confirms the direction of this kind of telling toward outsiders. As was noted earlier, Gunnar Jarring recalled the shaykhs of the Sultan Satūq Bughrā-khān shrine in Artush informally narrating the tazkirah to him from memory.[30] The second source introduces a type of audience that rarely appears in the historical record: children. The Uyghur playwright and novelist Säypidin Äzizi recalled hearing informal tales of Sultan Satūq Bughrā-khān from the shaykhs and elders around the shrine as a child in the 1920s.[31] Äzizi's recollection reminds us that our sources may have left other kinds of informal readings undocumented, and suggests that local shrine visitors learned the history of their neighborhood saint at a young age. It may have been that informal shrine narrations were not directed exclusively at outsiders but also were aimed at anyone who was assumed to be unfamiliar with the saint's tale.

Thus, the various roles of the shrine in the local community observed in contemporary Altishahr—as a site of regular grave tending, weekly market-related pilgrimage, holiday observance, *dhikr*, and informal narrations of the tazkirah tales—appear to have been equally significant in the region a century ago. While the historical documents provide the outlines of social systems connected with shrines, I have also taken advantage of ethnographic observation to understand what outcomes result when these systems, faintly sketched as they are in the historical record, are populated by living, believing humans, with all of their cares and aspirations. Of course, it is important to remember that there have been many changes in Altishahri society over the last one hundred years, and it cannot be assumed that a particular phenomenon, if undocumented in the historical sources, was also present a century ago, even if it is associated with a complex of phenomena that are historically well documented. But culture itself preserves information in its constant self-replication, even while it is subject to constant transformation. Culture is not unique in its susceptibility to transformation. Written historical sources, no matter their age, exist only in the present, and the body of those sources, the historical record, has undergone significant change over the decades and centuries, change that is no less profound or meaningful than the changes that cultures have undergone. Here the goal is to understand the human implications of the documented practices, and the reader may concede that a population living in the same cultural tradition and believing in the sanctity of the historically documented shrine rituals will be a better judge of those implications than an outsider such as this author.

Together, recent practice and older documentary evidence yields a rich picture of shrines' roles in the local and oasis-level communities. In the regular local functions of the shrine, history likely remained in the background and the saints' names would have been rarely heard. Such contexts, as opposed to the massive pilgrimage festivals associated with tazkirah recitations, allow us to see what kind of significance the shrine had outside textualized historical practice, and thus, what kind of meanings the shrine itself contributed to those historical practices linked to the shrine. Linking all of the various shrine activities was a sense of the sacred and liminal nature of the setting. The shrine was a point of connection with the spirit world. The common graves that surrounded most shrines were the sites of families' interactions with their deceased relatives, whose spirits they believed remained connected to the grave. The shaykhs who managed the shrine acted as intermediaries, pious experts who could facilitate interactions with powerful saintly spirits. Access to the deceased saints in turn offered the potential aid of their supernatural capabilities. The sick might be cured, the poor might be enriched, and sins might be forgiven. The holiness of the site also lent the visitors' own devotional activities additional strength. Thus, during the Barat vigil, people offered their thousands of repetitions of Quranic verses at the shrine rather than at home, in the hopes that such devotion would gain additional merit as the angels tallied their deeds of the previous year. The belief in the power of these holy places is well illustrated by the words of a nineteenth-century shaykh at the Ordam Padshah shrine near Yengisar, who reported that the enormous shifting sand dunes surrounding the shrine "have hitherto, out of respect to the sacred resting place of the holy martyrs, passed on in their course giving the hallowed spot a wide berth; and please God they will always do so to all eternity."[32] It was in this context that the texts of Altishahr's past were delivered. History shared in the unquestioned sacredness of the setting.

As we turn to the historical readings that took place during the annual festivals, it is important to remember that local history in particular was connected to the sacred and liminal shrine context. While the "jangnāmahs and legendary stories"[33] of world history were usually delivered on the streets of the bazaar or as entertainment in the barbershop, Altishahr's own past was associated with the hallowed environment described above, often by the shaykhs who mediated the rest of the shrine's powers. The close association between ancient places and holy places continues to operate today, with sometimes surprising results. So far, we have examined implications of the shrine's role for history, but the attachment of historical meaning and practice to the shrine also had implications for the interpretation of places in general.

In a world where historical practice is so intimately connected to sacred sites it is easy to assume the inverse, namely, that sacredness attaches to historical sites. One fall day in 2007, as I returned with a group of regular pilgrims from a trip to the Imam Shākir shrine, we passed a decaying *potai*, an enormous tower of solid brick, built and maintained under Qing and Republican Chinese rule to mark the old inter-oasis road as it crossed the desert. I was surprised to see that my companions stopped at this tower and rolled out a prayer carpet. They placed the tower between them and the setting sun and prayed the evening prayer. Few things could have been more surprising to me than seeing a group of Muslims prostrate themselves in front of a Chinese road marker. I had passed this very same marker before on my motorcycle pilgrimage, and those companions had known that the *potai* was simply a road marker. However, the leader of this group explained to me that the *potai* was, instead, an ancient minaret built in commemoration of the nearby Imam Shākir's martyrdom. Given the context, it was an understandable deduction, for in Altishahr there has long been little distinction between historical and sacred sites. All historical sites were sacred, and all sacred sites were historical. There is not that much difference between the shrine as history and the *potai* as minaret.

The sacred context of local historical practice must have lent great authority to the tazkirahs' visions of the past. Certainly, it did among the pilgrims I met. At the shrines, my occasional questions about the truth of tales about the saints were invariably met with incredulous surprise and one-word assertions of their accuracy: *rast* (they are true). Through the tazkirah's attachment to the shrine, local history became an integral part of the Islamic faith. For the participants in shrine worship, veneration of the saints was not some late accretion to a previously pure Islam. It was the essence of Islam. The tazkirahs themselves make this sacred authority clear, in conclusions that promise punishment in hell for anyone who doubts the truth of the tale. The *Tazkirah of the Four Sacrificed Imams*, for example, says "And those who doubt Their Holinesses the Imams will leave this world without faith, and on Judgment Day their faces will be black. . . ."[34] We may deduce from the tazkirah that veneration of the Four Imams was advertised as an integral part of Muslim faith. This does not mean that there were no doubters. The meaning of Islam was contested in Altishahr, as it has been everywhere.[35] Yet, for most of the huge numbers of regular Muslims who participated in the shrine tradition, the sacred context would have elevated local Altishahri history above world history both in importance and credibility.

The physical form of the shrine also brought its own meanings to historical practice. At Imam Shākir, the shaykh's embellishment about the wooden pole extending deep into the dunes is an example of the potential for the physicality of the shrine to enter the creative process of historical practice. Shrines take many forms, from low mud lumps decorated with rags to monumental mausoleums with green-tiled domes. But in every case their presence is, if not monumental, then certainly distinctive, marked as extraordinary by flags and the carcasses of sacrificed animals. This clear demarcation of the shrine as an extraordinary place demands explanation, and explanation of the shrine is history. The physical features of the shrine, themselves the products of prior pilgrimages and historical practices, become both a question about the past and a source of knowledge about the past. Most Altishahri experiences of history during pilgrimage would have been affected by this kind of dialogue with the physicality of the shrine. Thus, a marginal note in a copy of the Four Sacrificed Imams tazkirah evokes the connection between the physical expressions of the shrine and the pilgrim's knowledge in a short verse about the flags and banners of the shrine:

"I placed my head in my hand.
I placed the flags and banners in my knowledge."[36]

Altishahri history was also drawn into the liminality of the shrine as a connection to the spirit world. The characters of history were very literally present at the tazkirah readings. Not only did the saint's earthly remains lie beneath the soil but his or her immortal spirit was there, granting the requests of pilgrims and listening to the recitations of his or her own tale. History was a communication, not just among the living but between the living and the long dead protagonists of history. Thus, at the moment of each local Altishahri history's dissemination, text, place, and personage converged in literal and symbolic ways, each of the three doing its own work to connect the listener with the past, and to seamlessly integrate the past with the reality of the present.

Shrine Readings

While local historical narratives could be delivered at any time of the year, and especially, as we have seen, when outsiders arrived at a shrine, the concentrated pilgrimage festival was the most spectacular manifestation of historical practice. The readings that took place at such festivals, to which we now shift our focus, brought the tazkirahs to vast audiences. Many major shrines had their own particular time of the year when they hosted large groups of "pilgrims from all over the province."[37] Such shrine festivals could coincide with rest periods in the agricultural cycle, weather preferences, or Islamic holidays. The Ordam Padshah shrine's pilgrimage festival was held on the tenth of Muharram, the anniversary of Alī ibn Abī Ṭālib's martyrdom at Karbala and of the martyrdom of the shrine's own saint, 'Alī Arslān-khān. The shrine of Satūq Bughrā-khān held its annual festival at the end of August, when the figs ripened.[38] The numbers of pilgrims involved in such shrine festivals are astonishing for such a sparsely populated region. The British officer H. W. Bellew visited Kashgar in 1874–1875 and reported that the Ordam Padshah shrine in the desert near Kashgar was said to attract fifteen to twenty thousand pilgrims during its largest annual festival—this at time when the entire Kashgar oasis had a population of only about 112,000.[39] Gunnar Jarring, reported similarly large numbers based on his visit to Kashgar four decades later, writing that the same shrine hosted "tens of thousands" of pilgrims.[40] At the time of Jarring's visit, the entire Kashgar oasis had a population of only 450,000.[41] While local estimates of pilgrim numbers are likely inflated, it is clear that indigenous observers considered the attendance at shrine festivals to be remarkable in quantity alone. Located sixteen kilometers from the nearest cultivated land, Ordam Padshah could only be reached by a difficult trek over sandy wastes. The presence at an isolated and remote location of such large crowds, relative to the small population of Kashgaria, testifies to the popularity of these pilgrimage festivals, and to the freedom of movement enjoyed by a significant portion of the population.

The convergence of pilgrims from varying backgrounds made the shrine a powerful force for disseminating the information contained in tazkirahs across geographic and social boundaries. The potential cultural effects of the geographic mixing of people drew the attention of one of Altishahr's most famous foreign visitors, M. Aurel Stein, who stopped at a minor shrine along the Keriya River and wrote the following:

> While waiting for my baggage, which did not arrive till late in the evening, I had plenty of time to think of the curious inroad made by civilization, as represented by this sacred establishment, into the solitude of the desert. The shepherds who frequent the lonely grazing grounds of the Keriya River cannot fail to benefit largely as regards their knowledge of the outer world by the stream of pilgrims that passes in the autumn and spring to the local saint's tomb.[42]

As Stein's musing on shepherds hints, the mixing of people achieved by seasonal pilgrimage was not only geographic. Shrine gatherings attracted people from all walks of life for both sacred and mundane purposes.[43] Located in graveyards or at desolate locations in the desert, the shrines were liminal sites where people of all statuses mixed. One contemporary Altishahri author, Abdu Vali Akhon, complained about the variety of people who attended shrine festivals, writing:

> Some people come as though [the shrine] were a big bazaar, especially gamblers, hoodlums, thieves, cripples, prostitutes, fruit-sellers, bakers, and cooks. These do not bow in the direction of the shrine at all. They are busy, not with making pilgrimage or circling the shrine, but with their own professions and business. Thus, for them it is the same whether they get into a Chinaman's coat or a shrine.[44]

Abdu Vali Akhon also noted class differences in the ritual activities of pilgrims, whom he divided into the noble *(khaṣ)* and common *('am)*. The noble pilgrims followed more orthodox modes of devotion such as the recitation of "one or two suras" from the Quran, while the commoners engaged in activities such as "rubbing their face and eyes on the shrine's walls," which, from the perspective of madrassa-educated elites, bordered on superstition or even idolatry *(shirk)*.[45] In its separation of sacred and mundane activities, Abdu Vali Akhon's depiction resonates with the spatial arrangement at the last shrine festival to be closed by Chinese authorities, the Imam Asim festival, which I visited in 2010. At this early summer festival thousands of pilgrims were divided between two centers of activity, a main shrine and an associated temporary bazaar, separated by a ritual processional path just under one kilometer in length. Historical and hagiographical recitations occurred both in the immediate vicinity of the shrine and in an associated bazaar-like area where "hawkers, bakers, and cooks" plied their trades.

The presence of such diverse audiences at local history readings helped foster a sense of the past that could be shared across people of all backgrounds. The shrine system circumvented a major barrier to the creation of such shared views on the past, a barrier common to most premodern societies: the specialized localization of education along lines of class and profession. While tradesmen such as bakers were educated through apprenticeships, elites through the madrassa, and thieves presumably in less formal situations, members of all these groups were present at the readings of local history that took place at shrines. The mixing of classes, which perturbed Abdu Vali Akhon and threatened the sanctified nature of the shrine, was a mark of the shrine system's success in putting the saints at the center of history for all of Altishahr's inhabitants.

The British consul at Kashgar in the 1930s, C. P. Skrine, shared Abdu Vali Akhon's suspicion of pilgrims' motives, writing that "at the end of August . . . greedy pilgrims from all over the province congregate at the fair of 'Hazrat Sulṭānim' Sadiq Boghra Khan, to feast on the luscious figs of Astin Artush."[46] While the idea that people came from all over the province just to eat figs may be far-fetched at best, Skrine's account shares with Abdu Vali Akhon's a feeling that profane pursuits were driving many pilgrims to the shrines. Ildikó Bellér-Hann has pointed out that such irreverence appears to be at odds with the idea of the shrine as purely sanctified and holy, as it has been presented by Sawada Minoru.[47] The solution to the problem seems to be that sanctity of the shrine was contended among different groups with different goals and perceptions. On one extreme, the shaykhs who managed the shrines clearly believed in and promoted the sanctity of the shrine. On the other extreme, the thieves and hoodlums of Abdu Vali Akhon's account were uninhibited by the holy setting of the shrine. Probably the rules of reverence at a shrine were more difficult to enforce during the pilgrimage festivals, when the crowds of pilgrims from widely varied backgrounds arrived. Today one can see a difference in the level of reverence between members of a shrine's local community and visitors from farther away. I have often witnessed pilgrims from far away neglect to remove their shoes in parts of a shrine where members of the local community do so unfailingly, or shout in places where locals whisper. Each shrine is different, and the rules of reverence must be learned. Locals have often been trained from their youth to view their neighborhood shrine with deep respect, but may not feel the same inhibitions at a distant tomb. None of this robs the shrines of their sanctified stature. The negotiated nature of shrines' holiness does not mean that they are not holy at all. The bazaar-like atmosphere of some pilgrimage festivals allowed the tazkirah tradition to capitalize on both the crowd–drawing potential of entertainment (for the bazaar was notorious as a form of entertainment) and the authoritative power of the shrine's sanctity.

In the tazkirahs themselves, the idea of pilgrimage stands further away from the bazaar-like festival observed in practice, though there are some clues that a lively atmosphere was encouraged. The tazkirahs discuss the ritual role in passages that straddle the border between description of actual practices and prescription of ritual ideals. They often include brief instructions to the pilgrim for activities at the shrines, either through the example of holy figures who perform devotions at the shrine, or through blessings addressed to the reader. One of the more extensive blessing/instruction passages comes at the end of the *Tazkirah of the Four Sacrificed Imams*:

> Whoever is in need and makes pilgrimage to this blessed tomb, and enlivens the place, and makes the pots boil, and makes the lamps burn, and gives prayers [*du'a*] and praise, their needs in the world and in the afterlife will be satisfied, and taking a place in the shade of Their Holinesses the Imams they will receive [the saints'] intercession. Of that there is no doubt. And those who doubt Their Holinesses the Imams will leave this world without faith and on Judgment Day their faces will be black and they will be covered with shame, and deprived of [the saints'] intercession. Of this there is no doubt. And whoever reads or has read out to them the tazkirah of Their Holinesses the Imams, and weeps, and prays and glorifies God for Their Holinesses the Imams—they will have honor and esteem in this world and intercession in the next. Of this there is no doubt.[48]

It is hard to tell how much of this kind of passage is a description of typical shrine activity and how much represents the hopes of the author-copyist, or perhaps even the shaykhs. Certainly, some of the tazkirahs seem suspiciously promotional of the very people in charge of the shrine, as in the *Tazkirah of Imam Muhammad Ghazālī*, which says, "Whoever prays and glorifies God for them [the tomb keepers] and does honor to the shaykhs will have honor in both worlds."[49] Still, the activities mentioned fit quite well with the overall picture of shrine activities, and especially of the pilgrimage festivals, even mentioning the value of reciting the tazkirah. The blessing/instruction passages vary little across the taz-kirahs. Most mention the boiling of pots, burning of lamps, and praying, practices which are well attested.[50] The Ordam Padshah shrine for example, kept two large pots, dated 1281 (1864–1865) and 1328 (1910–1911), which were removed or destroyed sometime during the period from the Great Leap Forward through the Cultural Revolution.[51] The encouragement to "enliven the place" *(jā va yerlārini khūshvaqt qilip)* resonates with both the bazaar-like atmosphere described by Abdu Vali Akhon and a belief frequently encountered in Altishahr today, that the dead need to be kept company. If the manuscript quoted here is representative of feelings about shrine activities in the eighteenth to early twentieth centuries, then the lively activities of the shrine festival may not have been so irreverent after all.

Our sources provide little detail about the recitations that the pilgrims heard at shrines, and it is unclear whether most readings were undertaken by the pilgrims themselves, as Jarring records,[52] or by the shaykhs, as recorded in Abū al-Qāsim's 1830 tazkirah.[53] The possibility of pilgrims themselves reciting the tazkirah is supported by the vast numbers of tazkirah copies that have survived until today. A significant minority of tazkirah copies have the look of devotional handbooks, with the kinds of prayers used at shrines bound alongside several tazkirahs. One manuscript of Muhammad Sharīf even has alternating pages of tazkirah and prayer formulas.[54] The tazkirahs' narratives themselves often include prayers, such as the *munājāt* that Muhammad Sharīf offers when his ship is trapped in the whirlpool of the pillar of Iskandar.[55] In the case of a reading by a shaykh, such shifts from prose narrative to verse prayer would have been ideal points for audience participation. Indeed, in one copy of the Muhammad Sharīf tazkirah, the text claims that whoever recites Muhammad Sharīf's *munājāt* and prays for the saint will have his or her own wishes fulfilled.[56] Of course, as has already been discussed, the shaykhs' preservation of tazkirah manuscripts at the shrines is also well documented. In all likelihood, both pilgrim and shaykh readings took place.

The eighteenth-century poet Zalīlī mentioned a third type of reading in his poetic description of the weekly pilgrimage activities at the Yarkand shrine of the Seven Muhammads:

> And the storyteller [rawi] is also telling beautiful tales,
> Telling stories of those things seen and heard.
> Tell of the Seven Muhammads!
> Give signs of their pure tomb![57]

The term rawi (storyteller) has largely disappeared from Eastern Turki and Uyghur usage, though the related word riwayăt (in modern Uyghur, "story") has remained common. The storyteller's profession has also remained, though under different names. In his early-twentieth-century collection of poems about professions and titles, the poet Poskami did not include the rawi but instead described storytellers as maddā and qiṣṣakhvān (lit. "reciter of stories"). Poskami presents both professions as arbiters of "true knowledge" and declares that there is no qiṣṣakhvān of whom he can claim to be an equal.[58] The storyteller's participation in shrine gatherings has continued into the present. Such readings were delivered at the recently closed shrine festival of Imam Asim in 2010, and in 2013 at the weekly Friday market alongside the shrine of Imam Ăptăh, also in the Khotan oasis. The professional storytellers give dramatic recitations from popular devotional texts, including the saints' tazkirahs.[59] They recite from memory and offer prayers that earn contributions from the crowds that gather around them. Tazkirah recitation practices almost certainly varied to some extent between shrines and over time, and there is no reason to think that more than one form couldn't coexist. If the tazkirah recitations were anything like the hükmăt and munajăt recitations in today's dhikr gatherings, responsibility for recitation may have shifted between the shaykhs and members of the congregation who were well versed in the tradition. At the same time, professional storytellers could take advantage of the bazaar to ply their trade.

Another important shrine festival, the festival of the Ordam Padshah shrine, reappeared after the relaxation of state religious restrictions in the 1980s, and, supposedly, drew tens of thousands of worshippers again by the mid-1990s. Although the festival was shut down again by the time of my visits, it has been analyzed by Rahile Dawut and Rachel Harris, who published a valuable description of this three-day event as it was video-taped in 1995.[60] In this description, the bazaar aspect of the festival is present, but it is subordinated to powerful communal rituals of procession and *dhikr*, fueled by music, dance, and chanting. At the culmination of the festival, pilgrims marched to the tomb, organized into groups based on their hometowns and carrying tall flags *(tugh)*, a practice also attested in Jarring's observations.[61] The crowd was led by drummers playing the *dap* (a frame drum), and as they approached the tomb to plant their flags, many pilgrims entered ecstatic states or wept loudly. The planting of the flags is essentially a reenactment of saints' shrine foundations, as recorded in the tazkirahs and discussed in more detail below. While the procession is certainly a lively one, it is the power of community worship and the strong emotional effect that stand out as salient elements in this description, rather than the image of a chaotic and profane marketplace. This again resonates with Jarring's 1935 description of the pilgrims' "religious fanaticism" and their "crying and wailing, in honor of the holy martyrs."[62] Dawut and Harris also mention the large communal cooking pot, and the presence of the *maddā*, "telling religious stories."[63] All was not devotional ecstasy, however. Dawut records entertaining activities such as wrestling matches and cock fights.[64] Like other documented shrine gatherings, the festival at Ordam Padshah drew its massive crowds through a compelling mixture of sacred and profane pursuits.

Despite the relaxation of religious restrictions of the 1980s, in the beginning of the twenty-first century local officials have again severely curtailed the pilgrimage festivals. It is impossible to know exactly what motivates individual closures, but the restrictions on shrine worship fit well with Beijing's general approach to Islam in Xinjiang, which is aimed at curbing a perceived threat of violent politicized Islam. Any practice that falls outside the Islam promoted by state's Islamic association can be labeled "illegal religious activity." The Ordam Padshah shrine is among those that have been completely closed to pilgrims. When I tried to visit in 2007, the police officer who detained me and escorted me to the county police headquarters said that there was "something secret" out in the desert. His boss insisted that the ban on travel to the shrine was for the safety of the pilgrims. The closing of Ordam Padshah is typical of shrines that draw large crowds at their festival times and suggests that officials fear large public gatherings as much as "unorthodox" religious practices. Until at least 2010, local officials allowed the May-June festival at Imam Asim, near Khotan, to continue, but when I visited in

May 2013, police were preventing pilgrims from approaching the shrine. The shrine of Ujma, in the mountains southeast of Khotan, used to draw substantial crowds but has been shut completely.[65] The only shrine festival I know of that may still survive is the Imam Ja'far al-Ṣādiq festival, outside Niya, and it has come under close regulation. As of 2007, all pilgrims were required to register with the police and pay a hefty 50-yuan entrance fee. Due to the state's museumification of the shrines, such as those of Afaq Khoja and Sultan Satūq Bughrā-khān, some festivals never recovered from the disruption of religious activities that occurred during the Cultural Revolution. All told, state restrictions have thoroughly disrupted the festival traditions and removed the shrine festival from the experience of most Uyghurs, though a devoted minority, mostly rural, kept the traditions alive until the recent closing of the Imam Asim festival. Even now, some pilgrims refuse to give up their practices. During my 2013 visit to Imam Asim, I joined a group of about fifteen pilgrims who managed to sneak into the shrine compound by taking a tortuous alternate route on foot through the desert. Beyond such small acts of resistance, most individual elements of the festivals can still be found at certain weekly markets and holidays such as Barat.

In regard to the historical tradition, the confiscation of tazkirahs and the banning of recitations has been even more disruptive. As a result, many of the tazkirahs, which originally emerged from the oral tradition, have returned to their nonwritten origins. This is not to say that the books themselves have been forgotten. Shaykhs lament the disappearance of the physical tazkirahs and have asked me for copies. Pilgrims often still believe that the shaykhs have the texts. In some cases, the shaykhs may indeed have hidden copies, though the expectation persists even where the shaykhs are clearly desperate to acquire such texts. In one place, the shaykhs have found an alternative text to attach to the shrine. The shrine of Aṣḥāb al-Kahf, near Turpan, is the subject of at least two different tazkirahs, probably three, all of which have been denied to the shaykhs.[66] Fortunately, however, the story of the Aṣḥāb al-Kahf appears in the Quran, one of a limited number of Islamic books approved by the Chinese state, and the shaykhs have placed copies of the holy book in the shrine, where the relevant passages are presented or read out to visiting pilgrims. Despite the resourcefulness of the shaykhs in contemporary Altishahr, state policies have weakened the connection between popular historical knowledge and the shrine considerably. The banning of shrine books and shrine readings has also made it extremely difficult to investigate the traditional festival readings through ethnographic means. However, the persistence of the text-place connection in the minds of both pilgrims and shaykhs testifies to the importance of these books as a foundation of shrine rituals. The convergence of the place, the saint's presence, and the text gives the shrines their compelling attraction, and the presence of any one or two elements alone is an incomplete context for shrine devotions. The presence of the text has been the most difficult of the three elements to preserve, but pilgrims have adapted by replacing the physical book with an imagined book.

The eighteenth- through early twentieth-century sources, while sadly unspecific on the nature of shrine readings, at least confirm the prevalence and diversity of the practice, and explain the nostalgia for the text that persists at many shrines today. Such sources are more useful as catalogs of the various activities that took place at shrine festivals, and, in the case of the tazkirah sources, statements of the ideals for shrine worship. Together with our relatively scant ethnographic evidence, they paint a picture of enormous and complex community interactions in the presence of the saint. While the standards of propriety may have varied among the startlingly broad cross-section of society that participated in the festivals, the great crowds of worshippers undoubtedly reinforced the shaykhs' vision of a hallowed place. The mass participation in communal meals and processionals created an engrossing physical experience that engaged all of the senses. These crowds also ensured that the dissemination of the saints' histories reached diverse audiences in settings that created a personal connection to the past.

Conceptions of Shrine and Place

The reality of the shrine as a ritual site, constructed by the combined practices of individuals and communities, was complemented by the ideal of the shrine as presented in texts. The tazkirahs reveal Altishahri ideas about the shrine as a place, notions which influenced the shrines' ritual and social roles. Before proceeding with an investigation into the meaning of place, though, it is worth briefly addressing the conceptual connections between pilgrimage to saints' tombs *(ziyārat)* and the *hajj*, or pilgrimage to Mecca, which, according to the Quran (3:97), is the duty of all Muslims. The *hajj* and the esteem it inspired must have provided a model and an implicit blessing for *ziyārat*. Certainly, some Altishahris connected the two kinds of pilgrimage. Foreign travelers to Altishahr documented beliefs that a certain number of visits to an important Altishahri tomb could serve as a substitute for the *hajj*, a tradition which is still maintained.[67] While there were many differences between the ritual practices of *hajj* and *ziyārat*, some activities were shared, such as livestock sacrifices, circumambulation *(ṭawāf)*, and group pilgrimage, shared practices which may be attributed to the Altishahri inheritance of ritual practices from the wider Islamic world. Altishahri pilgrims continued to visit Mecca in small numbers under Qing rule, and returning pilgrims constantly refreshed knowledge of *hajj* practices, but such knowledge does not seem to have been a significant influence on Altishahri notions of pilgrimage. Overall, the connection between *hajj* and *ziyārat* seems to have been loose. We may note, for example, that none of the major Altishahri pilgrimage festivals occurred during the month of *hajj* pilgrimage, Dhu al-Hijja, and that the Qurban Heyt (Arabic: ʿĪd al-Aḍḥá) sacrifice associated with the *hajj* season was not known to be performed at the local Altishahri shrines. Furthermore, comparisons between the shrines and the Kaaba in Mecca, or the *ziyārat* and the *hajj*, do not appear in Altishahri texts.

While the tazkirahs are mostly silent on the *hajj*,[68] they provide a vivid picture of Altishahri conceptions of the shrine and place. Though Altishahri authors working in the eighteenth to early twentieth centuries left only sparse records of the practices associated with shrines, their treatment of the shrine as an ideal is somewhat richer. One of the few traits shared by all tazkirahs is that, in addition to recording the deeds and qualities of saint(s), they include some explanation of the origin or creation of the saint's shrine. In doing so, they address the question of how significance, in particular holiness and historical meaning, is attached to a point on the landscape. This question is what scholars outside the Altishahri tradition today might call the question of "place." Thus, in his study of the connections between ritual and place, Jonathan Z. Smith calls place "a locus of meaning," a fixing of meaning to a point in space.[69] The common Turki words for place were not used in this restrictive sense. The common word *makān*, for example, can refer to a locus of meaning but can also, in some contexts, indicate emptiness or "available space." Yet this does not mean that Turki speakers were uninterested in or unable to discuss the origins of a locus of meaning. When discussing the origins of shrines they relied on a special usage of the word *manzil*, which, among its other functions in the Turki dialect of Altishahr, could indicate an individual's deathplace.

The tazkirahs' discussions of place creation are best understood against the background of Altishahr's oasis geography. Surrounding the oases are vast stretches of land without focused points of meaning, and these stretches of empty desert space alternate with intense concentrations of meaningful land reclaimed from the desert. An arbitrarily chosen wheat farm in an Altishahri oasis may not have had great significance to the wider community, but to its own farmer it was a place. In this sense, any point in an oasis was meaningful to someone. On the other hand, the desert, which surrounds the inhabited parts of Altishahr and accounts for most of the Tarim Basin by area, was mostly devoid of such meaningful local distinctions. Altishahr's desert had no equivalent of the Tuareg or the Bedouin. Aside from a few shrines, along with the roads and inns constructed to enable its crossing, the desert contained vast expanses of meaningless space. The space itself, as a collective entity, had meanings, especially as a place of great danger.[70] But within this one enormous place there were few distinctions and fewer places. The desert was not owned or visited.[71] It was crossed, from one place to another place. In the tazkirahs, this empty space is notable for its absence. Despite the extensive travels undertaken by many of the saints, travels which necessarily included desert crossings, the desert itself appears only very rarely in the tazkirahs.[72]

The geography of Altishahr would thus seem to leave two geographically segregated options for the establishment of a shrine—the affixing of meaning to a point on the landscape. Within the oases, which were concentrations of places, the establishment of a shrine would necessarily amount to the transformation of a preexisting place. Perhaps a corner of a place known as Alimjan's apricot orchard is transformed into a shrine, or a village graveyard becomes a shrine when a grandee builds himself a fine tomb, to which stories of his greatness attach. In the desert, on the other hand, a place can be created in empty space. In the popular tazkirah tradition, narratives of place transformation on the oasis model are rare, even though a significant minority of shrines is located on cultivable land.[73] Instead, the most common explanation for shrine foundation follows the desert model. According to such tazkirahs, places are created out of empty space through the death of the saint, often during battle with unbelievers in the desert. Yet there are other tales that suggest a third way: the place was not created or transformed but discovered.

The establishment of a place and a shrine (the architectural expression of the place) in an empty space is a fairly straightforward process in the tazkirahs of saints whose shrines are located in the desert. The saint dies, often in battle, and often through some treachery of the enemy. The geographical setting is not described, though anyone familiar with the shrine would be aware of its desert location. The saint's associates, his deputies, or the ruling khan appoint personnel to the roles of tomb sweepers and shaykhs. The place is equipped with flags *(tūgh alām)* and cauldrons, and nearby lands are given to the newly established shrine as *waqf* endowments. The following excerpt from the *Tazkirah of Imam Muhammad Ghazālī* exemplifies this process as told in the tazkirahs:

> Then they prayed *namāz* for the martyrs who were under the leadership of His Holiness the Imam, and buried them. The great Shaykh Hasan built up an inn and gave all of the lands to the shrine in trust [*waqf awqāf qilip*] and he himself settled there. Becoming a devotee of His Holiness Imam Muhammad Ghazālī and all of the martyrs, he became the shaykh . . . and Shaykh Hasan and Zuhūrmūs Beg assigned shaykhs and sweepers to His Holiness the Imam. He assigned sixty households of people as shaykhs and sweepers . . . and he said, "Make [the martyrs'] pots boil and their lamps burn."[74]

Shrines such as Imam Ghazālī's are thus described as new places, created by the death of the saint, and developed by his companions.

Evidence suggests that many, perhaps even most, of the major shrines purported to have been founded in desert space were, in fact, transformations of earlier Buddhist religious sites, and in many cases, those locations were not yet deserts when the religious sites were founded. Archaeologist Aurel Stein identified several shrines with previous Buddhist sites. The shrine of Imam Shākir, which still had its sacred pigeons when Stein passed through, was, according to Stein's research, only a more recent manifestation of a Buddhist temple mentioned by the seventh-century Chinese pilgrim Xuan Zang. According to the pilgrim, the temple honored a rat-king who defended the Khotanese Buddhists against the Xiongnu, and in Xuan Zang's time the temple housed the rat-king's descendents. Whereas pilgrims to the Buddhist temple had fed sacred rats, the pilgrims to the more recent Islamic manifestation fed pigeons. This was, according to Stein, "the first striking instance of that tenacity of local worship which my subsequent researches showed for almost all sacred sites of Buddhist Khotan," though his publications do not detail all of these subsequent researches.[75] The phenomenon was not limited to Khotan. Stein carried out extensive archaeological investigations of Buddhist sites that had been replaced by the enormously popular Islamic Aṣḥāb al-Kahf shrine at Tuyuq, near Turpan.[76] Nor was the phenomenon limited to Stein's investigations. Grenard had previously argued that several shrines, including the shrine of Imam Ja'far Ṭayarān, were Islamic manifestations of earlier Buddhist sites.[77]

Despite numerous examples, the contradiction between the tazkirah tales and the evidence from archaeology and pre-Islamic texts is not reflected in the tazkirah tradition or in modern shrine culture. The Buddhist roots of shrines seem to have been unknown to, or forgotten by, Altishahri Muslims, at least by the time that the early tazkirahs were set in writing (around the turn of the seventeenth century). It is important to remember that while such shrines are frequently held up as examples of syncretism by scholars outside the tradition, within the tradition the shrines are considered wholly Islamic.[78] The tazkirah narratives of shrine foundation in empty space stand as authoritative. What the continuation of worship at these sites does demonstrate is the durability of holy places, even at remote desert locations. While the history of a place can be erased or altered, as the story of the rat-king at Imam Shākir has been, the historicalness of the place—its significance as a point of contact with the past—is much more difficult to eliminate. Though cultural outsiders—for example, the Muslim holy warriors in Buddhist Khotan—may not feel the need to maintain the stories they find attached to places, they often feel the need to attach some kind of story to a strongly "historical" place. As we shall see later, the present Chinese rulers of Xinjiang are also responding to the compelling power of the historicalness, as opposed to the history, of Altishahr's holy places.

Though the pre-Islamic roots of shrines are elided within the tradition, the tazkirahs do accommodate the idea of preexisting places, embraced through narratives of discovery. Altishahr's greatest tale of shrine discovery is the tazkirah of Khvājah Muhammad Sharīf, a sixteenth-century Sufi master whose career is also mentioned in Shāh Mahmūd Churās's more sober dynastic history.[79] In this tazkirah, the spirit of Sultan Satūq Bughrā-khān appears to Muhammad Sharīf one night and tells him to seek his tomb. Muhammad Sharīf then travels to Kashgar, where the general location of the tomb is widely known, but the exact spot remains a mystery. After three days of devotion in the stony area where the grave is thought to be, the sultan appears and shows Muhammad Sharīf the precise location of his tomb. Muhammad Sharīf appoints a caretaker for the tomb, thus making a shrine out of the sultan's previously hidden grave. In the rest of the tale, Muhammad Sharīf finds further graves of holy people with the help of the sultan and through his own interactions with other spirits. On the sites of their tombs he appoints caretakers and has mosques and *khaniqas* built. These discovery tales allow for a narrative that avoids the question of place creation. According to the tazkirah, the places already existed; Muhammad Sharīf simply makes shrines out of preexisting graves.[80]

The means by which a preexisting place becomes a shrine are well illustrated in the *Tazkirah of the Four Sacrificed Imams*. In between battles with the Buddhists of Khotan, the Four Imams discover the *manzil* of an earlier saint, Imam Ja'far Ṭayarān.[81] *Manzil* can mean a stopover point, a destination, or a place. In the tazkirah tradition, it is usually used to indicate a person's final resting place.[82] The *Tazkirah of the Four Sacrificed Imams* presents the place or manzil as a preexisting, pure locus of meaning, which is independent of the structures built upon it. When the Four Imams discover the manzil as an unmarked point in the desert, they develop it into a shrine by planting flags on it. Thus, the manzils underlying the shrines are almost purely places. They are not the buildings that mark them or even the graves. The shrine of Imam Mahdī-yi Ākhir-i Zamān (also discovered by the Four Imams, according to their tazkirah) does not even claim to hold the tomb of its namesake.[83] The significance of the place, as opposed to the structure, is clearly visible at the many shrines marked only by a few flag poles. The Imam Shākir shrine, for example, has survived for several hundred years with nothing more than these feeble wooden markers, bolstered not by a monumental memorial but by the memory of the communities that have frequented it. The strength and durability of that community memory is remarkable. Not only has the shrine survived the continuous shifting of the dunes on which it rests by means of a forest of flag poles, but it has done so in the face of outside pressures such as the upheaval of the Cultural Revolution. Large, permanent structures certainly encourage the preservation of place, and such structures are praised in the tazkirahs. However, as the more humble shrines demonstrate, it is enough for a saint to discover a locus of meaning, and for the community to preserve that meaning through regular pilgrimage.

The above examples of discovery, despite presenting holy places as preexisting, do not explicitly deny the possibility that the place was created within historical times. However, another major tazkirah portrays the saints' manzil, or deathplace, as existing even before the death of the saints. The tazkirah of the Seven Muhammads contains a typical story of tomb discovery. While the place of the Seven Muhammads' death is holy, it has been forgotten and thus lost to the people of Yarkand. A Sufi master appears hundreds of years after the Seven Muhammads' death, miraculously identifies their manzil, and creates there a shrine by planting flags. But the Seven Muhammads' tazkirah is unique for including both the tale of the manzil discovery and the tale of the saints' original death. Chapter 1 described how the Seven Muhammads were, according to their tazkirah, heavenly beings sent to earth to cure the prophet Muhammad's daughter Fatima of a deadly illness. Once they have done their job, however, God tells them that their places in heaven have already been occupied by others. The Seven Muhammads are told that they must wander the earth in search of their manzil. The prophet gives them a staff, telling them that they will know they have reached their manzil when the staff turns green. After years of wandering, the Seven Muhammads find their manzil, and settle there to concentrate on the spirit world. One day they lie down in their seven graves and die. Thus, the deathplace marked by the shrine of the Seven Muhammads not only existed before the shrine, but before the death of the saints.

The eternal nature of place in the saintly manzil has a parallel, and perhaps an explanation, in the nature of time and history as depicted in the *Tazkirah of Sultan Satūq Bughrā-khān*. The tazkirah is the story of the sultan's conversion to Islam and his subsequent holy wars to spread the faith. The sultan's first meeting with the man who will convert him, Abū al-Naṣr Sāmānī, is described from the latter's perspective: "Abū al-Naṣr Sāmānī looked: it is the holy personage whom I saw in history."[84] At this point in the tale, the twelve-year-old sultan has not yet converted nor achieved any other feats for which he is honored as holy, but Abū al-Naṣr Sāmānī is familiar with him from the reports of the prophet Muhammad's announcement that "Satūq" will be the first Turk to convert to Islam. The tradition is presented thus in the tazkirah: "Many years before His Holiness Sulṭān Satūq (God's gratitude be upon him) came to this world, his spirit was shown to His Holiness the Prophet (peace be upon him) during the *mi'raj*,[85] standing among the ranks of the prophets."[86] Later (but still centuries before the birth of Satūq), when the prophet's companions beg to meet the sultan, the prophet summons him, and the sultan arrives on horseback with forty followers. A certain Abū al-Naṣr Sāmānī was, according to the tazkirah, aware of this tradition. "When he looked at history he saw that not much time remained before the coming of His Holiness the Sulṭān."[87] Thus, the history of the sultan's worldly deeds existed before he entered the world, and it was known as history *(tārīkh)* rather than prediction or prophecy. The author's comfort with wrapping past, present, and future together into the term *history* is facilitated by the beginningless existence of the sultan's spirit. The ability of spiritual masters to communicate with the spirit world further encourages what may seem to us as a flattening of time. Saints are always reachable, whether dead or unborn. In the sultan's tazkirah, Abū al-Naṣr Sāmānī also enters the spirit world to speak to the deceased prophet Muhammad, asking him permission for a trip to "Turkestan" in search of the sultan. The eternal existence of the spirit, preceding worldly conception and surviving death, allows the saints and heroes of both the past and the future to affect the world of the present. While the explicit use of the term *history* in this way may be unique to the Sultan Satūq Bughrā-khān tazkirah, the idea of the saints preexisting their worldly birth is found in other tazkirahs, some of which have similar tales of the prophet Muhammad meeting the saint in a dream or vision, centuries before his birth.[88] In light of the eternal existence of saintly figures and the unification of past, present, and future through the spirit world, the eternal existence of the manzil, or deathplace, seems less unusual. The unbeginning and unending nature of the holy personage could also be shared by place and by history.

The last saints to be connected to a major tomb in Altishahr were probably the Seven Maidens of Uch Turpan (died late eighteenth century), and the next youngest major saint is Kashgar's Afaq Khoja (died 1694). This means that throughout the nineteenth and twentieth centuries, pilgrims were visiting a category of personage tied firmly to the past. It is even possible that, as in today's Uzbekistan, some Altishahris discounted the possibility of saints living in the present. In Louw's (2007, p. 132) keen analysis of pilgrimage in Uzbekistan, the impossibility of saints in the present "projected" "true sainthood . . . into the past, *avliyo* [saints] not only represented thresholds between human beings and God, but also between the present and an ideal past."[89] Thus, in Louw's Uzbekistan, pilgrimage is "virtual time travel." I have similarly argued that shrines were an important interface with history for Altishahris, and indeed facilitated interactions with the past. However, it would be inaccurate to transfer the notion of time travel to the Altishahri case from the example of Uzbekistan. Such a notion assumes a historiographical outlook that privileges chronology. Altishahri saints, however, were not understood as chronologically limited. Their physical presence on earth was but a small part of their existence, which began before their birth and continued into the pilgrim's own time after their death. The Altishahri shrine's link to the past was not so much a matter of traveling in time but of traveling in space to the presence of an extremely old personage, the ever-extant saint. Space, in Altishahr's local history, takes on the role that time plays in chronologically focused traditions.

It is also worth bringing up here the temporal–geographic parallels touched upon in the discussion of "oases of history." The content of the tazkirah tradition covered all places, that is, all of the major oases, but not all times. From the vast space of the past, authors attached significance to a limited number of personages and events, entexting them to create history. The creation of history in time is not unlike the creation of places in space. If a place is a "locus of meaning," we might call a history an assemblage of "moments of meaning." The parallels with Altishahr's oasis geography are striking. Links between conceptions of space and time are perhaps inevitable, as people in many cultures conceptualize time spatially, whether linearly or otherwise.[90] It seems fitting for a culture that inhabited concentrated islands of meaningful space in a sea of emptiness to colonize the past in a similar fashion, cultivating rich historical oases in concentrated portions of an enormous wilderness.

The performance of historical texts at shrines embedded the popular historical experience in daily, weekly, and annual rituals that were integral to the spiritual, economic, and social lives of all kinds of Altishahris, including beggars, prostitutes, bakers, thieves, kings,[91] merchants, and farmers. Though Altishahr had no social context devoted exclusively to the teaching of history, as in the history classes of modern public school systems, the shrine environment made local history a popular pursuit, which benefited from shrine culture's world of meanings and associations. These implications included a sense of deep sanctity and a belief in the presence of the prime movers of history, saints, at historical recitations. The latter phenomenon operated through the shrine's liminal potential. Not only were most shrines located in environments considered liminal in many cultures across the world—namely, deserts and graveyards—but worshipers imputed to them a special connection with the spirit world, and even a more direct route to God, through the immediate presence of the saint.[92] Accompanying this sense of presence was the pilgrim's own route, arrival, and attendance at the site of history. Once texts are successfully attached to a place, and especially a sacred place, it is easier to see them as emanations of reality. Pilgrims experienced the settings of history firsthand, and this could be taken as evidence for the truth of the tales. Their experiences could then be brought back to bear upon the physical text. A previously mentioned marginal note in a copy of the Four Imams tazkirah illustrates this potential, with the testimony, "I have seen the sands of the [Imam Mahdī-yi] Ākhir-i Zamān," penned in a rough hand alongside the story of the Imam Mahdī.[93] The tazkirah's tale of the Imam Mahdī was as real as the sand of Khotan, and perhaps more real, for example, than the foreign Rustam's exploits in some place called Balkh (as told in the *Shāhnāmah*). The deep connection of Altishahri histories to place, which we may call, as shorthand, their "localization," meant that history could not be told with equal authority in all places. While the tazkirah manuscripts display the efforts of authors, copyists, and readers to buttress the authority of the text, nothing could replace the sacred authenticity of a reading, or even an embellished retelling from memory, delivered at the shrine in the presence of the saint himself/herself, surrounded by the evidence of that history's reality. The convergence of text, personage, and place thus comprised the complete view of the past, as opposed to the text in isolation. Meanings that swirled around the institution of the shrine interacted with meanings attached to the text, as did the physicality of the shrine. The power to create and change these interlocking systems was diffuse. The shrine experience was created by the actions of thousands of pilgrims; the text was created by generations of readers and copyists.

The shrine institution also drew pilgrims into a participatory relationship with the past. The pilgrimage was often a reenactment of the saints' histories, for the act of pilgrimage was one of the noble pursuits that filled the histories of the saints. Most of the *Tazkirah of Muhammad Sharīf* consists of tales of his pilgrimages of discovery to the tombs of various saints. In most cases, the saints themselves had, according to the tazkirahs, only arrived at their tombs after long journeys. In the *Seven Muhammads* story, the saints even spent their lives in search of nothing other than their own tombs, only arriving after traversing the entire world. The ordinary pilgrims first traveled their own route from home to shrine and then often engaged in a ritual journey shared with other pilgrims, such as the flag-planting procession at Ordam Padshah. At the shrine of the Seven Muhammads, this ritual journey consisted of the curving route through vestibule, courtyard, shaykhs' platform, second courtyard, and tomb. At the shrine of Imam Shākir, pilgrims made an hour-long circular progression along the border of the martyrs' graves, kneeling and praying at the three most important graves. Such processional traditions certainly played other roles, such as lending solemnity to the rituals, but they also would have made it easy for pilgrims to situate their own narratives among those of the saints and bring the travels of the saints into the pilgrims' realm of experience.

In many parts of the world, museums and monuments provide extra-textual experience of the past and a site for community interaction with the past. These are important elements of popular historical practice, and in Altishahr they were made available by the shrine. Especially during festivals, the pilgrims' interaction with the places and personages of history was a holistic physical experience, involving the sounds of music, the smell and taste of the communal meal, which was feeding the saint as well as the pilgrim, the scent of burning oil lamps, the discomforts of a desert journey, and the sight of numerous flags, brought by fellow pilgrims over the years. The text was but one element in an elaborate communion with the past. Such immediate physical experiences reinforced the past's presence, and supported notions of time, place, and personage that emphasized permanence, even a sense of universal contemporaneity, through a focus on oases of significance in the past rather than a sequence of events in "homogeneous, empty time."[94] It was in this context that Altishahris maintained and negotiated a shared view of the past.

4

HISTORY IN MOTION

The deep connection of Altishahri histories to place—their localization—made them compelling vehicles for notions of rootedness and identity. In the shrine readings, not only were past and present connected but they were connected to a place. The audience was drawn into these interconnections as well. Whether audience members were locals (*yerliq*, literally "one of the place") or visitors from other oases, the act of pilgrimage linked each person's personal life history to the history of the saint, and thus to the saint's manzil. The connection between the saints and places was so powerful that popular epithets for most major towns referred to the saints buried there. Yarkand, for example, was the City of Patron Saints, and Khotan was the City of Martyrs. Turpan's name, the City of Strangers, referred to the many pilgrims who visited the town's shrines.[1] This place-heavy way of practicing history, of producing an "our history," was ideal for explaining the roots of the community that produced and consumed historical texts in Altishahr. Powerful stories of community roots were to be found in the tazkirahs, stories that located the roots of Altishahri identity at the shrines, where history was practiced in its most powerful form.

Another important implication of localization was that histories, and the pasts they represented, were put in geographic relationship to each other. Pilgrims navigated these relationships through travel, putting history in motion. While an individual tazkirah was rooted at the place of its associated shrine, knowledge of its contents, and, presumably, retellings, radiated outward along pilgrims' routes. These routes branched and crossed, forming networks. The geographic networks were, in turn, reflected in the organization of manuscript anthologies. Such works literally bound together the histories of the various shrines and oases in a

single manuscript to create a regional origin tale. Of course, books themselves traveled as well, and even if the most dramatic performance of a
tazkirah occurred at its own shrine, the geographically organized collections of tazkirahs provided a synoptic view of the network of localized
histories while maintaining the marks of the travel that bound them together figuratively.

This chapter examines the effects of deploying tales of community
origins along the networks of pilgrims' routes. Different roots at different oases might seem a tenuous basis for a view of the past shared across
a region. However, networks of sacred travel and the historical anthologies that mirrored them connected all of these roots into a larger complex that supported just such a regionally shared history.

Altishahri History and Identity

A shared view of the past is only a few short steps from a shared identity.
In nineteenth-century Altishahr, the shared view of the past was formed in
part through the creation of a new genre, the tazkirah, which made local
history imaginable. Equally important to the formation of the Altishahri
historical tradition was the pilgrimage system, which brought Altishahris
into a participatory and experiential relationship with that local past.
Yet there were two other important elements of Altishahr's historical tradition that allowed the shared view of the past to serve as a foundation
for a more complex and pervasive social phenomenon: a system of shared
identity. One of these was the originary aspect of the tales included in
Altishahr's tradition. The tazkirahs, while ostensibly the life stories of
individual saints, together provided an explanation of the origins of Altishahr's ordinary Muslims. The drawing together of these tales to create
a shared sense, not just of the past but also of common origins, was enabled by the flexibilities of manuscript technology, already described
above, as it articulated with the geography of pilgrimage. The second
important phenomenon for turning shared history into an element of
common identity was the record and display of participation in the historical tradition. Not only did people consume and reproduce the same
tales but they also learned that other people like them were consuming
those tales too, in faraway oases that they themselves might never visit.
I argue here that these two aspects of the historical tradition were important enablers of the construction of a particular kind of identity system in Altishahr, an imagined community.

Although the term *imagined community* is often used as shorthand for Benedict Anderson's 1983 formulation of modern nationalism, I use it here in the strict sense that Anderson intended when he described not only nations but also premodern religious communities, such as "Christendom," as "imagined communities."[2] By arguing for an imagined community in Altishahr I do not intend to suggest that there was an Altishahri nationalism before the twentieth century. There was probably no such thing in Altishahr until the fashioning of the Uyghur identity in the first half of the twentieth century, a project that took several decades to advance, and one that, in many ways, remains incomplete.[3] On the other hand, I do use the concept of the imagined community to contend that the Altishahri identity system was something other than just ethnicity. Influential scholarly concepts of ethnic groups, such as Weber's "groups that entertain a subjective belief in their common descent"[4] or Barth's less rigidly defined notion of an interaction between systems of identity and alterity,[5] omit one feature common among the largest identity systems of both the modern and nonmodern worlds: the explicit awareness of the extent of one's own identity group. This awareness is one important basis for the imagination that defines Anderson's imagined communities, members of which "never know their fellow members, meet them, or even hear of them, yet in the minds of each lives the image of their communion."[6]

The foundational work of demonstrating that a regional identity of some sort existed across Altishahr has already been done. Two important recent studies on Altishahri history before the Communist era have treated the prenationalist, Turki-speaking Muslims of Altishahr as an ethnic group, while still emphasizing that ethnicity was only one of several dimensions of identity.[7] Laura Newby, for instance, argues that this identity was marked by a common historical experience, "shared myths and legends," extensive inter-oasis mobility, and, most convincingly, consistent and explicit perceptions of alterity vis-à-vis other groups. She notes that Altishahris clearly differentiated themselves from Han Chinese by calling them Khitay, from Turkic and Mongolic nomadic groups whom they called Kirghiz and Qalmaq, and even from the settled Turkic speakers of Western Turkestan with whom they shared language, religion, and way of life. This last group they labeled Andijani, whether they came from Andijan or Khoqand or Samarqand or Bukhara. As Newby argues, the idea of an Altishahri "us" is clearly indicated in such designations of those from outside settled Altishahr as "them." A passage in the late seventeenth-century *Chinggiznamä* adds further weight to these claims by directly expressing the Altishahri identity. In summarizing the rule of a leader who had controlled all of Altishahr for only one year, it says he was "Khan of Kashgar for thirty-two years and Khan of the entire homeland *(yürt)* for one year."[8] Whereas Newby's essay focused on proving that an Altishahri identity did in fact exist, I analyze aspects of Altishahri pilgrimage culture and historical practice that shed light on what kind of identity system this was, leading to the conclusion that these systems supported a type of imagined community peculiar to Altishahr's own geographical, historiographical, and political contexts.

Of course, there were many other means by which identities were formed and enacted, involving the maintenance of both alterity at ethnic boundaries and identity within the group through shared symbols, stories, and practices.[9] To take one obvious example of identity maintenance through alterity, members of the Turkic Muslim population distinguished themselves from the Han Chinese minority in the towns through the taboo on pork. The popular historical tradition, on the other hand, brought the maintenance of identity beyond the realm of immediate personal interactions at ethnic boundaries. Through tales, rather than experience, of interactions with a "them" and the formation of an "us," the popular historical tradition advertised Altishahri identity to insiders, including those who never came into contact with the "other," and taught people that they were part of a larger community, shared with people they would never meet.

A Cosmopolitan Cul-de-sac

Mullah Hājī makes clear in his introduction to one of Altishahr's most popular tazkirahs, the *Tazkirat al-Bughrā-khān*, that this kind of book was intended to reveal to its readers the nature of their origins, writing:

> Records of the situation of the fathers and forefathers are found in ancient books. In order that they be known . . . I collected the true stories from the history of Hasan Bughrā-khān and other tazkirahs.[10]

But who were the fathers and forefathers of the Altishahris? We might reasonably expect them to be the saints, but, in fact, there was very little in the tazkirahs to suggest to readers that they were descendants of the saints. Mullah Hājī does not even tell his readers whether his heroes bore any offspring.[11] Yet, the tazkirah doesn't provide much information about any characters other than the saints, so it must be that the saints are the "fathers and forefathers" of which he wrote. Clearly, the Bughrā-khāns have an important originary role, but the nature of their fatherhood is vague.

One of the more surprising aspects of Altishahr's tazkirah-shrine tradition is its limited use of genealogy. While shrines in much of the Islamic world, and also in the Chinese world, are often associated with genealogies that trace the descendants of the saint or ancestor into the present day, this particular kind of genealogy was largely lacking in Altishahr. This is not to say that genealogies in general were absent. It is not at all unusual for a tazkirah to present a genealogy of the saint tracing his or her lineage backward in time (usually to the prophet Muhammad through Fatima and, in many cases, the first eleven imams of the Twelver Shia tradition).[12] However, the genealogies are rarely extended forward from the saints. Many of the saints do not even have children, according to the tazkirahs. In cases where the saints do have children, the children are themselves saints, with shrines, and often tazkirahs, of their own. The result is that the saintly genealogies either end with the first and only saint of the line to be buried in Altishahr, or proceed through a few generations of Altishahri saints before ending with a childless saint. The major ramification of this phenomenon is that, while the saints were often related to each other, the people who consumed the tazkirah tales, lay pilgrim and shaykh alike, were unlikely to be seen, or to see themselves, as descendants of the saints they venerated.

Here it is necessary to digress briefly and treat a very important exception to the trend of saints without descendants. Some of the latest saints to join the Altishahri pantheon were leaders of Naqshbandi Sufi orders, and for this group, the recognition of a line of descendants into the present was extremely important. The main figures in this group are Afaq Khoja, whose tomb in Kashgar is the most architecturally elaborate surviving shrine in Altishahr, and Ishāq Valī Khoja, who was considered to be buried in the royal tomb complex in Yarkand.[13] Members of these two holy lineages wielded great political power from the seventeenth century until late into the nineteenth century. Even today, it is said that there are claimants to the line of the Afaqi *khojas*.[14] Over the centuries, members of the main lines of *khojas* have tended to be buried at the shrines of their ancestors. When Jarring visited the Afaq Khoja shrine in 1929, he was introduced to a living descendant of the saint.[15] In the nineteenth century, at least until the Ya'qub Beg invasion, the living *khojas* of the Afaqi line wielded considerable influence, and frequently led rebellions against Qing rule.

The significance of a continuous genealogy was related to the Altishahri Naqshbandis' particular form of Sufism, in which the supreme position of authority over the sect was inherited. The tazkirahs of the Naqshbandi saints reflect this emphasis on a bloodline of Sufi leaders. In stark contrast to the more common kind of Altishahri tazkirah, with its focus on a single saint, or a group of contemporary saints that act as one, the Naqshbandi tazkirahs tend to treat entire lineages. Thus, the famous *Tazkirah-i 'Azīzān* (ca. 1770) treats saints from the father of Ishāq Valī, Makhdūm-i A'zam, down to his descendants at the time of the Qing conquest (1759). Some tazkirahs of the two Naqshbandi lineages were nearly as popular as any one of the tazkirahs that dominated the rest of Altishahr's historical world, but because of their concentrated connection to only two shrines, one at Kashgar and one at Yarkand, they did not represent the same kind of geographical coverage. They also tended not to be bound along with the other, more widespread type of tazkirah. At the same time, there was significant formal overlap. As will be seen later, one example of the Naqshbandi literature about Afaq Khoja was eventually embraced and transformed by the popular tazkirah tradition.[16]

The majority of popular tazkirahs, however, were not Naqshbandi tazkirahs. Most tazkirahs told the stories of saints with no living descendants in the reader's present. Thus, it was something other than genealogy that rooted the Altishahri community in the history of the saints. In part, such roots were apparent in shared place, and of course shared religion. Most of the saints of the tazkirahs were spreaders of Islam, either by sword or sermon, representing a kind of first Muslim in each place they visited. Altishahris may not have been the inheritors of the saints' blood, but they were the inheritors of their faith. The tazkirahs, in their roles as tales of the arrival of Islam, present a story of the origins of Altishahr's right faith. A second way that the saints were portrayed as originary figures was through their death, which necessarily entailed the establishment of a shrine. After their faith in Islam, what the people of Altishahr most shared among each other in relation to the saints was the veneration and guardianship of the saints' tombs.

The *Tazkirah of the Four Sacrificed Imams* provides an excellent example of how tazkirahs could provide Altishahri readers with explanations for the origins of their own identity group. It is important because it was widely consumed, and because in the nineteenth and early twentieth centuries, when this narrative reached its greatest popularity, the supposed tomb of the Four Imams had become an important gathering place where Muslims from Altishahr's widely spread oases converged and mingled. Like all Altishahri tazkirahs, the *Tazkirah of the Four Sacrificed Imams* was, furthermore, a text that circulated exclusively within Altishahr, its contents apparently irrelevant to Turkic-speaking Muslims outside Altishahr, who do not seem to have preserved or copied the text. The popularity of this text within Altishahr is shown by more than thirty copies in public archives[17] and more in private collections and antiquarian shops in Xinjiang.[18] In fact, it may have been the single most widely copied text explaining the historical origins of the "Muslims" in Altishahr.

The Four Imams tazkirah was likely committed to writing sometime between 1700 and 1820, drawing from oral sources of the epic tradition.[19] It tells of four imams who come from the city of Mada'in (in Iraq?) to assist the Qarakhanid ruler, Yūsuf Qādir-khān, in the conquest of Kashgar, Yarkand, and Khotan for Islam. The bulk of the work describes the battles that ensue against the native Buddhist inhabitants of Altishahr. At first, the outcome is in doubt, but after many years of grueling battles the imams and Yūsuf Qādir-khān push the infidels back to Khotan. However, just before victory is sealed, the Buddhists discover that the imams are vulnerable during the morning prayer and slaughter them like sheep. As the surviving Muslims lament the imams' passing, a voice comes from the unseen, saying,

> "Oh friends, we will become invisible to your eyes. Circle around us, and whoever mourns and humbles themselves will be companions and assistants of Islam." Then their bodies disappeared from sight. One person remained [i.e., one person could still see them]. His name was Khiẓr Bābā. His mother had been pregnant when she came from Mavarannahr [Western Turkestan] and gave birth to him in Khotan. Now he was forty-one years old. One day the Imams said to him "Oh Khiẓr Bābā, stay at our grave."[20]

Despite Khiẓr Bābā's protests that the task is too difficult for a lone man in a strange land, the imams command him to establish a shrine at their graves, consisting of candles and cooking pots, flags and banners, and endowments to fund the upkeep of the shrine. Yūsuf Qādir-khān learns of the imams' martyrdom, assigns Khiẓr Bābā as shaykh of the imams' shrine, and appoints the shrine with the items the imams had requested.

The short tale of Khiẓr Bābā stands out among the repetitive battle scenes that constitute the bulk of the Four Imams tazkirah. The personal details about Khiẓr Bābā are particularly remarkable. Usually, it is the protagonists' actions, the sizes of their armies, the number of enemies they slay, or the threats and vows they make that earn the attention of the author. Personal description is almost entirely absent. Age and place of birth are given for no other character in the tale, including the Four Imams themselves and the hero-king Yūsuf Qādir-khān. Thus, the details of the identity of Khiẓr Bābā, a character who appears for only a few pages, seem to be of great importance.

Coming immediately after the revelation of Khiẓr Bābā's unique power to see the deceased Four Imams, these details appear almost as an explanation of his visionary abilities, a list of qualities that led the imams to choose this particular man as the keeper of their shrine. Khiẓr Bābā's adulthood reveals that, within the logic of the narrative, his mother gave birth to him during the earliest incursions of Islamic Qarakhanid forces into Khotan.[21] The revelation of his first name hints at his visionary powers; "Khiẓr" is the name of a prophet who frequently appears in Islamic narratives of all kinds, wherein he guides seekers, be they Sufi mystics in search of God, Alexander the Great in search of the water of life, or Satūq Bughrā-khān in his predestined conversion to Islam.[22] The second name, Bābā, actually more of a nickname or title than a name, is certainly appropriate for an ancestor of the Muslims of Khotan. However, it is the circumstances of Khiẓr Bābā's conception and birth that are of the greatest interest to the discussion of Altishahri identity. Khiẓr Bābā's dual origin in Western Turkestan (conception) and Khotan (birth) provides both continuity with the greater Islamic world and a local specificity of origin that qualify him to hold a special connection with the imams and to act as steward of their tomb in Altishahr. He highlights at once the separation and the connection between Altishahris and the greater Islamic community. His genealogy is traceable to core Islamic lands, but he is of local birth, and it is this first locally born Muslim who is chosen to guard the tomb of the foreigners who made Altishahr holy through their deaths. The event brings together birth and death, humanity's most powerful means of creating permanent human connections to place, to fix both Khiẓr Bābā and the imams as locals of Altishahr.

Within the *Tazkirah of the Four Sacrificed Imams*, the Khiẓr Bābā episode stands at a pivotal moment for the story of Altishahri origins: the moment when the imams are transformed from foreign Muslims, born in some unspecified place abroad but fighting in Altishahr, to local saints, by virtue of their death and burial in the region. Here, death is a means of naturalization, in which the deathplace trumps all other connections to place (including birth). The close connection to Altishahr that the Four Imams earned through their local death is demonstrated by a copy of their tazkirah, which the copyist labeled as the *Tazkirah of the Imams of Khotan (Tazkirah–i Imāmān-i Khotan).*[23] Despite their foreign origin, the imams are now seen as saints of the Altishahri oasis of Khotan.[24] It is Khiẓr Bābā, the first descendent of foreign Muslims to be born in Altishahr, who, as shaykh, presides over the imams' transformation into locals.

The establishment of a manzil and then a shrine in Altishahr is, after being a Muslim, the major uniting factor in the identities of Altishahr's canon of local hero saints. Some saints of the tazkirah tradition were kings, others scholars, others mendicant Sufis, but all were Muslims and virtually all died in Altishahr.[25] By contrast, there are, for example, no tazkirahs describing heroes of Altishahri origin who found their end in foreign lands. As the most widely circulated and consumed works that treated the past of Altishahr, the tazkirahs established a canon of heroes who explain the history of a region through their shared local death. From their places of death sprang the new Altishahri identity. The people who were born and lived among those tombs, along with those who, like Khiẓr Bābā, tended those tombs or worshipped at them, were the readers and hearers of the tazkiras and the members of the Altishahri identity group.

Altishahri identity's foundation in death as well as birth evokes parallels with the phenomenon of diaspora, though there are also important divergences. In his work on the Hadrami diaspora around the Indian Ocean, Engseng Ho has linked cultural emphasis on the place of death to the diaspora, and contrasted this with the importance of birthplace to the nation.[26] In light of this divide, the story of *Khiẓr Bābā and the Four Imams* is the perfect originary metaphor for a society that had long ago ceased to be a diaspora but did not display the qualities of a nation.[27] The tales of khans and imams coming from the West to bring Islam to Altishahr, and becoming a part of Altishahr through their local deaths, in many ways resembles the story of a diaspora. The bearers of Islam who were destined for Altishahr had origins in places such as Western Turkestan or Iraq, places which themselves had once been destinations, rather than origins, for Muslims and their faith. We might even see these khans and imams as part of a larger Islamic diaspora that reached the edge of China from the West through warfare at the same time it reached the Southeastern coast of

China through trade. It is not surprising, given the importance of genealogy to other diasporas, not least among them the Hadrami, that the ancestry of these Altishahri hero saints is carefully recorded.

Yet there are important departures from the diasporic model, as well. While diasporas are characterized by their scattering of a people, the Altishahri identity was portrayed instead as a concentration of Muslims from diverse backgrounds: Turk, Arab, and Persian. It is perhaps also telling that, in the tazkirahs, the birthplaces of such foreign heroes are rarely given, while their places of death and burial are noted without fail. For all the hints of diaspora, when the heroes of Islam reached Altishahr, the genealogical and geographical expansion stopped, at least in the representations of the tazkirahs. The Altishahris did not attach themselves to the genealogies of the saints, but cared for the saints, building a shared identity around pillars of the Islamic pseudodiaspora, telling stories of their own birth among the tombs of the saints. The roots of those saints in other places were never entirely forgotten, but they receded into the background, as the saints' deathplaces were transformed into the birthplace of Altishahri identity.

Meanwhile, the abandonment of genealogy produced a society tied particularly strongly to place. Genealogy lends mobility to identity, allowing communities to stretch beyond homelands without sacrificing rootedness, stringing places along genealogical charts.[28] Altishahris, however, were connected to the saints not by genealogy but by presence, a presence enacted through everyday interaction at local tombs and through pilgrimage to the great shrines of the region. In this context, exile communities in Ferghana and in Yettisu, far from the tombs of the Altishahri saintly canon, were omitted from the picture of the Altishahri identity described in tazkirahs and on shrine walls.

According to the tazkirahs, the Four Imams were not the only outsiders to make a big mark on the landscape of Altishahr. There were also the Seven Muhammads from the Hejaz, who traveled the world in search of their own graves and found them in Yarkand. The Sufi master Muhammad Sharīf came from Ferghana and uncovered the lost tombs of other saints, both local and foreign, before being buried in Yarkand.[29] Abū al-Naṣr Samānī, a Samanid noble from Northeastern Iran, converted the prince of Kashgar to Islam and was buried alongside him in the royal town of Artush. All of these strangers became heroes in an identity system based on death as much as birth. Their graves grew into holy sites that attracted the prayers and donations of countless pilgrims.

Taken together, these histories weave a regional origin tale on a geographical weft of tombs and travel. It was a story that painted Altishahr as a cosmopolitan cul-de-sac that had embraced outsiders as locals but did not send its own luminaries back into the wider world to die abroad.[30] Through its integration with ritual and its links to networks of travel, it was also a story that supported a shared identity across wide desert wastes, long before the arrival of nationalism.

Routes

The stories of Altishahri origins gained power and organizational structure in their deployment across the landscape, their mobilization. We might expect the tazkirahs, through their connection to the shrine, to function exclusively as local tales at the oasis level. However, networks of travel built on pilgrimage and trade ensured that the tazkirah's narratives were spread throughout the region of Altishahr. This dissemination was no small accomplishment, for the geographical barriers to travel in Altishahr were extreme. The oases of Altishahr circle the enormous Taklamakan Desert, a sandy waste over 1,000 kilometers in length and 400 in width. On all sides, this desert is surrounded by imposing mountain ranges: the Tianshan, the Pamir, the Karakoram, and the Kunlun. Rivers, fed by glacial melt, empty from these mountains into the desert, where they eventually evaporate. The oases situated at the feet of these mountain ranges are man made, maintained by an elaborate system of canals that diverts river water to irrigate the land. Writing of his visit in 1904, Aurel Stein noted that the roads within rural parts of the oases appeared sunken, for the fields around the roads were raised by the continuous deposit of sediment carried down from the mountains in the river water.[31] Oases in Altishahr end suddenly, and the dramatic sight of sand dunes abutting apricot orchards and poplar-lined wheat fields is not uncommon. Travel between oases meant passing beyond this line and braving the harsh conditions of the Taklamakan, with its extreme heat in the day, extreme cold at night, lack of water, and sand storms that disoriented travelers and broke apart caravans.

We have two kinds of clues about the routes that pilgrims followed. The less specific kind of clue is the system of roads that connected the towns of Altishahr. These are particularly well documented in the works of British spies and travelers, who diligently noted each inn and well, in case British merchants, or perhaps even soldiers, might one day find themselves in the region.³² Vestiges of some of the old roads can still be seen in satellite photos. The roads, as reconstructed from textual evidence and surviving traces, are not too different from the roads maintained today by the People's Republic of China; humans have always been subject to the logic of the Tarim Basin's oasis geography. The roads skirted the feet of the mountains, maximizing the distance covered under the shelter of the oases' poplar trees while minimizing the length of desert segments. The distances between some oases could not be crossed in a single day's journey, and for these segments travelers stayed at a *langar*, or inn, typically a rudimentary stone shelter in the desert established by a *waqf* endowment. In the desert segments, shifting sands made proper roads impossible to maintain, so the "roads" were simply tracks marked by piles of stone or mudbrick towers (such as the *potai*), signs that guided pilgrims along the least treacherous routes through the desert. For travel between major towns, the network of roads was rather simple, essentially a single curving line that ran through each of the large towns. However, our second clue to the pilgrims' routes suggests that such a view of the roads oversimplifies the network of routes.

A small number of shrines preserve on their walls the graffiti of pilgrims, and these graffiti hint at patterns of travel on Altishahr's roads. Just as the manuscript tradition allowed people to write their own pasts into the margins of Altishahr's popular histories, pilgrimage permitted individuals to locate their own personal stories alongside those of the saints. Some pilgrims made this relationship a very literal reality by writing records of their visits on the walls, interior and exterior, of the shrines. Such graffiti provide a window onto the variety of journeys made by pilgrims. Typical graffiti record the date, the names of the pilgrims, their hometowns, and a very short account of their worship at the shrine. For example, a graffito on the interior wall of the Băysi Hekim Băg shrine in Yarkand's Altunluq cemetery (see Figure 2) reads,

> In the year 1304 [1886 AD] on Saturday, the fourth of the month of Safar, Mu'mīn Akhūnd, Qādir Akhūnd, and Jamāl Akhūnd from Kashgar, along with Mullā Muhammad Akhūnd of Upper Artush, these four travelers, requesting from God Almighty peace and security along with health and wellness, recited from the Qur'an, and returned.³³

This kind of graffiti writing seems to have been widespread. The handful of shrines that have preserved their original interior surfaces from the Qing period (usually due to neglect) bear graffiti in the same format, with the oldest surviving graffito dating to 1878, preserved on the wall of the Yunus Hekim Băg shrine in Yarkand. In the 1930s graffiti writers stopped using reed pens for their work, providing a convenient means of dating those graffiti that do not otherwise record their date. Based on this method, I have located the following shrines with late nineteenth-century to early twentieth-century graffiti: Yunus Hekim Băg (Yarkand, with dates), Bay Boba Khoqandi (Yarkand, no dates), Băysi Hekim Băg (Yarkand, with dates), and Iskăndăr Vang (Kashgar, no dates).[34] During his expedition of 1906–1908, C. G. Mannerheim noticed the same practice at the shrine of Kohmarim, near Khotan.[35] The practice continued through the twentieth century and remains a common feature of shrine visitation, except where shrines have been dressed up under Chinese government pressure for the benefit of tourists, such as the Afaq Khoja shrine near Kashgar.[36]

The graffiti tell a story of pilgrims from the farthest oases of Altishahr visiting even relatively minor shrines. For the period from the 1880s through the 1930s, the best collection of early graffiti, the Băysi Hekim Băg shrine in Yarkand, documents visitors from both nearby villages such as Poskam and the distant Altishahri towns of Merkit, Yangihissar, Kashgar, Artush, Khotan, Kucha, and Uch Turpan, along with pilgrims from Turpan who had established residences in Yangihissar. Shrines with greater reputations may have attracted pilgrims from an even greater diversity of towns. Since every major town had at least one important shrine, the clusters of routes encouraged by each shrine overlapped to create a dense network of moving people and information, which ensured that the histories associated with a particular oasis were disseminated to pilgrims from all corners of Altishahr. It is also important that this network of movement seems to have been largely limited to Altishahr. Of some fifty-seven pilgrims whom I have traced and whose place of origin is preserved and legible in 1930s or earlier graffiti, only one, a pilgrim from Bukhara, did not come from Altishahr (and among the much better preserved and more numerous graffiti from after the 1930s, I have found no pilgrims from outside Altishahr who recorded a visit). Systems of cultural interaction are almost never fully isolated, but the degree of geographic consistency that the surviving graffiti suggest for Altishahr's pilgrimage network was a powerful encouragement for the development of an identity that followed the same geography.

In the most basic sense, the sheer physical circulation of Altishahri people achieved by the pilgrimage tradition supported the region-wide identity through immediate encounters between people from diverse

places. The interaction of pilgrims of various origins is eloquently attested to in places where several pilgrims decided to chronicle their pilgrimage together in a shared graffito. The most striking of these is a graffito dated 1887–1888 from the Băysi Hekim Băg shrine, the legible parts
of which read,

> In the year 1302, year of the fish, on the sixth of the month of [unclear],
> Islām Akhūnd, the scribe, came from Poskam, recited the opening sura of
> the Quran, and, God willing, returned in health and wellness. The Kuchaliq
> from Kashgar, Maht Akhūnd ['s son?] Sābit, the Yengihissarliq . . . . . . son
> of Ṣādiq Beg, . . . Islām Akhūnd, the friend of the friends who came with
> us [?], [name?] Niyāz Akhūnd, ... Akhūnd. . . . . .
> . . . .

Here we have an artifact of the interaction of pilgrims from far-flung and
unconnected oases, who, for at least a moment, saw themselves as a group,
drawn together by the same saint. It is also worth noting that these pilgrims came from either side of Yarkand along Altishahr's major linear
route (for the Yangihissarliq, Poskam is beyond Yarkand). This suggests
that at least some of them met there (as opposed to traveling together), and
reminds us that, from the perspective of the shrine, the pilgrims' routes appear radial, with the shrine at the center. In any case, for these pilgrims, the
draw of shrine and saint were the impetus for the formation of a fleeting
inter-oasis group, an "us" preserved on the wall of the tomb.

And even though most people might not manage to travel between, say
Kashgar and Yarkand, like Maht Akhūnd, they would encounter such
travelers during pilgrimage festivals at their own local shrines, as Aurel
Stein had noted in 1904.[37] Those travelers would, in turn, bring back the
stories from the distant shrine's tazkirahs to their home communities.
The networks of pilgrimage kept the population of Altishahr in contact
with each other, while still maintaining an emphasis on the local community, for the majority of pilgrims would come from within the shrine's
own oasis or nearby oases.

The connection between mobility and history also added geographical implications to the acquisition and organization of historical
knowledge. Over their lifetimes, pilgrims would have acquired knowledge of different histories from the different shrines they had visited.
Today, in parts of Altishahr where shrine culture has best survived the
onslaught of Chinese religious restrictions, members of older genera-

tions will often speak of history in geographic terms, listing places by their saints, and saints by their places. A similar impulse is apparent in a tazkirah manuscript in which a reader has noted alongside several saints' names the locations of their tombs.[38] When today's pilgrims discuss history in terms of place, the saints in an individual's home oasis usually receive the most detailed treatment, with knowledge diminishing as the conversation moves to more distant oases. At the same time, most of the older participants in shrine culture are familiar with the biggest shrine in each major oasis (and of course its saint). It is likely that the effects of putting history in motion would have been the same a century ago. While some points on the historical landscape achieved near-universal fame, the idiosyncratic travels of individual pilgrims left traces in the structures of their personal historical imaginations, creating a locally weighted system extended along the networks of its participants' pilgrimages.

Reflections and Representations of Connection

In the manuscript era, such geographical arrangements of overlapping historical knowledge, concentrated for each participant in his or her home oasis, but including material from more distant oases with diminishing depth, were often mirrored in the arrangement of tazkirahs within composite manuscripts. Usually, such tazkirah compilations contained three to ten tazkirahs. The precise arrangements of the composite tazkirah manuscripts varied widely in Altishahr, but most demonstrate a measure of geographical consistency, based on the locations of the tombs of saints described in the texts. For example, one manuscript of the Four Imams tazkirah is a Kashgar-centered compilation, in which several tazkirahs of saints from the Kashgar area are joined by a tazkirah of a Yarkand saint, a Keriya saint, and a Khotan saint.[39] Another manuscript of the Four Imams is Khotan-centered, including tazkirahs of several Khotan imams alongside the tazkirah of Jalāl al-Dīn Katakī (whose shrine is in Aqsu) and a list of Kashgar rulers.[40] Yet another example of the Four Imams tazkirah is found in a manuscript with tazkirahs of Yarkand's major saints, Muhammad Sharīf, and the Seven Muhammads.[41] Not all tazkirah compilations showed such geographic variability, but most did.[42] The compilations often connected the Altishahri saints to the roots of sacred Islamic history by placing popular narratives about the prophet Muhammad and/or his family at the beginning of manuscript.[43]

In the late nineteenth and early twentieth centuries there was no widely available, vernacular, single-author history of the whole region.[44] That role was filled by the anthology—by bringing together diverse tazkirahs, which, once bound together, functioned as a history of all Altishahr, a comprehensive view of those parts of the past that mattered to people. In the Kashgar-centered example cited above, the tazkirahs describe the first royal convert to Islam in Kashgar, his descendents' martyrdom at the hands of the Buddhist armies of Yarkand and Khotan, the final conquest of Khotan with the help of the Four Imams, the supposed participation of the scholar Ghazālī in the spread of the faith to Khotan, and, hundreds of years later, the rediscovery of martyrs' graves by the Sufi master Muhammad Sharīf, who was buried in Yarkand.[45] Other composite manuscripts present a slightly different history. Since each anthology was made of a different combination of tazkirahs, there could be no single definitive history of the region, even though such region-wide composite histories were common. One could mix and match the building blocks of history, but the blocks were always chosen from the same set. It was a modular history from which an imagined community's narrative could be built with a local focus, but without the local emphases threatening the integrity of the larger story. Narrower oasis identities were preserved in the building of a large regional identity.

The strength of those narrower oasis identities is clear in the shrine graffiti. The graffiti writers maintained a distinction between being *of* an oasis and being *from* an oasis. People who are *of* an oasis (perhaps those born in that oasis, or from families whose graves were in that oasis), are labeled with a form of the oasis name ending in -*liq*. A person of Kashgar, for instance, is a *Kāshgharliq*, while someone of Turpan is a *Ṭurpānliq*, terms which remain in use today. This kind of oasis identity was apparently not dependent on the individual's current place of residence. It was something more permanent. Thus, we find graffiti that describe a "*Kūchārliq* from Kashgar" and Supurga Niyāz, "the *Ṭurpānliq* who came to *Yangṣiḥār* [*sic*], stopped, and stayed [permanently]."[46] Clearly the oasis identity named with the -*liq* suffix was more than a term of convenience to identify a person's place of residence. Supurga Niyāz did not become a *Yangihiṣārliq* by moving to that town. The oasis-*liq* term described something more essential, presumably based on a person's place of origin.

However, the very real significance of the oasis identities, as described here, should not be taken as support of a now widely known argument, advanced by the first modern ethnographer of the Uyghurs, Justin Rudelson, in 1997. Rudelson claimed that oasis identities and "geographic template divisions" trumped any regional identity, even as recently as the Altishahr of the 1980s that he described.[47] However, the existence and salience of oasis identities should not be mistaken for preeminence.[48] The Turki-speaking inhabitants of Altishahr in the nineteenth century maintained many different kinds of identities. Alongside the oasis-based identities, religious orders, such as the famous White and Black Mountain Naqshbandi *tariqats*, provided another kind of identity. Tradesmen identified with each other by profession, a system bolstered by guilds, trade manuals *(risālah),* and the master-apprentice relationship. At the broadest level, people identified with the wider Islamic world as believers in Islam. No one of these identities precluded or even overshadowed another. Instead, their salience grew or shrank depending on the context in which they were deployed. For example, the instances of oasis identity terms cited above were written on the walls of Altishahri shrines, places patronized by pilgrims from all over Altishahr, and, for the most part, Altishahr only. The oasis-*liq* terms on the shrine walls were used by Altishahris to communicate with Altishahris, and to differentiate among themselves. However, different terms were used in histories that describe encounters between the Altishahris and other Islamic peoples from outside Altishahr. In such contexts, Altishahris were called Muslims or locals, terms which we will explore in more detail momentarily. Here I want to emphasize that people of the various oases of Altishahr were connected together in ways that created an Altishahri identity *in addition to* the oasis identities.

Much has been made of the idea that Altishahris had no identity name for themselves beyond the oasis-*liq* terms.[49] However, this supposed lack of an ethnonym is not as clear as it seems at first glance. In fact, Altishahris employed a variety of terms to describe their collective identity, most of which were broad terms repurposed to distinguish between Altishahris and outsiders. Such terms included *Musulmān* (Muslim),[50] *Turki,*[51] *yerlik* (local),[52] and, in one 1935 source, *Altishahrlik* (person of Altishahr).[53] The adaptation of general terms is well illustrated by the eighteenth-century text, *Tazkirah-i 'Azīzān,* which denotes Altishahris by the term *Musulmān,* the most common name for the Altishahri identity before the 1930s. In a revealing passage, the author writes, "the Kirghiz are making many attacks . . . they will pillage the homeland [*yürt*]. Might we *Musulmāns* become prisoners of the Kirghiz?"[54] The Kirghiz whom the author excludes from the *Musulmān* identity were, at this time, not only adherents of Islam but even devotees of the same lines of Sufi spiritual leaders (the Naqshbandiyya) whose stories are the subject of his history. It is clear that in this context *Musulmān* does not indicate the wider community of believers in the Islamic faith, but instead denotes in particular the settled Turkic-speaking Muslims of Altishahr. *Musulmān* could be used to describe culture or ethnicity rather than faith,[55] and Kāshgharī used such lexical flexibility to facilitate his description of conflict between Altishahris and another Muslim identity group. The lack of a term devoted exclusively to naming the Altishahri identity did not stop authors from expressing that identity. Whether people called themselves *Turki, yerlik, Musulmān,* or *Altishahrlik,* or avoided naming their regional identity altogether, the notion that the settled Turki Muslims of Altishahr shared something that "Kirghiz," "Andijani," "Khitay" (Chinese), and other outsiders lacked demonstrates that oasis identities were neither the highest order identity group, nor an effective obstacle to the maintenance of such a group.

The significance of the missing ethnonym, if it can be said to be missing at all, has been overstated. As Laura Newby has persuasively argued, such a lacuna is no grounds for claiming that the Turkic speaking, settled Muslims of Altishahr, called Altishahris in this study for convenience, did not share in an identity. Expressions of alterity in the naming of outsider groups are clear enough evidence of a sense of shared identity. Despite Atishahris' unstable terminology for their own group, they were tied together by their tradition of shared origins, a tradition bound together by tazkirah anthologies and by networks of pilgrimage, which brought people to histories, and histories to people. More important than the existence or nature of ethnonyms was the expression of identity and alterity inherent in statements such as "the Kirghiz . . . will pillage the homeland." The modern fixation on stable ethnonyms is itself a product of nationalist thought. We should not be surprised to find a nonmodern, nonnationalist system of identity employing a less rigid vocabulary. As a projection of nationalist ways of thinking, the issue of the ethnonym is something of a distraction in our attempt to understand alternative modes of identity maintenance such as the Altishahri system under consideration here, and so, we return now to the exploration of Altishahri identity on its own terms.

In addition to documenting travels and inter-oasis friendships, the graffiti reveal further aspects of Altishahri historical practice that turned shared traditions into an imagined community. As much as the physical circulation of people would have helped to maintain a shared identity, perhaps the greatest significance of the shrine graffiti lay in the record and display of that circulation. By recording their acts of devotion involved in pilgrimage, pilgrims who wrote graffiti documented those small parts of their own histories that they shared with the saints. Just as the Four Imams' visit to the death site of Imam Ja'far Ṭayarān[56] and Muhammad Sharīf's pilgrimage to the tomb of Sultan Satūq Bughrā-khān[57] appeared in their tazkirahs, the pilgrims' visits to Muhammad Sharīf's tomb were displayed on the shrine walls. Thus, the historical experience was thick with the (brief) stories of ordinary people, fellow Altishahris. The walls of shrines were covered in small personal histories and the margins of manuscripts often bore the record of other people's readings, all of which was rich material for building an imagined community. Literate pilgrims could see for themselves on the shrine walls that Mu'mīn Akhūnd and his friends from Kashgar venerated the same Yarkand saint that they did, much like tazkirah readers could see the names of others who had performed ritualized readings of a book before them.

In at least one part of today's Altishahr, these personal stories have even been explicitly labeled as history. At the shrine called Hǎbbi Khojim, near Kashgar, pilgrims have begun to label their graffiti with the word *tarikh*. This practice likely grew out of an old formula for labeling the date, which begins most graffiti, for example, "*tarikhigǎ* 1970 *yili*. . . ." However, the word *tarikh*, which could in older usages signify "date" or "era" as well as "history," has in modern Uyghur become almost exclusively associated with "history." Pilgrims have separated the word from the date, placing it alone at the top of the graffito, interpolating other text in between the word *tarikh* and the date, and removing the dative suffix that was necessary for the date formula, thus changing the word *tarikh* into a label of "history" for the graffiti. The fact that *tarikh* has become a label rather than a date formulation is further supported by the graffiti at another shrine, the Alp Atta complex outside Turpan. At Alp Atta numerous graffiti are labeled *khatirǎ* (record or memorial), suggesting that a single word on the first line of a graffito should indeed be read as a genre label and not a part of the date formula. The date formula's transformation into the label "history" both suggests that pilgrims have themselves been open to viewing the graffiti as history and further bolsters the sense of ordinary individuals' participation in historical practice.

Returning to the early twentieth century, it is also significant that the vast majority of shrine graffiti recorded the writer's home village. This constant reminder of other pilgrims put pilgrimage and tazkirahs in a new light. The point is not only that the content of the tazkirahs told at the shrines created a shared sense of origins, but that the shrine-tazkirah system also created an awareness of that sharing. The imagination of an audience for the tazkirahs, of fellow readers in far-flung oases who shared those same origins, would have also contributed to a sense of shared identity, and a sense that this identity was shared with people whom one would never meet—an imagined community. It is also important to remember that this was a time and a place without maps. Maps are powerful tools in the creation of an imagined community.[58] They are images that give shape to the borders of "our" land. While these images were not available to Altishahris, the shrine graffiti performed a similar function. Pilgrims who entered the Băysi Hekim Băg shrine in the 1920s were surrounded by the names of Altishahr's oases, and they knew that people from those oases had come to venerate the same saint that they had come to venerate. In a land where stories of shared origins and identity were constructed around the tending and veneration of shrines, the record of pilgrims' hometowns on shrines walls demonstrated the breadth and limits of "us"ness. For literate pilgrims, the constellation of place names on the interior walls of the Băysi Hekim Băg shrine provided an image of the Altishahri imagined community.

Manuscript Technologies and Practices

We have already seen how the tradition of making composite manuscripts (anthologies) interacted with the geographic vectors of history to influence Altishahr's shared view of the past. Before moving on to the role of Qing rule in shaping Altishahri history and identity, it is worth pausing briefly here to recall the effects of manuscript technologies and practices, the critical enablers of the community authorship that created the tazkirahs as they existed in their most popular forms. The manuscript tradition was vital to the process of building a shared identity out of a shared past in three aspects: the creation of a new genre, refinement of texts through abbreviation, and wide community involvement in textual production.

The development of a shared historical tradition was not just a matter of composing texts that described the local past but also of forging a genre to convey such knowledge. As we have seen, Altishahr's genre of popular local history, the tazkirah, began to coalesce in the eighteenth century, as written tales about Altishahri shrines appeared and gained popularity. The interface of manuscript flexibilities, including titling, abbreviation, anthology production, talismanic marginalia, and postscripts, established important bonds of genre between the formally diverse works that were excerpted from encyclopedias and epics to become tazkirahs. The uses to which they were put and the social contexts in which they were deployed further linked the texts of Altishahr's shared history. Once the genre was well established, it further encouraged the production of new historical texts. In terms of creating a foundation for a regional identity, the creation of the tazkirah genre was important because it cleared a space for local history in a literary landscape that had long been dominated by the Persian tradition. Saints of Kashgar and Khotan began to populate a written past crowded with the Iranian heroes of the *Shāhnāmah* and the Semitic prophets of the *Qiṣaṣ al-Anbiyā'*.

The abbreviation that took place during copying not only gave the copyist a voice in the continued creation of texts but provided a mechanism by which the central tales of community origins were continuously, if subtly, updated. Presumably, this slow but widespread phenomenon, dispersed among the copyists of all Altishahr, would have also refined the tazkirahs into texts that were widely and supremely relevant to their audiences. The marginalia added by ordinary readers further bolstered the imagination of the Altishahri community. Even in the mundane instance of ownership marks, and especially in the common cases wherein readers documented their reading of the text, the marginalia demonstrated to readers that others, perhaps people they would never meet, shared their interest in the foundational stories of Altishahr's past. As we have seen, in some cases these marginalia even document the travels of books, for readers would sometimes record their hometowns in the margins, just as pilgrims did on shrine walls. The sum effect of the manuscripts' contribution to the construction of a local historical tradition is this: the tazkirahs were particularly suited to the role of supporting a community identity because they were so thoroughly shaped by the community.

Qing Rule as an Influence on Altishahri History and Identity

If one were to judge only from the overt narrative content of Altishahri popular history, it would be easy to conclude that the Altishahri view of the past had no connection at all to the Qing Empire under which it blossomed. The Qing and the Manchus go unmentioned in the popular histories. However, in the organization of that narrative content there is in fact a striking resonance with the Qing system of indirect rule. The basic geographical unit of Altishahri history, the oasis town, was also the point where China-based Qing rule articulated with local Altishahri structures of political authority. After the Qing conquest of Altishahr (1757–1759), local Altishahri nobles were set up as rulers over the major cities, with the Turki title of ḥākim beg (modern Uyghur: hekim băg). Below them were only fellow indigenous Altishahri officials, and above them only Manchu bannermen of the Qing, most notably the Qing councilor stationed at Kashgar.[59] The hakim begs were not only the highest indigenous political authorities, but also patrons of the Altishahri historical tradition. Several hakim begs are known to have patronized historical works. Hakim begs also financed the expansion of local shrines, and upon their deaths, their tombs often became shrines themselves, as in the case of the Yunus Hekim Băg shrine at Yarkand.[60] Thus, the hakim begs were well positioned to both influence and be influenced by the Altishahri system of popular history and identity maintenance outlined here.

The simplest way to understand the ramifications of Qing rule for local history is to note that the Qing conquest put an end to the sociopolitical context that perpetuated the classic dynastic histories. Altishahri histories in the dynastic tradition told the stories of locally born rulers who could claim power over all Altishahr. Both of the early dynastic histories whose authors are known were written by nobles involved in the political events they described.[61] While they were not precisely the kind of court-patronized works that dominated Western Turkestan, these histories were still products of their political environments, and they were designed to have an effect on those political environments.[62] At the end of the seventeenth century, Naqshbandi Sufi orders, in concert with Dzungar Mongol armies, overturned the political system that supported the dynastic tradition, and the Qing invasion firmly foreclosed the possibility of a return to dynastic rule. The dynastic histories in the classic form ceased to be widely produced. This left only the tazkirahs as survivors of Qing indirect rule. The tazkirahs were independent of the central court, connected politically only to shrine administration, which the Qing conquerors seem to have left undisturbed.[63] Even this political connection was weak. Because the tazkirahs were more firmly embedded in ritual and popular practices rather than the political sphere, and because they were created through the copying practices of the lowest literate ranks of society, they were unaffected by Qing indirect rule, if not encouraged.

A fuller picture of the shift from dynastic history to shrine-centered history emerges when we consider the hakim begs' situation at the border between Qing and Altishahri systems of political authority. This position presented them with special challenges to their political legitimacy, not least when it came to the sponsorship of historical writing. Both the Chinese historical tradition, as inherited by the Qing, and the Persian dynastic historical tradition, which had dominated Altishahr's written history production until the rise of the tazkirah-shrine system, were intimately bound up with notions of political legitimacy. In this sense, the two traditions were in fact remarkably similar. Chinese histories traced the Mandate of Heaven as it passed from one dynasty to the next, and the Persian dynastic histories similarly focused on the transfer of rule as it was ordained by God.[64] Both of these views of historical legitimacy regarded conquered or subjugated dynasties as those judged unworthy by Heaven or God. All historical writing necessarily entailed a claim of political legitimacy, for the occupation of the throne proved legitimacy. In the Persianate tradition of kingship, as in the Chinese tradition, the appropriate kind of history for a ruler to commission was an account of his own (or a previous) dynasty, an endeavor which was *ipso facto* an assertion of sovereignty.

This left the hakim begs in an interesting position as they patronized the production of Altishahri history. On the one hand, the Persian historical tradition that rulers had normally patronized in the hakim begs' own culture demanded that they be able to lay claim to unfettered independent Islamic rule by the grace of God. Since full sovereignty demonstrated the favor of God, they could not acknowledge Qing overlordship without bestowing legitimacy on the infidels. On the other hand, any claim to legitimacy in the Persian dynastic tradition would have been impossible to reconcile with the Chinese tradition as patronized by the Qing. The hakim begs could not have claimed legitimacy as rulers within the Persian historical tradition without tacitly advertising their failure as Islamic rulers in the face of the obvious practical reality of Qing rule.

Two solutions to this problem of history and legitimacy arose, one more successful than the other, both of which operated through a refusal to address Qing rule. One solution was that the hakim begs patronized historical works in the dynastic tradition that simply ended chronologically before the Qing conquest, altogether omitting the troublesome historical presence of the Qing by reaching back to a time before them. Such histories described the Muslim rulers who controlled the whole of

Altishahr in the fifteenth to eighteenth centuries. However, this kind of narrative preserved an implicit contradiction, for the story of the pre-Qing Muslim state in Altishahr established an ideal of Muslim rule that was obviously at odds with the situation obtaining in Qing Altishahr. In the end, few works were undertaken in this tradition, and those that did had only limited popularity, precluding the establishment of these variant dynastic histories as a cornerstone of popular historical consciousness.[65]

The other, more successful, solution to the problem of historical writing under Qing indirect rule was the tazkirah, which fully avoided the question of outsider rule by abandoning the larger politicohistorical unit of Altishahr. Like the less popular variant dynastic histories just mentioned, the tazkirahs also tended to describe pre-Qing times. However, through their connection to the oasis town, the largest indigenously controlled political unit, the tazkirahs also avoided the question of who should rule the whole of Altishahr in the Qing present. While dynastic histories of Altishahr's seventeenth-century rulers described a throne on which the Qing emperor now sat, the logical successor to the tazkirahs' hero saints of each oasis town was the hakim beg. There is not much evidence to suggest that the hakim begs patronized the tazkirah extensively (though some did), but their upkeep of the associated shrines and their own burial in elaborate tombs alongside the shrines reinforced their connection to the local saints.

The close connection between the hakim begs' patronage of shrines and the historical tradition is well illustrated by the tomb of Muhammad Sharīf, which was repaired and greatly enlarged by Yunus, hakim beg of Yarkand. Around 1808, on an interior wall, the hakim beg had inscribed a brief summary of the saint's life as presented in the tazkirah, along with a description of the hakim beg's repairs to the shrine. Although Yunus, the hakim beg, had not patronized the original composition of the tazkirah, he promoted it through the inscription and advertised his own connection to the saint, claiming to be a descendant, not of the saint himself, but of the "true followers" of the saint. With such support from the hakim begs, explicit or implicit, the tazkirahs gained wide readership, becoming the dominant vehicle of popular historical discourse through the system of shrine pilgrimage. At the same time, through their local focus, the tazkirahs were able to avoid the question of legitimacy beyond the level of the indigenous hakim begs. Though there are no grounds to claim that the Qing system of indirect rule through hakim begs directly caused the rise of the tazkirah, it is clear that the tazkirah system of historical texts was particularly well suited to Altishahr's Qing political context, and this may have been an influence on the success of the tazkirah and the weakness of dynastic history.

The correlation between indirect rule and the tazkirah's predominance over dynastic histories is perhaps even more striking when we consider the only extended interruption to Qing rule in Altishahr, the establishment of an independent kingdom under Ya'qub Beg, for during this brief interruption, the dynastic history quickly returned to prominence. In 1865 Ya'qub Beg, a military officer from the khanate of Khoqand (in Western Turkestan), managed to gain leadership of an uprising in Altishahr, and established there his own independent kingdom, which lasted until 1877. Though he called himself *amir* (*khan* would have implied descent from Genghis Khan), the state that Ya'qub Beg created was essentially an imitation of the khanate in Khoqand, an institution that owed much of its rhetoric and organization to the Persian tradition of kingship. Under Ya'qub Beg's version of the khanate, numerous changes came to Altishahr. Some, like the Islamic morality police in the markets and the rich state funding for mosques and madrassas, were the direct result of Ya'qub Beg's actions. Other changes resulted from the general shift in the political and cultural atmosphere. Among these was an explosion in history writing of types that had largely disappeared under Qing indirect rule. During Ya'qub Beg's reign, and in the twenty years after, over a dozen new histories appeared documenting the amir's rule, most of them grounded firmly in the tradition of dynastic history.[66] This was influenced in part by the influx of educated Andijani officials, people familiar with the dynastic tradition as patronized by the khan of Khoqand. Yet most of the writers were Altishahris. In his definitive survey of the Ya'qub Beg period, Hodong Kim attributes the expansion of history writing to Altishahris' excitement over the arrival of an "exuberant period" in which a Muslim ruler finally replaced the infidel Qing. However, although the amirate's establishment continued to inspire local historians for twenty years, their works never captured the public imagination, and most are known from a handful of copies or even a single manuscript. Even the well-read Mullah Mūsá Sayrāmī, author of his own history of the period, the *Tārīkh-i Amniyah,* seems to have been unaware of the historical works that had emerged from the Ya'qub Beg era. In his preface, justifying his own composition, he writes, "no sign or memorial [of the events of the Ya'qub Beg period] made by any of the wise men of the times or great scholars of the age is known. It has been 32 years since the [re-]taking of the throne [by the Qing]."[67] With the return of Qing rule, the dynastic history faded away again, and the tazkirah remained the most widely consumed type of historical text. The brief period of independent Muslim rule in Altishahr, and the large number of dynastic histories that emerged from it, would seem to confirm the correlation between the political system and the dominant forms of history writing, even in the absence of evidence for direct patronage. While other forms of history flourished under Ya'qub Beg, it was the tazkirah that seems to have best suited Qing indirect rule.

The formation of large-scale identity groups often articulates with the boundaries of political administrative units. The case of Altishahr is no exception. There the oasis town was a basic unit of both the local popular historical tradition and indigenous political administration. Just as oasis-based conceptions of history and identity were drawn together through the interaction of pilgrimage and manuscript technology, so too was the political system, with its oases-level hakim begs, tied together through a Qing superstructure of indirect rule. The boundaries of the tazkirah-shrine network were also strongly influenced by the boundaries of the Qing political unit of Xinjiang. Travel to Western Turkestan and interior China was always more restricted than travel within Xinjiang, encouraging the circulation of people within Altishahr, while creating barriers to intercourse with the rest of the Turkic and Islamic worlds. In many periods during Qing rule, travel outside the province was impossible. Altishahris also shared the economic and political realities of living in the Qing's only piece of settled Islamic Central Asia, an environment with significant differences from Western Turkestan and the Persian world. One of the most important would have been a disparity in educational resources. It is hard to imagine that the Qing begs would have been able to match the lavish support that independent khans of Western Turkestan continued to bestow upon educational institutions until the last quarter of the nineteenth century. While these institutions benefited greatly under the brief rule of the Khoqandi officer Ya'qub Beg,[68] they had already seriously atrophied again by the time of Martin Hartmann's visit in 1903.[69] While sources for Altishahr's scholarly environment are generally uneven, the poverty of higher education in Altishahr may go some way toward explaining the relative dearth of elite scholastic works, which many European visitors mistook for a lack of a historical tradition, and which made the popular works, especially the tazkirahs, all the more prominent.

This is not to say that the political unit in which Altishahris found themselves was the sole cause of the identity group's extent. Geography did its part, as well. Political barriers aside, inter-oasis communication was, if not always shorter, at least safer and easier than expeditions over the Pamir, Karakorum, or Tianshan mountain ranges. Most mountain routes were impassible for part of the year anyway. Language and culture also limited the extent of the Altishahri identity. The Northern parts of Xinjiang province, dominated as they were by nomadic Kazakh and Mongolic speakers on the one hand and Han Chinese colonists on the other, were hardly fertile ground for Turki texts and the rituals of settled Muslim agriculturalists. It was alongside such geographic and cultural influences that the context of Qing rule strongly influenced the course of Altishahri identity development, tightening bonds between Altishahri oases while reducing connections to the linguistically and culturally very similar peoples of Ferghana and Western Turkestan. For Altishahris, the borders of the Qing Empire made pilgrimage to Ferghana, or, for that matter, the Hui Sufi shrines of Gansu in the Chinese interior, far more difficult than pilgrimage to the oases within the administrative unit of Xinjiang. Thus, in its geographic extent, and, quite possibly, its modular, oasis-based organization, the Altishahri popular historical tradition was shaped by Qing indirect rule.

Although Altishahr's forms of community making through historical practice were influenced by the circumstances of Qing rule, these traditions were not the carefully orchestrated products of political projects. In Altishahr under Qing indirect rule, history's role as a weapon in struggles for legitimacy was overshadowed by other functions. Local historical practice was, instead, a ritual act linking the community to God through the presence of historical personages. It was also an explanation of the origins of group activities that brought people together. Though history in Altishahr differed from nationalist history in its functioning, it was no less intimately connected to people's imagination of their own community. And yet the differences are important. Most students of identity view higher order identities, especially nationalism, as constructions. This can lead to an assumption of intentionality or instrumentality, such that scholars say that identities are formed or maintained *in order to* achieve some end. Invented traditions have inventors promoting individual imaginations of their communities. For example, Manuel Castells argues that top-down nurturing of identity legitimizes a state, while bottom-up identity construction resists oppression.[70] The

Altishahri case, a regional identity tossed up by the jostling of pilgrims and scribes, shows us that complex identities can be formed without either of these forces. It appears almost incidental or accidental, given shape by Qing colonial boundaries and geographic barriers, yet kept largely separate from discourses of legitimation by outsider rule. It was cultivated by local loyalties to hometown saints, but only really knitted together into something larger through the extraordinary travels of pilgrims seeking supernatural aid. It was a system upheld by countless cultural idiosyncrasies, some borrowed, some uniquely Altishahri, which together quite arbitrarily linked a particular group of historical narratives into a shape that couldn't be manipulated by any ruler or class. Some individuals, for example, the shaykhs, boasted an outsized potential to intervene in the reproduction of knowledge, but their power was largely limited to individual tazkirahs, as opposed to the regional narrative, and it was subject to the ratification of the wider public through the diffuse powers of manuscript publication.

Thus, origin tales, manuscript technology, and pilgrimage practices interacted to create a shared sense of origins, along with a record and display of that sharing, across a large geographic unit shaped by China-based rule. The historical tradition that arose bore the traces of the context in which it developed. The localization of history created a spatial organization of Altishahri knowledge of the past. Chronology and even genealogy were replaced by geography as a way of organizing history. The Altishahri tradition also made history extremely personal. Pilgrimage was a participation in history, and the addition of one's own story to the pages or walls of history was sanctioned by custom and faith. History gained a special glow of authenticity because of its localization at sacred places, many of which had drawn worshipers for over a thousand years. Finally, history for each person was slightly weighted toward their local oasis, while still promoting the imagination of fellow Altishahris in other oases sharing the same past. Everyone in the system shared an identity with the same group, but each person would have had a slightly different sense of what that identity was, at least in terms of historical origins. This entire tradition was possible in part because it united Altishahr's greatest mechanism for moving and mixing ordinary people, the pilgrimage system, with its most powerful means of creating and disseminating historical knowledge, the manuscript.

The Altishahri system of identity maintenance outlined here fell short of the level of homogeneity that characterizes nationalism as a mode of community self-imagination. While Altishahris did share a regional identity, the view of that identity was slightly different depending on the home oasis from which it was regarded. Moreover, the Altishahri system of identity maintenance eschewed claims of a natural alignment between sovereignty and identity. It also depended on types of communication and imagination wholly foreign to the nationalism that would later conquer the region, including sacred texts embedded in ritual contexts, travel by foot or under animal power, manuscript rather than print technology, and concepts of indigeneity based on deathplace as much as birthplace. As we have seen, these features lent Altishahri identity a character quite foreign to nationalism. It may well be that the Altishahri identity has gone unnoticed for so long because our scholarly notions of identity were born in a world of nationalism, a world that expects secular histories and consistent ethnonyms, among other incidental features of our particular brand of identity. Altishahr's identity system also differs from what Anderson called "sacred imagined communities," such as medieval Christendom or the Islamic *ummah*, although the Altishahri people were also members of the latter. While these multilinguistic communities were bound together by a sacred literary language (Latin or Arabic), the Altishahri tradition depended heavily on the vernacular, even in ritual. Nor was Altishahr, governed as it was under the indirect rule of the Qing Empire, a dynastic community of the sort described by Gellner and Anderson, the kind of imagined community characterized by extensive vertical hierarchical ties. Yet in spite of all these things that it was not, Altishahr's circulation of people, record and display of the names and places of fellow Altishahris, and networked (though not quite uniform) teaching of common origins across all segments of society represent an identity system more complex than the classic Barthian view of an ethnicity negotiated at group boundaries. The Altishahri case presents an alternative kind of imagined community, one which did not develop out of the constellation of technological, historical, cultural, intellectual phenomena we call modernity, nor along the lines of the premodern supraethnic imagined communities that are commonly contrasted to nationalism. Yet it was an imagined community nonetheless, one which maintained a large, reasonably homogeneous identity across the region of Altishahr, formed in part through the mechanisms of community authorship, genre manipulation, and pilgrimage.

In the first half of the twentieth century, Altishahri intellectuals educated in Russian Turkestan reshaped this imagined community into what they called the Uyghur nation, and that Uyghur nation was, in turn, folded into the system of officially recognized ethnic categories that forms the cornerstone of the People's Republic of China's "multiethnic nation" *(duo minzu guojia)*. The ragged edges have been tidied up. Residents of Qumul and Ghulja, for example, had an uncertain status in the Altishahri identity system. They were culturally and linguistically extremely similar to the Altishahris, with local shrines of their own. However, no tazkirahs connected to these places have yet been discovered, and their lands did not appear in the most widely consumed textual representations of Altishahr's past. The new, Uyghur nation brought them firmly into the fold. Today the People's Republic claims the Uyghur identity as a constituent part of China by enumerating it among the fifty-six officially recognized "Chinese" ethnicities *(minzu)*. This incorporation of the Altishahri identity, via the Uyghur identity, into the modern Chinese nation necessarily brings with it the historical foundations of the Altishahri identity, for, as we have seen, that identity, the root of the official Uyghur "ethnicity," was created in part through an interaction of Altishahri historical practices and Qing indirect rule. Today the shrine and manuscript traditions persist, though they are hobbled by tight government restrictions. More importantly though, the tazkirah genre has reemerged in the print world, and remains a dominant presence in today's popular Uyghur historiography, competing and winning among Uyghur readers against the official histories of the People's Republic. This renewed tradition was born of the encounter between nationalism and the world of the tazkirah.

5

SAINTS OF THE NATION

The decades of the 1920s and 1930s were perhaps the zenith of the tazkirah-shrine tradition's power as a means of producing and reproducing a shared knowledge of the past. However, in those same decades new approaches to knowledge and communication were coming into their own, not least among them printing, professionalized education, and nationalist thought. These phenomena would rise quickly to the forefront of historical practice when outside forces began to suppress the tazkirah-shrine tradition. Beginning shortly after the arrival of Communist rule in 1949, large-scale disruptions to the practices of pilgrimage and manuscript copying began to seriously undermine the tazkirah-shrine tradition. Such disruptions, mostly in the form of state restrictions on religious practice and the confiscation of manuscripts, increased in the 1960s and 1970s, eventually leaving the shrines without tazkirahs, shaykhs, or, in some cases, even pilgrims. Since 1980 the pilgrimage tradition has recovered, but the tazkirahs are still beyond the reach of most ordinary people and the shaykhs. Some manuscripts continue to be copied, but in secret and in small numbers. Many young people have never seen such books. The shrine tradition is alive, and it is well enough to form the basis of the pilgrimage descriptions given earlier. However, the tazkirah-shrine tradition can no longer be said to represent the common or popular experience in Altishahr. The popular experience of historical practice has shifted into a new realm, the world of the printed word, dominated by a new genre, the novel. This is not to say that the tazkirah has been entirely displaced. It has instead been transformed, along with many of the associated features of the tazkirah-shrine tradition, into new forms that better suit the nationalist worldview that has taken hold in most Uyghur communities, along with new kinds of education, new modes of knowledge, and new technologies.

Perhaps the best example of the tazkirah's survival into more recent times is the hugely influential historical novel by Săypidin Ăzizi, named simply *Sutuq Bughrakhan*[1] after the king who had figured so prominently in tazkirahs of the manuscript age.[2] The term *historical novel*, which appears on the title page, is somewhat misleading; the book is better described as a fictionalized biography, presenting the life story of the tenth-century Satūq Bughrā-khān, extensively embellished with dialogue and fictional supporting characters. As a biography, and as a story of a central hero's marvelous deeds, it is a worthy successor to the tazkirah. Ăzizi's work appears to have been a surprise hit among Uyghur readers when it was published in 1987, as a second print run was undertaken within less than a year.[3] The book's role was clearly demonstrated to me during a 2007 conversation at a teahouse in Kashgar, where a server informed me that the city's central mosque was built on the site of a Buddhist temple. I asked where he had heard this, and he replied that he had read it, though he couldn't remember where. A patron chimed in, "Săypidin Ăzizi's novel," and I quickly ascertained that he recognized the server's tale from *Sutuq Bughrakhan*. Whenever the book was brought up, I was surprised to find that, despite the obvious fictionalization and the explicit label *historical novel*, this work was taken as a reliable source for knowledge about the past, to the extent that it shaped some people's understanding of Kashghar's main mosque. It is so trusted that it has even been cited as a source in one of the relatively few Uyghur historical monographs to include bibliographical information.[4] Ăzizi's *Sutuq Bughrakhan* was not the only "historical novel" to strongly influence Uyghur conceptions of the past. A host of authors followed in Ăzizi's footsteps, writing fictionalized accounts of historical "Uyghur" figures. That fantastic biographies could so command the attention of the Uyghur public should not be surprising in light of the tazkirah-shrine tradition. Indeed, we shall later trace the close connections between these fictionalized biographies and the tazkirah tradition.

For the moment, however, let us turn our attention to the differences between the two kinds of text. First, it is clear that in the more recent manifestation, biography has lost its old social context, or, more accurately, become embedded in new social contexts. The tomb of Sultan Satūq Bughrā-khān is well cared for in the town of Atush, but the novel *Sutuq Bughrakhan* is not read out to crowds there, or anywhere else for that matter. Nor are there many visitors at the tomb, even during the fig season of August and September, a season when, a century ago, the site would have been overrun with pilgrims. The new story of Sultan Satūq Bughrā-khān stands alone in an inexpensive print edition visually arranged for fast, silent, solitary reading. Presumably, in 1988 it was available at bookstores throughout Altishahr. The tale of Sultan Satūq Bughrā-khān came to tens of thousands of readers, rather than the other way around. Without the kind of rich social contexts, such as shrine readings, which helped categorize books in the manuscript tradition, the second major difference is hardly surprising: the Uyghur fictionalized biographies cohere as a genre not only in the uses to which they have been put but also in their form and content. That formal coherence is in part due to the adoption of the conventions of the novel, a literary form entirely absent from the manuscript world that flourished into the 1930s. A third difference lies in the choice of subjects. Only a few saints of the old tazkirah canon have been taken up in the fictionalized biographies, and new personages have appeared. This winnowing and replacement of Altishahr's heroes follows a pattern that reflects nationalist notions of identity: the saints who have survived into the new pantheon are from the small minority of saints connected to Altishahr not just by their death but also by their birth, as are most of the new heroes who have joined them. None of those great foreign heroes naturalized by their common death in Altishahr have survived into the new popular vehicle of Altishahri, now Uyghur, history and identity. This chapter examines the transformations of the tazkirah-shrine system and of historical practice in general during the twentieth century. It is both a tale of persistence, tracing the connections between the fictionalized biography and the tazkirah, and a story of change, examining the process by which the differences became naturalized to the tradition.

The reader will no doubt have noticed in these differences telltale preconditions and characteristics of nationalism: printing, the novel, a focus on birth in the homeland.[5] Indeed, nationalism has been a central theme in academic analyses of recent Uyghur historiography.[6] Altishahris embraced aspects of nationalist thought in increasing numbers as the twentieth century wore on, to the extent that today many see nationalism as a predominant characteristic of Uyghur identity construction, and we can say that virtually all Uyghur historical writing is either strongly nationalist in nature or clearly influenced by nationalist ideas. The story of this change—the arrival and development of nationalism—is an important and interesting one. However, it is not the full story. As the comparison of the tazkirah and the biographical novel suggests, nationalism did not take the same forms in Altishahr as it did in Europe or in the dominant Han discourse of central China. It would be a mistake to view late twentieth-century and early twenty-first-century Uyghur historical writing and practice as a simple adoption of (foreign) nationalist ways of imagining identity. Over time, the people of Altishahr did adopt much in the way of foreign nationalist approaches, but that is only part of the story. As successful as nationalist movements were in twentieth-century Altishahr, they competed against and merged with alternative ways of looking at Altishahr's past and the identity of its inhabitants. Uyghur identity today is shaped as much by these competing modes of thought as it is by nationalism. It will also be argued here that Altishahri systems of meaning and practice, especially the tazkirah-shrine tradition, transformed nationalism as much as nationalism transformed Altishahri traditions. There is much to be learned about the tazkirah tradition in the story of its transformation through the encounter with nationalism. Perhaps there is just as much to be learned about nationalism.

Alternatives

By the second half of the nineteenth century, the tazkirahs had come to represent the bulk of historical writing about the local past, at least in terms of the number of manuscripts produced, and they maintained their prominence at least through the 1930s. However, it is important to note that even during this period of dominance over local history's written dimension, the tazkirahs shared the stage with alternative approaches to the Altishahri past, and that these alternative approaches were embedded in their own social contexts.

To begin with, although the dynastic tradition largely disappeared with the arrival of the Qing, one dynastic work seems to have maintained a significant readership through the rest of the manuscript era: the sixteenth-century *Tārīkh-i Rashīdī*. This work was translated from the Persian to Turki and continued to be copied into the twentieth century, making it the lone example of its genre to maintain a significant readership. I have not been able to locate any references to the context in which it was read, but it lacked the fantastic and entertaining aspects of the works that were read in public commercial contexts. Its elevated language and style suggest that it would have been consumed by educated elites. We know of one such highly educated reader, for Mullah Mūsá Sayrāmī, author of the *Tārīkh-i Amniyah,* mentions the *Tārīkh-i Rashīdī* as a source of both information and inspiration.[7] However it was consumed, the *Tārīkh-i Rashīdī*'s persistence demonstrates that an alternative approach to understanding the past continued to circulate among the tazkirahs and is likely to have exerted some small influence on the tazkirah tradition, even if we cannot measure or describe it from our limited view of the literary landscape.

There were also short-lived innovations in historical writing, which did not result in viable traditions. One of these was a brief record of an uprising that took place in 1857, presented in a verse of *qasīdah* form. Shortly after a failed uprising in Kucha, a religious leader named Wali Khan entered Altishahr from the territory of the khanate of Khoqand and led further revolts in Kashgar and Yangihissar.[8] This work was probably the first written text to record recent events—namely, events that occurred within the memory of the author—since the dynastic histories of the 1690s. As in the case of the Ya'qub Beg period, we see here written history applied to the recent past at precisely the moment when the illegitimate (in the eyes of many Muslim inhabitants) Qing rulers were replaced by a Muslim leader.

Through its verse form, the Wali Kahn *qasīdah* recalls another tradition, the practice of writing songs about historical figures. An earlier uprising, also led by an Afaqi Khoja from Ferghana, Jahangir, resulted in no immediate written historical texts, but did enter the oral sphere. In 1828 Jahangir was lured by his Kirghiz father-in-law into a Qing trap, and this act of treachery was enshrined in a popular song.[9] Another song, which was still sung in the Khotan oasis in the first decade of the twenty-first century, describes the misdeeds of an oppressive local administrator in the 1890s.[10] We do not know how common this kind of song was, though we do know that such texts rarely made their way into the written realm.

The burst of historical writing that appeared in the wake of the 1864 rebellions and the government of Ya'qub Beg has already been outlined, but it is worth mentioning again here as one of several alternatives to the tazkirah tradition that never gained much popularity, but undoubtedly had some role, especially among elites, in the larger historical tradition. Certainly, these works would have great influence a century later, as Mullah Mūsá Sayrāmī's *Tārīkh-i Amniyah* was reprinted in the 1980s to a warm popular reception. It is also important to note here that this group of works was by no means homogeneous. Even in the midst of these events, the best way to document the new Muslim states of the 1864–1877 period was open for debate, and although the center of gravity was certainly in line with the dynastic court tradition, there were other approaches. The Ili revolution, for example, was most famously documented in a long verse format *(maṣnavī)*.[11]

While much of the interaction between the tazkirah tradition and various alternative approaches to the past is lost, we can see how these traditions articulated with each other, and the ways they were contested internally, in Mullah Mūsá Sayrāmī's fascinating statement about tazkirahs, from his own historical work in the dynastic tradition, the *Tārīkh-i Amniyah:*

> In this area of Yettishahr [i.e., Altishahr] there are numerous mazars and shaykhs. But the names and tazkirahs of most of them are unknown. And even in the cases where we know their names and tazkirahs, most of their tazkirahs are in disagreement with reliable [*mā taqaddam*] historical sources. Probably someone or other had at sometime or other willfully made up a tazkirah of his own, without consulting the historical sources.[12]

The manuscript corpus certainly supports Sayrāmī's claim of a lack of tazkirahs for most shrines. Even though the largest shrine *(mazar)* in each town had a tazkirah, there were hundreds, possibly thousands, of much smaller holy graves *(mazars)* that did not have associated tazkirahs.

Yet we should not take Sayrāmī's statement as a pure expression of skepticism. His apparent doubt of the tazkirahs is mitigated by his initial complaint that the tazkirahs are "unknown." We see here again, even in the eyes of a skeptic, the conceptual linkage between tazkirah and shrine, and the idea that a shrine *ought* to have a tazkirah. Sayrāmī's phrasing seems to imply that tazkirahs really should be there, and that, lamentably, in most cases they are missing. For a category of text that Sayrāmī finds generally in "disagreement with historical sources," the tazkirah still seems to have some attraction. In fact, the larger context of the above quote gives away the limits of Sayrāmī's skepticism, for this passage appears in Sayrāmī's geographical survey of Altishahr, the final section of his *Tārīkh-i Amniyah,* and the survey is almost entirely taken up with a tour of Altishahr's shrines. His descriptions of several shrines fall in line with the stories told in the popular tazkirahs. Indeed, the modern Uyghur editor of the *Tārīkh-i Hamīdī,* Ănvăr Baytur, wrote that

Sayrāmī had previously composed two works called tazkirahs: a *Taẕkirat al-Awliyā* and his own *Taẕkirah-i Aṣḥāb al-Kahf*.[13]

So we see that Sayrāmī, despite being the last major figure in the temporary revival of the dynastic tradition, was also a participant, in several ways, in the tazkirah tradition. However, his skepticism, limited though it may have been, is also telling. Sayrāmī's almost journalistic approach to understanding the past, visible especially in his sober description of the events of 1864–1877, is a marked break not only from the tazkirah tradition, but even from the dynastic tradition within which he explicitly situates his own work. In the passage quoted above, the phrase *mā taqaddam*, which Sayrāmī uses to describe the historical works with which the tazkirahs do not accord, and which Hamada Masami has translated "reliable," more literally indicates priority or antiquity. Sayrāmī may simply be describing these histories as "old histories," or he may be ascribing to the texts some other kind of authority. Elsewhere, however, he is clearer, speaking of "trustworthy histories" *(tārikh-i mu'tabar)*.[14] In both cases, what is unusual is the critical differentiation between texts that can be believed and those that cannot. Here a doubt has crept into the reading of sacred descriptions of the past, as Sayrāmī evinces a desire to know what "really" happened. The very idea of corroboration, comparing texts with an eye to inconsistencies, is also something new in Altishahr. Previous works, even tazkirahs, had cited specific sources, but never with a critical or investigative eye. On the contrary, the citation of sources in the older traditions, both tazkirahs and dynastic histories, served to borrow the assumed authority of those texts. Skeptical perspectives certainly existed elsewhere in the Islamic world before Sayrāmī's time, but they were new to Altishahr. History, which throughout the eighteenth and nineteenth centuries had become tightly integrated with Altishahri social practices, ritual, and geography, was for Sayrāmī to be separated from all other aspects of existence, to become a careful and critical pursuit of knowledge about what happened in the past, an "indispensable science" *('ilm-i ẕarūr)*.

Surely, Sayrāmī's approach was made possible in part by enormous social, economic, and technological changes that were taking place at the time. As has already been mentioned, Sayrāmī was an official in the Ya'qub Beg government, part of an officialdom staffed in part by Andijanis who had come from Khoqand with Ya'qub Beg. In terms of historical practice, it is noteworthy that the court tradition and the dynastic history were quite accessible in Khoqand, and that some of the Khoqandis who arrived in Altishahr wrote their own histories of the Ya'qub Beg period (though it must be remembered that Sayrāmī disavowed any knowledge of other histories written about that period). Yet there were other, broader shifts underway. The constellation of technological, social, and economic changes we think of as "modernity" were just beginning to take hold in Western Turkestan at the time of Ya'qub Beg's invasion. Many of these changes were hastened by the arrival of Russian rule, which encompassed Tashkent in 1865 and Samarkand in 1868, and brought the printing press (1868) and the telegraph. From its base in Altishahr, Ya'qub Beg's regime made strong efforts to establish international connections, hoping to fend off a Qing reconquest through diplomatic maneuvers.[15] Perhaps most significantly, Ya'qub Beg declared himself a vassal of the Ottoman sultan, and received in return a small number of cannon and Turkish military advisors, who worked on transforming and updating Ya'qub Beg's army. In the years between the Qing reconquest (1877) and Sayrāmī's first version of the *Tārīkh-i Amniyah* (1903–1904), these influences were augmented by a nascent modernist reform movement in Altishahr, and may account in part for Sayrāmī's innovative (for Altishahr) approach to history. While Sayrāmī's histories did not make any inroads into Altishahr's popular historical tradition, the growing international influences and emerging social changes that seem to be subtly reflected within his work would eventually revolutionize that popular approach to understanding the past, and, for that matter, all kinds of knowledge. It is to these changes we now turn in order to better understand how they would come to reshape the historical tradition.

A Century of Changes

Even before the tazkirah tradition entered what would be its height of popularity (in the first decades of the twentieth century), the seeds of its decline were already being sown. After the injection of foreign ideas that took place during the Ya'qub Beg period, signs of greater impending change began to appear in local Altishahri forms. Many of these changes were eventually to have a profound effect on visions of the past. New technologies, most notably the printing press, were slow to catch on, but, in the end, were extremely significant. They interacted with a revolution in modes of knowledge and education, and, eventually, the arrival of nationalist ideas, most of which came from the wider Turkic world, which was becoming interconnected to an extent perhaps never before seen. The following historical narrative spans most of the twentieth century, but it is not an exhaustive history of the period. Rather, it outlines particular changes in Altishahr's wider social context that would eventually come to bear on the historical tradition. It begins with a very brief introduction to the reform movements that took hold in Altishahr, then traces the development of printing in the region, and finally describes the Communist Party's suppression of tazkirahs and shrines, before returning to the main argument.

Reformers, Nationalism, and the "Uyghur" Identity

Between the fall of Ya'qub Beg's state in 1877 and the arrival of Chinese Communist rule in 1949, reform movements laid the groundwork for new ways of understanding the world, which would eventually reshape Altishahr's approach to the past. Among the new ideas that took root in Altishahr, nationalism represented perhaps the most profound reorganization of Altishahri self-imagination since the arrival of Islam.[16] Early ventures in nationalist thought appeared against the background of a dizzyingly complex succession of political upheavals, driven by actors as diverse as Han Chinese anti-Qing revolutionaries, disbanded Qing soldiers, military strongmen, Uyghur nationalists, and communist revolutionaries. In the first half of the twentieth century, Altishahr saw Qing imperial rule, tyrannical autocrats, loosely democratic experiments, and early moves toward socialism.[17] At the same time, printing, the telegraph, radio, film, and modern industry made their first inroads in the region. There is no room in this study for an in-depth look at all of these phenomena in their interaction, but it would be impossible to discuss the encounter between nationalism and Altishahri tazkirah-based historical practice without providing a thumbnail sketch of the processes by which nationalist thought became a central feature of the new Altishahri worldview.

The earliest proponents of cultural reform and nationalist thought were Altishahris whose worship, education, or business led them to travel widely. Altishahris traveling in the larger Muslim world at the beginning of the twentieth century encountered the new language of nationalism, which was developing in a cacophonous global conversation. For influence on Altishahri thought, no manifestation of this conversation was more important than the nationalisms developing in Western Turkestan. These nationalisms included Pan-Turkism, which saw peoples from Anatolia to Altishahr as part of a single Turkic nation, imaginations of a "Muslim Turkestani" nation (limited to Central Asia), and narrower ethnonationalisms such as Ozbek.[18] In the early years of Soviet rule in Western Turkestan, there was also a lively debate among émigré Altishahris about the nature of their own identity, and the significance of the increasingly popular term *Uyghur*, debates which would have great significance for Altishahri self-conceptions.[19] The multiple, overlapping, and often confusing notions of nationalism developing in Tsarist and Soviet Turkestan influenced Altishahri society along several vectors, including school reform programs, Soviet nationalities policies, the discourse among the large population of émigrés from Ghulja living in Soviet Yettisu, and the flow of Altishahris studying in Tashkent.

Altishahr's earliest connection to nationalist thought may have been through the Muslim cultural reformers of the Russian Empire, known as *Jadids* after the Persian term for the "new method" *(uṣūl-i jadīd)* of teaching the Arabic alphabet. The originator of the new method, a Crimean Tatar by the name of Ismail Bey Gasprinskii (1851–1914), was a Pan-Turkist, and many of the earliest Jadid intellectual projects shared Gasprinskii's interest in uniting a single Pan-Turkic nation. Many Central Asian intellectuals soon narrowed their focus to a "Turkestan" that excluded much of Gasprinskii's Turkic world.[20] It is difficult to know exactly how much Pan-Turkist or Turkestani nationalist thought arrived in Altishahr at what time, but many of today's Uyghur historians suggest that a school established near Kashgar by the Musabayov brothers, Husayn Bay and Bahā 'al-Dīn Bay, reflected a reformist program as early as 1885.[21] The Musabayovs' new school was eventually linked to a wider reformist network. Beginning in 1910 the Musabayovs' "Ḥusayniyya" school was led by an Altishahri who had studied in the Ottoman Empire, and in 1914 Husayn Bay helped the Ottoman reformist Ahmet Kemal (mentioned below for his printing press) establish another school in the Artush area. Graduates of the Musabayovs' and Kemal's schools eventually fanned out to found their own new schools in towns around Altishahr.

Of the reformers' programs in Altishahr only the new teaching movement has been studied in any detail, but it provides a rough measure of the spread of the Jadid influences in the region. The new schools multiplied despite difficulties from several quarters. Probably the most important resistance came from the administrations of Xinjiang's Republican-era Chinese rulers Yang Zengxin (1912–1928), Jin Shuren (1928–1933), and Sheng Shicai (1933–1944), who vacillated between support and suspicion. Many Altishahri elites also resisted the new schools, which undermined established Islamic educational norms, and these elites some-times looked to the Chinese governments for support in their opposition to the schools. The Altishahri educational movement continued with some strength through the 1910s, but its success was rather uneven. Cer-tainly, the traditional maktab remained the main form of education in Altishahr. Some of the larger towns lacked even a single new-style school, as it seems Qarghaliq still did in the late 1920s and early 1930s.[22] How-ever, even though the new schools could not have reached the majority of Altishahris, they likely succeeded in producing several generations of elites familiar with intellectual currents of the Turkic, Islamic, and Rus-sian worlds. These individuals would become influential in the indepen-dent East Turkestan Republics (1933–1934 and 1944–1949), establish Uyghur cultural organizations, dominate the national public discourse in the new newspapers, and produce much of the literature that eventually redefined Altishahri culture in its modern Uyghur form.

The new schools incorporated into their curricula a significant atten-tion to history as a distinct subject.[23] Sources on the nature of history teaching in Altishahr's new schools have yet to emerge, but the fact that history was included as a separate subject at all is significant. As Adeeb Khalid has pointed out, the new schools' separation of history (and other topics, including geography and arithmetic) from "religious instruction," which had its own time slot alongside the other subjects, marked the be-ginning of a "process of marking off Islam from the rest of knowledge."[24] This may in part explain why the teaching of "history and geography" was considered particularly offensive by Kashgar's opponents to the new-method schools.[25] Such desacralization of knowledge would later become an important aspect of the tazkirah's transformation into the nationalist novel. However, for the majority of Altishahris, who still at-tended the old-style maktab, historical practice remained embedded in sacred knowledge, dominated in the textual realm by the tazkirah.

A somewhat regular flow of Altishahri students to schools in Western Turkestan also encouraged the spread of new ideas to Altishahr, thanks both to the contact with new perspectives in Western Turkestan and to the often greater freedom of discourse in that area. A trickle of scholars and merchants had always traveled outside of Altishahr, and some of these began to encounter new ways of imagining identity in the late nineteenth century. Among these travelers, the famous reformist 'Abd al-Qādir Damollam was one of the most effective transmitters of new ideas to Altishahr. In 1889 he reached Bukhara, where he studied for eight years, and he later traveled to Istanbul and Cairo. 'Abd al-Qādir published educational materials abroad that circulated Altishahr, including a catechism that still circulates in Kashgar's underground book market. In the 1920s and especially in the late 1930s, the stream of traveling Altishahri scholars intensified, as hundreds of Altishahri students went to study in Western Turkestan, especially in Tashkent. During the time of warlord-governor Sheng Shicai's alliance with the Soviet Union, many students received financial support for their travel. The list of students each year may have even been personally approved by Sheng.[26] In dialogue with Soviet ethnic policies, intellectuals of Western Turkestan were shaping the Uzbek, Tajik, Kirghiz, and other national identities, and building for them new national literatures. In the Soviet socialist republics, Altishahri students were exposed to lively public discussions in newspapers and educational programs that included extensive interactions with political thought. The politicized atmosphere continued through the 1930s, when Sheng Shicai was sending over one hundred students each year. The memoir of a student during the Sheng era describes Altishahri students learning difficult Marxist texts and producing plays (it is not insignificant that theater was, along with the newspaper, the main form of reformist literature), and participating in a student union.[27]

There was already a great swell of interest in issues of identity in Western Turkestan before the revolution. Pan-Turkism from both Ottoman and Tatar scholars was popular, as were Pan-Islamic ideas. A "Turkestani" identity was under discussion, and articles appeared in newspapers discussing narrower identity terms such as *Sart*. The highly self-conscious and explicit examination of Central Asian identities was often paralleled by political aspirations. When Stalin's Soviet state went about creating the Central Asian Soviet Socialist Republics along ethnic lines, which involved an enormous project of classifying citizens, nationalist imaginings rose to even greater prominence, eventually becoming reified in the state's official categories. Soviet ethnic policy was influential in Altishahr in at least three ways. First, it encouraged discussions of identity among Central Asian intellectuals and pulled them closer into line with nationalism in the Russian, and thus European, tradition. It was in this intellectual environment that the Altishahri students in Tashkent became part of conversations surrounding national identity. Second, Sheng Shicai adopted much of Soviet ethnic policy, eventually classifying Xinjiang's ethnicities in much the same way that the Soviets had classified the people of Western Turkestan. Finally, there was a large population of Altishahri descent living within the Soviet Union, especially in the Yettisu region of the Kazakh Soviet Socialist Republic, who participated in the wider intellectual discourse of Soviet Central Asia, and whom the Soviets classified ethnically as "Uyghurs" or "Taranchis." This group probably had as much to do with the shaping of Uyghur identity as any segment of native-born Altishahri society.

The majority of Altishahris in Yettisu were Taranchis, descendants of the farmers whom the Dzungar Mongols and later the Qing forced to move from the Altishahri oases to cultivate the Ili valley in the Tianshan Mountains. The political vicissitudes of the nineteenth and twentieth centuries frequently forced large numbers of refugees to flee the Ili valley, and they usually ended up in the nearby and geographically similar Yettisu region. Other Taranchis arrived in Yettisu for seasonal work in factories. The discourse among the Taranchis has been thoroughly described by David Brophy, who demonstrates a similar interaction between indigenous intellectual debates over national identity and Soviet ethnic policies to the relationship that existed in the rest of Western Turkestan.[28] It was among this group that the word *Uyghur* came into use as an ethnonym for the Altishahris, including the Taranchis. Although the word *Uyghur*, a name associated with certain pre-Islamic Altishahri kingdoms, had maintained an ephemeral presence in Altishahr all the way into the twentieth century, it was not an ethnonym in wide use, and when it was used, it tended to be restricted to subgroups of inhabitants around the northern oases of Turpan and Qumul. The resurrection of the term as an ethnonym seems to have been influenced by European scholarship on the Uyghur Buddhist kingdoms, scholarship that was becoming available to intellectuals in Western Turkestan. In 1910 a Taranchi author published under the pen name Child of the Uyghur *(Uyghur Ballisi)*. By the 1920s, political and cultural organizations were using *Uyghur* as an ethnonym, and debating whether it should include Kashgaris (Altishahris exclusive of Taranchis) only, Kashgaris and Taranchis, or perhaps even all of the ethnic groups of Xinjiang, including Han. In 1935 Sheng Shicai enshrined the Uyghur category, essentially as it had developed among the Yettisu Taranchis, as an official ethnic category. This formulation of identity largely followed the limits of the Altishahri identity discussed earlier but also tied Turki speakers from places not known to have important tazkirahs, such as the Taranchis and the Turki inhabitants of the marginal oasis of Qumul, closely and explicitly to the Altishahri core.[29]

An anonymous 1934 article in Kashgar's *New Life* speaks at length of the state of nationalist thought in Altishahr:

> The children of Adam living across the whole face of the earth are divided from one another into sects [*mazhab*] and also separated into several peoples [*qawm*] and tribes [*urughlar*], for example Arab, Turk, English, French, Italian, Russian, Indian, Chinese, and the like. . . . Because most of our people here are in ignorance and unconsciousness we have forgotten what tribe we are from. If someone is asked what tribe we are from, he answers, "We are Muslims." It is correct to say of us that we are Muslims, but in terms of descent and tribe, it is surely also necessary to know what tribe we are from. Is it not futile for a man's child, upon forgetting his own father's name, to ask it of another person? So enough then. We are the children of the Uyghurs. *Uyghur* means our noble national [*milliy*] name.[30]

The *Uyghur* term was not entirely new to Altishahr when this essay appeared. In 1933 the failed East Turkestan Republic, for example, had called itself the *Islamic Republic of Uyghurstan* on some of its coins. Sheng Shicai, who, at the time of the article's publication, had recently solidified his control in Kashgar, supported the *Uyghur* label, and his government would officially establish the ethnonym shortly thereafter. The article suggests that most Altishahris still did not consider themselves to be Uyghurs at this time. Use of the *Uyghur* name was in all likelihood restricted to educated elites, perhaps those with access, even if indirect, to the intellectual trends in the Altishahri émigré community of Soviet Yettisu. Even the literate readership of the *New Life Newspaper* needed to be exhorted to promote the Uyghur identity.

By 1985 the *Uyghur* ethnonym was widely accepted by Altishahris. In that year, Justin Rudelson conducted a survey of eighty-one Turpan residents, in which all but five respondents ranked Uyghur among their three most salient identities (other choices being Muslim, Turpanliq, Junggoluq, and Turk).[31] However, the long journey from the situation that pertained in 1934 to the wide use of the ethnonym *Uyghur* in 1985 remains largely hidden. While scholars have paid plenty of attention to the development of elite Uyghur nationalist discourse and state ethnic policies, the process by which acceptance of the new (though presented as old) Uyghur identity spread among the ordinary Altishahri population has never been carefully studied, due mostly to a dire lack of accessible sources on the subject. Much of the spread of the Uyghur idea must have taken place during the first three decades of Chinese Communist rule (i.e., 1949–1979) a period for which we have only scant and little-studied sources.[32] Despite this dearth, however, it is worth noting a few obvious contributing factors. The People's Republic of China (PRC) essentially maintained the ethnic categories recognized by Sheng Shicai's regime. As an official ethnic category, the Uyghur notion must have been a major force in the dramatic reorganization of society that the PRC undertook in Xinjiang. PRC officials developed new alphabets for the language now called Uyghur, replacing the old alphabet, which had been used for both Persian and the various Turkic literary languages of Central Asia, including Altishahri Turki.[33] Compulsory schools taught material in Uyghur, from textbooks written in the new alphabets. Identification cards included (and still include) the official ethnic identity of each individual. Ethnic quotas were established for certain positions. We do not know what role Altishahri communities and social structures played in spreading the idea of Uyghurness. However, in one way or another, and with strong encouragement from state policies, the Uyghur identity, and with it, nationalist conceptions of the world, had spread widely among Altishahris by the 1980s.

Printing

Printing's eclipse of manuscript technology played an important role in the transformation of Altishahri historical traditions. The technologies of printing also interacted with, and amplified the effects of, the reform and nationalist movements just described. In order to examine print's role in the transformation of historical practice, it is necessary to look at the history of the print industry in some detail, because there has been no study that has focused on the role of the press in Altishahr.

The printing press was something of a failure in Altishahr for the first four decades of its presence (ca. 1890–1930). This is not to say that printed works were not available. Numerous printed books, especially from Tashkent, but also from Lahore, Bukhara, Samarkand, and other places, were available in Kashgar's markets.[34] From those markets Gunnar Jarring assembled a collection of fifty-nine printed books, but only two of them were produced in Altishahr. The demand for printed books does not seem to have been great enough to support a stable Altishahri press. In fact, if we examine the earliest printing operations in Altishahr, we see that in only a few cases did the impetus for print publication respond to a perceived customer demand.

The discovery of printed Buddhist texts from the ninth century in nearby Dunhuang makes it possible that Altishahr may have hosted one of the world's earliest printing presses. However, if printing did take place in ninth-century Altishahr, it almost certainly disappeared with the Islamization of region, and it remained absent until the end of the nineteenth century. In 1880 the Chinese general, Zuo Zongtang, who engineered the Qing reconquest of Xinjiang, established short-lived presses in Urumchi and Qumul, just north and northeast of Altishahr and within the Qing administrative unit of Xinjiang. These presses produced ephemeral editions of a treatise on smallpox vaccination, a treatise on the raising of silkworms, and a bilingual Chinese and Turki edition of the Kangxi emperor's moralizing work, the *Sacred Edict* (1670).[35] The publications were part of a two-pronged effort to develop Xinjiang economically and to integrate it culturally with the Chinese interior, most notably through the establishment of Confucian schools for Altishahri children. The Qing effort to promote Confucian morality through print, though initially based outside Altishahr, would eventually intersect with the efforts of Altishahr's own printing pioneer.

That pioneer was an Altishahri tailor named Nūr Muhammad Ḥājjī Ibn Sharīf Ḥājjī (hereafter Nur Muhammad), who had traveled to both Northwestern India and to Istanbul (and possibly, as his title suggests, to Mecca), learned the lithographic printing trade in India, and upon his return to his hometown of Yangihissar, set up his own lithograph press no later than 1893–1894.[36] According to an interview that Martin Hartmann conducted with Nur Muhammad in 1902, the first text printed on the press was a volume of Sufi verse, the *Ṣabāt al-'Ājizīn* of Sufi Allah Yār, an extremely popular book throughout Central Asia.[37] Interestingly, this was also the first work to be printed on an indigenously owned press in Western Turkestan (Tashkent, 1883).[38] For his second project, Nur Muhammad chose another popular verse work that would have no trouble finding an audience, a *divan* of verse by perhaps the greatest Turkic poet, Mīr 'Alī-Shīr Navā'ī. With these first two works, both classics in their own region, namely, Central Asia, we see Altishahri printing following a pattern of the more fully developed print industries of other parts of the Islamic world, where the most widely read titles of the manuscript tradition dominated early print markets. In all likelihood Nur Muhammad was simply imitating what he had seen elsewhere. But unlike those other parts of the world, Altishahr seems not to have had sufficient demand for cheap printed editions of the classics. Poor survival of these early editions suggests that the print runs were quite small; in 1902, Martin Hartmann was unable to locate any examples of Nur Muhammad's Yangihissar editions, nor have I have been able to trace any surviving specimens. Meanwhile, the same works survive in as many as a hundred copies in manuscript form.

However, Nur Muhammad's printing effort soon received a boost from outside forces. Around 1893–1894, the Qing government approached the printer-tailor with a commission to print a work Nur Muhammad called "the khan's words," a project he undertook at a new location in Kashgar.[39] Examples of multiple editions of "the khan's words" survive in the Hartmann collection, each with the full title *Important Sayings Composed by the Khan to Encourage Good Actions*. This work was a Turki translation of a morality text by the Shunzhi emperor (1638–1661), which had been widely distributed among Manchu bannermen.[40] Over a period of several years, starting in 1893–1894, Nur Muhammad printed 7500 copies. This figure may have represented an unusually large print run, for "the khan's words" has survived better than any other of Nur Muhammad's products.[41] Copies of "the khan's words" were distributed "for free everywhere" and the Qing government later ordered Nur Muhammad to produce an instruction manual for soldiers.[42] After Nur Muhammad began to receive commissions, the quality of his product increased dramatically, suggesting either direct assistance from his patrons or a reinvestment of the funds he received for the commissions. The earliest edition of "the "khan's words" is extremely crude, sometimes printed on local "Khotan" paper, and in places illegible.[43] In the same year, however, he produced another edition of the same work with high quality impression, calligraphy, and paper, rivaling even the products of printing centers such as Tashkent and Delhi.

The press's attractiveness to state actors was again demonstrated by a commission from the Russian consulate in Kashgar, which was, by the turn of the century, firmly entrenched in the local political scene. By the early 1900s, the Russians were such a presence that they offered a postal service connecting Kashgar and Ili to the rest of the world by means of an ordinary Russian imperial postage stamp, a service often used by other European visitors to Altishahr. The consulate's printing project for

Nur Muhammad was an internal newsletter for the consulate, a strange choice for a lithograph press.[44] The Qing state-making project had ironically kept Nur Muhammad's press in use long enough and visibly enough for the Russian Empire, the Qing's most threatening rival in Xinjiang, to make use of the press for its own ends.

In another ironic twist, Nur Muhammad's Qing-supported press may have been subsequently exploited by the reformist Musabayov brothers. At the very moment that the Qing state was working to displace Islamic schools with Confucian education, the Musabayov brothers were establishing new schools with curricula developed farther West in the Islamic world. According to Uyghur scholarly tradition, it was these Musabayov brothers who established a press, called the Brilliant Rising Sun Press, that published the work of a well-traveled local poet, Awlād Husayn Tajallī.[45] In his interview with Martin Hartmann, Nur Muhammad described printing an edition of Tajallī's poetry with exactly the same characteristics as the Brilliant Rising Sun Press edition.[46] The details of the edition are so precisely alike, in fact, that the Musabayovs' and Nur Muhammad's edition of Tajallī's verse, and thus their presses, must have been one and the same.[47] It is entirely likely that the wealthy Musabayovs arranged some kind of joint venture with Nur Muhammad, or simply financed Tajallī's work.[48] It's worth pointing out that all of the individuals involved in this venture had traveled extensively in the rest of the Islamic world, enabling all of them to envision the local author's poetry achieving wide circulation in print. It is also significant that the Tajallī project was another author-driven commission, much like the producer-driven Qing and Russian commissions. As of 1902, when Nur Muhammad was planning to undertake another printing job for Tajallī, he described the project as "to work for Awlād Husayn." The author's control over the process was further emphasized by the warning on the title page of the book that, "whoever prints this book without the license of the author will be called to account on judgment day."[49]

The competing influences of well-traveled Altishahri reformists, Russian imperialists, and the assimilationist Qing Empire had kept Nur Muhammad's Kashgar press in somewhat regular use through their commissions. During this period (ca. 1893–1901) Nur Muhammad again tried producing salable popular texts. According to Hartmann's interview with the Nur Muhammad, he produced new editions of the works he had printed at his first press in Yangihissar: the Sabāt al-ʿĀjizīn and the poetry of Mīr ʿAlī-Shīr Navāʾī.[50] Mentioned in the Hartmann interview, but not in Hartmann's catalog of his own collection, is a third popular work, an Arabic grammatical text featuring the famous *Kāfiya* of Ibn al-Hājib.[51] It seems that, with the aid of occasional commissions, the production of books aimed at a popular market was at least minimally viable as a business. However, printing does not appear to have made for very big business. Nur Muhammad kept his day job as a tailor, and when Martin Hartmann came to visit him in 1902, he found Nur Muhammad sitting at his sewing machine in Yangihissar, while the press he had assembled remained unused at a family member's house in Kashgar. Surviving examples of each of his editions number in the single digits. After 1902, Nur Muhammad and his press disappear from the historical record. His business gave rise to no competitors, and his experiments with popular, market-oriented printing represent the last editions of classic literature to be printed in book form in Xinjiang until the 1980s.

By contrast, printing on the producer-oriented model, funded by those who wished to spread their ideas rather than turn a profit, continued in the ensuing decades. At least four other printing ventures operated on this model before the 1930s. One of these was the press of the Swedish missionaries in Yarkand and Kashgar, which was primarily engaged in printing Turki translations of the Bible and Turki-language primers for the mission's school. The Musabayovs are said to have undertaken another printing project in 1910, a newspaper called *Ang Gezeti (Conscience Newspaper)*.[52] The Ottoman reformist, Ahmet Kemal, whose new-method school has already been mentioned, used a mimeograph press to issue a pamphlet *(risālah)*, entitled *Büyük Dīn* (The Great Religion), along with various announcements and pleas *(khitābnāmah)*, which he distributed "every four or five days."[53] Another immigrant, a Taranchi refugee from Soviet-controlled Yettisu, named Hüsäyinbäg Yunusov, printed textbooks and a newspaper in Ili with a press imported in 1918 from the Soviet Union. When Yunusov's paper was shut down, his press was used to print forms and decrees for the government.[54] As with many of the early presses' products, Yunusov's textbooks are at present known only from their mention in other sources. I have also been unable to locate any surviving examples of the earliest newspapers and pamphlets.

The first twenty-five years of book printing in Altishahr hardly suggested much promise for the technology. Printing projects were sporadic and ephemeral. No one seems to have made a sustainable business out of printing. The next decade would be even worse for printing. In the 1920s, governor Yang Zengxin (r. 1912–1928) grew increasingly fearful of the spread of ideas from the new Soviet Union, and banned all publication in Turki. Yang's successor, Jin Shuren (r. 1928–1933) continued Yang's system of tight control over political discourse and connections to the outside world.[55]

It is not surprising that, even before the censorship of Yang and Jin, the printed book simply did not catch on in Altishahr. The social practices in which books were embedded had developed in close connection with the manuscript tradition. They tapped the flexibility and community participation encouraged by the manuscript tradition, characteristics that were diminished in the printed book. To be sure, certain traditions could still be practiced with the printed book. Owners of printed works added marginalia, especially documentations of reading and ownership, just as they had in manuscripts.[56] Of course, the effect of these markings would have been different. Whereas in the manuscript tradition, the reader's contribution and the "original" text were nearly identical in their form and appearance (though usually distinguishable in their spatial layout—marginalia were, after all, found in the margins), in the printed text, there was a much starker difference between the mechanically produced words of the original text and the handwritten words of the readers. Other aspects of the manuscript tradition had no parallel in the printed book. Inherent in the technology of manuscript copying was an element of choice, which was lacking in the print industry as it developed in Altishahr. The composite manuscript, which often served as a custom anthology, simply could not be replaced by the printed book. The shifting, recombining, locally weighted tazkirahs, for example, could never be imitated by a rigid printed anthology. When it came to Altishahr's tazkirahs, no one even tried. In Western Turkestan, anthologies were produced, gathering several popular titles in one volume, though of course these couldn't reflect individual customers' tastes. The demand for such works never reached a level in Altishahr to support the burgeoning book printing industry there.

The path that printing did take in Altishahr makes sense when examined from the perspective of manuscript production. Manuscripts could be produced by the consumer or by a scribe whom the consumer commissioned to reproduce a text. In either case, it was the eventual consumer who controlled the production of the book. For each copy, the producer-commissioner and first consumer were the same. In a market-driven print industry, the producer-commissioner and consumer are separated; one producer creates a large number of books for a host of unknown consumers. Since the first printers were coming from the manuscript tradition, it is not surprising that they either acted as producer-consumers, printing texts for their own projects as a reader-copyist would have, or took commissions, as did the scribes of the same period, who lined a certain street waiting for customers in Kashgar.[57]

The producer-driven model that developed in Altishahr never resulted in the kind of fully fledged print industry, driven by a large market for printed books, that Benedict Anderson called "print-capitalism."[58] Yan Zengxin's and Jin Shuren's autocratic reigns (1912–1928 and 1928–1933, respectively) came to an end, and the tight control over the printed word was lifted, but the business of printing books still did not take off. All the way through the first decade of PRC rule (beginning in 1949), only a handful of books were ever printed in Altishahr (aside from the Swedes' missionary texts). Those that did emerge tended to be printed by presses in the business of newspaper publication. These books included, for example, a volume of works by the playwright and poet Aḥmad Ẓiyā'ī, which was printed in Kashgar by the Xinjiang Newspaper Office, in an edition of 500.[59] Here we see the real significance of printing technology in Altishahr: the newspaper.

The contrast between the printed book's lukewarm reception in Altishahr and the eventual success of the newspaper is startling. Early on, the newspaper industry was as ephemeral as the book printing business. The first indigenous newspaper in Altishahr was probably the aforementioned *Conscience Newspaper* supposedly produced at Kashgar under the patronage of the Musabayov brothers, beginning in 1910. Three other papers were founded in Ili shortly thereafter but were quickly shut down.[60] In the 1920s Yang Zengxin's prohibition on printing ended whatever newspaper industry had begun to develop. Indeed, Yang appears to have had an interest in stifling the newspapers in particular. A British observer noted that "not only is all written or printed matter dealing with current events excluded from the province, but the dissemination of 'news' in writing among the inhabitants is effectively prevented."[61] This observation also hints at some level of demand within Altishahr for information on current events.

The level of Altishahri (and Chinese state) interest in the newspaper became clear after Jin Shuren's rule came to an end in 1933. In that year, a chaotic series of rebellions and coups culminated in the establishment of the independent Islamic Republic of East Turkestan in Altishahr, and the warlord-governor Sheng Shicai's administration in Urumqi. In connection with the appearance of the new Republic, the *Sharqi Turkistān Hayāti (East Turkestan Life)* weekly newspaper was established, and other publications soon followed. The transition is described by Zunun Qadir, who was in his early twenties at the time: "Only after the changes of April 1933 was it possible for us to see newspapers, journals, and reading rooms. Up until that time we would gather at the barbershop and the cobbler's shop to tell and hear all kinds of epics and legends together."[62] After the fall of the Republic of East Turkestan, the *East Turkestan Life* newspaper continued under a new name, *Yangī Hayāt (New Life),* and by 1936 the paper had a circulation of 2200.[63] From the paper's original establishment in 1933, the interest in newspapers spread quickly (see Table 5.1), slightly faster even than technologies of printing; two of the new newspapers were written by hand. In Aqsu a group of modernist reformers started a newspaper called the *Sieve* without the benefit of a press in 1935. Twice per month they churned out a new handwritten edition in forty to fifty copies, and managed to keep their manuscript newspaper alive into 1936, when they acquired or built a printing press.[64] Under various names, this newspaper continued into the PRC period, and was eventually co-opted as the Chinese Communist Party's official party organ in Aqsu. Yarkand's first paper, the *Yăkăn Divar Geziti (Yarkand Wall Newspaper),* established by a group of reformers in 1935, is also said to have been handwritten, though the project was less ambitious than Aqsu's paper. The *Wall* was a one-page monthly, supposedly copied by a single scribe in ten copies per issue, and plastered on walls around the city of Yarkand. It seems to have survived only through the end of 1936.[65] Newspapers were also founded in Ili and Khotan, marking a great expansion of the genre. As the 1930s drew to a close, Sheng Shicai, who had managed to bring all of Xinjiang under his rule by 1934, tightened his control over political and social life. Some newspaper publishers were arrested, and others were simply replaced with publishers working for Sheng. The establishment of a newspaper became a dangerous activity, and remained so until a new political arrangement emerged in 1946, with the détente between the newly formed second East Turkestan Republic and the Guomindang. With the lifting of controls on publishing, five more newspapers appeared.[66]

The newspaper was an entirely new genre in Altishahr, and the lack of deeply rooted traditions concerning the newspaper may have made it possible for the genre to thrive. The change described by Zonun Qadir

Table 5.1. Turki newspapers founded in Altishahr before 1949

Town	Dates	Technology at founding	Name at founding	Founder
Kashgar	1910-?	Lithograph(?)	*Conscience*	Husayn Musabayov (Altishahr)
Ili	1910–1911	Mimeograph	*Ili Region*	Feng Temin/Tongmenghui (China)
Ili	1919–1920	Movable Type	*Free Word*	Hüsäyinbäg Yunusov (USSR)
Kashgar	1933–1949	Movable type	*East Turkestan Life*	East Turkestan government
Aqsu	1935–1949	Manuscript	*Sieve*	Uyghur Cultural Promotion Union
Ili	1934–1949	Movable Type	*Ili Shinjang*	Soviet Red Army elements
Yarkand	1935–1936	Manuscript	*Yarkand Wall*	Artuq Hajim (UCPU)
Khotan	1939–1949	Mimeograph	*Khotan Shinjang*	Välikhan Iminop
Ili	1945–1948	Mimeograph	*Qara Shahr*	Uyghur Cultural Promotion Union
Yarkand	1946–1949	Mimeograph	*Star of Fortune*	Locally elected government (?)
Qumul	1946–1948	Lithograph	*Qumul*	Advanced Youths (Ismayil Tahir)
Korla	1946–1947	Mimeograph	*Baghrash*	Uyghur Cultural Promotion Union
Lop Nur	1946–1947	Mimeograph	*Taklïmakan*	Uyghur Cultural Promotion Union

Note that most of these newspapers were taken over by other groups (or government authorities) at some point after their founding, and that they frequently changed names. The Aqsu information comes from Qadir Mäkit, "Azadliktin burunqi 'Aqsu Geziti' häqqidä," *Shinjang tarikhi materiyalliri* 42 (1999). The information for *East Turkestan Life* comes from the paper itself, an apparently complete set of which is preserved in the Jarring collection in the Lund University Library. The Ili information comes from Zerdin, "Ilida Gezitning barliqqa kelishi vä u besip ötkän musapä," 86–96. Most of the remaining information in this table comes from Ismayil Äsqäri, "Azadliqtin ilgiri Shinjangning härqaysi jaylirida näshir qilinghan gezit—zhurnallar häqqidä äslimilär," *Shinjang tarikhi materiyalliri* 32 (1992): 147–181. This source is quite important, but it is an oral history and some of the details, as remembered by the speakers, appear to be inaccurate. For example, the Aqsu information does not correspond to the more detailed depiction in the source above, which seems to have been based on examination of one or more actual newspapers. As with all materials published within the PRC, there is also the problem of political censorship, be it self-censorship or otherwise. This table is not exhaustive. Additional newspapers are mentioned in Liu Bin, *Uyghur adabiyat tarikhi*.

was not just a matter of new forms of communication becoming available. It was also a tearing away of the written word from its accustomed social contexts, a distancing of knowledge from immediate human interactions. The old forms of knowledge reproduction, such as the tazkirah-shrine system, defined not only what words were used but also how they were said and how were they written. Printing, and especially movable type, proved unfit for the tasks of the tazkirahs, and so the tazkirahs continued to flourish in the world of the manuscript, even as book printing ventures died and the newspaper spread across Altishahr. The newspaper genre, on the other hand, represented precisely that separation of the word from social contexts that made printing inappropriate for the tazkirahs. In the form of the newspaper, writing was no longer sacred or talismanic, no longer used for repeat performances or lifelong storage, and no longer open to reader and author alike. Separated as it was from the traditional sacred and social contexts of writing, the newspaper even managed to succeed without the *bismillah* ("in the name of God," written at the head of all manuscript and even lithograph books), the lack of which Altishahris had used to condemn the books printed by the Swedish Missionary Press.[67] Moreover, the newspaper broke free of calligraphic constraints that dictated the forms of the letters in the manuscript tradition. Writing in the newspaper genre could now take multiple technical forms—lithograph, movable type, mimeograph, and manuscript—though in the end it was movable type that won out, just as it had in most of the rest of the world.[68]

The story of new technologies of the word is important to our understanding of Altishahri approaches to history because of its profound implications for modes of communication and knowledge. The print revolution, which gained its strongest foothold in Altishahr through the newspaper, would eventually come to serve popular Altishahri historical writing, as in the case of Äzizi's *Sutuq Bughrakhan* (1987). However, it must be emphasized that, with one very important exception (a serial newspaper history described below), there was little historical writing in print before the arrival of Communist Chinese rule in Altishahr. History, for most people, remained in the realm of the manuscript, even as newspaper printing gathered momentum in the 1930s and 1940s. During that time, the mix of *ḥikayāt*, prophet stories, foreign dynastic histories, and epics continued to provide Altishahris with information about the foreign past, while the tazkirahs (and to a lesser extent the *Tārīkh-i Rashīdī*) continued to dominate Altishahr's textual representation of the local past.[69] Even the alternative tradition of the dynastic history as practiced by Mullah Mūsá Sayrāmī was not entirely forgotten, though it remained an exception to the dominant trends.[70] The limited circulation of printed works before PRC rule is reflected in Xinjiang's thriving second-hand-book market today. In a decade of frequent visits to book dealers across the region, I encountered countless manuscripts, as well as early lithographs from elsewhere in Central Asia, and recent illegal home-made publications, but never a single pre-1949 product of an Altishahri press. Around half of the printed books documented in the sources are not to be found in any accessible or published library collections. Printed genres would not fully overshadow the manuscript until the late 1970s and early 1980s, at which time they would have a hand in transforming the practices of understanding the past.

The shifts in historical practice that would eventually saturate modern Uyghur society were, however, initially cultivated in the medium of print, even if the circulation of printed works did not extend beyond a small, highly educated elite in the early days. In 1916 and 1917, Nūshīrvān Yāvshev of Khotan published a semi-regular feature, "A Selection from the History of Altishahr," in *Shūrā*, a reformist journal published in Orenburg, Russia. In this series Yāvshev presented translations and summaries of other historical works, namely an Altishahri extension of the *Tārīkh-i Rashīdī* and an Ottoman history of Kashgar with nationalist overtones.[71] Nationalist historical works were also written and published among the Taranchi Uyghur community in Soviet Yettisu (Semirech'e, now Kazakhstan).[72] Some of these works may have been smuggled into Altishahr, and they must have influenced some of the more well-traveled and internationally connected members of Altishahr's intelligentsia. Another important nationalist history that appeared outside Altishahr was written by Muhammad Amīn Bughrā from exile in Kashmir and published in 1946.[73] This text doesn't seem to have made its way back to Altishahr in significant numbers, but Bughrā's history formed the foundation for another hard-to-find book of nationalist history, published by the newspaper editor Polat Qadiri in Urumchi in 1948.[74] Among the small but growing number of highly educated reformists and nationalists, printed works were beginning to reshape the historical landscape.

The Arrival of Nationalist History

It was the newspaper that brought what appears to have been the first nationalist history to print in Altishahr itself.[75] The newspapers of Alt-

ishahr were usually established as tools for creating social or political
change. In addition to news items, they carried essays debating reform
issues, political programs, government proclamations, and in at least one
case, historical essays. One paper republished stories from reformist papers in Western Turkestan.[76] Most shared in the goal of creating a break
with old forms of social organization and knowledge reproduction. The
newspaper's separation of the word from ritual and traditional social
contexts was ideal for this purpose. Reform took many shapes. There
were reformers in the Jadid tradition, scripturalist religious reformers,
nationalists, communists, and even the Chinese warlord governments,
which had their own plans for reshaping Altishahri society.[77] All of these
(often overlapping) groups took advantage of the newspaper as a tool for
producing change.

One of the major intellectual efforts to bring about Altishahr's stark
break with its past was the writing of a new history for the region. In
September 1933, the editor of *East Turkestan Life* began publishing a
history of East Turkestan in serial form, the first part of which appeared in issue number four of the paper. Both the form and content of
this new history represented perhaps the greatest single change to the
practice of history in Altishahr since the arrival of Islam. Though many
of this history's innovations had already appeared in publications outside of Altishahr, the serial in *East Turkestan Life* seems to have been
the first nationalist history to be published in Altishahr itself. It was
clear from the introduction to the first installment that this history was
intended for entirely different purposes than those of the tazkirahs or
dynastic histories:

> Each people [*qawm*] and each nation [*millat*] has its own known history of
> the political and economic situations that have gone before. If a nation is
> uninformed of its historical situation, its strength will dwindle and its spirit
> will break, and thus it will not be able to prepare for the future. [The peo-
> ple of the nation] cannot give importance to the shared national good and
> everyone is occupied with their own concerns. The national bonds are
> broken, and the nation becomes vile and a plaything before the bordering
> nations. We, the nation of East Turkestan also had great glory in former
> times. . . . [Our subjugation by foreign nations] came from disunity and
> from everyone following their own private desires and forgetting the na-
> tion's general goals and profit. And also from not giving importance to our
> past history. . . . [Thus] we recognized our duty to collect in this, our na-
> tional paper, our national history in concise form.[78]

Here history has become a separate branch of knowledge, completely desacralized. There is no *bismillah,* no request for the forgiveness of God or blessing for the historical actors. History is not written to glorify holy personages or to record the deeds of a dynasty chosen by God. But this does not mean history has lost its significance. On the contrary, it has become a matter of life and death. It is the foundation of national unity and sovereignty. History is no longer the story of great individuals, as it was in the tazkirahs. The protagonist of history is now the nation, and the supporting characters are the bordering nations. Above all, history is now a matter of politics. Knowledge or ignorance of history is a key determinant of who will rule Altishahr and how. The author of this particular article, writing in the "national paper" of the independent East Turkestan Republic, uses history to underpin the legitimacy of the new state.

As it unfolds over fourteen issues, the history traces the story of the East Turkestan nation in cycles of unity, during which the nation grows and conquers other lands from China to Europe, and disunity, during which other nations subjugate the nation of East Turkestan. The history begins by stating of the people of East Turkestan that "we are the children of the soldiers of Oghuzkhan who settled in our East Turkestan." The "we," which frequently appears throughout the history, is alternately associated with the "Turk people" and the East Turkestan nation. The nation of East Turkestan is equated with great empires of Eurasia, including those of the Huns and Genghis Khan, who are claimed to be Turks. The only individuals of importance in this history are political leaders, particularly leaders who caused the nation to expand its power. Lists of territory controlled or reduced to tributary status are strewn throughout the narrative, with special attention to the times when China *(Khitay)* came under the rule of the "nation of East Turkestan." The nation is thus given a physical shape. Borders surround a continuous stretch of land, all of which is equally part of the nation.

There is very little in this history that can be explained by reference to earlier Altishahri traditions. It is in most respects no different from nationalist histories around the world, which have been described in countless other scholarly essays and analyzed in more detail than the scope of the present study recommends. Here it is important to note that this now-familiar form of historical practice entered Altishahr rather suddenly, as it did Western Turkestan, and that there were important connections to discourses in the wider Turkic world. In particular, the new nationalist history was indebted to Pan-Turkic imaginings of the past as they had developed in the Ottoman Turkish and Tatar spheres. Indeed, the newspaper's editor and probable author of the serial history, Qūtlūgh Shawqī, though born in Kashgar, was educated in Istanbul, and the language of his essays is strongly influenced by Ottoman Turkish.[79] According to one scholar, Shawqī also wrote a stand-alone history, *Vaqi'i Qǎshqǎr,* during his time as newspaper editor, though I have been unable to locate any surviving copies of such a work, and the citation may refer to his newspaper serial.[80]

Qūtlūgh Shawqī may have authored the first nationalist history to be printed in Altishahr itself, but he was not the first person to apply a Pan-Turkist perspective to the history of the region. Such influences made a relatively subtle appearance in the summary histories that Nūshīrvan Yāvshev had published in Orenburg's *Shūrā* journal. More explicit discussions of the connection between the nation and history can be found among the publications of the Taranchis of Yettisu. We find, for example, an earlier Altishahri expression of ideas about the importance of history to the nation in the works of Naẓar Khvājah 'Abd al-Ṣamad Oghli (Nǎzǎrghoja Abdusemǎtov, Child of the Uyghur) who was writing in Soviet Yettisu. In the introduction to his 1920s *History of the Taranchis,* he argued that a "national history for all the Uyghurs" was necessary for the success of the nation.[81] The *East Turkestan Life* history's claims on Genghis Khan for the Turkish people were also preceded by similar a statement from 'Abd al-Ṣamad Oghli. In 1912 he had argued in the Tatar periodical *Shūrā* that the word *chinggiz* in Chinggiz Khan (Genghis Khan) was a Turkic word. In his essay, Abdusemetov cited related claims about *chinggiz* from other articles in *Shura* and the Istanbul newspaper *Türk Yurdu.*[82] Exactly how and when such Pan-Turkist ideas of history reached Altishahr is unclear. Several early reformers in Altishahr, such as the Turk Ahmet Kemal (arrived 1914), were known Pan-Turkist sympathizers, but earlier nationalist historical texts, if any were written, have not come to my attention.

Until more newspapers from the first half of the twentieth century become available to researchers, it is also impossible to say with certainty just how widespread or limited the practice of history writing in newspapers was. It is possible that such politicized historical writing only flourished under the relative freedom of expression that seems to have obtained under the East Turkestan Republic government. Certainly, such works were discontinued in the Kashgar paper's new version as *New Life* under Sheng Shicai. The 1933 history in *East Turkestan Life,* however, represents the first significant application of Pan-Turkist and nationalist ideas to the writing of history within Altishahr. These ideas would appear again briefly in the ephemeral publications of Bughrā and Qadiri (mentioned above) and then reemerge in the 1980s, after a long publishing silence imposed by the People's Republic of China. With the expansion of Uyghur-language publishing in the 1980s, nationalist ideas would merge with the tazkirah tradition to create a new, Uyghur way of understanding the past.

Disruption of the Tazkirah-Shrine System

The upheavals of the first three decades of PRC rule in Altishahr, though largely hidden by state restrictions on document access and interviewing, are at least known from their broad outlines to have thoroughly disrupted the system of tazkirah production and shrine pilgrimage that had served as ordinary Altishahris' connection to the region's own past. The first serious challenge came through the PRC's land reform campaigns. The main shrines held sometimes enormous amounts of land in trust *(waqf)*, the income from which paid for physical upkeep of the shrine and the services of shaykhs, sweepers, and other personnel. The Imam Ja'far al-Ṣādiq shrine was said to own the entire town of Niya at the turn of the century.[83] In 1952 the Afaq Khoja shrine near Kashgar held 16,750 mu (1,117 hectares) of arable land in *waqf,* along with thirty mills, two shops, and buildings totaling 515 rooms.[84] The new PRC rulers started the process of confiscating and redistributing such *waqf* lands in 1953. Without a means of financial support, Islamic institutions and their personnel were more easily integrated into the state's religious bureaucracy. However, notwithstanding land reform and the state incorporation of Islamic institutions, the early 1950s were a time of relative tolerance on the part of PRC toward the shrines and Islamic culture in general, at least in comparison to the storms that were to come. Shaykhs still survived on the donations of pilgrims, who continued to visit shrines without restriction until the Religious Reform Campaign of 1958.

The Religious Reform Campaign initiated a radical shift in the state's approach to religious activities, inaugurating two decades of assimilationist campaigns and attacks on religious institutions.[85] Such attacks reached their peak in the Great Proletarian Cultural Revolution (1966–1976), when Mao's calls for young people to "bombard the headquarters" and "smash the four olds" plunged all of China into near anarchy. Little detail has emerged concerning the attacks on the shrine system during this period, but the vague outlines suggest a devastating blow. Mosques and shrines were converted to other purposes. The shaykh at one shrine told me that his predecessor had been forced to flee and that the shrine's attached mosque had been converted into an office for cadres. Other survivors of the period have told of mosques converted to pig sties.[86] Many shrines were simply shut down and left to crumble, while others seem to bear the signs of deliberate destruction, for example the Alp Ata complex near Turpan. A tour of Altishahr's shrines today turns up a common tale among the shaykhs: they took up their posts after the Cultural Revolution, replacing shaykhs who had been chased out during the turmoil of that period. Shrine graffiti from the period of the Cultural Revolution are all but absent. Perhaps many people continued to perform the daily or weekly rituals associated with the shrines, if only in secret. However, with shrines officially closed and shaykhs removed, the practices of long distance pilgrimage and pilgrimage festivals must have ceased entirely, and with them the tazkirah readings.

It is hard to say when, but, at some point, the tazkirahs kept at shrines were also confiscated or destroyed. I never once encountered a shrine or shaykh who claimed to preserve a manuscript tazkirah. When asked about tazkirahs, shaykhs invariably answered that "the government has it." Indeed, the government controls a large number of tazkirahs, and manuscripts in general, which seem to be preserved for their value as cultural property. The Xinjiang Minorities Ancient Works Gathering, Organizing, and Publishing Workshop in Urumchi preserves over 1,500 manuscripts, including numerous tazkirahs, although, according to the director, these are only accessible to employees of the "workshop." Other institutions, such as Xinjiang University and the Xinjiang Academy of Social Sciences keep additional books. Precisely how these institutions acquired their works remains a mystery, though provenience statements in Mukhlisov's 1957 catalog suggest that confiscation was an important means.[87]

Thus, in ways that will only become clear at some point in the future, the PRC put an end to the tazkirah-shrine system as it had existed for hundreds of years. Then, in the liberalization and reforms of the late 1970s and the 1980s, religious institutions in Altishahr sprang back to life. By the 1990s, major shrine festivals were taking place again. However, the revived traditions bear the scars of the trauma that they endured in the Cultural Revolution. The tazkirahs have never been replaced; most are still considered "illegal religious books," namely, Islamic books that have not been through the censorship process. The current shaykhs took their positions years after their predecessors had been eliminated, breaking the transmission of expert knowledge across generations. The size and popularity of shrine pilgrimage festivals never reached the levels seen in the first half of the twentieth century, partly due to continued restrictions. Still, this hobbled version of the shrine system, along with memories of the tazkirahs and the older, fuller tradition, contributed to the reemergence of the tazkirah in its new form.

New Historical Writing and the New Tazkirah

The tazkirah reemerged in a new environment of openness that permitted the convergence of the important trends described above, especially printing and nationalist imaginations of "Uyghur" identity, with the tazkirah tradition. The same PRC policies that allowed the revival of mosques and shrines also opened up the printed word to Uyghur writers and thinkers. For the first three decades of PRC rule, Uyghur-language texts were largely limited to state newspapers and journals, which included some literary products, mostly of an ideological nature. Very few books were printed before 1978. One of these was a history of Ya'qub Beg printed in 1958, which, unfortunately, I have been unable to access.[88] Beyond this lone work, no historical monographs were published under PRC rule before the reform era. Nor were there more than a handful of novels, and those were propagandistic vehicles of praise for the socialist project.

Clearly, there was a latent interest in publishing, though, because a flood of new Uyghur literary products appeared during the political reforms of the late 1970s and early 1980s. At least a dozen new literary and scholarly journals were established in the years 1978–1980, eight of them in 1980 alone. In the same year, the Xinjiang People's Press published the first issue of an occasional series called *Shinjang Tarikh Matiriyalliri (Xinjiang Historical Materials),* a combination of academic and propagandistic historical articles, oral histories, and memoirs focused on the 1920s through 1949. Novels also began to appear in the 1980s, with at least ten published by the end of 1985. Most of these were historical novels set in the same period covered by the *Historical Materials* series. They tended to recount the adventures of an ordinary "Uyghur" character navigating the political turmoil of the times. Two of the early novels were set in the Cultural Revolution.[89] Some of the historical novels contained disguised nationalistic content and became extremely popular. Among these, *The Awakening Land* of Abdurehim Ötkür (1988) has probably left the deepest impression among Uyghurs, and with four editions totaling 68,000 copies, may be the most widely read novel in the Uyghur language. This work has been analyzed in some depth elsewhere, but it is worth noting here that it took up the thread of nationalist writing that had characterized the *East Turkestan Life* serial history, and that it remains one of the most accessible vehicles of nationalist history for Uyghur readers.[90] It is a major source of Uyghur popular visions of the past.

A more explicit form of nationalist history also emerged in the late 1980s, and more closely followed the example of the *East Turkestan Life* serial history: studies that aimed to trace the roots of the Uyghur people, demonstrate the existence of a continuous and ancient Uyghur nation, claim great accomplishments for that nation, and connect the nation to a fixed geographic homeland. Most important among these was Turghun Almas's *The Uyghurs,* which, in addition to drawing from Turkic nationalist discourse, also borrowed language from Chinese nationalist claims to civilizational greatness.[91] The historical works of Almas and other overt Uyghur nationalists were quickly suppressed. Almas himself was put under house arrest because his writings quickly came to be recognized as a threat to the PRC's vision of a multiethnic "Chinese" nation, of which the Uyghurs were only one small part. The fate of Turghun Almas had a chilling effect on explicitly historical nationalist writing among Uyghur intellectuals. However, history writing continued, and even flourished, under the guise of fiction.

Before turning to the new biographical fiction, however, it is worth pausing to look at the fate of the tazkirah during the 1980s boom in print publishing. In 1984 the journal *Bulaq (Wellspring)* published the versified *Tazkirah of the Four Imams* by Mullah Niyāz, and in the ensuing decades a handful of other tazkirahs have been published.[92] However, these manifestations of the tazkirah were unconnected to the functions that had created the genre. Shaykhs, who often complain about the banning of tazkirahs in manuscript form, seem to be unfamiliar with the availability of the tazkirahs in these journals. The social and institutional forces that led to the tazkirahs' republication simply do not articulate with the world of the shrine, in which the shaykhs live. The

contexts of the tazkirahs' publication indicate purposes other than rees-
tablishing the connection between text and shrine. The tazkirahs appear
in two kinds of journal. One group consists of literary journals, mainly
Bulaq (Wellspring), which are building a canon of state-approved "Uyghur" literature and tend to print the versified, rather than prose, tazkirahs as specimens of fine Uyghur poetry. The other important journals
for reproducing the tazkirahs are the "old books research" reports, issued by local (Kashgar and Aqsu) offices of "collecting, organizing, and
publishing old books." These offices are engaged in a scientific and antiquarian project of preservation that dovetails with both Uyghur nationalist and PRC ethnopolitical goals of regularizing and cataloging the
cultural heritage of the Uyghur ethnicity. While such a project certainly
has its value, the aims are not so much to preserve cultural practices
such as the tazkirah-shrine tradition but to create a supply of easily accessible texts that can be used to buttress nationalist (PRC or Uyghur)
imaginations of the Uyghur identity.

Of course, once the printed texts leave the press, they can end up being
used in different ways than intended, and undoubtedly, some of these tazkirahs have been used in ways more appropriate to the old manuscript
tazkirah's social context. For example, I encountered a hand-bound composite book that included four tazkirahs bound alongside each other. One
was a mechanically reproduced manuscript (photocopy or mimeograph).
The other three were printed tazkirahs removed from the journals cited in
Table 5.2 and rebound together, just as tazkirahs had been in the old
manuscript tazkirah anthologies. Still, for the most part, these printed tazkirahs have not reached beyond a specialized literary or technical audience, and they remain largely cut off from the traditions that originally
generated them.

Not all tazkirah revivals were as divorced from the earlier traditions
as the journal editions. A native of Uch Turpan, Ibrahim Qurban, took
advantage of the growing publishing opportunities to address one of the
classic ideals of the tazkirah-shrine tradition, the notion that important
shrines should have tazkirahs. In 1984 he published a tazkirah of his
own original composition for his hometown shrine, named (both book
and shrine) after the shrine's occupants, the Seven Maidens *(Yättä Qizlirim)*. Qurban did not explicitly use the word *tazkirah*, but his verse
tale of the Seven Maidens' heroic deeds fit the bill, and was written with
the shrine in mind. Thus, Qurban wrote in the conclusion of the work,

Table 5.2.   Tazkirahs republished in journals during the 1980s

Title	Author	Date	Journal
Tazkirah of the Four Imams (verse)	Mullah Niyāz	1984	*Wellspring*
Tazkirah of Muhammad Sharīf (verse)	Zalīlī	1984	*News on Research on Old Books*
Tazkirah of Arshidīn Valī	Anonymous	1986	*Research on Old Books*
Tazkirah of Qirmish Ātā	Anonymous	1986	*Research on Old Books*
Tazkirah of the Four Imams (prose)	Anonymous	1989	*Research on Old Books*

Sources: Molla Niyaz Khotăni, "Töt Imam Tăzkirisi," *Bulaq* 11 (1984): 68–106; Muhămmăt Sidiq Zălili, "Tăzkiră Khoja Muhămmăt Shirip Büzrükvar," *Qădimqi kitaplar tătqiqat khăviri* 1 (1984): 39–73; Abdirishit Măhămmăd, ed., "Măvlana Ărshidin Veli Tăzkirisi," *Qădimqi kitaplar tătqiqati* 2 (1986): 82–128; Măhămmăd Usman, ed., "Sultani Qirmish Ata' Tăzkirisi," *Qădimqi kitaplar tătqiqati* 2 (1986): 31–61; Abdurishit Muhămmăd and Muhămmăd Usman, eds., "Yüsüp Qadirkhan Ghazi Tăzkirisi," *Qădimqi kitablar tătqiqati* 1 (1989): 1–27.

> Forgetting is a sin against ancestors and descendants.
> For this reason, dear reader, I wrote the "Seven Maidens"
> Because they have a martyrs' tomb,
> And this tomb has descendant guards.
> If there is so much respect for them among their people *(ăl),*
> How has an account of them not been put to paper?[93]

The connection between text and tomb could hardly be clearer. Yet this is not a pure revival of the tazkirah tradition as it stood before state intervention. We see in this passage a new imagination of lineal descent from the saint, combined with the older imagination of Altishahris as guardians or venerators of the saints' tombs. The nature of the printed book also set Qurban's tazkirah off from its forerunners. Like the author of the *Tazkirah of the Companions of the Cave,* Qurban was careful to record his fear that he might make an error, writing in the last line of the work, "If there be an error, forgive me, dear reader!" Unlike the *Companions* author, who wrote for the manuscript medium, Qurban did not invite the reader to correct his mistakes. Qurban's tazkirah was expected to multiply through the machinery of the press, not the continued copying of its consumers. It is difficult to know how Qurban's tazkirah was received, but it is clear that this kind of writing did not spread. Qurban's book was printed in a large quantity—15,000—but it is hard to find today. No one, to my knowledge, has published a new tazkirah of his or her own since.

This does not necessarily mean that there has been no demand for the tazkirahs, even in print. In 1988 the Kashgar Uyghur Press published four tazkirahs in an edited version of a manuscript anthology from a state collection, translated into modern Uyghur orthography and vocabulary.[94] Not only was the work printed in large numbers—14,150—but pirated versions have appeared in Yarkand's market since the original supply disappeared from official bookstore shelves. In addition to this publication, people still satisfy the demand for tazkirahs through manuscript copying. One manuscript, copied in 2006, embraces both traditions; it is a manuscript copy of the printed tazkirah anthology just described, marking the end of a remarkable chain of transmission from oral epic to manuscript to print and back to manuscript.[95]

Meanwhile, the meaning of the modern Uyghur word *tăzkiră* has drifted away from those genres that preserve the old tazkirah tradition. In modern Uyghur, *tăzkiră* can now be used to indicate any writing about the past.[96] However, it is most prominently used to describe writing in the Chinese historiographical tradition of the local gazetteer. One Uyghur scholar has even traced the birth of "the science of the tăzkira," *tăzkirishunasliq*, to the Qing historian Zhang Xuecheng (1738–1801), author of the essay, "Ten Proposals for the Compilation of Local Histories."[97] The adaptation of the Uyghur term to a form of historical practice rooted in the Chinese tradition has proceeded with state support. Beginning in 1984, the official Gazetteer *(Uy: tăzkiră, Ch: difangzhi)* Committee of the Xinjiang Uyghur Autonomous Region published a quarterly journal, *Shinjang Tăzkirisi* (later, *Shinjang Tăzkirichilik*), which started as an internal government publication but switched to public distribution in 1999.[98] The word *tăzkirichilik*, found in the later form of the journal's title, indicates the science of compiling local gazetteers, namely, documenting local history and culture through approaches as varied as biography, geography, toponym studies, and the cataloging of historical documents.

However, while the modern Uyghur *tăzkirichilik* may have little to do with the old Altishahri tazkirah, and while few Uyghurs may have access to the academic edited tazkirahs or Qurban's verse hagiography, another new genre has managed to successfully fuse historical approaches of the Altishahri tazkirahs with popular nationalist depictions of the Uyghur identity, and to take advantage of the print technology that has finally taken root in Altishahr. The new genre, which in this study is called "biographical novel," is essentially a subtype of the historical novel, and indeed these works are labeled in Uyghur as historical novels *(tarikhiy roman).*[99] Unlike most historical novels, which take as their protagonists fictional characters and follow their actions through a historical setting, the Uyghur biographical novel trains its attention on well-known historical figures. The plots of these books follow the historical record in its broad outlines and fill in the gaps with fictional events. In this regard, the biographical novel is quite similar to Hollywood's "biopics," such as *Alexander the Great* or *The Last Emperor.* The Uyghur biographical novel tends to maintain a close focus on the title character and to follow him or her from youth or even birth until death. The books are often quite faithful to the historical record where events are documented in the sources but interpolate sometimes wildly fantastic and anachronistic fictional events between the historically attested elements.

The creation of Uyghur biographical novels began rather suddenly, with at least three such works completed in the first years of the 1980s. These were Abdulla Talip's *Qaynam Urkishi,* published in October 1982; Săypidin Ăzizi's *Sutuq Bughrakhan,* written in 1979–1982 but not published until 1987; and Khevir Tömür's *Baldur Oyghanghan Adăm,* completed in 1983 and published in 1987.[100] Undoubtedly, multiple influences shaped the Uyghur biographical novel, some of which will be discussed in more or less detail below. In general, however, the full genealogy of modern Uyghur literature's ancestors remains to be studied in depth. The focus here will be on the ways that the biographical novel provided a new venue for important elements of the tazkirah tradition, keeping alive certain strains of Altishahri historical practice in the new, print-dominated, nationalist world.

The single most important continuation of the tazkirah tradition in these novels is the centrality of personage and, in particular, characters of monumental stature. In order to understand the resonance of outsized heroes, it is worth returning for a moment to the content of the tazkirahs to examine the nature of personage. For all of the tazkirahs' diversity in form and content, the popular examples do hold in common their use of what Walter Ong called "heavy" characters, individuals whose extraordinary deeds are "monumental, memorable, and commonly public."[101] This kind of character anchors Altishahri tazkirahs of all types. The saints of the epic-style tazkirahs perform incredible feats of violence, dispatching outrageous numbers of infidels in a single day's battle while remaining unscathed themselves. Muhammad Sharīf, whose tazkirah resembles the Persian romance, not only has miraculous spiritual powers, allowing him to communicate with spirits of the dead and cause water to flow from the dry earth, but also demonstrates extraordinary physical prowess enabling him to jump onto the "column of Iskandar." In the taz-kirah of Arshadīn Valī, Jamāl al-Dīn Katakī demonstrates his power by riding on the back of a tiger. The author of the *Tazkirah of Sultan Satūq Bughrā-khān* establishes Satūq's greatness early on by reference to "heavy" characters from romances and epics. He is given "the power of Rustam" the "strength of ʿAlī" and the "bravery of Amīr Hamzah."[102] In all of the popular tazkirahs, the characters are not only great, the best of the best, the strongest ever, but they are without personal failings of any kind. In fact, there is very little at all to these characters aside from their great deeds and heroic qualities. There is, for example, almost no physical de-scription. As Ong points out, this kind of character is typical of oral and orally influenced works around the world.[103]

In the Uyghur biographical novel, the "heavy" character makes its re-turn. This is particularly true of Äzizi's *Sutuq Bughrakhan* and the many works that followed in its wake. Sutuq is not only good; he is good at everything he tries. He is a master hunter, scholar, swordsman, and tacti-cian. The author also devised new episodes in Satuq's life that demon-strate his moral qualities. For example, we learn of Sutuq's concern for the poor and the weak when he frees a pair of slaves in the market.[104] Äzizi's adoption of the novel, a genre that had become a global phenom-enon long before 1979, led him to add extensive physical description of the sort that was absent from the tazkirahs. However, we are still dealing with a "heavy" character, for Satuq has no flaws whatsoever. A connois-seur of the Western novel might consider Satuq a one-dimensional char-acter and a mark of poor writing, but *Sutuq Bughrakhan* is not a West-ern novel. It is an Altishahri biographical novel, drawing from a combination of multiple cultural resources, chief among them the novel and the tazkirah.

In the case of Äzizi's *Sutuq Bughrakhan,* the connection to the tazkirah and to the saint's tomb is direct and explicit. Äzizi rewrote the tale of Sultan Satūq Bughrā-khān, one of the few saints of the popular tazkirahs who was said to be a native of Altishahr.[105] The basic outlines of Satūq's life story in the novel are taken from the *Tazkirah of Sultan Satūq Bughrā-khān* (originally an excerpt from the *Tazkirah-i Uvaysīya*).[106] The central elements of the tazkirah—Satūq's conversion at the hands of Abū al-Naṣr Sāmānī, his establishment of a glorious khanate in Kashgar, and his holy wars against the Buddhists—are all emphasized heavily in the novel. The timescale of the story also closely follows the tazkirah. In both the novel and the tazkirah the reader meets Satūq in his teens and the tale continues to the end of his life. However, Ăzizi greatly expanded the tale. Whereas the tazkirah occupies forty pages in the 1988 printed modern Uyghur translation, Ăzizi's novel is an epic 1007 pages long. In terms of plot, much has been added to increase Satūq's significance, such as a conquest of Samarqand (for which there is no historical evidence). Ăzizi also abandoned parts of the tazkirah tradition, giving Satūq a son named Musa Bughrakhan, who does not appear in other sources, while omitting sons of Satūq who are described in tazkirahs.[107] Ăzizi also added lengthy descriptions of settings, physiognomy, clothing, and so on, along with extensive dialogue.

The importance of the tazkirah-shrine tradition to Ăzizi's biographical novel is not only visible in the direct borrowings from the *Tazkirah of Sultan Satūq Bughrā-khān* and the shared focus on monumental personage. Ăzizi was a native of Artush, the town in which Satūq Bughrā-khān's shrine is located. He described his inspiration for the novel in its introduction, which begins thus:

> I have hoped to write a novel about Sutuq Bughrakhan for a long time. Because the shrine [*mazar*] of Sutuq Bugrakhan is in Artush, where I was born and raised, I had heard many stories and tales about him from the time when I was little onwards. To this mazar, which was famous not only in Kashgar but all over Xinjiang, people would come from great distances to make pilgrimage, calling the mazar "Hăzsultunum."[108] The people of Artush esteemed this mazar even more.[109]

Later in the introduction, Ăzizi adds that,

> When I was little, I would go to this "Hăzsultunum" with other children and we would play there. Later, we would listen to the long, fascinating stories about "Hăzsultunum" from the shrine's old shaykhs and aqsaqals. Thus, this influence concerning Sutuq Bughrakhan that permeated my youth produced a desire in me to write something when I became an adult.[110]

The connection between this early Altishahri biographical novel and the tazkirah-shrine system could hardly be more explicit. Ăzizi's experience overlaps nicely with Jarring's report on the same shrine, mentioned earlier. Ăzizi, who was born in 1915, would have been fourteen years old when Jarring made his visit to the shrine at Artush in February 1930.

When Jarring arrived, followed by an enormous crowd of onlookers, "with a high shrill voice, the sheikh lectured about all of Satuq Bughra Khan's good deeds and he described his life, according to the biography, tazkirah, which I had looked into previously."[111] It is tempting to imagine a young Äzizi in the crowd, which, according to Jarring, "must have ended up by encompassing half the population of the town."[112]

Säypidin Äzizi was the kind of man who was often in the right place at the right time. In part due to his fame and political power, we have far more information about his life than about the other two authors of early biographical novels. His literary and political careers are emblematic of the confluence of ideas that would determine the trajectory of Uyghur historical practice. In 1935, after a youth marked by a traditional maktab education and exposure to the tazkirah tradition at his hometown shrine, Äzizi joined the second group of Altishahri students sent to study in Tashkent. It was a pivotal event for what would become the most successful career of any Uyghur political figure in the twentieth century. In addition to joining the Communist Party and studying Marxist ideology, in Tashkent, Äzizi was exposed to new forms of literature. From his memoirs we know that he read Uzbek plays, the genre par-excellence of Western Turkestan's modernist reformers, Jadid and communist. He also acted in and helped write a play about new-method education.[113] This experience foreshadowed his later (1980) publication of a biographical play about the sixteenth-century queen in Yarkand, Amannisakhan, an early harbinger of the return of biography as a predominant form of popular history.[114]

Äzizi may have also been exposed to the novel in Tashkent. The first Central Asian novel, Abdulla Qodiriĭ's *Ötkän Kunlăr (Days Past)*, appeared in book form in 1925 (it first came out as a serial). According to Qodiriĭ himself, *Ötkän Kunlăr* was a conscious attempt to acquaint his countrymen with the "modern novel," which he emphasized was not a part of the old literary canon.[115] Other authors followed Qodiriĭ, and while Altishahri writers labored under the strict publication controls of the warlord governments and the PRC, Soviet Turkestan became the proving ground for the novel in Central Asia. Historical novels were a major component of the emerging tradition. Äzizi returned to Tashkent twice after his schooling there, but for novelistic influence on his *Sutuq Bughrakhan*, Äzizi did not have to leave Altishahr at all. In 1954 a Uyghur translation of the Uzbek novel *Navoiy*, by Oybek, was distributed in Xinjiang.[116] This work was a biographical novel about the poet 'Alī-Shīr Navā'ī, an early example of a substantial trend of fictionalized biography among the Uzbeks of the Soviet Union.[117] Though it lacked the extreme hagiographical hyperbole of the Altishahri biographical novel, Oybek's work may have introduced to several future Uyghur writers the novelistic technique of fictionalizing a national hero's biography.

However Săypidin Äzizi may have first encountered the novel, he seems to have recognized fully its potential as a vehicle for nationalist representations of the past. In *Sutuq Bughrakhan* we see the kind of community imagining that led Benedict Anderson to consider the novel as the quintessential genre of nationalism.[118] The book begins with something at once utterly foreign to the tazkirah and perfectly characteristic of the novel as an engine of national imaginings: a description of the setting, whose inhabitants go about their varied lives simultaneously and anonymously, connected by their shared membership in a single community, a nation marching together through homogeneous, empty time. It begins thus: "The first half of the tenth century, the year of the cow, autumn—the morning sun's fresh, golden light adorns the Kashgar valley and stings the eye."[119]

A falcon flies over the valley, and Äzizi describes the world from its vantage point. The sound of girls singing resounds throughout the valley: "In the fields, canals, and deserts beneath the falcon's wings, serfs, awoken at dawn and already now engaged in exhausting labor, half hungry and half naked, move about together with difficulty. The bazaars, with their heart-wrenching beggars in tattered clothes, are just now beginning to bustle."[120]

Guards at the palace begin their day. Destitute worshippers pray for relief at a Buddhist temple. The sound of the girls singing continues to float through the valley. The falcon begins to descend, and the reader's view is diverted to Satūq Bughrā-khān, himself descending on horseback from the mountains that overlook the scene of the nation.

Äzizi is obviously trying to paint a picture of an oppressive social order here. It is the tip of a thread that runs throughout the novel—the establishment of feudal inequality as one of the enemies against which the hero struggles. However, these first pages are also a classic example of the novel's potential for depicting an imagined community. All of the anonymous strangers described are a part of a single nation, even if it is a nation in which oppression is rife. Anderson's famous analysis of the novel *Noli Me Tangere* as an expression of nationalist imagining would apply equally well to Äzizi's novel, with only a change of place names: "The image of . . . hundreds of unnamed people, who do not know each other, in quite different parts of Manila, in a particular month of a particular decade, immediately conjures up an imagined community."[121]

For all the similarities of setting and community description, though, the relation of Äzizi's protagonist to this community is entirely different from what one finds in the typical nationalist novel outside Altishahr. Whereas the novel genre is distinguished by its tendency to focus on more ordinary characters who navigate the imagined community as members, in Äzizi's biographical novel the "heavy" protagonist is, throughout the novel, shown as the leader and embodiment of that community, both above and constitutive of the community. The effect of such a juxtaposition of tazkirah and historical novel forms is striking. We see the tazkirah-like character, the "heavy," one-dimensional, timeless, omnibenevolent, fantastically strong Satūq Bughrā-khān walking around in a minutely described, finely detailed, community of ordinary people fixed in abstract time.

The other two early biographical novels, *Qaynam Orkishi* and *Baldur Oyghanghan Adăm,* feature similarly hagiographical protagonists and share Äzizi's nationalist sentiments, but in their opening chapters they lack the elaborate community portrait seen in *Sutuq Bughrakhan.* Several of the most important authors of biographical novels, however, followed Äzizi's example, sometimes slavishly.[122] The first of these was Părhat Jilan, whose biographical novel, *Măhmut Qăshqări,* about the great Qarakhanid scholar Maḥmūd Kāshgharī, appeared in print in 1994. As in the case of *Sutuq Bughrakhan,* a second print run was undertaken within less than a year, and the book has a strong reputation among Uyghur readers. The novel displayed the same juxtaposition of the inhumanly great central character with finely detailed national imagining. In an opening chapter strongly reminiscent of *Sutuq Bughrakhan,* the author describes "the pigeons of my imagination flying in the sky of thought," bringing into his view the Kashgar of the Qarakhanid period. He gives a bird's-eye view of miners working in the mountains, herders driving their animals, farmers tending their fields, children playing in the towns' neighborhoods, and merchants bargaining in their shops. The hagiographically perfect Maḥmūd Kāshgharī navigates not only this homeland, but, in the second half of the novel, ventures forth and represents his nation to the wider Islamic world. Unlike Săypidin Äzizi, however, Părhat Jilan chose a protagonist with no tazkirah.[123]

The title characters of the ensuing biographical novels reveal a new pattern in the selection of personages around which identity was built (see Table 5.3). In a sharp break from the tazkirah tradition, all but one of the authors (Abduväli Äli)[124] wrote exclusively on title characters who were considered to have been born in Altishahr or the Ili valley. As we have noted already, the notion of local birth is critical to nationalist imagination of who is one of "us." The biographical novels were part of a process of selecting new heroes for the imagined community in its recent reorganization as a nation. History—and most Uyghur readers in this genre consider the biographical novels historically reliable—remained organized around the axes of monumental personages, as it had in the tazkirah tradition, but nationalist history demanded a new kind of personage, a child of the nation. Through the biographical novels, Uyghur authors chose a new set of personages. They are a new kind of saint: saints of the nation.

The biographical novels bear the marks of the print world into which they were born. They tend to be enormously long texts, which cannot be read in one sitting, or even one week. Many, in fact, are printed in two

Table 5.3. Biographical novels, 1987–2003

Title	Author(s)	Date of first publication	Date of completion
Qaynam urkishi	Abdulla Talip	1982	unknown
Sutuq Bughrakhan	Säypidin Äzizi	1987	1982
Baldur oyghanghan Adäm	Khevir Tömür	1987	1983
Mähmut Qäshqäri	Pärhat Jilan	1994	unknown
Mälikä Amannisakhanim	Tursun Yunus	1996	1995
Sadir Palwan	Tursun Yasin	1997	1991
Sä'idkhan	Haji Mirjahid Kerimi and Sawut Dawut	1997	1994
Bädölät	Abduväli Äli	1997	unknown
Muhämmät Beshir Chingvang	Aishäm Äkhmät	1999	1998
Sultan Abdureshitkhan	Haji Mirzahid Kerimi	2000	1998
Apaq Khoja	Abduväli Äli	2000	1999
Turghaq Khojilar	Abduväli Äli	2000	1999
Mäkhdum Äzäm vä uning ävladliri	Abduväli Äli	2000	2000
Yüsüp Khas Hajip	Haji Mirjahid Kerimi	2002	2000
Jallat Khenim	Yasinjan Sadiq Chughlan	2003	2001

volumes. This marked departure from the brevity of the manuscript tazkirahs was allowed by a change in the way books are consumed. Most tazkirahs could be heard or read in less than an hour or two. Their brevity was ideally suited to public performances that took place within the time limitations of pilgrimage, and to maintaining the interest of listeners, who could not receive the text away from the presence of the reciter. So it was that Abū al-Qāsim, in his 1829 recasting of the Bughrā-khān tazkirah, substituted "one line for a thousand."[125] Săypidin Ăzizi, in his own version of the Bughrā-khān story, has done the opposite. He has substituted a thousand pages for forty. His book is written for the new world of print technology, which, thanks to the economy of scale, is capable of producing such long works relatively cheaply. The community in which it is propagated is highly literate, not dependent on public recitations. The book, in its physical and technical aspects, is designed for the fast, silent reading that has become the dominant mode of book consumption. Since its primary venue is private reading, it can easily be absorbed over a long period of time.

The private nature of reading in the print world does not, however, mean that texts have become a hermetically sealed universe unto themselves. Like the tazkirahs before them, the biographical novels have their own important social contexts. The silently read, printed word certainly removed much of historical practice from the interpersonal world and changed the dynamic between author and readership. No longer does the community have a significant role in shaping the text as it was written. Used, printed books in Altishahr are remarkably free of marginal notations. No longer is the context in which a reader consumes a text shared with others, or even necessarily consistent from one person to another. Some may read at home, others at work, and others at the bookshop. Yet new historical practices have emerged around the new form of historical text.

The closest practice to silent, insular reading that I observed in Altishahr was bookstore reading. The state-run bookstores were often full of young men and women (about twelve to thirty years of age) using the shop as a library, for there are few public libraries in the region and their holdings are very limited. During the holidays and school vacations the numbers of readers swelled, with more readers consuming biographical novels than any other genre of book. Very little verbal communication went on in this context, though readers did seem to pay some attention to what others were reading. The sense of shared participation in a historical tradition was not entirely lost with the disappearance of shrine readings and manuscript marginalia, but persisted among those who assembled around this new node of knowledge reproduction and witnessed each other's participation.

The integration of texts into social settings has also been encouraged by the fact the printed books are still physical objects which must be handled and owned. The prices of the most recently published biographical novels range from eighteen to fifty-four yuan (about three to nine dollars as of 2013), a low price compared to manuscripts, for sure, but still out of the range of many younger readers, such as university students and the large numbers of unemployed young men. For this reason the private trading and lending of books was extremely common. After talking with Uyghur readers about a book they had read, I often asked to see or borrow the work, and discovered that they themselves had read a borrowed copy. Some voracious readers whom I met could knowledgably discuss most books in print but themselves owned half a dozen books or fewer, which they used for trade or as collateral for borrowed books. Among the readers I knew in Kashgar, book trading and lending was connected to historical discussion. Such discussion often took place in private settings; history, even as published by the government's official presses, is considered very politically sensitive.

Historical discussion, could, however, occur in public spaces when participants felt comfortable. One of the more intimate public venues was the teahouse, a deeply rooted fixture of Altishahri social life, mainly among older men. Teahouses had largely disappeared by the time I first visited Altishahr in 2000, but around 2007 their numbers grew in Kashgar, and some teahouses became vibrant arenas of public discussion, ranging from gossip to discussion of prices to historical talk and sometimes even political debate. There remained at all times a fear of "spies" from the PRC government, but the fear was not strong enough to stifle all conversation. More often than not, historical talk was undertaken with reference to books, and in this way, the meaning of those books was negotiated among the members of the community. Although the printed text is fixed, its interpretation is not. Readers debated which personages were the best among the saints of the Uyghur nation. With biographical novels acting as major sources of historical knowledge, personages have become the units of discussion, the frames of the debate.

Just as important to establishing the meaning of the printed historical texts was the discussion of the truthfulness of books. Unlike the manuscript era, during which a general trust of written sources was the norm, the reading environment of the early twenty-first century has been marked by textual distrust. This is almost entirely the result of PRC censorship. Han-Chinese-authored historical works are viewed as highly distorting of the historical record, and Uyghurs are aware that works in their own language go through extensive censorship processes, which are rumored to involve significant editorial manipulation. In the words of one teahouse customer, who was talking with his friend about the biographical novels of Abduvăli Ăli, "most books published are just lies, but these have lots of truth." In this environment, the community's judgment on the reliability of a text strongly affects its meaning. Books condemned as government propaganda are assumed to be wrong in all or nearly all of their assertions. The history textbook used at Xinjiang University, which, from the perspective of a Western academic historian, contains a great deal of reliable factual information on the history of Altishahr (more so than many biographical novels), is frequently condemned as fully dishonest because it represents the PRC's official history of Xinjiang.[126] As a result, its narrative is seen by many readers as a reliable source of what did *not* happen in Altishahr. The biographical novels of Abduvăli Ăli and the university textbook are extremes on a spectrum of trustworthiness among books. In between, there are many books that are seen as honest in authorial intent but adulterated by censors. These are books, which, in the words of an Uyghur security guard who commented on a novel I was carrying, "do not have the words that originally came from the author's pen." In historical discussions, the mixed reliability of such works leaves individual passages open to debate. The discussion of the authenticity and reliability of works has left the meaning of the new historical texts in the hands of the community again, despite the fixed nature of print.

The biographical novels are also connected to a changing geography of pilgrimage. A new kind of pilgrimage, mostly tourism with a small component of worship, is emerging among the educated and the well-to-do. With this new pilgrimage has come a new selection of sites, including new heroes such as Amannisakhan (Yarkand) and Maḥmūd Kāshgharī (Opal). It is not always easy to tell whether the site selection reflects the biographical novels or vice versa, but the correlation can be compelling. A friend in Khotan, who had just returned from a pilgrimage around the province, listed for me the shrines he had visited by the name of their saints. Of the six, five were title characters of biographical

novels, and four were personages whose tombs were not objects of popular veneration before PRC rule.[127] The shift of attention from the
foreign-born Altishahri saints of the manuscript era to native "Uyghur"
national heroes may be shifting the geography of the pilgrimage circuits
that lie at the roots of the new personage-centered national history.

In the second half of the twentieth century, two important pillars of
the tazkirah-shrine tradition were removed: the free circulation of manuscript texts and mass participation in regional pilgrimage. The ways
that Altishahris, or Uyghurs, as the people of Altishahr began to call
themselves, adapted and preserved the tazkirah tradition speak to the
natures of both alternative influences and the tradition itself. We saw
how texts and places organized the Altishahri experience of history and
acted as fulcra around which a community-negotiated history turned. It
should be remembered, though, that the tazkirahs—the building blocks
of the Altishahri modular history—were named after their saints. The
tazkirah anthologies represented not just a spectrum of places but a spectrum of personages. When we turn to the convergence of nationalist history, printing, and the tazkirah-shrine tradition, we see what happened
when the connection between text and place was broken. Personage had
always been important, be it in the intimate communication between pilgrim and saint or the titling of tazkirahs with the names of saints, but
when the oases disappeared as a frame for the organization of history,
the significance of personage became even more visible. It is not surprising that the oases should fade from importance in the face of nationalism. Nationalism involves a striving for homogeneous identity and regular distribution of sovereignty across even space. The Altishahri historical
sense of an interconnected archipelago of places (oases and shrines) surrounded by a sea of empty space has been replaced by the single, fully
and evenly Uyghur nation. It is hard to imagine a point in the middle of
the Taklamakan Desert as a part of Altishahr, the "Six Cities," but it is
easy to imagine such a point as a place within the Uyghur nation, and no
less a part of that nation than Kashgar. Place receded as a unit of history,
leaving personage to bear the weight alone. An archipelago of history
was replaced by a portrait gallery.

The story of the tazkirah in the twentieth century also reminds us of the
adaptability and diversity of nationalism. In his history of nationalism,
Benedict Anderson described several different modes of nationalism, each
shaped by the cultures and political systems among which it flourished,
including Creole nationalisms, linguistic nationalisms, official national-

isms, and colonial nationalisms.[128] However, this historical diversity is suppressed when we treat nationalism as a universal language of political struggle. Gardner Bovingdon has described conflicting Chinese and Uyghur visions of Altishahr's past as "competing nationalisms," arguing that "histories written by Uyghur nationalists depict a starkly different past from that found in official Chinese histories, yet the structures and narrative strategies of the opposed texts strikingly recall each other."[129] This kind of analysis is certainly pertinent to much of the Uyghur historical writing Bovingdon analyzed, especially the suppressed attempts to revive the *East Turkestan Life* strain of nationalist historiography (for example in Turghun Almas's *The Uyghurs*).[130] However, in light of the biographical novels, it is clear that such an interpretation ignores much of what is Uyghur (or at least Altishahri) about Uyghur nationalism, namely deeply rooted and particularly Altishahri/Uyghur ways of cultivating a shared history. Clifford Geertz wrote that "religious faith, even when it is fed from a common source, is as much a particularizing force as a generalizing one."[131] The Uyghur historical tradition reminds us that the same should be said about nationalism.

6

THE STATE

Just as it always has been, popular Uyghur historical practice is in a state of transition. The complex of phenomena that together constituted the Altishahri possession of the past in the nineteenth and early twentieth centuries persists today in various forms. In the rare remaining outposts of shrine culture it has changed little since its heyday, while in urban environments such as Kashgar and Urumchi the old approaches to the past appear only as the vestigial roots of a newer, nationalist tradition. The shrine-based Altishahri historical tradition was never pure or exclusive. It always shared the stage with the older, dwindling Persian and epic traditions and, later, the rising forces of printing and nationalism. It also faced coeval rival systems of historical knowledge production, such as the brief resurgence of the chronicle under Ya'qub Beg and the longer flourishing of two important Sufi lineages, the White Mountain and Black Mountain Khojas. In order to illustrate the interaction of these historical practices across time, along with their influence on the present, we turn now to an example that has drawn the attention of numerous Xinjiang specialists: the shrine and reputation of a saint turned villain, Afaq Khoja.[1] This example also facilitates an exposition of the main nodes of the shrine-based tradition, namely, place, text, and personage, in their natural state of interaction. These have largely been treated separately so far, but the case of Afaq Khoja demonstrates the power and durability the system gained from the interplay between such forces.

The example of Apaq Khoja will also introduce the rise of a newly central influence in the shaping of Altishahri/Uyghur historical practice: the Chinese state. The state had always been present, if only as a distant force, diluted through the Qing system of indirect rule and unevenly applied in the oasis capitals. The structure of this power distribution mechanism was at least coincidentally reflected in the modular organization of popular historical knowledge. However, under the rule of the Chinese Communist Party, the state acquired a new role of direct and often conscious intervention in local historical discourse, which has changed both the content and form of historical practice. Moreover, the relation between Chinese state and Uyghur subjects has not been unidirectional. As the Afaq Khoja example will demonstrate, the old nexus of text-place-personage still has a powerful hold on Uyghur historical writing, one that has served to circumvent censors but has also influenced the Chinese state's own approach to the Uyghur past.

Perhaps the best way to begin an investigation of the history of Afaq Khoja is to follow the Altishahri model. In one of my first inquiries into Uyghur historical practice, I asked an Uyghur friend, call him "Tursun," what he knew about Satūq Bughrā-khān, and he told me I should just go to the shrine. So let us do the same for Afaq, and turn our gaze toward his burial place, the tomb of the so-called White Mountain Khojas. It is perhaps the most beautiful example of Altishahri architecture standing, set among tall, slim poplars on the rural outskirts of Kashgar. While clearly related to its Timurid predecessors in Western Turkestan, the mausoleum has unusually stout minarets that evoke Doric columns, a massive dome on a broad, low hall, and simple glazed tiles in an unusual palette of green, yellow, blue, and brown, all of which lend the structure a distinctly local character. This beautiful site witnesses daily a surprising manifestation of historical practices at the junction of Uyghur and Chinese cultures. The White Mountain Khojas, who lie beneath the massive dome, were a line of Sufi leaders responsible for more uprisings against China-based rule than any other movement in the history of Altishahr. Today, one might expect the shrine to attract the veneration of Uyghur nationalists resentful of Chinese rule, or to number among the several Uyghur shrines that the Chinese government has closed to all visitors. Instead, it is a favorite destination among well-heeled Han Chinese tourists, many of whom arrive in groups, shading themselves from the sun with umbrellas and straw cowboy hats stamped with "Marlboro," perhaps even sitting for a photograph in Qing-style clothing or on the back of a colorfully attired camel that is tied up in front of the shrine. At the same time, this potential site of resistance is scorned by many young Uyghurs. The repulsion is so strong that one Uyghur tour guide told me, "I ask forgiveness from God every time I go there." Even some of the Uyghur staff at the shrine will express disgust with the place when out of earshot of their supervisors. These Uyghurs are not concerned with tourist desecration. Rather, they abhor a particular saint buried under the dome. It is a surprising turn for a shrine that once hosted thousands of Altishahri/Uyghur pilgrims.

The details of this ironic shift in historical significance are even more astonishing. Both Chinese and Uyghur visitors to the shrine ignore the original function of the building as a tomb for an entire lineage of religious and political leaders. Instead, each group has reshaped the site as a stand-in for a single famous personage. On the Uyghur side, at least, this makes a great deal of sense, considering the role of monumental personages in the tazkirah-shrine system. Indeed the concentration of historical meaning in exemplary individuals is common throughout the world. Yet in the case of the White Mountain Shrine, the choice of personages and the symbolic meaning attributed to them is counterintuitive. The Han Chinese visitors to the tomb come for *Xiang Fei,* Fragrant Concubine, an Altishahri woman from the White Mountain lineage, who, according to popular Chinese legend, was captured for the Qianlong emperor during the conquest of Altishahr, sent to join the imperial harem in Beijing, and eventually strangled by the emperor's mother for not fulfilling her new sexual duties. Archival sources tell a different story, but the state-approved signs at the site leave most details to the visitors' preconceptions, saying merely that Fragrant Concubine "was selected for the harem" and died of an illness.[2] However, the signs are clear that visitors should see in the story of Fragrant Concubine a precedent of ethnic unity, noting that "afterward so many stories about the Fragrant Concubine circulated, and expressed every ethnicity's aspiration from time immemorial for unity and mutual love."[3] The government has promoted the message of ethnic unity widely in Xinjiang, in everything from newspaper advertisements to signs on military vehicles, in an attempt to reduce hostility between Uyghurs and Han.[4]

It's probably a good thing for China's "ethnic unity" that most Uyghurs are unaware of the full story of sexual enslavement that constitutes the standard Han Chinese take on Fragrant Concubine. Since the state's promotion of Fragrant Concubine stories at the tomb began, some Uyghurs have developed their own understandings of the woman they now call *Iparkhan* (Fragrant Queen), but most Uyghurs associate the shrine with another figure, the White Mountain leader called Apaq Khoja (originally Afaq Khoja). The connection of the White Mountain line with the rebellions of the nineteenth century is forgotten today. In his own time, and for centuries after his death (1694), Afaq Khoja was revered by the people of Kashgar as the holiest man of his era. Later, he was honored in the *Tazkirah of Sayyid Āfāq Khwāja*.[5] However, for most Uyghurs today, he is a national villain, a schemer who came to power on the coattails of an infidel Mongol army, paved the way for Chinese conquest, and committed countless atrocities. These evil deeds are often imagined in exquisite hyperbole, as when my friend Tursun told me that Afaq killed so many Uyghurs that their flowing blood turned a water wheel.

How could the situation at the White Mountain shrine have come about? How did a saint become a villain and a victim of imperialist conquest become a symbol of interethnic harmony? Several scholars have made important contributions to answering this question.[6] These scholars, along with others studying contemporary Uyghur historiography in general, have given Orientalism (on the part of the Chinese), anticolonial resistance (on the part of the Uyghurs), and/or nationalism (and "competing nationalisms") central explanatory significance in their treatments of Uyghur approaches to the past.[7] Indeed Orientalism, resistance, and nationalism (though of a uniquely Uyghur hue) have played their part. However, all of these analyses do their work without the help of an investigation of Uyghur notions of history, text, place, or personage, concepts that have played decisive roles in forming the curious historical environment that surrounds the White Mountain shrine today. In addition to illuminating the role of the state, the effects of interaction between text, place, and personage, and the nature of the interface between the tazkirah-shrine tradition with other currents of Altishahri historical practice, an analysis of Altishahri historical practice in relation to Afaq Khoja provides new explanations of the strange reception of his shrine today. This unexpected reception is a product not only of nationalism and state interventions in the practice of history but also of the tazkirah-shrine tradition in its interaction with those forces and others.

The Arrival of the White Mountain Sufis

Before examining the reputation of Afaq Khoja, it is worth pausing to recall an important (but by no means the only) source of raw material for this historical tradition: the lived life of Afaq Khoja, the past out of which history has been elaborated. Of course, our access to this past is limited, because it is filtered through local histories whose complexities and biases will become more apparent below. However, across all of the earliest sources some consistencies arise, which, in the eyes of an outsider at least, seem to grant us glimpses of the past, distorted though they may be.

Like most of Altishahr's premodern hero-saints, Afaq Khoja had foreign roots. Though he was born in the oasis of Qumul (*Hami* in Chinese), on Altishahr's traditional border with China, Afaq partly retained the status of a foreigner (in addition to claims of indigeneity), because his father, Muhammad Yūsuf, was born in Dahbid, in the environs of Samarqand.[8] The circumstances of his father's arrival in Altishahr would have profound effects on Afaq's integration into the local historical tradition. Afaq and Muhammad Yūsuf were adepts in the Naqshbandi Sufi path *(tarīqat)*, a very politically active order of mystics who, like many Sufi orders, sought union with God through remembrance of the deity and the study of mystical poetry and recognized an unbroken succession of sanctified leaders linking back to the namesake of the path, Bahā' al-Dīn Naqshband, and ultimately, to the prophet Muhammad. Afaq's father, Muhammad Yūsuf, seems to have believed that he was entitled to succession to the leadership of the *tarīqat,* and when he was thwarted in that goal by the Naqshbandi elites and the temporal rulers of Western Turkestan, he made his way to Altishahr. However, Altishahr already had its own branch of the Naqshbandi path, whose leaders shared an ancestor in Muhammad Yūsuf's grandfather, the Makhdūm al-A'ẓam. Despite their resistance, Muhammad Yūsuf was able to build a powerful following stretching from Gansu to Yarkand, and he even gained the support of the khan of Yarkand, who at that time ruled virtually all of Altishahr. In the end, however, Muhammad Yūsuf was poisoned by his Naqshbandi rivals, and he passed his authority on to his son Afaq Khoja.

The succession of Naqshbandi leaders that Muhammad Yūsuf established in Altishahr eventually came to be known as the White Mountain Khojas, while the rival branch that had arrived in Altishahr one hundred years earlier were called the Black Mountain Khojas. In a departure from the Naqshbandi tradition of Western Turkestan, both Altishahri branches made leadership of their paths hereditary, introducing into Altishahr a new role for genealogy that would surface in the local historical tradition.[9] Once the rivalry between Black and White Mountain lineages was initiated, much of Altishahri society, especially the political elite, was divided by loyalty to one or the other lineage. The influence of the Naqshbandis reached a crescendo in 1679, when Afaq managed to temporarily exile the Black Mountain leaders and install himself as the political ruler of Altishahr. In what would become the most controversial act of his life,

Afaq achieved this seizure of power with the aid of non-Muslim forces: the Dalai Lama and the Dzungar Mongols. Afaq's arrival in Kashgar at the head of a Dzungar Mongol army initiated a period of instability marked by frequent Dzungar domination of Altishahr. Afaq Khoja died in 1694, but for the next sixty-five years, Altishahr saw an endless succession of wars between the White Mountain and Black Mountain leaders, with frequent shifts in alliances to the Dzungars, the real military power in the region. The back-and-forth came to an end when Afaq's old rivals, the Black Mountain Sufis, collaborated with the Qing conquerors in 1757–1759. With their rivals backed by an overwhelmingly strong new infidel power, Qing China, the White Mountain leaders escaped to Western Turkestan (primarily to the Ferghana Valley), from where they would launch invasions and rebellions in Qing-controlled Altishahr throughout the nineteenth century.

In some respects, the activities of Afaq and his father made excellent raw material for the tazkirah tradition. For one, both saints made enormous investments in their own personal, individual reputations. During extensive travels in Altishahr, Kokonur, and China, Afaq built up the White Mountain following by crafting his own reputation, through charismatic preaching and the performance of miracles. Attachment to one or the other of the Naqshbandi orders in Altishahr was not a question of doctrine, but rather of personal loyalty, characterized by a belief in the supreme holiness of the order's leader. When he died in 1694, Afaq had both enemies and supporters in large numbers, but whatever people thought of him, Afaq's personage was firmly planted in the Altishahri understanding of the past. The former "axis of axes" had become a fulcrum of historical meaning, around which overlapping and competing narratives could turn. A significant segment of Altishahr's past would henceforth be understood in terms of the sacred and political status of the personage known as Afaq Khoja. The attention that both Muhammad Yūsuf and Afaq paid to their shared tomb, including the procurement of a sufficiently rich sacred endowment, was also important to the tazkirah tradition, for obvious reasons. So were their origins in foreign lands, their claims to bringing religious purity, and their death in Altishahr. A widely recognized personage, a wealthy tomb, and a story of naturalization by death cried out for treatment in Altishahr's popular tazkirah form.

However, in other respects, Afaq's Naqshbandi politicoreligious order in Altishahr made difficult source material for the tazkirah-shrine tradition that was beginning to emerge in the decades after the saint's death.

First, the earliest literature to glorify Afaq was designed to perpetuate his reputation as a Naqshbandi, and followed hagiographical genre norms that came with the Naqshbandis from Western Turkestan. Second, Afaq's reputation threatened to bring the state into the tazkirah. The acts of recording or learning the details of Afaq's life had political ramifications, for his descendants continued to vie for supreme political power. Meanwhile, the tazkirah tradition was growing up, instead, around saints who were either outside the state (e.g., the Seven Muhammads) or had been incorporated long after their political rule (e.g., Satūq Bughrā-khān). The typical distance of the tazkirah from the state may have even helped the genre to flourish under the volatile periods of Naqshbandi dominance and subsequent Qing indirect rule. Finally, the importance of genealogy to the Naqshbandis made for an awkward fit with the tazkirahs' vision of originary saints without descendants. Despite these challenges, by beginning of the twentieth century the tazkirah-shrine system seems to have co-opted the shrine and reputation of Afaq, though never to the same extent as it had earlier saints. The larger White Mountain Naqshbandi tradition met its own obstacles, most notably the opposition of Altishahr's Qing rulers, and this may have provided the space for the tazkirah tradition to slowly make inroads into the history of Afaq Khoja. Ironically, the tazkirah tradition finally overtook the reputation of Afaq at a time when the state had become thoroughly invested in the saint's history again. In 2000 a biographical novel, fully permeated by the influence of the tazkirah and entitled *Apaq Khoja,* was published by the state's flagship Xinjiang press, and in the following year it was publicly burned by the Chinese state.[10]

Becoming History

Long before Afaq became a part of the popular tazkirah-shrine tradition, which was only just emerging at his death, he was embraced by other historical traditions. Thus, when the tazkirah tradition began to dominate Afaq's reputation, probably in the nineteenth century, it encountered an already-dense entanglement of divergent historical appropriations of the saint. These began in Afaq's own lifetime in forms now lost to us: gossip, legal documents, letters, and followers' stories about the great teacher. When Afaq Khoja died of natural causes in 1694, his personage immediately became a locus of more consciously historical practice. Both his followers and his enemies retained memories of his actions, either witnessed or reported. Those memories were the product of experiences, and the lived experiences of Afaq Khoja must have been remarkably diverse and profound. They included enlightenment and inspiration, sudden conversions that turned scoffers into followers, and moving religious experiences that brought followers closer to God. Some were awestruck in the presence of a man they believed to be the holiest person alive, the "axis of axes." Meanwhile others experienced Afaq Khoja's deeds through their economic and political ramifications, whether through sudden enrichment via the empowerment of a certain faction of nobles, or through starvation, death, and loss in the wars that Afaq prosecuted. A small circle had more intimate experiences with Afaq as father, son, or husband. However, all of this diversity of experience would soon be distilled into a narrow range of flattened representations, dry manipulations of the past for the goals of the future, goals that only demanded interest in a tiny range of experiences.

Afaq's followers made early use of their experiences with the master, before and after his death. Naqshbandi traditions throughout Central Asia had long placed great stock in the words and deeds of the leader (pīr) of the order. This we know from the numerous books, entitled maqāmāt or manāqib, that preserve such tales of deceased saints as an example to followers (murid).[11] Since so much Naqshbandi learning revolved around the sayings and deeds of former leaders, it is likely that Afaq's followers often told each other stories about their deceased master. Some memories presumably formed the seeds of an oral tradition, for the later, popular Tazkirah of Sayyid Āfāq Khwāja contains much material with the hallmarks of oral transmission. Memories of Afaq would also eventually make their way into written histories that were composed by survivors of Afaq's era, one composed two years after his death, another within twenty years, and a third about thirty-six years after Afaq's death.[12] It is not unlikely that short poems commemorating his death also circulated among Afaq's literate followers, as had happened in the case of Afaq's great grandfather.[13]

The earliest surviving physical recording of Afaq's life and death, however, was the elaboration of the shrine complex that would hold his body at the same site where his father was already buried. According to Afaq's tazkirah, toward the end of his own life Afaq ordered the construction of a large domed structure to cover his and his father's graves. This act was itself a historical practice, recording the presence of the saint in the body-sized grave marker, expounding upon his power through the size of the structure, and upon his holiness through the minaret-like towers at the corners of the tomb. The shrine also attracted further historical practices, particularly pilgrimage, which was a part of both the Central Asian Naqshbandi tradition and the broader Altishahri culture.

In its early days, when Muhammad Yūsuf was the only occupant, the White Mountain shrine would have attracted mostly followers of the White Mountain order. That audience grew as Muhammad Yūsuf's son Afaq traveled throughout Altishahr, Gansu, and Tibet, seeking followers.[14] With Afaq's ascent to political power, and his transfer of Altishahr's capital from Yarkand to Kashgar, the influence of the White Mountain order in the environs of the shrine became pervasive. By the time of Afaq's death in 1694, most of Kashgar's population was loyal to the White Mountain Sufi lineage. Though Afaq and his father brought with them traditions from Western Turkestan, the ordinary Kashgaris they won over brought Altishahri customs of shrine veneration with them to the White Mountain tomb, eventually bringing Afaq into the popular tazkirah tradition.

However, Afaq appeared in a written text very quickly after his death, before the Altishahri popular tazkirah genre had fully emerged. Around the first half of the year 1696, an anonymous author wrote a Persian-style dynastic history, known today as the *Chinggiznamă*, documenting the fate of the ruling dynasty of Yarkand, which traced its origins to Genghis Khan.[15] True to its generic roots, this work subordinates Afaq's story to the narrative of the Chinggisid khans. Though Afaq had stolen power from the Chinggisid khans, he also quickly renounced any official political role, and maintained puppet khans for much of his rule, as did several of his successors. As a typical dynastic history, the *Chinggiznamă* uses dynastic time rooted in the succession of rulers, and the account of Afaq's rule is thus spread across subsections named after his puppet khans, namely the sections called "The Accession of 'Abd al-Rashīd Khān to the Throne of Yarkand" and "The Accession of Muhammad Īmīn Khān, Son of Bābākhān."[16] Another dynastic chronicle, by a Black Mountain devotee, Shāh Mahmūd Churās, shows its bias by largely omitting Afaq from the historical record.

Despite its claim to chronological precedence, however, the chronicle is an outlier among the written artifacts of Afaq's early historical tradition. Most of the texts written by contemporaries of Afaq were rooted in the conventions of the *maqāmāt,* or *manāqib,* a genre that had entered Altishahr from Western Turkestan along with the Naqshbandi Khojas of both Black and White Mountain lineages. These texts were, in effect, byproducts of the mystical tradition that Afaq himself spread, tailored to the needs of Afaq's followers or enemies. Instruction for devotees was an important function of the *maqāmāt/manāqib* genre. Unlike the popular tazkirah genre, which often painted a caricatured superhuman saint from the distant past for purposes of veneration, the *maqāmāt/manāqib* works relied on the first-person voice of a devotee who relayed personal recollections or secondhand eyewitness reports of more ordinary occurrences. The works document mystically significant teachings and less bombastic miracles, all for the education of the devotee.

While they share a single genre, the two clearly dated *maqāmāt/manāqib* histories of Afaq promote starkly differing views of the saint. The earlier text is the *Companion of the Seekers (Anīs al-Ṭālibīn)*, written by a Black Mountain partisan during the Black Mountain Khoja Dāniyāl's first period of ascendance (ca. 1695–1713). Although the main purpose of the work is to promote the genealogy, deeds, and sayings of important Black Mountain saints, the constant competition between the Naqshbandi sects required some mention of Afaq. The author's loyalties show plainly, and Afaq, as the most prominent leader of the rival White Mountain sect, is reviled as an "impostor and traitor of heaven,"[17] bringing explicit anti-Afaq views into the written historical record for the first time.[18] The other early *maqāmāt/manāqib* work is the *Hidāyatnāmah (Book of Hidāyat*, referring to Afaq Khoja's birth name, Hidāyatallah), of 1729–1730, which, in the fifth chapter *(bāb)* refers to itself as *maqāmāt*. The author, a White Mountain devotee, was dedicated to preserving Afaq's deeds and sayings as instruction for future followers. The *Book of Hidāyat* contains extensive accounts of Afaq's teachings, including sections on abstract theological themes such as love, perfection, and the permissibility of ecstatic dance. Another, derivative, White Mountain *maqāmāt/manāqib* appeared soon after.[19] None of the *maqāmāt/manāqib* artifacts of Afaq's life mentioned so far ever achieved that most basic indicator and enabler of popular participation: translation into the vernacular. Yet if the Persian language, the lingua franca of Central Asia, Muslim India, and Iran, was a barrier to popular Altishahri participation, it also permitted a wider, transregional reputation for Afaq.

Domesticating an International Saint

Unlike most Altishahri saints, Afaq became something of a transregional and transcultural hero after his death. The frequent and sudden swings in power between Naqshbandi politicoreligious factions often resulted in migrations of thousands of White Mountain followers to Badakhshan, India, and the Ferghana Valley. The first of these migrations to result in a longstanding community took place shortly after the death of Afaq Khoja's widow in 1695, when his youngest son Khoja Hasan fled to India and then the Ferghana Valley. The community that Hasan established remained in contact with Altishahr, and was occasionally supplemented by further exiles, most notably the large number of White Mountain refugees who resulted from the Qing conquest. Hagiographical accounts of Afaq and Hasan thus found a readership in the Ferghana Valley's White Mountain community through at least the nineteenth century.[20] To the east of Altishahr, in China proper, Afaq left behind communities of believers in Qinghai and Gansu, where both Afaq and his father had preached widely among Chinese Muslims and the Salars.

Afaq's international linkages, forged both before his birth and after his death, made their mark on the literature that grew up around his reputation. After his death, Afaq's reputation began to separate into three distinct traditions. One was the *maqāmāt/manāqib* tradition, patronized by the White Mountain communities of both Altishahr and Western Turkestan.[21] Another survived among the Chinese Muslim Naqshbandi branch that Afaq had founded in Gansu.[22] A third historical tradition flourished within Altishahr alone, where a hagiographical text was shaped to fit the local tazkirah-shrine tradition. Here I will focus on the first and third of these traditions, describing Afaq's transregional reputation as a Naqshbandi saint before going on to show how Afaq was transformed into a local through the tazkirah-shrine tradition.[23]

The White and Black Mountain orders created communities through genealogy, both physical and spiritual, which, through travel, enmeshed several cultural regions, and thus held out the prospect of a closely interconnected community straddling Altishahr and the Ferghana valley. The scope of this interconnection was limited considerably by the Qing conquest of 1759, which created a fixed border between the two regions that has survived down to the present. However, on either side of that border, some White Mountain followers continued to read the same works, namely the White Mountain *maqāmāt/manāqib* texts described above. In Western Turkestan, Afaqi texts largely continued the seventeenth-century Naqshbandi approach to understanding saintly forbears, an approach well suited to the continued White Mountain Sufi practices and politicoreligious organization that survived in the Ferghana Valley through the nineteenth century. The two White Mountain *maqāmāt/manāqib* works discussed above were the main texts available, though even they were copied in small numbers. Despite the state suppression of White Mountain activities in Altishahr, the White Mountain community maintained contact across the border. Even in Altishahr, the Persian *maqāmāt/ manāqib* works continued to be copied in small numbers.

It was the tazkirah in its popular Altishahri form that would come to dominate the Altishahri textual imagination of Afaq Khoja in the nineteenth and early twentieth centuries and finally naturalize the saint as a uniquely Altishahri personage. The most commonly encountered account of Afaq Khoja among Altishahri manuscripts is a Turki book that goes under several titles, all translated and adapted from a Persian-language text entitled *Lives of the Loyal (Siyar al-Mukhliṣīn)*. The *Lives of the Loyal,* written by a follower of the White Mountain Khoja line, Ibn ʿAlī Khvājah Akhūnd, is known from two Altishahri copies.[24] It narrates the biography of Muhammad Yūsuf, his son Afaq, and Afaq's son Hasan in succession, with a focus on their miracles and great deeds. The work begins with an introduction copied wholesale from an earlier *maqāmāt* text, but in a distinct departure from the *maqāmāt/manāqib* tradition, it includes virtually no reporting of the words and wisdom of the saints. By the end of the nineteenth century, the *Lives of the Loyal* had been translated into the vernacular and renamed as a tazkirah. In the translated copies, the *maqāmāt* introduction is omitted. The record of Afaq's ancestry has been altered to include the first eleven of the Twelve Shiʾite Imams, a genealogical preference common to many Altishahri popular tazkirahs. Some copies are abbreviated, always maintaining the section on the work's most famous subject, Afaq Khoja.[25] The transformation of the *Lives of the Loyal* into a popular Altishahri tazkirah, a text suitable for connection to the tomb of Afaq and the practices of pilgrimage, is visible in the titles that copyists gave to the Turki version, such as the *Tazkirah of Sayyid Afaq Khojam*.[26] Indeed, all of the titles found on Altishahri copies of the popular Turki version include some form of the word *tazkirah*, and all of them name the book after Afaq (or by his formal name, Hidāyatallah), despite the equal space devoted to his father and his son in the original Persian work.[27] The history of the first three generations of the White Mountain leadership had been transformed in the minds of readers and copyists into a tazkirah of Afaq Khoja.

The Shrine Co-opts a Reputation

The tazkirah tradition's inroads into the Afaqi tradition probably would not have been so extensive were it not for the simultaneous accretion of typical Altishahri shrine activities and resonances to the tomb of the White Mountain Khojas. Though Afaq and his father brought with them traditions from Western Turkestan, the ordinary Kashgaris they won over brought their own Altishahri forms of shrine veneration to the tomb of the White Mountain Khojas. According to Afaq's tazkirah, the shrine was founded upon the death of his father, Muhammad Yūsuf, on a nameless plot of Kashgar farmland that had been donated by a follower.[28] In the ensuing decades many of Afaq's successors were buried there, and local notables reserved places for their own tombs as near as possible to the saints. Over the following centuries, through the continuing sacred presence of these saints and the localization of history at their graves, that nameless plot of land was made permanently meaningful, a reality even the Chinese state has come to embrace. Eventually the fame of the shrine advanced beyond the circle of White Mountain devotees, and the tomb became a major site of pilgrimage in the popular Altishahri tradition.

The earliest evidence of the White Mountain tomb's integration into local shrine traditions is its incorporation into pilgrimage circuits that included popular local saints unconnected to the Naqshbandi tradition. In the first quarter of the eighteenth century, two famous Sufi poets placed the tomb of Afaq on their pilgrimage itineraries alongside Yarkand's popular tomb of the Seven Muhammads.[29] One of these pilgrims, Muhammad Zalīlī, also linked Afaq's shrine to several other popular saints of Kashgar, Yarkand, and Khotan.[30] Zalīlī's mention of flags and banners (tugh-'alam) at the White Mountain tomb also resonates with popular Altishahri shrine practices. There is more evidence regarding such practices from the late nineteenth century, when European visitors began to arrive, by which time the White Mountain tomb seems to have become a typical Altishahri shrine. One important change was the reconceptualization of the White Mountain family shrine as an individual's shrine. Altishahris began to associate the tomb with the prominent personage of Afaq Khoja, whose careful reputation building had accrued lasting fame to himself, over and above his politicoreligious movement. Thus, the shrine was widely known as the Tomb of Afaq Khoja by the late nineteenth century.[31]

In the early twentieth century the shrine saw the kinds of enormous gatherings that have been described for other popular shrines in Altishahr.

The skeptical C. P. Skrine wrote that "Hazrat Afaq is really a kind of coun-try club for Kashgar; the *tawwuf* [sic] or 'circling' of the shrines is sup-posed to be performed by every visitor, but the famous apricots and mel-ons of Besh Karim are the real attraction rather than the exhortations of the mullahs."[32] While Skrine was clearly indulging in either exaggeration or extraordinary cynicism, his account is tame compared to the memoir of Ahmet Kemal, the Ottoman reformist. Describing his 1914–1917 stay in Kashgar, Kemal wrote that people performed the same practices at Afaq Khoja as at other Kashgar shrines, such as those of ʿAlī Arslān-khān, Bībī Maryām, and Quṭbullah, including "rubbing the face on sheep horns . . . and on cow tails."[33] He also complained about the "pleasure and ease and debauchery" at the gathering for the Barat vigil, during which he claimed "Afaq Khoja's so-called ʿÜzümlük' garden is a field of squalor. In the center of the garden, masses of people with open shirts gamble. In the four cor-ners of the garden, around kindled fires, drug addicts smoke until morn-ing."[34] Kemal's screed is a typical expression of reformist distaste for shrine practices, but, like Skrine's cynical comments, it reflects the well-known role of the shrine as a site of entertainment in Altishahr. Both authors were reacting to the mixing of leisure and devotion in large fair-like gatherings *(sayla)* at the tomb, a phenomenon that reflected the full incorporation of Afaq's shrine into the local Altishahri traditions of pilgrimage. By trans-forming the White Mountain lineage's tomb complex into the tomb of Afaq Khoja and recasting the *Lives of the Loyal* as the *Tazkirah of Afaq Khoja*, an image emerged of Afaq as an Altishahri saint, an individual of supernatural potency, who possessed a special connection to Kashgar, and, via the pilgrimage routes, to much of the rest of Altishahr.

The Manuscript Tradition and the Afaq Tazkirahs

Compared to other popular tazkirahs, the Afaq Khoja tazkirahs were not copied in such large numbers, limiting our access to the popular written-oral tradition of which the manuscripts are artifacts. The somewhat small number of specimens of the Turki translation also leaves us few clues about how this particular group of works was used, and thus how it was transformed from the *Lives of the Loyal* to the *Tazkirah of Sayyid Afaq Khojam*. Though at least eleven copies have come down to us, two of those were copied at the request of Swedish visitors,[35] and most of the remaining copies were collected within a few years of their copying, leav-ing little time for the accumulation of marginalia. Nonetheless, those copies that have survived give hints of complex textual histories that match quite neatly with the patterns of manuscript technology described earlier. Afaq (d. 1694) is among the most recent of the popularly venerated saints in Altishahr, but the forces of community authorship in the manuscript tradition had already reshaped his tazkirah by the early twentieth century. Among the surviving Afaq tazkirah copies we find several unusually strong expressions of the copyists' power to reshape texts.

As is typical for popular Altishahri literature, the Turki version of Afaq's tazkirah tells us nothing about its author, who, as a mere conduit for transmission, is not considered worthy of mention. In this particular case, however, the authorial silence was imposed by the translator. In the Persian original *(Lives of the Loyal),* the author, who called himself Ibn 'Alī, reported a dream in which he was told the title of his work, thus establishing his role as a transmitter of knowledge from the realm of the unseen. The translator excised this information entirely, along with the title and the name of the author. The resulting text is more extreme in its disavowal of authorship than most works in that it provides absolutely no introduction, nor, in most copies, even formulaic statements of origin. At least one copyist addressed this deficit himself, expressing the popular predilection for authoritative transmission by adding phrases such as "the historians say that . . ." to his copy of the book.[36]

Though marginalia are few in the surviving Afaq tazkirahs, the colophons are particularly rich. The author did not invite readers to emend the book, but again, in a bold demonstration of the power of the scribe, a copyist has taken this normally authorial role upon himself. In verses appended after the final *tamām* (finished), the copyist recorded his name and the following message:

> If there are many mistakes in my writing forgive me,
> If, reading, it is full of errors, erase them.

> Do not make faults; in my writing faults are plenty,
> When reading, don't forget [to say] a prayer.

This is, to my knowledge, the only appearance in Altishahri literature of an acknowledgment that future copyists or readers might introduce errors, in addition to correcting the text. More typical are the copyist's expressions of the feebleness of the human conduit of historical transmission and the sacredness of reading.

The copyist's invitation to change the text of an author he likely never met is striking, yet nothing could demonstrate the power of the copyist more than the fact that these verses of his were included, with some alterations, in at least two other copies of the Afaq tazkirah. It's not possible to know what copyist was first responsible for these verses, but two of them inserted their own names into the verse, a certain Mullah Qurbān Kāshgharī in 1888 and a Ḥakīm Jān in 1918–1919.[37] Perhaps both were repeating an earlier copyist's poetry. Despite some changes, certain verses remained unaltered from one manuscript to the next, displaying that aspect of the manuscript most foreign to the print world, namely, that the textual additions of an individual, when they are seen as appropriate by the community, can multiply and become a part of further specimens of the book. This phenomenon even extended to highly specific information about the act of copying, as can be seen in a group of Afaq manuscripts that retained the same copyist's name. A manuscript from the India Office Library says that Muhammad ʿAlī completed it in 1893 "at His Holiness Sayyid Afaq Khoja's tomb."[38] Another scribe later copied this colophon, including both the copyist's name, Muhammad ʿAlī, and the record of copying at the shrine, while changing the date.[39] Here the authority that seems to have accrued to a manuscript copied at the shrine may have encouraged the appropriation of the copyist's colophon in further specimens.

The narrative contents of the manuscripts of the Afaq tazkirah show a typical variability nurtured by the flexibility of the manuscript tradition, variability with rather strong repercussions for the reputation of the saint himself and for the role of the text. A copy in the Jarring collection (Prov. 369), for example, contains two stories about Afaq that show him as dangerously vengeful, stories that are missing from other copies in Lund, Berlin, and the India Office Library.[40] In one of these stories a five-year-old Afaq kills children who mock his outsider status and in another, he miraculously sends a piece of wood flying through the air from Kashgar to kill the king of Dahbid, who had exiled his father. These are the only two vengeful acts in the catalog of Afaq's miracles, and they are absent from most manuscripts of his tazkirah. By omitting the vengeance tales, the majority of Afaq tazkirah manuscripts present a more magnanimous view of the saint. Another example of copyist influence is found in two copies in the Jarring collection that share a similar abbreviation, cutting out the long section on Afaq's son Hasan, a third of the book in most copies, and ending instead with the death of Afaq.[41] This abbreviation effectively brought the text closer to the culture of shrine veneration, for, as we have seen, by the late nineteenth century, the shrine of the White Mountain Khoja family began to be seen as the shrine of

Afaq Khoja in particular. Another manuscript, Jarring's Prov. 22, accommodated shrine culture by introducing a phrase encouraging the burning of lamps as an offering.[42]

The copyist was not, of course, the only extra-authorial influence on the text, for hallmarks of the oral tradition are scattered throughout the tazkirah. The recentness of the events in the text reminds us of the continuously active role of oral narratives in Altishahri historical practice. Under the influence of scholars such as Walter Ong, who suggested a teleological pattern of progress from oral to written technologies, it would be easy to assume that oral material in the tazkirahs survived from some time before the widespread use of writing, only to be reshaped into written versions much later. However, in the Afaq tazkirah we have a text with strong oral tendencies that was produced during an era in which written texts were quite normal. It may be that unwritten forerunners of the Afaq tazkirah did precede its earliest written manifestations, but even those oral tales would have been created in a time of extensive book use, and indeed after the *Hidayatname* (1729–1730) had already captured many of the events of Afaq and his son Hasan's lives in writing. It is also possible that the text was first created in written form, but its author had absorbed stylistic influences from the oral tradition, or even that some of the oral influences accreted to the text later.

In most senses, the transformation of the Afaq tazkirah through the first decades of the twentieth century followed the patterns seen in other popular tazkirahs. The shrine-tazkirah tradition was well on its way to fully co-opting Afaq's reputation. Yet Afaq Khwaja's death had not occurred so long ago, and his reputation had not been molded by the tazkirah tradition as long as other saints' personages had. The earthly Afaq's religious and political programs were not, as far as we can tell, centered on the discovery or patronage of the shrines scattered across Altishahr,[43] as Muhammad Sharīf's had been. Afaq seems to have cultivated followers through preaching, the display of miracles, the biweekly teaching of Sufi principles from further West,[44] a claim to inherited spiritual authority, political maneuvers, and military campaigns. The Afaq tazkirahs still bear traces of the Naqshbandi tradition that Afaq had promoted during his lifetime. To begin with, the subject of the Afaq tazkirah, in its most extensive versions, is properly the White Mountain lineage, including Muhammad Yūsuf, his son Afaq, and Afaq's son Hasan. Copyists deemphasized this to some extent by renaming the *Lives of the Loyal* as the *Tazkirah of Sayyid Āfāq Khwāja,* but in most copies, the stories of Afaq's father and son remained as a testament to the genealogically focused order they led. The concern for genealogy, especially continuing genealogy, also led to an otherwise unusual (for Altishahr) genealogical linking of past and present. Thus, the tazkirah says of the deputies of Hasan Khoja that "their descendants exist now today,"[45] a claim of descent absent from other Altishahri tazkirahs. At the same time, it's worth remembering that few of Altishahr's tazkirahs were originally written specifically for the tazkirah-shrine tradition, so these traces are not really so unusual. The tazkirahs derived from biographical dictionary entries retain aspects of that genre, and the tazkirahs derived from oral epics retain elements of the epic tradition. It's also fitting that Afaq's tazkirah mentions the descendents of his son's companions and deputies rather than his own descendants. Even in the face of the Altishahri Naqshbandi emphasis on saintly genealogy, the tazkirah describes a lineage that ends with a saint, leaving the community to build itself around tombs instead of living descendants. The presence of living people claiming descent from Afaq, which is documented elsewhere, does not seem to have made a mark on the tazkirah.[46]

There is, however, one way in which the Afaq tazkirah departs from the shrine-tazkirah tradition unexpectedly: none of the copies I have traced were bound together with other tazkirahs.[47] While there is no way to know for sure why Afaq's written reputation managed to hold out against the co-opting pressure of the tazkirah tradition in this one regard, an explanation may lie in the factional competition between the Black and White Mountain orders. Among Altishahr's saints, the Black and White Mountain Khojas are exceptional for promoting exclusive, rather than inclusive, claims to sanctity. From Afaq's time down to the Qing conquest, devotees of Afaq were in open competition, often war, with the Black Mountain order and its supporters. According to the Afaq tazkirah, Afaq, his father Muhammad Yūsuf, and his son Hasan were all poisoned by Black Mountain Sufis. A devotee of Afaq was expected to be an opponent of the Black Mountain Khojas, and a Black Mountain devotee was an enemy of Afaq's followers. This was quite different from the world of saint veneration that was growing at the same time through the tazkirahs, wherein the tombs of several saints could be linked through a single pilgrimage (such as the one Zalīlī documented), and the tazkirahs of several saints could be bound together—usually saints with very different cultural, linguistic, and genealogical backgrounds.

The exclusivity claimed by the Naqshbandi saints seems to be a result of the attachment of saintly sanctity to explicit claims on political power, in particular, sovereignty. The pursuit of power is by nature a search for exclusive rights, and the exclusive rights that the Khojas claimed as sovereigns were mirrored in their exclusive claims to veneration. This connection is clear in the White Mountain invasions of the nineteenth century, which often began with a pilgrimage to the tomb of Afaq Khoja, and grew in strength as the masses of ordinary White Mountain devotees revolted in support of the invaders. It is no surprise, then, to find that the Afaqi tazkirahs are never bound alongside texts of the Black Mountain tradition. Nonetheless, it is still startling that the Afaqi tazkirahs I have traced were not bound together with any other hagiographical works at all. It hardly seems possible that Afaqi claims on exclusivity even prevented their tazkirahs from being bound together with such universally revered figures as Satūq Bughrā-khān.

The tazkirah's unfinished embrace of Afaq prevented the full range of the tazkirah-shrine tradition's repercussions from playing out in regard to this particular saint. The fact that Afaq's tazkirah was not bound with others limited its potential as material for building the shared identity described earlier. In this sense, the claims to exclusive legitimacy inherent in the local Naqshbandi tradition may have prevented Afaq's reputation from contributing to the maintenance of Altishahri identity through the tazkirah system. However, there is no reason to think that people could not see themselves as both White Mountain followers and Altishahris (musulmān in the restrictive, local sense). The numerous White and Black Mountain partisan texts, despite their rancor against the opposing group, never excluded their Altishahri enemies from the category of musulmān in the same way they excluded the Kirghiz. As it stood in the early twentieth century, the tazkirah of Afaq straddled the two traditions, local Naqshbandi and tazkirah-shrine, permitting the partial operation of both systems, but the complete or ideal operation of neither. The hybrid nature of Afaq's reputation in his tazkirah will explain some of the strange things that have happened to this personage in recent years. First, however, we must examine the influence of a younger tradition, which overtook Afaq's reputation, at least in the written form, beginning in the 1930s: nationalism.

The Encounter between Afaq Khoja and Nationalism

The earliest nationalist histories of Afaq Khoja applied the logic of nationalist thought to elements of the Naqshbandi tradition, initially bypassing the tazkirah tradition entirely. For nationalist authors trying to reshape the modular, un-named, uneven Altishahri identity into a new "Uyghur" nation, Afaq Khoja's collaboration with non-Altishahri, non-Muslim, non-Turk forces (the Dzunghar Mongols) in the conquest of Altishahr must have seemed an obvious act of treachery. It was not presented as such in Afaq's popular tazkirah. The non-Naqshbandi hagiographies of Altishahr clearly treated all Muslim figures as heroes, saving the role of villain for the infidel. Afaq's cooperation with infidel forces did not, in and of itself, raise a challenge to the saint's holiness. Rather, the tazkirah tells that Afaq demonstrated his power and holiness by defeating the Dalai Lama in a contest of magical or miraculous powers and that the Dalai Lama, having been thus mastered, agreed to call his followers, the Dzungar Mongols, to Afaq's aid. Afaq's Dzungar-assisted rise to political power is thus presented as a sign of his strength and righteousness. The fact that Altishahr effectively became a Dzungar dependency for the next seventy years is not mentioned.

It is easy for us, in our nation-dominated present, to understand how nationalists would have seen the issue differently. The nationalist logic linking identity and polity is strong enough that one might even expect the early Uyghur nationalist historians to arrive at an innovatively jaundiced view of Afaq on their own. However, such creative analysis was not necessary. The preexisting Naqshbandi tradition provided a clear path to the anti-Afaq view that nationalist writers developed. The Altishahri form of the Naqshbandi tradition was to a large extent influenced by the actual deeds of Afaq and his father, such that in this case Afaq's lived past played a role in determining the nature of the later Uyghur embrace of that past. The antagonistic factionalism of the Naqshbandi tradition in Altishahr, stoked by Muhammad Yūsuf and perpetuated by his son Afaq, provided something that the usual popular tazkirahs did not: negative views of the saint. White Mountain followers in Altishahr had their *maqāmāts, manāqibs,* and tazkirahs of Afaq, but Black Mountain followers created their own texts. We have seen that an early Black Mountain text, *Anis al-Ṭalibīn,* called Afaq an "impostor." A later Black Mountain text, *Tazkirah-i 'Azīzān,* treats Afaq differently in different copies. Some copies take a neutral tone while noting that Afaq came to power with the aid of an infidel army. One version is explicitly negative, reporting the transfer of power to Afaq thus:

Afaq Khoja said, 'If you make me master I will take and give you one hundred thousand *tenga*s from these cities.' The Qalmaqs[48] accepted his words and made Afaq Khoja master and returned. Until this time this country *(yürt)* has been giving one hundred thousand *tenga*s. Afaq Khoja invented this evil *(bad)* thing.⁴⁹

Such texts show that disparaging views of Afaq did circulate, perhaps primarily among Black Mountain followers, and provided a precedent for nationalist authors' accusations against Afaq long before the emergence of nationalist thought.

The logic of nationalism made the Black Mountain attacks on Afaq particularly attractive. The claim that Afaq subjected Altishahr to outside rule has a special resonance with one of the central characteristics of nationalism, the notion that the nation should align with the state, that only members of the nation, accepted by the nation, may legitimately rule the nation. By contrast, the earlier, nonnationalist Altishahri tradition of saint veneration easily accommodated foreign conquerors as heroes within the tazkirah system, such as the armies of the Four Imams or those of Muhammad Ghazālī, not to mention Afaq Khoja's Dzunghar army.⁵⁰ But the logic of nationalism meant that the outside rule brought by Afaq Khoja made the saint a traitor, and the negative view of Afaq would thus grow throughout the twentieth century alongside nationalism, eventually displacing the widespread popular veneration that was evidenced at his tomb.

Nationalist interest in Afaq Khoja can be traced to the very roots of Uyghur nationalism, and was maintained in succeeding nationalist histories written throughout the twentieth century. 'Abd al-Ṣamad Oghli, whose adoption in 1911 of the pen name Child of the Uyghur *(Uyghur ballisi)* represents perhaps the earliest-known modern usage of the Uyghur ethnonym, believed that a "national history for all the Uyghurs" was necessary for the success of the nation. To this end he published his *History of the Taranchis,* which presents Afaq's historical role in a matter-of-fact tone, but with unmistakable implications. According to 'Abd al-Ṣamad Oghli, Afaq's alliance with the Dzunghars was the end of an "independent Altishahr."⁵¹ In 1933 the newspaper of the nationalist state of East Turkestan took a similar attitude in its serial "Our History," writing that "Afaq's side was victorious and the khan was defeated and Yarkand, the capital of Altishahr, went over to the side of the Mongols and Afaq, and the Chinggisid country of independent East Turkestan, which had lasted continuously for 400 years, came to an end."⁵² This evaluation of Afaq's significance was repeated again in 1946 in *The History of East*

Turkestan, written by Muhammad Amīn Bughrā and published in Kashmir during his exile.[53] Bughrā credited Afaq Khoja with bringing about the end of the *Sa'idiya* (a term for the Moghul Yarkand khanate) "nation" *(milli dölăt).* After moving to Turkey, Bughrā ratcheted up the anti-Afaq rhetoric, calling Afaq's followers "traitorous" in an updated version of his history.[54] The appearance of the word *independence* in these works is a new phenomenon in Altishahri history, which highlights the concern for aligning state and identity. It was this notion that turned Afaq's invasion from an act of greatness to an act of national betrayal.

That turn was made easier by the social decontextualization that accompanied history's entrance into the world of print. Afaq's tazkirah and the rival Black Mountain historical texts were imbedded in their own social systems. There is no space here to analyze the Black Mountain tradition, but we can note that Afaq's tazkirah was firmly attached to place. It was copied and presumably read at Afaq's shrine, and it was associated with Afaq's historical power base of Kashgar, just as other tazkirahs were associated with the oases in which their saints were buried. In a work shaped to be copied or read at the grave of its saint, namely, in the very real and continuing presence of that saint, it would have been inconceivable to denigrate the holy figure. The newspaper, which probably enjoyed a wider readership in Altishahr than the other nationalist works mentioned here, tore Afaq's reputation away from the tomb context and from other social contexts, including the dwindling Black Mountain Sufi order that had nurtured anti-Afaq sentiment since the eighteenth century. It could only have helped that the genre that impugned this holy man, the newspaper, was desacralized, produced in mechanical print rather than hallowed calligraphy, lacking the *bismillah,* and made of impermanent material. Without the participation of the scribal class and readership in the continued reproduction of the text, the widespread veneration for Afaq in the very city where the newspaper was printed could not leave its mark on the new text. Where the meaning of Afaq's personage had previously been negotiated around the pivots of his shrine and his tazkirah, it was now influenced by the producer-dominated medium of print. The change in textual technology represented by the newspaper was the perfect vehicle for a change in the reputation of Afaq.

After Bughrā's book, nationalist views of Afaq disappear temporarily from Altishahr's historical record, as the People's Republic of China annexed the region and established its strict control over publication. Even ignoring the obvious problems faced by an ideology based on Uyghur independence, all potential authors faced a censorship regime that was extremely hostile to anything that could be considered ethnic "chauvinism."[55] In any case, restrictions on publication were so severe that almost no history at all was produced in the Uyghur language until the 1980s. The Afaq tazkirah also receded from prominence under the People's Republic. The last known copy was made for a Swedish missionary in 1929. At the same time, worship at the Afaq Khoja shrine was restricted and, during the Cultural Revolution, brought almost to a complete halt. At a moment when neither nationalist nor tazkirah-driven imaginations of Afaq Khoja had completely won out, Uyghur historical writing was put on hold.

The story told so far suggests a rough schematic division of historical approaches into local Naqshbandi, popular tazkirah-shrine, and nationalist traditions, but it also demonstrates that the borders between these systems were never entirely clear, that they interacted and fed off each other, and that an idealized description of any one of these strains is misleading without an investigation of how it articulated with competing approaches. The present study has devoted much of its space to the tazkirah-shrine tradition, because that tradition explains so much of what has previously seemed mysterious about Uyghur approaches to the past. However, the case study of Afaq Khoja shows how that tradition plays out when it is not operating in an idealized or stereotypical form, and emphasizes its influence on, and influence by, other ways of doing history. Indeed all three of these strains of history making have influenced the current politicohistorical discourse in Xinjiang. After a lull following the arrival of PRC rule, all three returned with renewed power at the turn of the twenty-first century and created new forms in interaction with the state, taking the Uyghurs' new Chinese rulers by surprise.

The Recent Fate of Afaq and His Shrine: State Appropriation

Afaq Khoja seems to have drawn the attention of China's new Communist rulers in the same way that he attracted the local tazkirah tradition: through the family mausoleum that he founded. The state began redistributing the shrine's extensive *waqf* landholdings in 1953.[56] The shrine itself, however, seems to have been respected during the PRC's initial toleration for local religious practices, and the government was actually responsible for repairing the dome in 1956.[57] Like so many other cultural phenomena, Afaq and his shrine disappear from the historian's view during the Great Proletarian Cultural Revolution, when shrine worship was curtailed and the publishing of literature in Uyghur ground to a halt, with the exception of a handful of politically correct revolutionary novels. However, with the advent of the reform era, Afaq and his shrine emerged with new and prominent roles, as a result of two major changes: the explosion of Uyghur-language publishing and the rise of tourism, both domestic and international.

Tourism at the White Mountain shrine was not entirely new in the reform era. Even in the last days of the Cultural Revolution, in the summer of 1976, Jan Myrdal witnessed a busload of visitors at the shrine. However, in the ensuing three decades, as China welcomed ever-increasing numbers of foreign visitors, and as rising living standards turned domestic tourism into a major economic force,[58] the shrine became critical to the state's promotion of Kashgar as a tourist destination. Whereas the local governments in several parts of Altishahr have treated major shrines as a threat to the security of Chinese rule, the Kashgar government has treated the White Mountain shrine, with its imposing architectural beauty, as an opportunity for economic development through tourism. Ironically, there has probably been no other shrine more closely tied to rebellion against China-based rule than the White Mountain shrine. Both Jahāngīr Khoja, a White Mountain Khoja who led an uprising in 1826, and Ya'qub Beg, who hijacked the 1864 rebellions, began their short reigns with pilgrimages to the shrine, which remained a symbol of White Mountain sovereignty long after the arrival of Qing rule. The state has managed this potential threat by pressing changes in both the function and the meaning of the shrine.

The state's attempt to change the function of the shrine from a place of ritual pilgrimage to a destination for tourism has been extremely successful. The old artifacts of pilgrimage—flags, sheep's horns, offerings—have long ago been removed, perhaps during the Cultural Revolution.[59] A hefty entry fee of 15 yuan dissuades the poorer rural visitors who make up the majority of pilgrims at other shrines. A guard at the site reported in 2007 that the few pilgrims who still arrive to worship at the shrine are senior citizens, who are exempt from the entry fee. Irreverent Han and foreign tourists undermine any sense of ritual gravity. Shaykhs have been replaced by tour guides and security guards. In 2003 the local government of Kashgar ceded control of the site to a private company, Zhongkun, which was headed by a former official of the Propaganda Department of the Communist Party's Central Committee. Little has changed under Zhongkun's management, which is restricted by state policies regarding preservation and tourism.

The persistence of place in Altishahr, represented best by shrines with pre-Islamic roots surviving on shifting dunes with little architectural construction, is in part a result of the mutual reinforcement of personage and place that characterizes the tazkirah-shrine tradition. Every important place has a person, and nearly every historical personage has a place. Through this link, the memory of the individual and the significance of the place bolster one another. As long as the memory of Apaq Khoja survives, the significance of his grave site cannot be erased, and as long as the White Mountain cemetery remains holy, Apaq cannot be entirely forgotten. The Kashgar government has, for the most part, chosen not to challenge this durability of place, preferring instead to co-opt the phenomenon as a rich opportunity for conveying cultural and political meaning.[60] Thus, despite a general drive to undermine the influence of Sufi orders in Xinjiang, the Chinese government has chosen neither to close the Apaq Khoja shrine nor to entirely dissociate Apaq from it. Rather, the government has adapted admirably to the tradition, promoting its own exemplary personality, Xiang Fei, the Kashgarian woman who entered the Qianlong emperor's court as a concubine in the 1760s. A Chinese-language document from Kashgar shows that Chinese inhabitants of that town had already connected popular Xiang Fei legends to the shrine by 1903.[61] However, the historical traditions of the small Han population in Kashgar had so little effect on the shrine that foreign observers (aside from Hartmann, who collected the document and recorded the connection in his unpublished diary) failed to note the Xiang Fei legend. The story may even have died out, only to be reimported from China proper after the rising popularity of plays about Xiang Fei.[62] Not only was the Xiang Fei legend's connection to the White Mountain shrine weak, reliable historical evidence for any actual connection in Xiang Fei's own day is nonexistent. However, Xiang Fei's value to the communist party as a symbol of "the unity of every ethnicity of China"[63] far outweighs the difficulties of commemorating in a Kashgar mausoleum a woman who is actually buried near Beijing (where, ironically, she is given far less attention). The official tour guides at the Apaq Khoja shrine devote the majority of their standardized speeches to the story of Xiang Fei, and the multitude of souvenir shops sell an impressive variety of Xiang Fei images. One poorly translated tour book even goes so far as to state in English that "Apaq Khoja Tomb has a local name: The Tomb of Xiang Fei."[64]

Authorities employed a similar strategy at the central cemetery and shrine of Apaq's Sufi rivals, the Black Mountain Khojas. This shrine complex, called *Altunluq* (Golden), was previously known best as the burial site of the Seven Muhammads, the Black Mountain Khojas, and the khans of Yarkand. Here again, authorities shifted emphasis from Sufi and political personages to a more agreeable exemplary female character, in this case the sixteenth-century queen and patroness of the arts, Amannisakhan. Today at the Altunluq complex, the graves of the Black Mountain Sufi leaders are entirely unmarked, and those of the khans are dwarfed by Amannisakhan's new mausoleum.

In the case of Xiang Fei, the government's promotion efforts have been quite successful, as they tapped into both preexisting legend and the power of a sanctified site. Xiang Fei now has a very real presence in local Uyghur historical consciousness, even if attitudes toward her are somewhat ambivalent. Amannisakhan has also made her mark as a historical personage for the Uyghurs of Yarkand. In a fascinating interplay of PRC Orientalizing ethnic policy, and Altishahri historical tradition, the promotion of Amannisakhan paved the way for the appearance of a Uyghur biographical novel.[65] Amannisakhan, largely a forgotten personage in the era of the tazkirah, has now been fitted with both tomb and tazkirah (in the form of the novel). In the cases of both Xiang Fei and Amannisakhan, authorities chose figures who wielded limited power in their own time to replace the politicized and distinctly Islamic figures that originally dominated the significance of these shrines. The choice of female characters is also reminiscent of Orientalism as described by Edward Said, which is characterized in part by a tendency to feminize the other, a phenomenon also noted by Steven Harrell in his examination of Han Chinese approaches to other cultures as a "civilizing project."[66] Yet, however we interpret the authorities' choice of these two women, it is significant that they have reemerged in Uyghur popular imagination in part as a result of Han Chinese influence. Young men in Kashgar exhibited curiosity about the role of Xiang Fei, though a consensus has yet to emerge as to whether she is a hero or a traitor. The grave and place of pilgrimage is a traditional site of the Uyghur encounter with the past, and this resonance has acted as a fulcrum of meaning for Xiang Fei's promotion, contributing to Xiang Fei's reemergence as a topic of historical discussion in Kashgar.

Xiang Fei is emblematic of the Chinese state's approach to the history of Altishahr in general, in that she represents a historical category from central China imposed on the conquered region. By choosing a personage,

Xiang Fei, as framework for co-opting the White Mountain shrine's history, the state adapted in a small way to the Uyghur/Altishahri historical tradition. However, Xiang Fei's story is distinctly Chinese; her story reached the present, not in Altishahri texts or monuments, but in Chinese-language histories and dramas that circulated in central China. The popular Xiang Fei legend reflects the long tradition of Chinese writing about women who gave up their lives to protect their chastity. Outside the shrine context, in the state's primary knowledge-production institution, the university, state-sponsored histories are further divorced from the indigenous language and practice of history. Professional academic historians in China's officially sanctioned venues write about "Xinjiang local history" *(Xinjiang difang shi)*, stressing that the region is merely "the northwest border region of our great motherland," which cannot have its own history, but can have a local history as a component of the history of the Chinese nation.[67] Moreover, Chinese categories of historical time are imposed on a history that had always been more concerned with geography and personage. Reflecting Chinese traditions that extend back to the Han dynasty, Chinese scholars organize Altishahr's ("Xinjiang's") history by the dynasties of China proper. Thus, the period of Qarakhanid rule in Altishahr is discussed as Xinjiang local history of the Song dynasty, despite the complete absence of Chinese power in Altishahr during the Song. This approach has doomed standard histories in the eyes of most Uyghurs. In the case of Xiang Fei, on the other hand, the state's admixture of local forms of historical practice with imported Chinese themes has resulted in a more viable history.

Uyghur Nationalist Appropriation

However successful Zhongkun and the relevant governmental ministries may have been at promoting Xiang Fei's connection to the shrine, other views flourish as well. There still exist among the older generations many Muslims who regard Apaq as a saint,[68] and according to staff at the shrine, there is still a trickle of pilgrims during the appropriate holidays. Inhabitants of the surrounding village also still seem to view Apaq as an important and positive figure despite (in many cases) a lack of specific knowledge about his activities.[69] Perhaps most interesting, though, is the viewpoint of the young Uyghur men among the shrine's employees, for whom Apaq is a national villain, a view shared by many urban Uyghurs. When questioned about the source of their distaste for Apaq Khoja, young men throughout Xinjiang referred to a historical novel published in 2000, written by a certain Abdulvǎli Ǎli, and entitled simply *Apaq Khoja*.[70] As we have seen, the view that Apaq was a national traitor is not new, but it was Abduvǎli Ǎli's novel that managed to popularize the idea of the villainous Apaq, bringing it to the brink of ubiquity among urban youths. The book's authority only grew when, in 2001, authorities in Kashgar staged a public burning of Ǎli's works.

Ǎli's novel, which tends to be viewed by Uyghur readers as historically reliable despite its explicit labeling as a novel *(roman)*, is probably the most popular and influential historical text shaping views of Afaq Khoja today.[71] During regular and extended visits to Altishahr between 2000 and 2010, I frequently encountered intense animosity toward Afaq Khoja, a phenomenon I am not the first to record.[72] When questioned about their sources of information, informants more often than not cited Abduvǎli Ǎli's novel, and often encouraged me to read it myself. This anecdotal, but remarkably consistent, evidence suggests that the Kashgar authorities' burning of Ǎli's novels has been quite an ineffective tactic for suppressing the novel's influence. Indeed, many privately owned bookshops in Urumchi and Kashgar continued to stock the book in quantity. A disproportionate number of my contacts in Altishahr have been males between the ages of sixteen and fifty, but readership of the novel seems to bridge divisions of gender, class, and age.[73] The influence of the novel is eloquently attested in another biographical novel, published in 2003,[74] which includes a series of photos of the author, Yasinkhan Sadiq Choghlan, engaged in activities that demonstrate his prestige and authority, including an image of the author "listening to a story from his forerunners" and interviewing with a famous Uyghur newscaster. One photo shows Choghlan "together with writers of Yarkand," listening to a man who reads from Ǎli's *Apaq Khoja*.

The publication of this book was a curious event, because most Uyghur readers have attributed to the novel strongly Uyghur nationalist messages, but it was written by a trusted member of the government's propaganda and publishing apparatus. Beginning in 1979, Abduvǎli Ǎli spent a little over a year working in the Kashgar County propaganda bureau before starting two decades of work at the Xinjiang People's Press.[75] Whatever the author's motives may have been, it seems that in the authorities' willingness to publish a work that might undermine Afaq as a potential Uyghur national hero or Islamic hero, they let something equally dangerous occur—the creation of a national villain.

Abduvăli Ăli did not start from scratch but elaborated on the anti-Afaq tradition as it had developed through the nationalist period. In the 1980s, several Uyghur historians began to discuss Afaq much as Muhammad Amīn Bughrā had presented him in 1946, with a traitorous Afaq betraying an idealized "Uyghur" Yarkand (Sa'idiyya) Khanate.[76] Following these influential works, Ăli's novel presents the Yarkand Khanate of the late seventeenth century as an ideal Uyghur state. A benevolent Abdullah Khan presides over a time of economic plenty and flourishing arts, until the evil Afaq begins to undermine his authority through heresies and trickery. Eventually, Afaq betrays the Uyghur people by bringing an infidel Dzungar army to conquer the Uyghur motherland. In the attempt to maintain his new position, Afaq then commits various atrocities, such as destroying shrines and burning books. Because the Yarkand Khanate was the last independent state geographically coterminous with Altishahr and ruled by Turki-speaking Muslims, most Uyghur readers have naturally concluded, based on Ăli's narrative, that Afaq Khoja's "traitorous" act was the real cause of the incorporation of the "Uyghurs" into foreign empires, first the Dzungar Empire, and then the China-based Qing Empire. Thus, in the popular interpretation of Ăli's book—and here I strongly emphasize that the popular interpretation is not necessarily Ăli's intended meaning—Afaq is ultimately to blame for the indignities suffered by the Uyghur nation at the hands of the Chinese state today. Ăli's use of the words *milliy* (national), *wătăn* (nation), and *ana makan/ ana wătăn* (motherland) allows readers to decide for themselves whether he is referring to the Chinese nation or the Uyghur nation.[77] The former interpretation may perhaps explain why the book made it past the censors, while the latter goes some way to explaining the book's popularity among Uyghur readers. Numerous long allegorical fables, adapted from Aesop and from *Kalīlah and Dimnah,* are sprinkled throughout, and are easily interpreted as commentaries on the oppression of the Uyghur nation. When Chinese authorities eventually discovered how Uyghurs were interpreting the novel, books by Ăli were publicly burned in Kashgar in 2001.[78] For witnesses who had read Ăli's *Apaq Khoja,* this can only have tied the Chinese state even more firmly to the evil Afaq of the novel, whose own burning of books cemented his status as villain.

Beyond a literal vocabulary of nationalism with words such as *motherland* and *nation*, the novel displays the same elements of national imagination that Ăzizi used in *Sutuq Bughrakhan.* At the beginnings of chapters, detailed settings imply the whole of an imagined community:

smoke issues from chimneys as families start their days, and during scenes that take place at night, the author is careful to remind the reader of all the citizens sleeping quietly in their beds. But as in *Sutuq Bughra-khan,* the style of Ăli's novel is mixed, and such archetypical community imaginings end after the first few pages of each chapter, where the more traditional "straightforward, single-file narrative" picks up,[79] only to give way to a classic element of the tazkirah tradition, the fabulous deed. As in the biographical novels that preceded it, Ăli's novel presents a tazkirah-like "heavy" character carrying out his fabulous deeds in a finely drawn, sometimes even realist, national setting. However, in Ăli's *Afaq Khoja,* the moral character of the protagonist is reversed. Rather than relating the life of a national hero, Ăli pursues his nationalist message through an equally powerful symbol, the national villain. Afaq is portrayed as purely evil, bent on nothing other than the acquisition of power, inspired by destruction and tyranny, cruel without limit, and enabled by a Machiavellian cleverness that is unsurpassed.

For inspiration, Ăli himself tapped the tazkirah tradition, to the extent that he cites several tazkirahs in his novel, along with chronicles and *maqāmāt/manāqib* texts. In one case Ăli even uses a motif from the Black Mountain *Tazkirah-i Azīzān,* in which Aqbash Khan killed so many followers of Afaq that their flowing blood powered a flour mill.[80] Ăli switches victim and perpetrator, crediting Afaq with the gory achievement. Other aspects of Ăli's caricature of an evil Afaq seem to be invented afresh, as when he has Afaq order henchmen to cut out the still-beating hearts of his Uyghur enemies for the satisfaction of the infidel Dzungar ruler, who, Ăli writes, delighted in eating human hearts.[81] The biographical novel's connection to the popular tazkirah, with its long tradition of heavy-handed characterization, goes some way to explaining how such exaggerated works, which present themselves explicitly as novels, have been received as reliable historical sources by huge numbers of Uyghur readers.

The example of Afaq Khoja shows how the tazkirah-shrine tradition, in concert with other strains of deeply rooted Altishahri historical thought, have served as a historical resource, both to the state, which has co-opted shrines to promote "ethnic unity" and tourism, and to Uyghurs who use the new novelistic incarnation of the tazkirah tradition to express resentment of Chinese rule and dreams of an independent Uyghur nation. Through the use of particularly Uyghur (Altishahri) systems of historical meaning, Uyghur authors have managed to create a large nationalist literature that is both deeply inspiring to readers and largely invisible to the Han-dominated government. In the nineteenth and early twentieth centuries, the shrine-tazkirah system supported an Altishahri historical identity through the stories of a constellation of saints, who, when seen as a group, provided a vision of an "our history" that was shared across the "six" cities in spite of outsider rule. In the last two decades, the biographies of a new kind of saint (and villain), the saint of the nation, have allowed Uyghurs to maintain a remarkably public discussion of identity in an environment where the state only permits the imagination of one particular nation: the multiethnic Chinese nation of the People's Republic of China.

Much of what is unusual about the case of Afaq Khoja stems from his chronological proximity to the present and to the tazkirah tradition. Traces of political strife and factionalism that have been smoothed over by time in other saints' traditions are raw in the Afaq tradition. Afaq is a boundary figure. He is perhaps last person to attain the status of a major popular saint with both tazkirah and shrine.[82] His lateness gives us greater access to the past, for more writing has survived from Afaq's period than from earlier saints' lifetimes, and this access offers us a more detailed picture of the long process by which the tazkirah tradition embraced individuals' reputations. In many cases, the tazkirahs have a monopoly on history in that they are the only surviving record of particular saints. The obstacles to becoming a tazkirah-worthy saint are thus smoothed over. Afaq's case shows the troubled and incomplete rise to prominence of one view of the saint from among a multiplicity of competing discourses. Presumably, other tazkirahs faced similar obstacles now elided in the surviving historical record.

In retrospect, the popular reappropriation of Afaq's personage through the Altishahri tazkirah tradition almost seems inevitable. Given that Afaq and his lineage depended on both the manuscript tradition and the shrine, it is not surprising that particularly Altishahri approaches to these phenomena made their mark on his reputation. Though it remained incomplete, the incorporation of Afaq into the tazkirah tradition shows the power of popular tradition as enabled by manuscript technology, and the magnetism of the shrine as an extraordinary place that demanded explanation. Ultimately, the expectation that such a large shrine should be paired with a work that focused on the great deeds of the saint in an easily recitable form found its expression in the *Tazkirah of Sayyid Āfāq Khwāja*. Yet the tazkirah tradition exists today only in a highly modified form. The strange situation that pertains at Afaq's grave today highlights the role of the state in that transformation, with the Chinese state enlisting Uyghur forms of historical practice to promote "ethnic unity" *(minzu tuanjie)* while simultaneously destroying key nodes of the those traditions. As many scholars have noted, Uyghur historical practice has taken refuge in nationalist discourse, but, as the present story of Afaq's reputation should make clear, recent Uyghur historians have also tapped deeper veins of Altishahri historical traditions, stretching all the way back to Afaq's own day. The earlier Altishahri historical approaches were shaped by other states—Qing indirect rule, Afaq's demitheocracy—but these were state forces with a lighter historiographical touch. The heavy hand of the modern Chinese state, which managed to shut down shrines and end the manuscript tradition within the brief span of a decade, should probably receive some credit for the unusually stark transformation of Altishahri traditions into the Uyghur discourses we see today. Whereas the tazkirah overtook Afaq's reputation over the course of two and a half centuries, never fully displacing the alternatives, the biographical novel appeared less than half a century after the imposition of Chinese Communist Party rule and monopolized Afaq's reputation almost entirely. The power of the new vision of Afaq was most vividly demonstrated by the Chinese state's reaction to it: the public burning of Ăli's novels in 2001. However, it must be remembered that this is a tradition transformed, not created, by the state, and much of what is interesting resides in the roots of the tradition. The Chinese state itself has recognized this in its manipulation of the tradition for its own ends.

Despite transformation, there is continuity. We see in all phases of Afaq's historiography the strong role of personage in the Altishahri tradition. Through the presence of the saint at the shrine, the historical personage shared in the shrine's demand for explanation, and the significance of personage projected itself onto conceptions of shrine and text. The White Mountain shrine became the Afaq Khoja shrine and the *Lives of the Loyal* became the *Tazkirah of Sayyid Āfāq Khwāja*. Personage also functioned as an organizational framework for information about the past. Altishahr's cultivated oases of history were personages as well as places. As we have seen, the localization of history created strong links, even equivalences between the two: Afaq and Kashgar, the Seven Muhammads and Yarkand, Satūq and Artush, and so on.[83] The history of Afaq's personage is the story of the attachment of a huge range of information and argumentation to the reputation of a single prominent figure. The titles of written texts testify to the centrality of personage, even outside the tazkirah tradition: the *Book of Hidāyat* (Afaq's birth name), the *Tazkirah of Hidāyat,* the *Tazkirah of Sayyid Āfāq Khwāja, The Lives of the Loyal,* and *Apaq Khoja.* While the authors of these texts presented vastly different views of Afaq, they all agreed on the centrality of his personage as a site of debate. His personage thus functioned as a fulcrum of historical practice, a center point around which competing visions turned. The simultaneous mutability and durability of Afaq's reputation allowed a continuity of historical practice despite the passage of a succession of discourses and power structures.

The Chinese state has forced personage to carry more historical weight in the last three decades through its control of texts and places. With the end of the Cultural Revolution, the state removed the shrine of Afaq permanently from popular historical practice through what has been called its "disneyfication"[84] and through its marketing to Han tourists via the promotion of Xiang Fei. The manuscript, by the end of the Cultural Revolution, was very much a thing of the past, with most private copies transferred to state archives and the production of new manuscripts nearly eliminated.[85] However, while the state undermined both the manuscript and the shrine, it left the personage of Afaq largely untouched (although one might argue that it was not for lack of effort— the importation of the Xiang Fei myth from China might best be seen as an effort to erode the prominence of Afaq). But if it was separated from place and text, the personage of Afaq did not lose its role as a fulcrum of historical practice. Just as Jonathan Z. Smith has argued that meaning embedded in place can be transplanted to ritual,[86] I would argue that in the case of Afaq Khoja, much of the historical meaning that had been localized at his shrine survived through its attachment to the last standing pillar of the tazkirah-shrine tradition: personage, the critical mnemonic that survived the elimination of text and place.

As should be clear, this phenomenon was not unique to the case of Afaq Khoja. Recent historical practice, in the form of historical talk, has placed the personage of Afaq and all of its associated meanings in interaction with a new set of key personages. These are the saints of the nation, monumental figures born in Altishahr[87] and promoted through the new tazkirah in its novelized form. Afaq's old Black Mountain foils have been replaced by figures, such as Maḥmūd Kāshgharī, who were largely unknown in Afaq's day. With this in mind, let us revisit a statement documented by another researcher, Edmund Waite, in 2006, reporting the words of a young hotel worker in Kashgar:

Many people believe Apaq Khoja destroyed our culture. Many people believe that before Apaq Khoja our culture was very developed. For example at the time of the Qarakhanid dynasty there was Mähmut Qäshqäri, who wrote the Turkic dictionary and Yusup Khass Hajib who was a famous poet. Then also at the time of the Säidiyakhan there was Amansahan [sic] who compiled the twelve Mukams [sic] and Abdurâshid Khan. However, Apaq Khoja encouraged Sufism—Xinjiang became very backward. Apaq Khoja also burnt books and made people ignorant. He sided with the Chinese and supported them—he brought them to Xinjiang. Although later descendants of Apaq Khoja rebelled against the Chinese government in the nineteenth century it was too late. That is why we hate Apaq Khoja.[88]

For Waite, this statement demonstrates a mixing of oral and printed sources of history, a rising tide of ethnic sentiment, and "the power of oral transmission in a context where the dissemination of state-sanctioned information is discredited by the local populace." Indeed, all of these phenomena are reflected to a greater or lesser extent in this statement. Yet further significance should be obvious in light of the traditions analyzed in the present study. The bulk of the content of the hotel employee's statement is derived from texts, in particular, texts shaped by the tazkirah tradition. Like Afaq, all four saints of the nation mentioned by the young narrator are to be found in popular biographical novels. The logic of Afaq's sins against the nation follows Ăli's novel precisely, including the charge of book burning, which is found in no other source on Afaq. The only change of detail, the transmutation of Dzungars to Chinese, surely represents the effects of circulation in the oral world. It is a reminder that, like the tazkirahs before them, the biographical novels circulate in oral as well as physical forms. However, I reproduce the hotel employee's statement here mainly to point out the operation of personage. Just as we orient ourselves geographically by relating one place to another, the speaker orients us historically by relating one personage to another. Chronology has crept in,[89] but personages from the thirteenth century articulate with others from the sixteenth and seventeenth centuries. Afaq cannot be fully understood except in relation to other human fulcra of history.

I too have been drawn into this tradition by the gravity of Afaq's personage in Altishahr. My own manipulations of the past, like those analyzed in this chapter, are intended to say something about the people of Altishahr. To do so I have felt compelled to organize my arguments around the idea of Afaq Khoja, as opposed to, say, the notions of a Khoja period, Uyghur Sufism, or Chinese colonialism. I recently discovered that an earlier and condensed version of this chapter, published in *Central Asian Survey*, has been translated by a Uyghur reader, and it may therefore one day join the swirl of voices that contend over the reputation of Afaq Khoja in Altishahr itself.

The long, durable tradition of attaching meaning to Afaq has created a richly layered historical resource for the present. Each successive approach to history left traces in the traditions that followed: Afaq's popular tazkirah inherited the multigenerational approach of the Naqshbandi tradition, and the novel inherited the heavy characters of the tazkirah tradition. Much was discarded along the way, but traces of all of the traditions appeared in the latest manifestation, the novel. From the dynastic chronicles, Ăli borrowed noble Chinggisid rulers; from the Naqshbandi literature, factional intrigue; from the tazkirah, the "heavy" protagonist; and from later works the discourse of nationalism. The layered historiography of Afaq, embracing flattering and damning views, along with mutually alien discourses and vocabularies, presented Ăli with a treasury of alternative pasts that gained new power in their recombination. Recognizing these as wellsprings for alternative futures, Ăli deployed sources from all traditions selectively. As the anthropologist Valerio Valeri noted, both the past and history are storehouses for alternative ways of acting, of behaviors that can spark change, even as actors imagine themselves reproducing the old.[90] What Ăli presented as a utopian, independent, Uyghur khanate of Yarkand, destroyed by Afaq through collaboration with ethnic and religious others, may not actually have been Uyghur or paradisiacal, but in its novelistic incarnation it proposes an appealing alternative future. And for all of its factual divergences from the past, the novel is deeply rooted in that past. There is even something of Afaq Khoja in *Apaq Khoja*.

CONCLUSION

The story of Altishahri and Uyghur history is unusual in part because of the long connection between *popular* historical practice and the manuscript tradition. In so many of the world's historical traditions, especially manuscript-based historical traditions, written history was the domain of elites, distant from the popular historical practices that flourished beyond the manuscript. Indeed, the written word has often served as a barrier to popular participation in the shaping of societies' histories. In Altishahr, on the other hand, the manuscript both fed the popular tradition and reflected it. The integral role of the manuscript has provided us with particularly rich clues to the ways ordinary people understood their society's past. It also presents us with an example of an alternative way of interacting with the past. While no one element of Altishahri historical practice was unique to Altishahr, the particular constellation of phenomena created a distinctive tradition that offers to expand our notion of what history can be. The flexible traditions of manuscript production, the role of the manuscript in pilgrimage and shrine rituals, and the connection of history to those shrines together yielded a very particular way of embracing the past, which was open to a large community. It was a mode of historical practice that survived the arrival of print technology and government interference in pilgrimage and publishing, eventually finding new expression in the genre of biographical fiction.

Most of the historical texts that comprised the popular canon emerged in their Altishahri forms with the rise of the vernacular in the eighteenth century. During that time, old foreign works were recast in the local Turki dialect and a large number of local works were composed anew or adapted from the oral tradition. As the concerns of Abū al-Qāsim, translator-author of the *Ūlūgh Taẕkirah-i Bughrā-khān,* indicate, some of the vernacular's rise can even be attributed to a conscious desire to increase ordinary people's access to the world of the manuscript. Popular historical practices no doubt flourished in Altishahr long before the manuscript became a familiar force in the lives of ordinary people. Perhaps shrines such as that of the Seven Muhammads in Yarkand, whose popularity Mirza Haydar Dūghlāt documented in 1546, were important sites of such historical practices. However, it was in the eighteenth century that such popular practices began to pass more regularly through the realm of the written text, giving us a sudden, if partial, glimpse of the world of tales that Altishahris were telling about the local past. This view is partial because we see it through the lens of the late nineteenth-century and early twentieth-century manuscript corpus, but it provides valuable clues to the origins of that corpus.

The increasing linkage between the manuscript and popular history in the eighteenth century represented a simultaneous popularization of the written text and writing of the popular tradition. That is to say that the emergence of the manuscript as a popular medium involved both the vernacularization of written texts previously limited to elites and the entrance of popular unwritten texts into the written form. To return to two examples we have already seen, the *Shāhnāmah,* previously known in its Persian form to elites such as Abul Muḥammada Khan of Turpan (r. 1641–1646), was fully translated into Turki by 1796,[1] while the popular unwritten holy war tales about the sons of Sultan Satūq Bughrā-khān were written down by 1812.[2] The convergence of such varied texts, some with deep and distant roots in places such as India and Arabia, others with origins in the Turkic milieu of Altishahr, was an important element in the formation of Altishahr's historical tradition. Although, to the outsider, the hybrid works inherited from other cultures often appear distinct from Altishahr's home-grown histories, for Altishahri consumers, they were equally constituent of "our history." The tears shed by the shaykh over the Persian Siyāvush are emblematic of just how thoroughly inherited heroes can be reconciled to local genres and how deeply connected the inhabitants of Altishahr can feel to their hybrid histories.

Of course, one of the central conclusions of this study is that the written text is only one phenomenon among several in the practice of history. Despite the well-known value of unwritten narratives as historical evidence,[3] the written text continues to loom large in professional academic historians' imagination of what it means to do history. Among the many reasons for this is the fact that written evidence tends to be seen (often rightly so) as the richest source for knowledge of the past. It is also of obvious significance that the academic historian's own end-product is considered to be a written text such as this one.[4] However, another cause may lie in the nature of the print culture in which academic history developed. In the dominant culture of print, the written text is easily delimited from the rest of human activity. The seeming rigid stability of authorship, the notion of a "final" text, and the apparent faithfulness of individual books to a single ideal original make it easy to imagine a separate dimension of discourse, in which texts address other texts and stand as the ultimate representation of a historian's thought, independent of the social contexts that inevitably govern the creation and use of objects such as books. The historiographer may take interest in biographical or institutional contexts that influenced the creation of the text (as a way of understanding the text), but it is the world of these texts, interacting with each other, that is typically construed as the subject of inquiry.

Such a separation between textual and social worlds is impossible to imagine in a manuscript tradition such as that of Altishahr. The manuscript has been a flexible means of transmitting texts wherever it was used, but the Altishahri context demonstrates just how extensive and powerful this flexibility can be. The boundary between reader and book, so clear in the printed book, is blurred completely in the Altishahri manuscript. It was often difficult to tell if a correction in the text was part of the "original" manuscript or a reader's addition to an earlier copy, not to mention the fact that producer (copyist) and consumer (reader) were commonly the same person. More importantly, the written text was primarily used as a script for oral recitation, moving written texts directly into social settings. When such social activities as tazkirah recitations at shrines have the potential to influence new written texts at the points of authorship (as in the case of Abū al-Qāsim's written challenge to the recitations of the shaykhs) or of copying, we have a situation in which the written text is fully and *obviously* merged with the social world. In ways that are readily apparent to its users, the written text is both a byproduct of and a participant in historical practice, but it is not, as history in the print tradition is so often imagined, the very fabric of history.

Increasingly, the textual environment of the print world is looking like a short and geographically limited interlude in humanity's history. As print rapidly cedes territory to networked digital communication (before print has even reached every corner of the globe), ever larger swathes of our social activities are carried out in electronic forms of writing, while written texts are regaining the flexibility that characterized the manuscript tradition. The wiki is a fantastic example of the latter phenomenon, with community authorship at a scale that dwarfs that found in Altishahri manuscripts. The print world's illusion of a separate realm of the text is giving way to an experience far more reminiscent of the manuscript tradition.

The present study also serves as an example of how previous historians shape our view of the past. It is worth recalling that we often write about the same subjects that were written about in the past, if from different perspectives. Shrines are as important in my own work as they were in the tazkirahs. Of course, this pattern does not always hold; holy war is central to many tazkirahs, but gets little attention here. Still, the selective preservation created by authors and archives exerts a strong pull on the historians of the present. Both authors and archives are genre-driven. Texts that fit established genres are more likely to get written, more likely to get preserved, and more likely to be understood. We have seen that the boundaries of the Altishahri local historical genre par-excellence, the tazkirah, were formed through the extratextual practices of a large community. The authors of Altishahr's local history were, in that sense, the entire community, and a wide range of traditions of saint veneration had implications for the texts left behind by Altishahris' historical practice. My engagement with the past has thus been influenced by the pilgrimages of the past.

Of all the extratextual activities associated with history in Altishahr, I have focused on pilgrimage because it created the one social setting most securely connected to the practice of local history. Just as narratives passed in and out of manuscripts, changing as they moved, they also passed through the environs of the shrine. People brought their own notions of the saint's history with them and left with new ones. Recitations by pilgrims, shaykhs, and professional singer-storytellers are all documented in the historical record, revealing the shrine as a site at which historical meaning was negotiated. For these reasons I have referred to both text (manuscript) and place (shrine) as fulcra of meaning, to emphasize the idea that they served similar roles as meeting points for narratives about the past. Since both texts and shrines were seen as sources of authenticity and authority, the most important ones became fixed, unquestioned axes of a slowly but constantly shifting community imagination of the past. The staff and pilgrims at a shrine might change, and the text of a tazkirah might change as it was copied into a new manuscript, but the abstracted ideals of these things retained their authenticity. So it was, for example, that Abū al-Qāsim could question the shaykhs of the shrines and call for his own rewriting of the holy tazkirah, and yet the shrine and original tazkirah remained as sources of authenticity within his rewriting.

The enormous significance of place was instrumental in lending Altishahri historical practice two of its salient characteristics: sacredness and presence. We have seen that, both in the past and present, shrines have been tightly integrated into the daily, weekly, and annual activities of the villages in which they are situated. Daily and weekly care for the dead, ordinary supplication and prayer for health or wealth, weekly pilgrimage in connection with regional markets, and the celebration of annual holidays such as Barat/Tünăk at shrines constantly reinforced the holiness of the shrine and its connection to the world of the supernatural. Such activities defined the performative context in which the tazkirah was widely disseminated to ordinary and nonliterate people. At the same time, the tazkirahs were narratives that climaxed in the death of the saint and the establishment of the shrine. The continuous community construction of the shrine as a sacred place (through ritual) along with the connections to the shrine and the supernatural within the tazkirahs meant that in Altishahr, popular, local history was sacred history. There was no profane historical practice that could rival the influence of the ritualized, sacred system of the tazkirah and shrine. In this context, antiquity and sacredness have merged, with surprising results such as the pilgrims' prayers in the direction of a Chinese road marker. A society's approach to history can affect its understanding of place as well as the reverse.

The tradition of tazkirah recitation at the shrine also meant that historical practice in its most powerful form was undertaken at the sites where the events of the past were said to have taken place, hence my emphasis on presence. Mass learning about Altishahr's own past took place not in a schoolhouse remote from the setting of history, but at the very places where the tazkirah narratives reached their climaxes: the manzils, or deathplaces, of the saints. Pilgrims brought themselves into the very real presence of the saint, linking their own personal lives into the narratives of the past. The smells of oil lamps, the taste of food from the communal cooking pot, the sounds of songs and prayers, the sight of forests of flags, all of which are aspects of saint veneration mentioned in important tazkirahs, made the past present for pilgrims in ways that texts alone could not.

Once we recognize that Altishahri notions of history were tightly linked to notions of place and that place could serve as a fulcrum of historical meaning in ways similar to texts, travel emerges as an important element of historical practice. It was not only narratives that intersected at the shrine, but also itineraries. The meeting of narratives and journeys created a network, which was reflected in Altishahri history's geographic organization. This network of travel, writing, and recitation also supported a group identity from within by assembling and disseminating stories of a shared past in forms that appeared comprehensive but accommodated local emphases. It created an identity maintained by phenomena that have been rare in most times and places: wide popular access to written texts in the vernacular and an extensive mobility of ordinary people that ensured those written texts would be disseminated along networks of travel, and across class boundaries. Most importantly, the system bore obvious markers of its own functioning. Not only did people in different places practice the same historical tradition but in many cases they could see who was sharing in that tradition with them, not just in face-to-face interactions, but through the marginalia of other readers, the flags of other pilgrims, and the graffiti on shrine walls. The Altishahri identity was relatively homogeneous, built, as it was, in every instance from the same stock of modular historical building blocks, and maintained in ways that spread awareness of who was included and where.

Scholars tend to associate complex homogeneous identity systems with modernity. Thus, in the influential formulations of Gellner and Anderson, nations are products of the social and technological transformations of modernity. Those who seek complex identity systems in the premodern world focus on large kingdoms, "civilizations," such as that of the Greeks, or religious communities. The premodern "imagined communities" that Anderson describes are religious communities of continental scale or dynastic realms. Anthony Smith's broader notion of "ethnies" has allowed him to compare a wider set of premodern complex identity systems, including those of the Greeks, the Jewish diaspora, Sassanid Persia, and the Normans.[5] These authors and others have been important not only for exploring the notion of nationalism, for which they are best known, but also for broadening our understanding of complex identity systems other than nationalism. The Altishahri system adds to their examples another kind of complex identity system, which developed in another context: a long period of indirect rule.[6] The example of Altishahri identity invites us to resurrect Anderson's original formulation of the imagined community, with the nation as one *kind* of imagined community, and look for other kinds of imagined community and other associations between such identities and common historical contexts.

Since so many arguments about identity involve notions of modernity, it is interesting to ask whether Altishahri society of 1700 to 1930 should be considered "modern." In this period, many of the social, economic, and technological phenomena commonly associated with modernity were absent in Altishahr, and yet Altishahri society must have been shaped to some extent by these phenomena, which were taking hold in the surrounding societies of interior China, the Russian Empire, and British India. On the one hand, Altishahr certainly lacked or eschewed much of what scholars most frequently associate with modernity, such as industrialization, the nation-state, secularization, and, especially important in this study, tools of intensive information dissemination such as print and public education. On the other hand, Altishahr's incorporation into the Qing Empire was tied to the closing of the steppe, the final absorption of all Eurasian nomadic peoples into bordered agrarian states. This transformation, which was completed when the British, Russian, and Qing Empires butted up against one another, put an end to the steppe-sown dynamic that had so deeply influenced Eurasian societies for two thousand years. The closing of the steppe was also a crucial element in the creation of the modern concept of a world consisting entirely of bounded nation-states, and perhaps should be considered a characteristic of modernity in Eurasia. As we have seen, the Qing expansion into Altishahr and the establishment there of indirect rule influenced the shape of the Altishahri identity.

The past as it was made relevant to the settled Turkic speakers of Altishahr—the popular Altishahri and Uyghur visions of "our history"—is itself both a reflection and engine of identity. Perhaps the history of a place, when it is practiced by an inhabitant of that place, is always a negotiation of identity. Indeed, in the world of the early twenty-first century, which is still dominated by nationalist imaginings, it is difficult to imagine identity maintenance without history, for claims about the legitimacy of a nation's ties to place, like so many other claims of legitimacy, are nearly always built upon history. History's power for legitimation arises in part from the ability of the past to play both self and other. Arguments based on the past and arguments based on the other both have a sheen of impartiality. They are both outside authorities, which we marshal to judge (usually to praise) our own societies. These outside authorities, supposedly cordoned off from the bias of our own self-image, are also a source of justification for a society's aspirations. Citation of the other also does this job just fine. The Uyghurs can say, "the Kazakhs have an independent state and so should we," and many do so. But how much more powerful it is to say, "*We once had* an independent state!" The disinterested authority of the past, when it is "our history," can be connected, even equated, with the society's notion of self, all the while preserving its apparent neutrality. The truth, of course, is that it is not the past that is doing the heavy lifting in such cases, but, instead, history. Historical practice is a far cry from the dispassionate impartiality of the past. In any case, nationalist battles over the past, using history as a weapon for national legitimation, make the link between identity and history obvious to the inhabitants of a world of nation-states. Perhaps then, few will be surprised that even in a nonmodern, nonnationalist society such as eighteenth-century to early twentieth-century Altishahr, an examination of local history leads inexorably to a study of that identity. In Altishahr under Qing indirect rule, history's role as a weapon in struggles for legitimacy was overshadowed by other functions. Local historical practice was, instead, a ritual act linking the community to God through the presence of historical personages. It was also an explanation of the origins of group activities that brought people together. Though history in Altishahr differed from nationalist history in its functioning, it was no less intimately connected to people's imagination of their own community.

Despite my having said so much about tazkirahs and shrines, it should also be clear that the tazkirah-shrine system of historical practice was not the only one current in Altishahr during the nineteenth and twentieth centuries. There were always elite scholarly circles, some of whose members would have scoffed at the works that are the focus of this study (though many also embraced them). We have seen that the invasion of Ya'qub Beg brought about a significant injection of literary influences from Western Turkestan, most obvious in the flood of chronicles that emerged in its wake. This wave brought hints of modernism that were reinforced in a big way, beginning in the 1890s, and especially when Altishahri students began returning from study in Soviet Tashkent in the 1930s. However, the system of knowledge emphasized in this study was the most widely deployed one during the period in question. More people participated in this historical tradition than did in the Ya'qub Beg officials' circles or the reform movements of the twentieth century's first three decades.

My distinguishing of the popular tradition from these other trends could be somewhat deceptive, if it is seen to imply isolation. For this reason it must be emphasized that there was perpetual interaction. Mullah Mūsá Sayrāmī's critique of the tazkirah-shrine system is evidence enough of that. And, as we have seen, by the late twentieth century, it was a blending of the tazkirah-shrine tradition and modern nationalist historical approaches that came to represent most Uyghur engagement with the past. However, at least until the 1930s, and probably for a decade or two thereafter, the new approaches to the past were inaccessible to the vast majority of Altishahris. It has been my aim to explore the common experience of the local past, and the tazkirah-shrine tradition stands out as predominant. This tradition should not be seen simply as a background against which modernity made its blustery entrance into Altishahr. The tazkirah-shrine tradition was not stagnant. It was subject to constant community renewal through manuscript practices, and occasional ruptures through independent authorship. At the moment that reformers were trying to change the manuscript tradition, the manuscript tradition was itself changing, as it always had been.

During the second half of the twentieth century, the pace of change quickened. The kinds of changes resulting from community authorship within the tradition of Altishahri historical practice were overshadowed by major interruptions that entered from outside Altishahr entirely. Chief among these were nationalist thought, printing, and finally, the rule of the Chinese Communist Party, which accelerated the adoption of printing and nationalist thought while attacking the ritual basis of the popular local historical tradition. By the mid-1960s, the actions of the Chinese Communist Party rulers of Altishahr had gravely circumscribed two of the main fulcra of historical practice in Altishahr: the text in the form of the manuscript and place in the form of the shrine. Yet the Altishahri approach to local history survived, in part through the use of personage as an organizing principle.

Personage had been an important fulcrum of historical meaning long before the challenges of the later twentieth century. Though tazkirahs were organized in their composite manuscripts by place and geographical networks, they were labeled with the names of the saints. The stories of those great personages, added together, constituted the history of Alt-ishahr. As the narratives changed, the heroes remained the same. Certain personages, like certain texts and places, were unquestioned axes around which the community's constantly renegotiated history turned. The role of personage became more apparent as the people of Altishahr, under the name "Uyghur," adapted their popular historical tradition to new political and social contexts. Personages still lend their names to popular historical texts, the biographical novels, and young men debate historical questions through discussion of those personages. The tazkirah, stripped of the flexibility of the manuscript tradition and the power of massive sacred recitations, has reemerged in the nationalist biographical novel by arranging historical narrative around the ideal personages of Uyghur heroes such as Sultan Satūq Bughrā-khān, or, in the case of Afaq Khoja, an ideal national traitor.

The importance of shrine, pilgrimage, and manuscript in shaping to-day's nationalist histories should serve as a warning, to both Western and Chinese analysts, that a focus on the conflicts between Uyghurs and the Chinese state can distort our understanding of Uyghur identity. To be sure, the histories that Uyghurs most avidly produce and consume stand in opposition to Beijing's official image of China as an eternal and harmo-nious multiethnic nation. However, this does not mean that such a histori-cal tradition was primarily constructed as a form of opposition. Popular Uyghur historical practice is a very real expression of cultural systems that were already developing before the arrival of China-based subjugation. Although influenced by its political context, Uyghur historical practice is neither a reaction to subjugation nor a simple artifact of resistance. Much Chinese political and scholarly discourse seeks to quarantine what is pre-sented as a minor strain of dangerous oppositional historiography, while promoting a "real" history of the Uyghurs that buttresses the official nar-rative. Meanwhile, Western scholars seek in Uyghur historiography a con-scious resistance to the colonial Chinese state. Both approaches find what they seek, and, in doing so, remain blind to the ways that Uyghurness it-self resists. But Uyghurness does not only resist. Uyghur notions of history also offer to expand our sense of how humans can and do interact with the past, a contribution that would be no less valuable or striking had it developed entirely in the absence of Chinese domination.

There is little chance that the prominence of Chinese domination, both in scholarly analyses and in the lives of Uyghurs, will diminish any-time soon. In response to acts of violent resistance from 2009 to 2014,

Beijing has redoubled its reliance on security services and increased the very restrictions on cultural expression and mobility that magnify Uyghur discontent. As the state creates more constraints for Uyghurs to resist, resistance will only become more worthy of study. But we cannot give up hope that a greater understanding of Uyghur culture on its own terms, including Uyghur Islam, Uyghur identity, and even Uyghur historical practice, may one day contribute to more informed, if not more ethical, policy decisions.

NOTES

Abbreviations

Archives

Al-Biruni Institute of Oriental Studies, Academy of Sciences, Republic of
   Uzbekistan (IVANRUz)

Bancroft Library, University of California, Berkeley (Bancroft)

Bodleian Library, Oxford University (Bodleian)

Former holdings of the British Museum, now in the British Library (BM)

Hartmann collection, Staatsbibliothek zu Berlin—Preussischer Kulturbesitz
   (Hartmann)

Indian Institute Library collection, Bodleian Library, Oxford University (Ms
   Ind Inst)

India Office Library collection, British Library (IOL)

Jarring Collection, Lund University Library (Jarring Prov.)

Library of the Nationalities Research Institute, Central University of Nationalities, Beijing (MZXY)

Mannerheim Collection, National Library of Finland (Mannerheim)

St. Petersburg branch of the Institute of Oriental Studies of the Russian
   Academy of Sciences (SP)

University and State Library of Saxony-Anhalt in Halle (Saale): Library of the
   German Oriental Society (Halle)

Xinjiang Branch of the Chinese Academy of Social Science, Nationalities
   Research Institute (XJCASS)

Individual Manuscripts

HMShSM: Harvard University Libraries, uncataloged manuscript containing the
   Tazkirah of Muhammad Sharīf and the *Tazkirah of the Seven Muhammads.*

KhMSh: Private collection in Khotan, manuscript of the *Tazkirah of Muhammad Sharīf.*

MFSI: uncataloged, paginated manuscript containing tazkirahs of the Four Sacrificed Imams, *Imām Ja'far Ṣādiq*, the Seven Muhammads, and Muhammad Sharīf in the Library of the Nationalities Research Institute, Central University of Nationalities, Beijing.

Introduction

1. A few examples: History as writing: Paul Ricoeur, *Memory, History, Forgetting,* trans. Kathleen Blamey and David Pellauer (Chicago: University of Chicago Press, 2004), 234; History as a science: Numa Denis Fustel De Coulanges, cited in Marc Bloch, *The Historian's Craft: Reflections on the Nature and Uses of History and the Techniques and Methods of Those Who Write It,* trans. Peter Putnam (Manchester: Manchester University Press, 1992), 25; history as common to all societies: Michel Foucault, *The Archaeology of Knowledge; and the Discourse on Language,* trans. A. M. Sheridan Smith (New York: Pantheon Books, 1982), 7.

2. Greg Dening, *The Death of William Gooch: A History's Anthropology* (Honolulu: University of Hawai'i Press, 1995).

3. Maurice Halbwachs, *On Collective Memory*, trans. and ed. Lewis A. Coser (Chicago: University of Chicago Press, 1992); Jan Assmann, *Religion and Cultural Memory: Ten Studies* (Stanford: Stanford University Press, 2005).

4. This sense has survived from the original Greek *historia,* which indicated either learning by inquiry or the narration that results from such inquiry; Henry Liddell and Robert Scott, *Greek-English Lexicon* (New York: Harper and Brothers, 1870), 676.

5. Benedict Anderson, *Imagined Communities: Reflections on the Origin and Spread of Nationalism* (London: Verso, 1991), 86.

6. Xinjiang Weiwu'er Zizhiqu Jaioyu Ting and Xinjiang Lishi Jiaocai Bianxie Zu, *Xinjiang Difang Shi* (Ürümchi: Xinjiang Daxue Chubanshe, 1991), 9.

7. Both of these characteristics of the term may be changing. *Altishahr* is the name of the most successful Uyghur hip-hop group.

8. *Moghūlistān* was also common, especially in the earlier texts treated below.

9. David Brophy, "Rebirth of a Nation: The Modern Revival of Uyghur Ethnicity," (MA thesis, Harvard University, Cambridge, MA, 2005).

10. India Office Records: L/P&S/7/91, British Library.

11. The most influential formulation of this argument is by Dru C. Gladney, "The Ethnogenesis of the Uighur," *Central Asian Survey* 9, no. 1 (1990): 1–28.

12. That is to say, relying primarily on records created by the state or governing elites, for example, James Millward, *Beyond the Pass: Economy, Ethnicity, and Empire in Qing Central Asia, 1759–1864* (Stanford: Stanford University Press, 1998); Justin Matthew Jacobs, "Empire Besieged: The Preservation of Chinese Rule in Xinjiang, 1884–1971" (PhD dissertation, University of California, San Diego, 2011).

13. For example, Michael Dillon, *China's Muslims* (New York: Oxford University Press, 1996); Graham E. Fuller and Jonathan N. Lipman, "Islam in Xinjiang," in *Xinjiang: China's Muslim Borderland,* ed. S. Frederick Starr, new edition (Armonk, NY: M. E. Sharpe, 2004), 320–352.

14. Shahzad Bashir, *Sufi Bodies: Religion and Society in Medieval Islam* (New York: Columbia University Press, 2011); A. Azfar Moin, *The Millennial Sovereign: Sacred Kingship and Sainthood in Islam* (New York: Columbia University Press, 2012).

15. Nile Green, *Indian Sufism since the Seventeenth Century: Saints, Books and Empires in the Muslim Deccan* (London: Routledge, 2006); Nile Green, *Making Space: Sufis and Settlers in Early Modern India* (Oxford: Oxford University Press, 2012).

16. Exemplary works that do take such traditions seriously as history include: Renato Rosaldo, *Ilongot Headhunting, 1883–1974: A Study in Society and History* (Stanford: Stanford University Press, 1980); Kirsten Hastrup, *Other Histories* (New York: Routledge, 1992); Andrew Shryock, *Nationalism and the Genealogical Imagination: Oral History and Textual Authority in Tribal Jordan* (Berkeley: University of California Press, 1997).

1. The Historical Canon

1. The only one of these not to pass on significant material to the Uyghur *historical* tradition was the Chinese tradition. There is, however, in the British Library, an Altishahri translation of a Chinese tale, which bears a date of 1270 AH (1853–1854): manuscript no. Or. 5329.

2. For example, Mirza Haydar Dūghlāt, the Kashgarian author of the sixteenth century *Tārīkh-i Rashīdī,* used important Persian-language works from Western Turkestan, such as Yazdi's *Zafarnāma* and the *Tārīkh-i Jahāngushāy,* but aside from excerpts reproduced within the *Tārīkh-i Rashīdī,* these works didn't find a place in the later Eastern Turki historical canon. Mirza Haydar Dūghlāt, *Mirza Haydar Dughlat's Tarikh-I Rashidi: A History of the Khans of Moghulistan,* trans. W. M. Thackston (Cambridge, MA: Harvard University, Dept. of Near Eastern Languages and Civilizations, 1996). I have been unable to trace any Altishahri copies of the *Zafarnāma* or the *Tārīkh-i Jahāngushāy* in the collections of Gunnar Jarring, Martin Hartmann, or the Urumchi Ancient Text Office.

3. Abu'l-Qāsim Firdawsī, *The Shahnama of Firdawsī* trans. A. G. Warner and E. Warner. (London: Kegan Paul et. al., 1905–1915 [ca. 1000]), 311.

4. For the shrine's location on the old Khotan to Chira road, see the "Map Showing Portions of Chinese Turkestan" in the back pocket of M. Aurel Stein, *Sand-Buried Ruins of Khotan: Personal Narrative of a Journey of Archaeological and Geographical Exploration in Chinese Turkestan* (London: Hurst and Blackett, 1904).

5. The shrine is described in Rahilă Davut, *Uyghur mazarliri* (Ürümchi: Shinjang khălq năshriyati, 2001), 135.

6. In Altishahr, "shaykh" is a religious title and position usually reserved for a man or men in charge of a shrine or saint's tomb. The title implies great knowledge and devotion to the holy personage associated with the shrine.

7. In quoting the shaykh's tale, I have approximated his pronunciation of the main characters' names. In the tradition of Arabic names like 'Abdallah (slave of God) and 'Fazlallah (favor of God), the shaykh's tale added the combining form of "Allah" to the name of Siyāvush.

8. Whereas *Altishahr* literally means "six cities," *Yettishahr* means "seven cities." Both terms refer to the same region.

9. Harold Scheub, *The Poem in the Story: Music, Poetry, and Narrative* (Madison: University of Wisconsin Press, 2002), 18–19.

10. Rahilă Davut, *Uyghur mazarliri* (Ürümchi: Shinjang khălq năshriyati, 2001), 135–138.

11. Uyghur: *kona kitablar.*

12. For example, a carbon-copy manuscript in of Mullah Ḥājī's *Tazkirat al-Bughrā-khān,* calling itself the *Tăzkiră Hăzriti Sultan Săyd Ăli Arisilankhan,* copied in 1983, bears the phrase "written according to the original text" (Ăsli tikisti buyichă yizildi). Prov. 580.

13. Shinjang Uyghur Aptonom Rayonluq Az Sanliq Millăt Qădimki Ăsărlirini Toplash, Rătlăsh, Năshir Qilishni Pilanlash Răhbărlik Guruppa Ishkhanisi, *Uyghur, özbek, tatar qădimki ăsărlăr tizimliki* (Kashgar: Qăshqăr Uyghur năshriyati, 1989). This catalog represents the most extensive record of manuscripts preserved in Xinjiang today, encompassing 1,550 books (a small minority of which are lithographs). Many of the entries in this catalog are too vague to determine origins of the texts they describe, but roughly two thirds of those that are identifiable have origins outside Altishahr. A similarly large proportion of works in the Jarring collection, which has a much clearer catalog, are of non-Altishahri origin, despite a slight bias in the collection toward Altishahri works. Gunnar Jarring, Handwritten Catalog of the Gunnar Jarring Collection of Manuscripts from Eastern Turkestan in the Lund University Library, 1997. Taking a count of foreign versus local works is of course more of an art than a science, as it is always difficult to decide where to draw the line, especially where foreign seed material has been reworked by Altishahri authors.

14. P. Oktor Skjaervo, "Eastern Iranian Epic Traditions I. Siyāvaš and Kunāla," in *Mír Curad. Studies in Honor of Calvert Watkins,* ed. J. Jasanoff, H. C. Melchert, and L. Oliver (Innsbruck: Innsbr. Beitr. z.Sprachwiss, 1998).

15. Mirza Ḥaydar, *Tārīkh-I Rashīdī: tarīkh-i khavānīn-i Mughūlistān: Matn-i Fārsī,* ed. W. M. Thackston (Cambridge, MA: Dānishgāh-i Hārvārd, bakhsh-i zabānhā va farhang'hā-yi khāvar-i nazdīk, 1996), 154 (f. 87r).

16. Skjaervo, "Eastern Iranian Epic Traditions I"; M. Aurel Stein, *Ancient Khotan: Detailed Report of Archaeological Explorations in Chinese Turkestan* (Oxford: Clarendon Press, 1907), 159.

17. For a collection of foundation stories of other cities in Altishahr, see Ghăyrătjan Osman, ed., *Uyghur khălq rivayătliri: shăkhslăr, văqălăr hăqqidiki rivayătlăr* (Ürümchi: Shinjang yashlar—ösmürlăr năshriyati, 1998). Most of the tales in this collection derive from Altishahri oral tradition, but some are culled from written sources.

18. This number excludes the products of the Swedish missionaries who printed Turki-language Bibles, hymnals, and schoolbooks at their press in Kashgar. The surviving lithographs are to be found in the Hartmann collection and the Jarring collection, with one important specimen preserved in the Princeton University Library.

19. Jack Dabbs, *History of the Discovery and Exploration of Chinese Turkestan* (The Hague: Mouton and Co., 1963).

20. Few details about this process have come to light, but some hints are to be found in Mukhlisov, *Uyghur klassik ădibiyati qolyazmilirining katalogi* ([Ürümchi?]: Shinjang yerlik muzeygha tăyarliq korush basqarmisi, 1957).

21. This situation may not last. I have seen PRC government documents claiming that thousands of "illegal books" have been confiscated, and some Uyghurs report that local authorities have threatened house-by-house searches for such books.

22. A. M. Muginov, *Opisanie uĭgurskikh rukopiseĭ Instituta Narodov Azii* (Moscow: Izdatel'stvo vostochnoĭ literatury, 1962); Muhammad Haidar Dughlát, *The Tarikh-I-Rashidi: A History of the Moghuls of Central Asia,* trans. E. Denison Ross (London: S. Low, Marston and Company, 1895).

23. Martin Hartmann, "Die Osttürkischen Handschriften der Sammlung Hartmann," *Mitteilungen des Seminars für Orientalische Sprachen an der Königlichen Friedrich-Wilhelms-Universität zu Berlin* 7, no. 2 (1904): 1–21.

24. Thomas Douglas Forsyth, *Report of a Mission to Yarkund in 1873* (Calcutta: Foreign Department Press, 1875), 87. A partial translation into Turki may be found in St. Petersburg D23, but this appears to be a rare exception: Dmitrieva, *Katalog tiurkskikh rukopiseĭ Instituta Vostokovedeniia Rossiĭskoĭ Akademii Nauk,* 428.

25. Martin Hartmann, *Chinesisch-Turkestan: Geschichte, Verwaltung, Geistesleben und Wirtschaft* (Halle: Gebauer-Schwetschke Druckerei und Verlag, 1908), 47–52.

26. Mirza Haydar Dūghlāt, *Mirza Haydar Dughlat's Tarikh-I Rashidi,* 3.

27. Alongside the Arabic-only Qurans and Quranic selections, there circulated a smaller number of Quranic selections with Persian or Turki interlinear commentary or explanation. Still, it seems that such works had limited impact. The writer Saddriddin Ayni describes a similar situation in Western Turkestan,

where he made his way through the various levels of the educational system without learning the meaning of the Quranic verses he had memorized. Sadriddin Aini, *The Sands of Oxus: Boyhood Reminiscences of Sadriddin Aini* (Costa Mesa, CA: Mazda Publishers, 1998). Even the occasional *ḥāfiẓ* (person who has memorized the entire Quran) whom I encountered in Altishahr said that he was not taught the meaning of the Quran.

28. Jarring Prov. 570, f. 51r–51v.

29. Jeanine Elif Dagyeli, *"Gott liebt das Handwerk": Moral, Identität und religiöse Legitimierung in der mittelasiatischen Handwerks-risala* (Wiesbaden, Germany: Dr. Ludwig Reichert Verlag, 2011); Adeeb Khalid, *The Politics of Muslim Cultural Reform: Jadidism in Central Asia* (Berkeley: University of California Press, 1998), 25–26.

30. For example, Jarring Prov. 570, ff. 40r–41r. See also, above, Khalid, *The Politics of Muslim Cultural Reform,* 26.

31. This is further confirmed by the large number of *risālahs* (over 40 volumes) in the Urumchi Ancient Text Office: Shinjang Uyghur Aptonom Rayonluq Az Sanliq Millät Qädimki Äsärlirini Toplash, Rätläsh, Näshir Qilishni Pilanlash Rähbärlik Guruppa ishkhanisi, *Uyghur, özbek, tatar qädimki äsärlär tizimliki,* 540–554.

32. For distribution of the *risalas,* see Dagyeli, *Gott liebt das Handwerk.* For other popular Central Asian works, many of which were also read widely in Altishahr, see Sigrid Kleinmichel, *Halpa in Choresm (Hwarazm) und Atin Ayi in Ferganatal: Zur Geschichte des Lesens in Usbekistan im 20. Jahrhundert* (Berlin: Das Arabische Buch, 2000).

33. Many Altishahri manuscripts of the *Qisas ul-Anbiyā'* clearly descend from the text compiled by al-Rabghūzī around 1310 in Western Turkestan, though they are marked by significant deviations and interpolations. For an extensive discussion and bibliography, see Gunnar Jarring, *Literary Texts from Kashghar* (Lund: CWK Gleerup, 1980), 14–15. Al-Rabghūzī's work is, in turn, a recasting of Persian version of an Arabic work of the same name. Nosiruddin Burhonuddin Rabghuzii, *The Stories of the Prophets: Qisas Al-Anbiya': An Eastern Turkish Version,* ed. Semih Tezcan, trans. M. Vandamme, J. O'Kane, and H. E. Boeschoten (Leiden; New York: Brill, 1995).

34. The popularity of this book among Turki readers and listeners from all walks of life was noted by European travelers to the region in the late nineteenth and early twentieth centuries, and this popularity is reflected in the large number of manuscripts surviving in various archives. Jarring, recounting his 1929–1930 visit to Kashgar, wrote that the *Qiṣaṣ ul-Anbiyā'* was the "best known, most read, and most copied" of the "Islamic religious and morality works." Gunnar Jarring, *Return to Kashgar: Central Asian Memoirs in the Present,* trans. Eva Claeson (Durham: Duke University Press, 1986), 198. The Urumchi Ancient Text Office holds ten copies: Shinjang Uyghur Aptonom Ray-

onluq Az Sanliq Millăt Qădimki Ăsărlirini Toplash, Rătlăsh, Năshir Qilishni Pilanlash Răhbărlik Guruppa Ishkhanisi, *Uyghur, özbek, tatar qădimki ăsărlăr tizimliki,* 111–115. There are ten in Lund, one of which was commissioned by the Swedish missionary Gustaf Ahlbert (Jarring, Handwritten Catalog of the Gunnar Jarring Collection of Manuscripts from Eastern Turkestan in the Lund University Library), three in St. Petersburg (Muginov, *Opisanie uĭgurskikh rukopiseĭ Instituta Narodov Azii.*), and two in the Hartmann collection in Berlin (Hartmann, "Die Osttürkischen Handschriften der Sammlung Hartmann," 1–21).

35. Ṭabarī's famous *History of the Prophets and Kings* was also known but seems to represent a historiographical dead end in Altishahr. Although the book was translated into Eastern Turki around 1800, it was a scarce book and never imitated. One copy is preserved in the Jarring collection, Prov. 439. The translation is mentioned in the *Tārīkh-i Rashīdī-i Turkī.* There is also one copy of Balʿamī's Persian version from Altishahr listed in Shinjang Uyghur Aptonom Rayonluq Az Sanliq Millăt Qădimki Ăsărlirini Toplash, Rătlăsh, Năshir Qilishni Pilanlash Răhbărlik Guruppa ishkhanisi, *Uyghur, özbek, tatar qădimki ăsărlăr tizimliki,* 191.

36. Kleinmichel, *Halpa in Choresm (Hwarazm) und Atin Ayi in Ferganatal.*

37. Prov. 98 calls itself the *Jamiʿ al-Ḥikayat Turkī.* Adding the word *Turkī* to a title was a convention that indicated a work was a translation—thus, *Shāhnāmah-i Turkī, Tārīkh-i Rashīdī-i Turkī,* and so on. The presence of numerous sections of Persian verse preserved within the translations also suggests a Persian original. See, for example, Abdurakhman Aqsu'i, *Jami'i hekayă* (Ürümchi: Shinjang khălq năshriyati, 1998).

38. See, for example, Jarring Prov. 568.

39. Aqsu'i, *Jami'i hekayă,* 243.

40. Richard Stoneman, trans., *The Greek Alexander Romance* (London: Penguin Books, 1991), 28.

41. In any case, holy figures who preceded the prophet Muhammad, especially prophets such as Moses, were seen as Muslims.

42. Seeger A. Bonebakker, "Some Medieval Views on Fantastic Stories," *Quaderni Di Studi Arabi* 10 (1992): 21–43.

43. Prov. 324, f. 46r.

44. Greg Dening, *The Death of William Gooch: A History's Anthropology* (Honolulu: University of Hawai'i Press, 1995), 12.

45. Aqsu'i, *Jami'i hekayă,* 255.

46. For example, the *Tārīkh-i Ḥamīdī.* Jarring Prov. 163.

47. Both have been translated into English. Kai-Kā'ūs bin Iskandar, *A Mirror for Princes: The Qābūs Nāma,* trans. Reuben Levy (London: The Cresset Press, 1951); Ṭabarī, *The History of Al-Tabari,* ed. Ehsan Yarshater, 40 vols. (Albany: SUNY Press, 1985).

48. Jarring, *Return to Kashgar,* 198.

49. A similarly titled work, *Rāhat al-Qulūb,* was quite popular in Altishahr, but seems to be different from Huwaydā's *Rāḥat-i Dil,* described in Kleinmichel, *Halpa in Choresm (Hwarazm) und Atin Ayi in Ferganatal,* 255. Though not all of the works described by Kleinmichel as popular in Ferghana and Khwarezm found readership in Altishahr, most did. They are here subsumed under the categories of stories about the prophet and his family and *ḥikayāt.* For the *Rāhat al-Qulūb,* see Jarring, *Literary Texts from Kashghar,* 69–84.

50. Reşid Rahmeti Arat, *Kutadgu Bilig, I: Metin* (Istanbul: Millî Eğitim Basımevi, 1947); Khāṣṣ-Hājib, *Wisdom of Royal Glory: A Turco-Islamic Mirror for Princes—Kutadgu Bilig.*

51. Maḥmūd Kāšǧarī, *Compendium of the Turkic Dialects: (Dīwān luǧāt atturk),* ed. James Kelly and Robert Dankoff (Cambridge, MA: Harvard University Printing Office, 1982).

52. T. I. Sultanov, "Medieval Historiography in Manuscripts from East Turkestan," *Manuscripta Orientalia* 2, no. 1 (1996): 25–30.

53. A. B. Khalidov, *Arabskie rukopisi Instituta Vostokovedeniia: kratkiĭ katalog* (Moscow: Nauka, Glavnaia redaktsiia vostochnoĭ literatury, 1986), 422. Nos. 9338 and 9339; Mirza Haydar Dūghlāt, *Mirza Haydar Dughlat's Tarikh-i Rashidi,* 225, 251.

54. Mirza Haydar Dūghlāt, *Mirza Haydar Dughlat's Tarikh-i Rashidi.*

55. Ibid., 3.

56. Julie Meisami, *Persian Historiography to the End of the Twelfth Century* (Edinburgh: Edinburgh University Press, 1999).

57. Mirza Haydar Dūghlāt, *Mirza Haydar Dughlat's Tarikh-i Rashidi,* 3.

58. Churās, *Khronika.*

59. O. F Akimushkin, ed., *Tārīkh-i Kāshghar: Anonimnaia Tiurkskaia khronika vladeteleĭ Vostochnogo Turkestana po konets XVII veka: Faksimile Rukopisi Sankt-Peterburgskogo Filiala Instituta Vostokovedeniia Akademii Nauk Rossii* (Sankt-Peterburg: TSentr Peterburgskoe Vostokovedenie, 2001), 294.

60. Churās's work is known from one Persian original (Russian State Library Pers. 11) and two Turkic translations: Tursunmuhămmăt Sawut, *Uyghur ădăbiyati tarikhi materiallar katalogi* (Ürümchi: Shinjang dashö til-ădăbiyat fakulteti, 1991), 328, #3547; Churās, *Khronika,* 333, IVANRuz 7586. The so-called *Chinggiznamă* is known from the following manuscripts: XJCASS MS 00679, SP C576, SP B2472, and SP C577. Molla Mir Salih Kashghări, *Chinggiznamă* (Kashgar: Qăshqăr Uyghur năshriyati, 1986), 1; Dmitrieva, *Katalog tiurkskikh rukopiseĭ Instituta Vostokovedeniia Rossiĭskoĭ Akademii Nauk,* 55.

61. Dmitrieva, *Katalog tiurkskikh rukopiseĭ Instituta Vostokovedeniia Rossiĭskoĭ Akademii Nauk,* 39–41. Jarring Prov. 77; Tashkent IVANRUz 1430 10191/II; Jarring Prov. 77; Sawut, *Uyghur ădăbiyati tarikhi materiallar katalogi,* 329, #3552.

62. Sultanov, "Medieval Historiography in Manuscripts from East Turkestan," 27.

63. SP nos. D120, D121, and D122.

64. T. I. Sultanov, "Medieval Historiography in Manuscripts from East Turkestan," 29; T. I. Sultanov, "'Tārīkh-i Rashīdī' Mīrzā Khaidara Dūghlāta (Literaturnaiâ istoriiâ pamiâtnika)," *Pis'mennye pamiâtniki vostoka* (1982): 116–135.

65. The last ruler of the independent "Sa'idiya," Moghul Khanate, was defeated in 1678. The *Chinggiznāmah* was written around 1696. Nīyazī's *Qiṣaṣ al-Gharā'ib* of 1852 could be considered an exception. Its blending of universal history, the history of Chinggis Khan's descendants, and records of "strange" occurrences, strays far from the standard form of dynastic history, but it was commissioned by a ruler with claims to descent from the Chinggisids who are the subject of the work's second section. For more on Nīyazī, see Sultanov, "Medieval Historiography in Manuscripts from East Turkestan." On the role of the "strange" in Islamic Central Asia, see A. Azfar Moin, *The Millennial Sovereign: Sacred Kingship and Sainthood in Islam* (New York: Columbia University Press, 2012), 60–62.

66. During the dozen years (1865–1877) in which Ya'qub Beg built an Islamic State in Altishahr, dynastic history made a brief return to Altishahr. More than a dozen histories of Ya'qub Beg's military intervention in the region were written, many of them by authors who arrived with Ya'qub Beg from Andijan. These works never gained much currency; most are known only from single autographs. For a description of the histories of the Ya'qub beg era, see Hodong Kim, *Holy War in China: The Muslim Rebellion and State in Chinese Central Asia, 1864–1877* (Stanford: Stanford University Press, 2004), 263–266.

67. There are, of course, rare exceptions, in the form of both works usually called tazkirah but not labeled as such, and, more rarely, works that are only called *tazkirah* in a single copy, for example, a lone copy of a biography of Fāṭima, labeled *tazkirah* in St. Petersburg (SP C551, 1v).

68. The addition of titles at the hands of copyists, compilers, or collectors was also common elsewhere in the Islamic world during the manuscript age. In the Arabic tradition such titles were often alterations or abbreviations of an original title supplied by the author within the text. Nikolaj Serikoff, "Beobachtungen über die Marginal- und Schnittmittel in christlich-arabischen und islamischen Büchersammlungen," in *Manuscript Notes as Documentary Sources,* ed. Andreas Görke and Konrad Hirschler (Beirut: Ergon Verlag, 2011).

69. The prose *Tazkirah of the Four Sacrificed Imams,* for example, has been labeled:

..... imāmlāri türt imām ẕabīḥlārning Khotan diyārighā kälgänlärining
   wāqi'ātlāri (MS in a private Khotan collection).
taẕkīra'i Ḥaẕrat Imām Nāṣr al-Dīn Imām Ẕahir al-Dīn Imām Mu'īn al-Dīin Imām
   Qawām al-Dīn bayānidā (Prov. 102, f. 48v)
taẕkira-yi Ḥaẕrat Padshāh Jahāngīr u Ṣaḥib-i Qirān u Qātil-i Kuffār u Nām-i
   Mashhūr (Prov. 349, f. 48r)

türt imām ẓabīh Allahning taẓkirahlari (Prov. 327, f. 31r)
taẓkirah-i imāmān-i Khotan (Prov. 565)
taẓkirah-i ḥaẓrat imām ẓabīhlar (MZXY T70, SP C551, Prov. 73, f. 123v)

Note that only one of these label/titles does not include the word *tazkirah*.

70. Anonymous. *Tazkirah-i Sut Bībī Padishāhim,* Hartmann, MS Or. Oct. 1727. f. 1v.

71. The earliest biographical Persian work to use the tazkirah designation in its title is Farīd al-Dīn 'Aṭṭār's *Taẓkirat al-Awliyā'.* For a translation of this work, which was also available in Altishahr, see Farid-ud-Din 'Attar, *Le Mémorial Des Saints,* trans. A. Pavet de Courteille (Paris: Éditions du Seuil, 1976).

72. For example, in eighteenth- and nineteenth-century India, a tazkirah was usually a biographical dictionary of poets, whereas in Western Turkestan the genre was equally likely to focus on Sufi saints.

73. For a useful discussion of the questions surrounding the authorship of this work, see Devin DeWeese, "The Tadhkira-i Bughrā-Khān and the 'Uvaysī' Sufis of Central Asia: Notes in Review of Imaginary Muslims," *Central Asiatic Journal* 40 (1996): 87–127.

74. The Khwajagan and their followers were, of course, not the only people to employ these common Arabic terms for titles and genres. The semantic range of *maqāmāt* and *manāqib* across various societies from pre-Islamic Arabia to Islamic Spain, North Africa, and the Turko-Persian world is vast. See, for example A. F. L. Beeston, "The Genesis of the Maqāmāt Genre," *Journal of Arabic Literature* 2 (1971): 1–12; Asma Afsaruddin, "In Praise of the Caliphs: Re-Creating History from the Manaqib Literature," *International Journal of Middle East Studies* 31, no. 3 (n.d.): 329–350. Here I will use the combination of the two words *(maqāmāt/manāqib),* which in other contexts indicated separate genres, to indicate the sixteenth- to eighteenth-century Central Asian tradition.

75. Mawlānā Shaykh, *Maqāmāt-i Khvājah Aḥrār: Tazkirah-'i Khvājah Nāṣir Al-Dīn 'Ubayd Allāh Aḥrār (806 Tā 895 Q.),* (Tokyo: Institute for the Study of Languages and Cultures of Asia and Africa, 2004). For *Ẓiyā' al-Qulūb,* see C. A. Storey, *Persian Literature: A Bio-Bibliographical Survey,* vol. 1, part 2 (London: Luzac and Company, 1972), 981.

76. Among the Turki tazkirahs whose Altishahri origin has never been called into question, the *Tazkirah of Muhammad Sharīf Khvājah* appears to have the earliest *terminus ante quem.* The work must have been in existence as of 1724, when it was versified by Muhammad Zalīlī. For the dating and editing in modern Uyghur orthography of Zalīlī's works, see Muhammad Zalīlī, *Zălili Divani,* trans. Imin Tursun (Beijing: Millătlăr năshriyati, 1985). Several manuscripts of Zalīlī's works survive, the most complete being that used for the modern Uyghur edition. Other examples are to be found in Lund: Prov. 76 and Prov. 414. The *Tazkirah of Muhammad Sharīf* must have been written after the last event

recorded therein, the death of 'Abd al-Raḥīm Khan. According to the *Ching-giznāmah,* this occurred in 967 AH (1559–1560 AD). Akimushkin, *Tārīkh-i Kāshghar: Anonimnaia Tiurkskaia khronika vladetelei Vostochnogo Turkestana po konets XVII veka: Faksimile Rukopisi Sankt-Peterburgskogo Filiala Instituta Vostokovedeniia Akademii Nauk Rossii,* f. 64a. Since all known copies of the *Tazkirah of Muhammad Sharīf* are written in Turki, and the earliest known Turki literary product from the region *(Chinggiznāmah)* was written at the end of the seventeenth century, it is likely that it was written in the later portion of the date range given here, namely, from the last quarter of the seventeenth century to 1724. The possibility remains, however, that a hitherto unknown Persian original may yet be discovered, potentially pushing the date back much further.

77. The summary here is based on the following manuscripts: HMShSM; KhMSh; MFSI; Jarring Prov. 73.

78. Probably he is meant to be Khiẓr, who also guided Alexander the Great in the *Iskandarnamah,* and Sultan Satūq Bughrā-khan in the *Tazkirah of Sultan Satūq Bughrā-khān.* See Patrick Franke, *Begegnung mit Khidr: Quellenstudien zum Imagindren im Traditionellen Islam* (Stuttgart: Franz Steiner Verlag, 2000).

79. The *munājāt* genre has been common in much of the Islamic world. For more on its Central Asian manifestations, see Thierry Zarcone, "The Invocation of Saints and/or Spirits by the Sufis and the Shamans: About the Munâjât Literary Genre in Central Asia," *Kyoto Bulletin of Islamic Area Studies* 1, no. 1 (2007): 52–61.

80. This tazkirah has been published in a modern Uyghur translation. Molla Haji, *Bughrakhanlar tăzkirisi,* trans. Abdurehim Sabit (Kashgar: Qăshqăr uyghur năshriyati, 1988). The editors have clearly mistaken a collection of works bound together in one manuscript for a single work. The work that Mullah Ḥājī called *Tazkirat al-Bughrā-khān* is probably only the section labeled *ikkinchi bab* (chapter 2) in the Uyghur translation, although it is possible that the *Tazkirah of the Four Sacrificed Imams* (the *khatima* in the Uyghur *Bughrakhanlar tăzkirisi*) was originally part of Mullah Ḥājī's work. See Rian Thum, "Untangling the Bughrā-Khān Manuscripts," in *Mazars: Studies on Islamic Sacred Sites in Central Eurasia,* ed. Jun Sugawara (Tokyo: Tokyo University of Foreign Studies Press, forthcoming). The summary presented here is based on Jarring Prov. 73, Jarring Prov. 148, and the Uyghur translation.

81. Jarring Prov. 73, f. 89v; Jarring Prov. 148, 149v.

82. Mehmed Fuad Köprülü, *Early Mystics in Turkish Literature,* trans. Gary Leiser and Robert Dankoff (New York: Routledge, 2006), 12.

83. *Tazkirah of Imam Ja'far Ṭayaranī:* SP C554. *Tazkirah of Ḥaẓ rat Begim:* Prov. 576. *Tazkirah of Muhammad Ghazālī:* SP B775.

84. This dating is based on the same evidence as the dating of the *Tazkirah of Muhammad Sharīf.* The *Tazkirah of the Seven Muhammads* is also known only in Turki, so we may set the late seventeenth century as a likely *terminus post*

quem, based on the fact that earlier works were composed in Persian. Zalīlī, who versified the *Tazkirah of the Seven Muhammads* (Jarring Prov. 76), was active in the first half of the eighteenth century. My summary of the *Tazkirah of the Seven Muhammads* is based on HMShSM and Jarring Prov. 566.

85. All seven of their names, each beginning with "Muhammad," are given in a MS in the Jarring collection, Prov. 414, f. 18r.

86. Thum, "Untangling the Bughrā-Khān Manuscripts." Eighteenth-century versified tazkirahs include the *Tazkirah of the Seven Muhammads,* the *Tazkirah of Sut Bībī,* the *Tazkirah of Muhammad Sharīf,* and the *Tazkirah of the Four Sacrificed Imams.* The versified *Tazkirah of the Four Sacrificed Imams* can be found in the following manuscripts: MZXY T50, and Mannerheim I. A versification of the *Tazkirah of the Companions of the Cave* also exists, though its dating is uncertain: SP C562, and also Muhămmătturdi Mirzi'ăkhmăt, ed., "Tăzkirǎ'i Ăshabul Kăhf," *Bulaq* 113, no. 2 (2007): 39–48. Another versification of uncertain date is a tazkirah of Abū al-Naṣr Samānī: SP C546. The other three versified tazkirahs mentioned here are the works of Zalīlī and can be found in Prov. 76. Two of these, the tazkirahs of Muhammad Sharīf and the Seven Muhammads, are published in Zalīlī, *Zǎlili Divani.*

87. There is also a small group of texts called *wafātnāmah,* roughly meaning "death book," which describe the circumstances leading up to the death of a holy figure.

88. Mirza Haydar Dūghlāt, *Mirza Haydar Dughlat's Tarikh-i Rashidi.*

89. Prov. 148, ff. 135r–135v.

90. For example, Jarring Prov. 73, 102, 103, 143, 148, 155, 203, 349, 355, 413, 414, 504, 565, 567.

91. Gunnar Jarring, "The Ordam-Padishah-System of Eastern Turkistan Shrines," *Geografiska Annaler* 17 (1935): 348–354.

92. Mannerheim bought a tazkirah at the shrine of Imam Mūsá Kāẓim. G. Raquette, "Collection of Manuscripts from Eastern Turkestan. An Account of the Contents," in *Across Asia from West to East in 1906–1908,* ed. C. G. Mannerheim (Helsinki: Suomalais-Ugrilainen Seura, 1940), 3–15. Hartmann bought one of two copies of the Sut Bībī Pāshim tazkirah kept at the Sut Bībī shrine: Hartmann, "Die Osttürkischen Handschriften der Sammlung Hartmann."

93. The biggest exception is the *Tazkirah of Imam A'zam* (Abu Hanifa). This work does not appear to have been of Altishahri origin, and it was also popular in Western Turkestan. A handful of chapters about saints buried elsewhere were also excerpted from the *Tazkirah of the Uwaysīs* and labeled as individual tazkirahs. However, these are always excerpted together with the chapter containing the biography of Sultan Satūq Bughrā-khān, who is buried in Artush, near Kashgar.

94. SP B775. 47v, 48r.

95. Jarring, *Literary Texts from Kashghar,* 85.

96. Marginal notation, MFSI p. 50.

97. Namely the dynastic histories, especially the *Chinggiznāmah,* which includes the history of Genghis Khan.

2. Manuscript Technology

1. This account is based on Abū al-Qāsim's introduction to his *Ūlūgh Tazkirah-'i Bughrā-khān* (*Great Tazkirah of the Bughrā-khān[s]*), 1829–1830. The manuscript used in this study is Jarring Prov. 563. Based on Muginov's catalog descriptions, SP B734 and C543 seem to be the same work. A. M. Muginov, *Opisanie uĭgurskikh rukopiseĭ Instituta Narodov Azii* (Moscow: Izdatel'stvo vostochnoĭ literatury, 1962).

2. Mukhlisov reports a manuscript of Mullah Ḥājī's *Tazkirat al-Bughrā-khān* copied in 1812, which means that Mullah Ḥājī's tazkirah had been around for at least a decade when Abū al-Qāsim finished his own work. Abū al-Qāsim's complaint that there is no Turki version of the tazkirah would seem to indicate that he was unaware of Mullah Ḥājī's work, which would suggest that Mullah Ḥājī's version was not yet widely propagated. Of course, there is also the possibility that Abū al-Qāsim was aware of Mullah Ḥājī's tazkirah but chose not to mention it, perhaps because he disapproved of it. Mukhlisov also suggested that Mullah Ḥājī was a shaykh at the shrine of Yūsuf Qādir-khān in Kashgar, though he does not say how he came upon this information. If this is true, it is possible that Mullah Ḥājī was among the shaykhs whose additions bothered Abū al-Qāsim. Yusupbeg Mukhlisov, *Uyghur klassik ădibiyati qolyazmilirining katalogi* ([Ürümchi?]: Shinjang yerlik muzeygha tăyarliq korush basqarmisi, 1957), 44.

3. This would seem too obvious to be worth stating were it not for the fact that our own culture of books, represented by this book itself, purports the opposite, presenting books as unobtrusive vehicles for texts that are final, stable formulations of a single "author's" thought. Work on the subject is far too extensive to cite exhaustively, but the following influential works represent a sample of the numerous directions from which these problems have been approached: Roger Chartier, "Laborers and Voyagers: From the Text to the Reader," *Diacritics* 22, no. 2 (1992): 49–61; Elizabeth L. Eisenstein, *The Printing Press as an Agent of Change* (Cambridge: Cambridge University Press, 1980); Adrian Johns, *The Nature of the Book: Print and Knowledge in the Making* (Chicago: University of Chicago Press, 1998); Michell Foucault, "What Is an Author?" in *Textual Strategies: Perspectives in Post-structuralist Criticism,* ed. and trans. Josué V. Harari (Ithaca, NY: Cornell University Press, 1979); D. F. McKenzie, *Bibliography and the Sociology of Texts* (Cambridge: Cambridge University Press, 1999); Walter J. Ong, *Orality and Literacy,* 2nd ed. (New York: Routledge, 2002).

4. As far as possible I have avoided the oral-written binary, a categorization scheme that many scholars have found problematic. One problem is that each

term characterizes transmission, preservation, and reception all at once, leaving little room for the particular constellations evident in Altishahr. Thus, when discussing what has often been called the "oral tradition," I have reserved the adjective "oral" for acts of transmission that actually involve speech, while characterizing textual preservation separately as "memorized" or "unwritten," and reception as "aural." For an important alternative to the oral-written binary in the Islamic context, see Gregor Schoeler, *The Genesis of Literature in Islam: From the Aural to the Read* (Edinburgh: Edinburgh University Press, 2009).

5. Ildikó Bellér-Hann, *The Written and the Spoken: Literacy and Oral Transmission among the Uyghur* (Berlin: Das Arabische Buch, 2000), 41. The close interconnection of oral and written transmission is common throughout Central Asia. M. Nazif Shahrani, "Local Knowledge of Islam and Social Discourse in Afghanistan and Turkistan in the Modern Period," in *Turko-Persia in Historical Perspective,* ed. Robert L. Canfield (Cambridge: Cambridge University Press, 2002), 169.

6. A similar situation pertained in the Arabic-speaking world. See, for example, Edward Lane, *The Manners and Customs of the Modern Egyptians* (London: J. M. Dent & Company, 1908), 397–398.

7. Fernand Grenard, "Histoire, linguistique, archéologie, géographie," in *Mission Scientifique dans la haute Asie, 1890–1895,* ed. J. L. Dutreuil de Rhins (Paris: Ernest Leroux, 1898), 85–86.

8. Abdikerim Rakhman, ed., *Uyghur khălq dastanliri* (Ürümchi: Shinjang khălq năshriyati, 1995); Osman Ismayil, ed., *Uyghur khălq rivayătliri: Nam-ataqlar hăqqidiki rivayătlăr* (Ürümchi: Shinjang yashlar—ösmürlăr năshriyati, 1995); Ghăyrătjan Osman, ed., *Uyghur khălq rivayătliri: Shăkhslăr, văqălăr hăqqidiki rivayătlăr* (Ürümchi: Shinjang yashlar—ösmürlăr năshriyati, 1998); Ăkhmăt Imin, ed., *Uyghur khălq apsană—rivayătliri: Kök gümbăz* (Ürümchi: Shinjang khălq năshriyati, 2006). Such collections are numerous, though there is much duplication of material, and the majority of the works recorded are mirrored by, or directly derived from, well-known written texts. This is very much appropriate to the Altishahri/Uyghur story-telling tradition, but it means that only a small number of tales that circulated exclusively in unwritten forms are preserved within these collections, and most appear to be retellings by the collectors and editors.

9. Grenard, "Histoire, linguistique, archéologie, géographie," 81.

10. Rahilă Davut, *Uyghur mazarliri* (Ürümchi: Shinjang khălq năshriyati, 2001); Osman, *Uyghur khălq rivayătliri.*

11. For one such tale from contemporary Altishahr see Imin, *Uyghur khălq ăpsană—rivayătliri: kök gümbăz,* 88–89.

12. Davut, *Uyghur mazarliri.*

13. In addition to Grenard (cited above), Hartman noted written sources for the ghazalchis' tales. Martin Hartmann, *Chinesisch-Turkestan: Geschichte, Ver-*

waltung, Geistesleben und Wirtschaft (Halle: Gebauer-Schwetschke Druckerei und Verlag, 1908), 40. Olufsen documented the storytellers' written sources in Western Turkestan. Ole Olufsen, *The Emir of Bokhara and His Country* (London: William Heinemann, 1911), 434.

14. Brinkley Messick, *The Calligraphic State: Textual Domination and History in a Muslim Society* (Berkeley: University of California Press, 1996); Dennis Howard Green, *Medieval Listening and Reading: The Primary Reception of German Literature 800–1300* (Cambridge: Cambridge University Press, 2005); Jessica Brantley, *Reading in the Wilderness: Private Devotion and Public Performance in Late Medieval England* (Chicago: University of Chicago Press, 2007); Schoeler, *The Genesis of Literature in Islam*; Konrad Hirschler, *The Written Word in the Medieval Arabic Lands: A Social and Cultural History of Reading Practices* (Edinburgh: Edinburgh University Press, 2012).

15. Of course, this blending does not need to be seen as a stage along an inexorable march from "orality" to the printed word. The "mixing" conceptualization does not preclude recognizing oral performances as a flourishing and integral part of manuscript technology, as opposed to "residual" vestiges of an obsolete technology on the wane, as Walter Ong famously presented them. Ong, *Orality and Literacy*; Jack Goody, *The Interface between the Written and the Oral* (Cambridge: Cambridge University Press, 1987).

16. Daniel Hobbins, *Authorship and Publicity before Print: Jean Gerson and the Transformation of Late Medieval Learning* (Philadelphia: University of Pennsylvania Press, 2009), 8.

17. Translation of the *Tārīkh-i Rashīdī*: SP nos. C569, C570. For the plausible but undocumented claim that Kāshgharī translated Ṭabarī's *History*, see Nijat Mukhlis and Shämsidin Ämät, "Näshirgä täyyarlighuchidin," in *Täzkirä'i Äzizan* (Kashgar: Qāshqār uyghur näshriyati, 1988), 2. Jarring's manuscript collection includes a Turki translation of Ṭabarī's *History*: Prov. 439.

18. 'Ibn 'Alī's *Siyar al-Mukhliṣīn*. The only accessible manuscript I have located is in the Bancroft Library of the University of California, Berkeley (call number 4MS BP189.7.N35.A23 1700z).

19. Shinjang Uyghur Aptonom Rayonluq Az Sanliq Millät Qädimki Äsärlirini Toplash, Rätläsh, Näshir Qilishni Pilanlash Rähbärlik Guruppa ishkhanisi, *Uyghur, özbek, tatar qädimki äsärlär tizimliki* (Kashgar: Qāshqār Uyghur näshriyati, 1989); Tursunmuhämmät Sawut, *Uyghur ädäbiyati tarikhi materiallar katalogi* (Ürümchi: Shinjang Dashö Til-Ädäbiyat fakulteti, 1991).

20. There are probably about a thousand Altishahri manuscripts outside China.

21. Arved Schultz, *Kaschgar (Chinesisch Turkestan): Stadt u. Landschaft* (Hamburg: Meißner, 1921), 27; Grenard, "histoire, linguistique, archéologie, géographie," 260–261. Kuropatkin estimated 1.2 million, and Forsyth 1,015,000, in Thomas Douglas Forsyth, *Report of a Mission to Yarkund in 1873* (Calcutta: Foreign Department Press, 1875), 62. For an overview of population figures, see

Ildikó Bellér-Hann, *Community Matters in Xinjiang 1880–1949: Towards a Historical Anthropology of the Uyghur* (Leiden: Brill, 2008), 61–63.

22. No manuscript-era inventories of books have surfaced, making it impossible to calculate even a rough survival rate, and thus the number of books in circulation, as has been done for medieval Europe. See, for example, Uwe Neddermeyer, *Von der Handschrift zum gedruckten Buch: Schriftlichkeit und Leseinteresse im Mittelalter und in der frühen Neuzeit; quantitative und qualitative Aspekte* (Wiesbaden: Otto Harrassowitz Verlag, 1998).

23. Forsyth, *Report of a Mission to Yarkund in 1873,* 87; Ella C. Sykes and Percy Molesworth Sykes, *Through Deserts and Oases of Central Asia* (London: Macmillan, 1920), 316. In Qadir's description, every student had his or her own book. Zunun Qadir, *Zunun Qadir ăsărliri,* ed. Muhămmăt Polat (Ürümchi: Shinjang khălq năshriyati, 1992), 481.

24. Henry Walter Bellew, *Kashmir and Kashghar: A Narrative of the Journey of the Embassy to Kashghar in 1873–74* (London: Trübner, 1875); Bellér-Hann, *Community Matters in Xinjiang 1880–1949.*

25. Alekseĭ Nikolaevich Kuropatkin, *Kashgaria, Eastern or Chinese Turkistan: Historical and Geographical Sketch of the Country, Its Military Strength, Industries, and Trade* (Calcutta: Thacker, Spink and Co., 1882), 45.

26. Brian Street, *Literacy in Theory and Practice* (Cambridge: Cambridge University Press, 1985).

27. The vernacular literacy of Altishahr is slightly different from Street's "maktab literacy" in that it allowed wide written transmission of texts that were outside the maktab cannon. Thus, literacy extended to popular epics and romances, allowing those genres to be reshaped through their association with the book into tazkirahs.

28. M. Aurel Stein, *Ancient Khotan: Detailed Report of Archaeological Explorations in Chinese Turkestan,* vol. 1 (Oxford: Clarendon Press, 1907), 143.

29. Altishahr: Zunun Qadir, *Khatirilăr* (Ürümchi: Shinjang khălq năshriyati, 1985), 8. Western Turkestan: Sadriddin Aini, *The Sands of Oxus: Boyhood Reminiscences of Sadriddin Aini* (Costa Mesa, CA: Mazda Publishers, 1998).

30. Qadir, *Khatirilăr,* 6–28.

31. Shinjang Uyghur Aptonom Rayonluq Az Sanliq Millăt Qădimki Ăsărlirini Toplash, Rătlăsh, Năshir Qilishni Pilanlash Răhbărlik Guruppa ishkhanisi, *Uyghur, Özbek, tatar qădimki ăsărlăr tizimliki,* 163, 343–346.

32. Adeeb Khalid, *The Politics of Muslim Cultural Reform: Jadidism in Central Asia* (Berkeley: University of California Press, 1998), 23.

33. Aini, *The Sands of Oxus.*

34. Hartmann recorded that Nasāfī's work was studied in Yarkand. Hartmann, *Chinesisch-Turkestan,* 50.

35. Abdurishit Khojăhmăt, "Qarghiliq Nahiyisining 1926 yildin 1936 yilghichă bolghan 10 yilliq tarikhidin ăslimă," *Shinjang tarikhi materiyalliri* 12 (1983): 203.

36. Gunnar Jarring, *Materials to the Knowledge of Eastern Turki: Tales, Poetry, Proverbs, Riddles, Ethnological and Historical Texts from the Southern Parts of Eastern Turkestan*, vol. 4 (Lund: C. W. K. Gleerup, 1951), 117–126. Maqsud Hadji's characterization of the curriculum differs somewhat from the other sources described here but also includes a significant vernacular component.

37. Hartmann, *Chinesisch-Turkestan*, 52.

38. This outline of the madrassa curriculum comes from Hartmann's detailed survey, undertaken in Kashgar and Yarkand in 1903. Hartmann records one exception to the absence of history, Jāmī's biographical compendium, *Nafaḥāt al-Uns*. Hartmann, *Chinesisch-Turkestan*.

39. Jarring Prov. 207, translated in Wolfgang E. Scharlipp, "Two Eastern Turki Texts about Reading and Writing," *Turkic Languages* 2, no. 1 (1998): 109–125.

40. While Ong and Goody saw this as a trait of newly or partially literate cultures, subsequent scholarship has shown audible reading to be the norm for most manuscript traditions, even after as much as a millennium of manuscript use (e.g., nineteenth-century Yemen); Messick, *The Calligraphic State;* Goody, *The Interface between the Written and the Oral;* Ong, *Orality and Literacy*. The most notable exception is the practice of silent reading as it developed in late medieval Europe. See Paul Saenger, *Space between Words: The Origins of Silent Reading* (Stanford: Stanford University Press, 2000).

41. Mizra Haydar Dūghlāt, *Mirza Haydar Dughlat's Tarikh-i Rashidi: A History of the Khans of Moghulistan*, ed. W. M. Thackston (Cambridge, MA: Harvard University, Department of Near Eastern Languages and Civilizations, 1996), 3.

42. Jarring Prov. 73, f. 83r; Emine Gürsoy-Naskali, "Ashabu'l-Kahf: A Treatise in Eastern Turki," *Suomalais-ugrilaisen Seuran Toimituksia* 192 (1985): 34.

43. Jarring Prov. 73, f. 83r.

44. Gürsoy-Naskali, "Ashabu'l-Kahf: A Treatise in Eastern Turki," 34.

45. "rāwīlār āndāgh riwāyat qilūrlār kim . . ." Jarring Prov. 73, f. 55v, and many others. Another common version of the narration formula is the shorter "āndāgh riwāyat qilūrlār kim" (they relate such a tradition that), found, for example, in Jarring Prov. 102 and Mannerheim V, f. 1b, among many others.

46. For example, the *Tazkirah of Imam Ja'far Ṭayaranī*, St. Petersburg B774, f. 15r and C554, f. 1v.

47. Dūghlāt, *Mirza Haydar Dughlat's Tarikh-i Rashidi*, 190 (f. 141r).

48. Uzghanī, Bodleian 2497, f. 3v.

49. Hirschler, *The Written Word in the Medieval Arabic Lands;* Johannes Pedersen, *The Arabic Book* (Princeton, NJ: Princeton University Press, 1984). I have found no evidence of this kind of activity in the Altishahri context.

50. In fact, Uzghanī complained that while there were many collections of saints' biographies, such as the Farīd al-Dīn 'Aṭṭār's *Tazkirat al-Awliyā'*, and

Jāmī's *Nafaḥāt al-Uns,* there was no existing biography of this group of saints (the Uvaysīs), and cites this gap as a motive for writing the work.

51. Devin Deweese has convincingly refuted claims that the Uvaysīs constituted a clearly defined "order." Devin DeWeese, "The Tadhkira-i Bughrā-khān and the 'Uvaysī' Sufis of Central Asia: Notes in Review of Imaginary Muslims," *Central Asiatic Journal* 40, no. 1 (1996): 87–127; Devin DeWeese, "The 'Competitors' of Isḥāq Khwāja in Eastern Turkestan: Hagiographies, Shrines, and Sufi Affiliations in the Late Sixteenth Century," in *Horizons of the World: Festschrift for İsenbike Togan,* ed. İlker Evrim Binbaş and Nurten Kılıç-Schubel (Istanbul: İthaki, 2011), 133–215; Julian Baldick, *Imaginary Muslims: The Uwaysi Mystics of Central Asia* (New York: New York University Press, 1993).

52. Jarring Prov. 563. The Persian original is unknown. Abū al-Qāsīm's material, which focuses on Sultan Satūq Bughrā-khān's descendants, is much different from the *Tazkirah-i Uvaysīya* (more popularly known as *Tazkirah-i Bughrā-khān*). There is no known Persian prototype for Mullah Ḥājī's *Tazkirat al-Bughrā-khān.*

53. The Uyghur editor of Mullah Ḥājī's *Tazkirat al-Bughrā-khān* interpreted this phrase as a reference to a patron.

54. Dūghlāt, *Mirza Haydar Dughlat's Tarikh-i Rashidi,* 3.

55. Sayrāmī's history served as the main source for Kim Hodong's definitive study of this period: Hodong Kim, *Holy War in China: The Muslim Rebellion and State in Chinese Central Asia, 1864–1877* (Stanford: Stanford University Press, 2004).

56. Jarring Prov. 327, f. 31v.

57. Hodong Kim, who based much of his *Holy War in China* on Sayrāmī's history, concluded that "Sayrami continuously revised his work throughout his life." Kim, *Holy War in China,* 194. Kim provides a chart of the chapter arrangements of several versions of Sayrāmī's work: Ibid., 194–195.

58. The date of completion is found at the end of the work in Pantusov's 1904–1905 lithograph edition of the same. Mullah Mūsá Sayrāmī, *Tā'rīkh-i Amaniyah* (Kazan: Tipographīĭa imperatorskago universiteta, 1905), 325.

59. Bibliotheque Nationale, Paris: Collection Pelliot B 1740. Cataloged as an autograph, though the "(?)" in Kim's citation (p. 265) suggests some doubt on this point. Another autograph, in an unspecified PRC archive, is mentioned in Mukhlisov, *Uyghur klassik ădibiyati qolyazmilirining katalogi,* 45–46. It is unclear what evidence suggests either of these texts are autographs. If they are autographs, and the PRC manuscript is not Sayrāmī's autograph of 1903–1904, then we can say that Sayrāmī produced at least five autographs of the history, including the two *Tārīkh-i Ḥamīdī* autographs cited below.

60. *Tārīkh-i Ḥamīdī,* uncataloged manuscript in MZXY, accessed for this study through a partial facsimile thereof in the author's collection. Sayrāmī dates the completion of this manuscript to 1911 but writes that the work was

first completed in 1908. This suggests a fifth autograph in the form of a 1908 manuscript of the *Tārīkh-i Ḥamīdī*.

61. Jarring Prov. 478 (1331/1912–1913). It is important to note, though, that this copy was probably made by request of the Swedish missionary Gosta Raquette. Other known copies of the *Tārīkh-i Amniyyah,* as recorded by Kim (265–266): St. Petersburg (Muginov 27) 1328/1910; PRC in Mukhlisov by copyist Tashmaliq, 1907. Another copy of the *Tā'rīkh-i Amniyya* is in the Ürümqi Ancient Text Office: Shinjang Uyghur Aptonom Rayonluq Az Sanliq Millăt Qădimki Ăsărlirini Toplash, Rătlăsh, Năshir Qilishni Pilanlash Răhbărlik Guruppa ishkhanisi, *Uyghur, Özbek, tatar qădimki ăsărlăr tizimliki,* 192–193. Aside from an autograph in the PRC, the only other known copy of the *Tārīkh-i Ḥamīdī* seems to be Jarring Prov. 163, 1345/1927. It is written on a Swedish notebook, suggesting missionary involvement. This makes a total of three autographs and five copies surviving, with two of the copies likely produced at the request of Swedish missionaries.

62. Harold Love, *Scribal Publication in Seventeenth-Century England* (New York: Oxford University Press, 1993), 53.

63. The notion of community authorship advanced here refers to a large community's alteration and even production of widely circulating texts, involving the uncoordinated reshaping of publicly available texts by people of all classes and professions over long periods of time. This is in contrast to Margaret Ezell's "social authorship" of early modern England, which refers to the individual author's production of a text for circulation in a restricted social group or network. Margaret J. M. Ezell, *Social Authorship and the Advent of Print* (Baltimore: Johns Hopkins University Press, 2003). It also differs from the more widely used term, "collective authorship," which usually designates the intentional or unintentional collaboration of a small number of individual authors, often scholarly elites.

64. Eisenstein, *The Printing Press as an Agent of Change,* 114.

65. Paul Zumthor, *Oral Poetry: An Introduction,* trans. Kathryn Murphy-Judy (Minneapolis: University of Minnesota Press, 1990), 203–205. Jan Assman applied the term *mouvance* to written texts. Jan Assmann, *Religion and Cultural Memory: Ten Studies,* trans. Rodney Livingstone (Stanford: Stanford University Press, 2006).

66. Unpublished notes by Tony Stewart, quoted in Sheldon Pollock, "Literary Culture and Manuscript Culture in Precolonial India," in *Literary Cultures and the Material Book,* ed. Simon Eliot, Andrew Nash, and Ian Willison (London: British Library, 2007), 88.

67. This neatly fits Jan Assman's assignment of *mouvance* to "cultural texts" and literal reproduction to "sacred texts." Assmann, *Religion and Cultural Memory,* 118. On the other hand, the extensive *mouvance* of the tazkirahs, themselves nothing if not sacred, represents a notable exception to Assman's rule. The great

accuracy of Quran reproduction in manuscript form is, ironically, a result of the distrust of the written word alone. Schoeler, *The Genesis of Literature in Islam,* 36. The greatest variation I have discovered in Altishahri Qurans is a disagreement in the use of dagger *alifs* versus full *alifs.*

68. Assmann, *Religion and Cultural Memory,* 118–119.

69. For example, the *Iskandarnāmah* and its pre-Islamic forerunners, the *Thousand and One Nights,* and popular epics discussed in Lane, *The Manners and Customs of the Modern Egyptians.* But there is an important difference: whereas the tazkirahs were considered sacred and their variation was condoned, the shifting popular works in the core Arabic-speaking regions were generally seen as illicit. Hirschler, *The Written Word in the Medieval Arabic Lands,* 166–168.

70. Shāh Maḥmūd Churās, *Khronika,* ed. O. F. Akimushkin (Moscow: Nauka, 1976); Dūghlāt, *Mirza Haydar Dughlat's Tarikh-i Rashidi.*

71. A later example is the continuation of Sayrāmī's *Tārīkh-i Ḥamīdī,* found in Prov. 163. The extension of the tazkirah of Kohmarim in BM Or. 9230 could also be considered a part of this tradition.

72. Gursoy-Naskali, "*Ashabu 'l-Kahf: A Treatise in Eastern Turki.*" The translation is Gursoy-Naskali's, though I have left *tazkīr,* a form closely related to *tazkirah,* untranslated rather than rendering it "[book of] memoirs." This tazkirah may have been written by Muhammad Ṣādiq Kāshgharī, whose *Tazkirah-i Azīzān* includes a similar passage. Mullah Mūsá Sayrāmī also has similar requests in both his *Tārīkh-i Amniyya* and the *Tārīkh-i Ḥamīdī.* Musa Sayrami, *Tārikh-i Ḥamīdī,* (Beijing: Millātlār ăshriyati, 1986), 37. It also appears that in medieval England, calling on the copyist to edit a text was not unknown. However, in the English case, this call was directed to a particular stationer whom the author knew and trusted, such as the prolific stationer John Shirley. C. Greenberg, "John Shirley and the English Book Trade," *The Library* 6, no. 4 (1982): 377.

73. MFSI, page 145.

74. Ibid. While respectful forms were used for holy figures such as prophets and saints, God was supposed to be addressed in the familiar.

75. KhMSh.

76. See Chapter 1 for the dating of the *Tazkirah of Muhammad Sharīf.*

77. Such is the case with HMShSM.

78. The former version appears in KhMSh, the later in HMShSM.

79. HMShSM, KhMSh, MFSI. Also *ḥazrat payghambar* vs. *ānḥazrat* in MFSI and KhMSh.

80. By "corruption" I intend to indicate changes that unintentionally eliminate or obscure meaning without providing any alternate message, all the while maintaining some traces of an earlier more meaningful manifestation.

81. The story in question begins on f. 25v of Prov. 369. The only accessible manuscript of the Persian original is in Berkeley's Bancroft Library: 4MS BP189.7.N35.A23 1700z.

82. BM Or. 9230. The British Museum's "oriental" manuscripts are now housed in the British Library.

83. Another manuscript cataloged as the *Tazkirah of Kohmārim* is held at XJCASS, but I was not permitted to examine it.

84. Lucien Febvre and Henri-Jean Martin, *The Coming of the Book: The Impact of Printing 1450–1800,* trans. David Gerard (London: NLB, 1976), 320.

85. A. Görke and K. Hirschler, eds., *Manuscript Notes as Documentary Sources* (Würzburg: Ergon Verlag, 2011); Hirschler, *The Written Word in the Medieval Arabic Lands.*

86. C. H. Talbot, "The Universities and the Mediaeval Library," in *The English Library before 1700: Studies in Its History,* ed. Francis Wormald and C. E. Wright (London: Athlone Press, University of London, 1958), 69.

87. Gunnar Jarring, *Return to Kashgar: Central Asian Memoirs in the Present,* trans. Eva Claeson. (Durham: Duke University Press, 1986), 78.

88. Gunnar Jarring, Handwritten Catalog of the Gunnar Jarring Collection of Manuscripts from Eastern Turkestan in the Lund University Library (1997), 464. The copyist also calls himself a beggar, but this is a common formula to express modesty.

89. Z. Jasiewicz, "Professional Beliefs and Rituals among Craftsmen in Central Asia: Genetic and Functional Interpretation," in *Cultural Change and Continuity in Central Asia,* ed. Shirin Akiner, 1991, 171–180.

90. Jarring, *Return to Kashgar: Central Asian Memoirs in the Present,* 198.

91. H. W. Bellew, *Kashmir and Kashghar: A Narrative of the Journey of the Embassy to Kashghar in 1873–74* (Lahore: Sang-e-Meel Publications, 1999 [1875]), 278.

92. Kuropatkin, *Kashgaria, Eastern or Chinese Turkistan,* 36.

93. Jarring Prov. 372, Prov. 327, Prov. 250, Prov. 437.

94. For example, a book dealer showed me a manuscript of Mullah Ḥājī's *Tazkirat al-Bughrā-khān,* copied in 2003, priced at 100 yuan. The same bookseller offered me a printed version for 50 yuan. In the same market, pirated print copies of the text could be had for 10 yuan. Another contemporary manuscript, a copy of a *Tazkirah of the Companions of the Cave,* was priced at 500 yuan.

95. Jarring attributed to Khotan the paper in manuscripts with dates as early as 1145–1146/1732–1734, also a manuscript with a copying date of 1226/1811–1812, and others with copying dates in the 1820s, suggesting that the indigenous papermaking industry predated the book boom of the late nineteenth century by at least a century. Gunnar Jarring, Handwritten Catalog of the Gunnar

Jarring Collection of Manuscripts from Eastern Turkestan in the Lund University Library (1997), 152, 343, 560, 574, 576, 678–679.

96. Prov. 207, translated in Scharlipp, "Two Eastern Turki Texts about Reading and Writing." Russian paper goes unmentioned in this description, but at least as early as 1905, Russian paper was being used for some manuscripts, for example, Bancroft 4MS BP193.16.A3 1800zb.

97. During his 1906–1908 expedition to Altishahr, Mannerheim recorded prices for locally made paper from the town of Guma at one copper coin *(pul)* for four sheets or 90 *pul* for a jin (1¼ pounds). For purposes of comparison, we may note that Mannerheim recorded a daily wage of 10 *pul* plus board for a workman in Kashgar and a price of 15 *pul* for a hen. C. G. Mannerheim, *Across Asia from West to East: 1906–1908* (Helsinki: Suomalais-Ugrilainen Seura, 1940), 57, 81, 180, 195. In Altishahri manuscripts, sheets of paper were folded in half and bound in quires, yielding two folios (four pages) per sheet. The average number of folios in manuscripts for which we have price information is 156. Based on the per-sheet prices of Guma paper, and conservatively assuming that the Guma sheets were less than double the minimum size required for a manuscript, the cost of paper for such a book would be 19.5 *pul,* about two days of unskilled labor wages and 33 percent more than the price of a hen. If the Guma sheets were double or more than the minimum size required for a manuscript, then the cost of paper for book making would have been one half or even one quarter of this price.

98. It is interesting to compare the Altishahri case to northern Nigeria, which has relied entirely on imported paper and experienced many periods of "book famine" over the last five centuries. In both cases, however, it is impossible to establish a direct causal relationship with any real certainty. Murray Last, "The Book and the Nature of Knowledge in Muslim Northern Nigeria, 1457–2007," in *The Trans-Saharan Book Trade: Manuscript Culture, Arabic Literacy and Intellectual History in Muslim Africa,* ed. Graziano Krätli and Ghislaine Lydon (Leiden: Brill, 2011).

99. For book prices, I use data from Jarring, Handwritten Catalog of the Gunnar Jarring Collection of Manuscripts from Eastern Turkestan in the Lund University Library.

100. Brian Richardson, *Manuscript Culture in Renaissance Italy,* 1st ed. (Cambridge: Cambridge University Press, 2009), 4; Ann Komaromi, "The Material Existence of Soviet Samizdat," *Slavic Review* (2004): 597–618.

101. Prov. 576, a manuscript of Mullah Ḥājī's *Taẕkīrat al-Bughrā-Khān,* completed April 1, 2006, and copied from the modern Uyghur translation published under the title *Bughrakhanlar Tazkirisi* (Kashgar: Uyghur Press, 1988). Even the footnotes were copied.

102. Jarring, *Return to Kashgar: Central Asian Memoirs in the Present,* 110.

103. A detailed description of writing by Muhammad ʻAlī Damolla can be found in Prov. 207. It is translated in Scharlipp, "Two Eastern Turki Texts about Reading and Writing."

104. This absence was, however, not complete. A rare historical work in the chronicle tradition, along with a translation of the *Tārīkh-i Rashīdī*, was written under the patronage of the indigenous local rulers who governed for the Qing. T. I. Sultanov, "Medieval Historiography in Manuscripts from East Turkestan," *Manuscripta Orientalia* 2, no. 1 (1996): 25–30.

105. Love, *Scribal Publication in Seventeenth-Century England*. Margaret Ezell has questioned the notion of scribal "publication." Ezell, *Social Authorship and the Advent of Print*.

106. Pollock, "Literary Culture and Manuscript Culture in Precolonial India."

107. Prov. 297, f. 20r.

108. MFSI, 50.

109. Endpaper of Prov. 565.

110. MFSI, page 91.

111. For example, borrowers marks, lenders fees, and purchase records can be found in the margins and flyleaves of medieval English manuscripts: C. H. Talbot, "The Universities and the Medieval Library," in *The English Library before 1700*, ed. Francis Wormald and C. E. Wright, (London: Athlone Press, University of London, 1958), 68,72,73. Early modern manuscripts are covered in finding aids. William H. Sherman, *Used Books: Marking Readers in Renaissance England* (Philadelphia: University of Pennsylvania Press, 2009). Altishahri marginalia are not directed at "the *manipulation of information* . . . selecting, ordering and applying resources gleaned from a wide variety of text" (Sherman, p. 47), but rather the interface of reader experience with sacred writing and the narratives contained in the manuscript. These histories were not made for manipulation, not seen as stores of information to be rearranged for new purposes, but as sources for sacred narrative, information deployed in a meaningful and continuous sequence.

112. Görke and Hirschler, *Manuscript Notes as Documentary Sources*; Sherman, *Used Books*.

113. H. J. Jackson, *Marginalia: Readers Writing in Books* (New Haven: Yale University Press, 2001) considers the ethical and aesthetic ramifications of marginalia in our own time; Sherman, *Used Books*, considers collector impressions of marginalia in Renaissance and early modern books as they survived into much later contexts.

114. Paul Ricoeur, *Memory, History, Forgetting*, trans. Kathleen Blamey and David Pellauer (Chicago: University of Chicago Press, 2004), 642.

115. E. D. Hirsch, *The Philosophy of Composition* (Chicago: University of Chicago Press, 1977).

116. While not properly part of Altishahr, these areas were part of the same culture area and were inhabited by the Taranchis, descendents of those Altishahris who had been forcibly moved by the Dzungar Mongols in the eighteenth century to the mountainous areas just north of Altishahr proper.

117. Qadir, *Khatirilăr,* 51.

118. Ibid., 1–2.

119. Ibid., 67.

120. Presumably a Turki translation of the Persian epic, *'Abū Muslim Nāmah.* Many Eastern Turki manuscripts of this work are known, including Prov. 534, Prov. 230, Prov. 437, and Hartmann 2o 3300.

121. Perhaps "Shāh-i Mardān," one of 'Alī ibn Abī Ṭālib's titles. Romances recounting 'Alī's great deeds were not rare in Central Asia.

122. Qadir, *Khatirilăr,* 68.

123. Theodore Roosevelt and Kermit Roosevelt, *East of the Sun and West of the Moon* (New York: Blue Ribbon Books, 1926), 209.

124. Grenard, "Histoire, linguistique, archéologie, géographie," 86.

125. N. N. Pantusov, *Materialy k izucheniiu narīechīia Tancheĭ Ilīūkago okruga,* vol. 9 (Kazan: Tipo-litografīia Imperatorskago Universiteta, 1907), 5, 11. For the *mashrab* in recent times, see Sean R. Roberts, "Negotiating Locality, Islam, and National Culture in a Changing Borderland: The Revival of the Mäshräp Ritual among Young Uighur Men in the Ili Valley," *Central Asian Survey* 17, no. 4 (1998): 673–699.

126. Jarring Prov. 563, f. 50v.

127. Ibid., f. 50v.

128. Gunnar Jarring, "The Ordam-Padishah System of Eastern Turkistan Shrines," *Geografiska Annaler* 17, Supplement: Hyllningsskrift Tillagnad Sven Hedin (1935): 348.

129. Jarring, *Return to Kashgar: Central Asian Memoirs in the Present,* 136.

130. Săypidin Ăzizi, *Sutuq Bughrakhan* (Beijing: Millătlăr năshriyati, 1987), 2.

131. Ismayil, *Uyghur khălq rivayătliri: Nam-ataqlar hăqqidiki rivayătlăr,* 167–168.

132. Martin Hartmann, "Die osttürkischen Handschriften der Sammlung Hartmann," *Mitteilungen des Seminars für Orientalische Sprachen an der Königlichen Friedrich-Wilhelms-Universität zu Berlin* 7, no. 2 (1904): 1–21.

133. Bellew, *Kashmir and Kashghar: A Narrative of the Journey of the Embassy to Kashghar in 1873–74,* 278.

134. Hasan and Husayn tales were also kept at some shrines, though they are not mentioned as often. See Hartmann, *Chinesisch-Turkestan: Geschichte, Verwaltung, Geistesleben und Wirtschaft,* 40 and Mannerheim 2.49.1 VIII. These works are still recited at some shrines today.

135. Mannerheim 2.49.1 II.

136. Bancroft 4MS BP193.16.A3 1800zb; IOL MS Turki 9; IVAN RUz 3426.

137. Dawut, 2001.

138. Hedin, *Central Asia and Tibet* (London: Hurst and Blackett, 1903).

139. For example, Jarring Prov. 570, ff. 40r–41r; Jarring Prov. 567, f. 163v; Hartmann MS Or. Oct. 1727, p. 2.

140. Prov. 58, f. 71a. Also Jarring, Handwritten Catalog of the Gunnar Jarring Collection of Manuscripts from Eastern Turkestan in the Lund University Library, 85.

141. Jarring Prov. 297, f. 60r.

142. Jarring Prov. 275. Jarring's translation in Jarring, Handwritten Catalog of the Gunnar Jarring Collection of Manuscripts from Eastern Turkestan in the Lund University Library. For further examples of this formula, see Prov. 50, Prov. 302, Prov. 331, and Prov. 390.

143. See Jarring Prov. 567.

144. For a similar phenomenon in the medieval English context, see G. S. Ivy, "The Bibliography of the Manuscript Book," in Wormald and Wright, *The English Library before 1700*, 54–55.

145. Jarring Prov. 565.

146. Jarring Prov. 522. See Jarring, Handwritten Catalog of the Gunnar Jarring Collection of Manuscripts from Eastern Turkestan in the Lund University Library, 920.

147. The Jarring collection, which is reasonably representative of the manuscript corpus as of about 1930, very well documented, and extremely accessible, is probably the best resource for estimating the prevalence of composite manuscripts (at least until archives in Urumchi become accessible). About 23 percent of physical manuscripts are anthologies. Measured by individual works, rather than physical books, the proportion is more significant. Of the individual works in the Jarring collection, 72 percent are to be found in anthologies. In addition to the works I counted as anthologies, there are books made up of one main work with one or two very short (several folios) works, usually poetry, preceding and/or following the main text.

148. SP C547, C549.

149. Jarring Prov. 148.

150. A sense of antiquity also contributed to textual authority for anonymous "literary" texts in medieval Europe. Foucault, "What Is an Author?" 148.

151. Persian inscription on the wall of the tomb of Muhammad Sharīf, summarizing the *Tazkirah of Muhammad Sharīf* and commemorating the patronage of the Beg of Yarkand.

3. The Shrine

1. The Imam Shākir shrine is also known as *Qum Rabat Padshahim* (My King of the Fort in the Sands) or *Kăptăr Mazari* (Pigeon shrine).

2. This date (1289 AH) is carved into one of the columns in the mosque in fine calligraphy. The architectural style is typical of the Yaqub Beg period, with its mix of local and Khoqandi forms. Mirza Haydar mentioned the Seven Muhammads shrine in his 1553 *Tarīkh-i Rashīdī*. Mirza Haydar Dūghlāt, *Mirza*

Haydar Dughlat's Tarikh-i Rashidi: A History of the Khans of Moghulistan, ed. W. M. Thackston (Cambridge, MA: Harvard University, Department of Near Eastern Languages and Civilizations, 1996), 190.

3. More precisely, these visits took place July 2004–July 2005, June 2007–January 2008, and late summer 2009. Most of the visits were concentrated in the 2007–2008 period.

4. I was not able to undertake a thorough study of the *hükmät* material, but much of it seems to be taken from a canon of popular devotional verse very similar to that documented in Sigrid Kleinmichel, *Halpa in Choresm (Hwarazm) und Atin Ayi in Ferganatal: Zur Geschichte des Lesens in Usbekistan im 20. Jahrhundert* (Berlin: Das Arabische Buch, 2000). For Yasavi see Devin DeWeese, "Ahmad Yasavi and the Divan-i Hikmat in Soviet Scholarship," in *The Heritage of Soviet Oriental Studies,* ed. Michael Kemper and Stephan Conermann (New York: Routledge, 2011), 262–290.

5. Shohret Hoshur and Joshua Lipes, "Uyghurs Targeted over Desert Prayers," trans. Dolkun Kamberi, *Radio Free Asia,* accessed December 1, 2013, http://www.rfa.org/english/news/uyghur/uyghurstargeted-04022009162642.html.

6. I have changed the name of the village to protect my hosts.

7. It is commonly claimed that twelve imams are buried around Khotan, though the number twelve is merely a convention. The most popular Khotan-area saints called *imam* are (in transliteration from modern Uyghur orthography): Musa Kazim, Ghazali, Ăskări, Asim, Hashim, Qasim, Ăptăh with his six brother imams, Jafari Sadiq, Jafari Tayrani, Măhdi, and the Four Imams who fought alongside Yūsuf Qādir-khān. A *Tazkirah of the Twelve Imams* also exists describing twelve additional saints (e.g., Jarring Prov. 349). For the connection between Khotan's imam-saints and Twelver Shiism, see Fernand Grenard, "Histoire, linguistique, archéologie, géographie," in *Mission Scientifique dans la Haute Asie, 1890–1895,* ed. J. L. Dutreuil de Rhins (Paris: Ernest Leroux, 1898).

8. This is the Hasan al-ʿAskarī of the Twelver Shia tradition, which places his tomb in Samarra, Iraq. Shaykh al-Mufīd, *Kitāb al-Irshād: The Book of Guidance into the Lives of the Twelve Imams,* trans. I. K. A. Howard (Elmhurst, NY: Tahrike Tarsile Qur'an, 1981), 523.

9. Throughout this book, I use the term "liminal" in the more general sense of relating to a threshold, rather than the specific Turnerian sense of a moment outside structure. Victor W. Turner, *The Ritual Process: Structure and Antistructure* (New York: Aldine de Gruyter, 1995).

10. Gunnar Jarring, *Return to Kashgar: Central Asian Memoirs in the Present,* trans. Eva Claeson (Durham: Duke University Press, 1986), 189.

11. A Swedish missionary photograph from the early 1900s in the collection of Gertrude Raquette shows the ordinary graves outside the Seven Muhammads shrine, looking much as they do today.

12. M. Aurel Stein, *Sand-Buried Ruins of Khotan: Personal Narrative of a Journey of Archaeological and Geographical Exploration in Chinese Turkestan* (London: Hurst and Blackett, 1904), 132.

13. Ildikó Bellér-Hann, "'Making the Oil Fragrant': Dealings with the Supernatural among the Uyghurs in Xinjiang," *Asian Ethnicity* 2, no. 1 (2001): 15; Fernand Grenard, "Le Turkestan et le Tibet, étude ethnographique et sociologique," in *Mission Scientifique dans la haute Asie,* ed. J.-L. Dutreuil de Rhins. (Paris: Ernest Leroux, 1898), 129; Thomas Douglas Forsyth, *Report of a Mission to Yarkund in 1873* (Calcutta: Foreign Department Press, 1875), 36.

14. Forsyth, *Report of a Mission to Yarkund in 1873,* 39.

15. Stein, *Sand-Buried Ruins of Khotan,* 160, 464; Robert Shaw, *Visits to High Tartary, Yarkand, and Kashghar (Formerly Chinese Tartary) and Return Journey over the Karakorum Pass* (London: John Murray, 1871), 155.

16. R. C. F. Schomberg, *Peaks and Plains of Central Asia* (Gilgit: G. M. Beg Sons, 1996), 155.

17. Zalīlī's *Safarnāmah.* This translation is based primarily on Muhammad Zalīlī, *Zălili divani,* trans. Imin Tursun (Beijing: Millătlăr năshriyati, 1985), in which the original Chaghatay has been squeezed into modern Uyghur orthography. I also worked from Jarring Prov. 76, but this was of limited use because Jarring's manuscript is missing most of the section translated here. A partial translation into French can be found in Alexandre Papas, *Mystiques et vagabonds en islam: Portraits de trois soufis qalandar* (Paris: Cerf, 2010), 152–154.

18. Forsyth, *Report of a Mission to Yarkund in 1873,* 496, 502.

19. Dūghlāt, *Mirza Haydar Dughlat's Tarikh-i Rashidi,* 190.

20. Bellér-Hann, "'Making the Oil Fragrant': Dealings with the Supernatural among the Uyghurs in Xinjiang"; Ildikó Bellér-Hann, *Community Matters in Xinjiang 1880–1949: Towards a Historical Anthropology of the Uyghur* (Leiden: Brill, 2008), 355–362.

21. Jarring Prov. 207, no. 56.

22. Grenard, "Le Turkestan et le Tibet, étude ethnographique et sociologique," 247.

23. Ella C. Sykes and Percy Molesworth Sykes, *Through Deserts and Oases of Central Asia* (London: Macmillan, 1920), 206.

24. The first asphalt road on the Kashgar–Khotan route seems to have been laid between 1966 and 1979, and it may have been during this construction that the road's route was moved away from the shrine. Măqsut Tiyipov, "Shinjang tashyol tărăqqiyati tughrisida āslimă," *Shinjang tarikhi materiyalliri* 28 (1990): 89. The situation has recently changed again. The new Khotan rail line passes within a few hundred meters of the shrine.

25. Bellér-Hann, *Community Matters in Xinjiang 1880–1949,* 323, citing Sigrid Högberg, *På Obanade Stigar* (Stockholm: Svenska Missionsförbundets Förlag, 1912).

26. For example, the *Tazkirah of Muhammad Sharīf*, and the *Tazkirah of Imam Muhammad Ghazālī*.

27. Gunnar Jarring, *Matters of Ethnological Interest in Swedish Missionary Reports from Southern Sinkiang*, vol. 4, *Scripta Minora Regiae Societatis Humaniorum Litterarum Lundensis* (Lund: C. W. K. Gleerup, 1979), 323.

28. Gunnar Jarring, "The Ordam-Padishah-System of Eastern Turkistan Shrines," *Geografiska Annaler* 17 (1935): 350.

29. Zalīlī, *Zălili divani*, 593–652. Jarring Prov. 76, ff. 72r–77r.

30. Jarring, *Return to Kashgar*, 136.

31. Săypidin Ăzizi, *Sutuq Bughrakhan* (Beijing: Millătlăr Năshriyati, 1987), 2.

32. Forsyth, *Report of a Mission to Yarkund in 1873*, 37.

33. Zunun Qadir, *Khatirilăr* (Ürümchi: Shinjang khălq năshriyati, 1985), 68.

34. Jarring Prov. 349, f. 71v.

35. Most Altishahri authors seem to accept the authenticity of the shrines and their stories, but Mullah Mūsá Sayrāmī challenged them in his *Tarīkh-i Ḥamīdī*, uncataloged manuscript in MZXY, 1911, facsimile. Still, Sayrāmī accepted the basic sanctity of most shrines, as when he wrote in the *Tarīkh-i Ḥamīdī* that "whatever the name, this place certainly is not a normal place but has miraculous powers and wondrous occurrences."

36. Bancroft f4MS.BP137 1800z (v. 2) (unfoliated). The head in hand may be a reference to the weeping that is a conventional form of devotion at the shrines.

37. Clarmont Percival Skrine, *Chinese Central Asia* (New York: Houghton Mifflin, 1926), 183.

38. Ibid.

39. Forsyth, *Report of a Mission to Yarkund in 1873*, 38.

40. Jarring, *Return to Kashgar*, 112; Jarring, "The Ordam-Padishah-System of Eastern Turkistan Shrines."

41. Ludwig Golomb, *Die Bodenkultur in Ost-Turkestan. Oasenwirtschaft und Nomadentum* (Freiburg: Verlag des Anthropos-Instituts, 1959), 37–38; Bellér-Hann, *Community Matters in Xinjiang 1880–1949*, 63.

42. Stein, *Sand-Buried Ruins of Khotan*, 312.

43. Bellér-Hann, *Community Matters in Xinjiang 1880–1949*, 376.

44. Jarring Prov. 207, no. 36, 1. This is clearly a polemical passage, which may reflect reformist tendencies that were just beginning to take hold in Altishahr at this time, and it likely includes some exaggeration. However, it is clear that the mixing of classes and professions is itself an irritant to the author, as opposed to simple hyperbole in the service of argument.

45. Jarring Prov. 207, no. 36, 1.

46. Skrine, *Chinese Central Asia*, 183–184.

47. Bellér-Hann, *Community Matters in Xinjiang 1880–1949*, 376; Minoru Sawada, "A Study of the Current Ordam-Padishah System," *Journal of the History of Sufism* 3 (2001): 89–111.

48. Jarring Prov. 349, f. 71v.

49. St. Petersburg B775, ff. 47r–47v.

50. Other tazkirahs with such blessing/instructions include the tazkirahs of the Seven Muhammads, Ja'fari Ṭayarān, Twelve Imams, and Mullah Hājī's *Taẓkīrat al-Bughrā-khān*.

51. Rahilä Davut, *Uyghur mazarliri* (Ürümchi: Shinjang khălq nǎshriyati, 2001), 51.

52. Jarring, "The Ordam-Padishah-System of Eastern Turkistan Shrines," 348.

53. Abū al-Qāsīm's versified *Tazkirah of the Bughrā-khāns*, Jarring Prov. 563, f. 50v.

54. HMShSM.

55. Zarcone argues that these were intended specifically for recitation at the shrines, and that both pilgrims and shaykhs would have recited these *munājāt*. Thierry Zarcone, "The Invocation of Saints and/or Spirits by the Sufis and the Shamans: About the Munâjât Literary Genre in Central Asia," *Kyoto Bulletin of Islamic Area Studies* 1, no. 1 (2007): 55.

56. Jarring Prov. 413, f. 134v.

57. Zalīlī, *Zǎlili divani*, 605.

58. Ăbdullah Poskami, *Kitabi Ăbdullah* (Ürümchi: Shinjang khălq nǎshriyati, 2004), 260–261.

59. Rahile Dawut, personal communication, 2009, documented the telling of the tazkirah at Imam Asim. When I visited this festival in 2010, a *maddah* was telling the story of Abdulqadir Gilani. Nearby a group of musicians performed the ballad of Nochi Beg. In 2013 I heard the same performers sing the story of the *Kiyik* (deer), for which see Kleinmichel, *Halpa in Choresm (Hwarazm) und Atin Ayi in Ferganatal,* 263–265.

60. Rachel Harris and Rahilä Dawut, "Mazar Festivals of the Uyghurs: Music, Islam and the Chinese State," *British Journal of Ethnomusicology* 11, no. 1 (2002): 101–118.

61. Jarring, *Return to Kashgar,* 112.

62. Jarring, "The Ordam-Padishah-System of Eastern Turkistan Shrines," 348.

63. Harris and Dawut, "Mazar Festivals of the Uyghurs."

64. Davut, *Uyghur mazarliri,* 53.

65. Personal communication with police officers preventing access to the road to Ujma, 2007.

66. Mannerheim X, published in Emine Gürsoy-Naskali, "Ashabu'l-Kahf: A Treatise in Eastern Turki," *Suomalais-ugrilaisen Seuran Toimituksia* 192 (1985); Muhǎmmǎtturdi Mirzi'ǎkhmǎt, ed., "Tǎzkirǎ'i Ăshabul Kǎhf," *Bulaq* 113, no. 2 (2007): 39–48. A possible third is mentioned by Ănvǎr Baytur in Mūsá Sayrāmī, *Tārikh-i Ḥamīdī,* trans. Ănvǎr Baytur (Beijing: Millǎtlǎr Nǎshriyati, 1986), 10.

67. Jarring, *Return to Kashgar*, 112; Schomberg, *Peaks and Plains of Central Asia*, 66; Jarring, "The Ordam-Padishah-System of Eastern Turkistan Shrines."

68. The exception occurs where a tazkirah relates the story of a saint's pilgrimage to Mecca, as in the *Tazkirah of Muhammad Sharīf*.

69. Jonathan Z. Smith, *To Take Place: Toward Theory in Ritual* (Chicago: University of Chicago Press, 1987), 30, 183.

70. For example, the common folk etymology for the desert's name, Taklamakan, is "go in and never come back."

71. Interestingly, ownership of land was often imagined as ownership of water, which in turn was measured by the area (in *batman*) of land it could irrigate. For example, a text might describe a shrine's landholding as "20 *batman* of water."

72. A notable exception is the story of the Four Imams' discovery of the *manzil* of the Imam Mahdī-'i Ākhir-i Zamān, which is said to occur in the sands of the desert: MFSI, page 91.

73. One exception may be the Black Mountain tradition regarding their graves in Altunluq, where the Khvājahs' graves were placed next to the khans' graves.

74. *Tazkirah of Imam Muhammad Ghazālī*, SP B775.

75. Stein, *Sand-Buried Ruins of Khotan*, 180.

76. Aurel Stein, *Innermost Asia* (Oxford: Clarendon Press, 1928), 614.

77. Grenard, "Le Turkestan et le Tibet, étude ethnographique et sociologique," 240–241.

78. See the discussion of this issue in Devin DeWeese, *Islamization and Native Religion in the Golden Horde: Baba Tükles and Conversion to Islam in Historical and Epic Tradition* (University Park: Pennsylvania State University Press, 1994), and in Bellér-Hann, "'Making the Oil Fragrant': Dealings with the Supernatural among the Uyghurs in Xinjiang."

79. Shāh Maḥmūd Churās, *Khronika*, ed. O. F. Akimushkin (Moscow: Nauka, 1976).

80. For another, similar tale of extensive shrine discovery, see the tradition of Ishāq Valī reported in Davut, *Uyghur mazarliri*, 195.

81. Jarring Prov. 349, f. 66r.

82. However, the "stopover point" usage is not entirely absent. See the *Tazkirah of 'Abd al-Raḥmān* in Bancroft f4MS.BP137 1800z (v.2).

83. *Tazkirah of the Imam Mahdī-yi Ākhir-i Zamān*, twenty-first-century manuscript, Jarring Prov. 576.

84. Jarring Prov. 148, f. 115r.

85. The prophet's temporary ascension into heaven on the winged creature Burāq.

86. *Tazkirah of Sultan Satūq Bughrā-khān* (chapter 7 of the *Tazkirah-i Uvaysīya*), from Jarring Prov. 148, f. 109v. The preexistence of Satūq Bughrā-khān has a clear precedent in Islamic traditions regarding the prophet Muhammad. God was said

to have created the "Light of Muhammad" before any other creatures. Marion Holmes Katz, *The Birth of the Prophet Muhammad: Devotional Piety in Sunni Islam* (New York: Routledge, 2007), 12–15.

87. Jarring Prov. 148, f. 112r.

88. An unfoliated manuscript of the *Tazkirah of the Twelve Imams* (Berkeley 4MS BP193.16.A3 1800zb) uses this trope both for the Twelve Imams generally, and for Imam Qāsim in particular, who is described as preexisting in eternity *(tarīkh biqār)* while the companions of the prophet await his entry into physical existence *(wujūd)*. The Seven Muhammads tazkirah also describes the saints as existing as heavenly personages before becoming incarnate.

89. Maria Elisabeth Louw, *Everyday Islam in Post-Soviet Central Asia* (New York: Routledge, 2007), 132.

90. For a spatial conception of the past in terms of migration routes, see Renato Rosaldo, *Ilongot Headhunting, 1883–1974: A Study in Society and History* (Stanford: Stanford University Press, 1980).

91. Among the more famous rulers known to visit the shrines were Abd al-Rashīd Khan, Jahangir, and Ya'qub Beg.

92. McChesney notes that shrines in Afghanistan hold a greater claim on the popular imagination to linkages with the eternal realm than do mosques or other sites of worship. R. D. McChesney, *Waqf in Central Asia: Four Hundred Years in the History of a Muslim Shrine, 1480–1889* (Princeton, NJ: Princeton University Press, 1991). In my experience, the same situation pertains in Altishahr.

93. MFSI, page 91.

94. Walter Benjamin, *Illuminations,* trans. Harry Zohn (New York: Schocken Books, 1969), 261–262. Here I follow Anderson's usage of the phrase. Benedict Anderson, *Imagined Communities: Reflections on the Origin and Spread of Nationalism* (London: Verso, 1991), 24–26.

4. History in Motion

1. Nikolai Katanov, *Volkskundliche Texte aus Ost Türkistan I–II,* vol. 1 (Leipzig: Zentralantiquariat der Deutschen Demokratischen Republik, 1976), 220–221. Also cited in Ildikó Bellér-Hann, *Community Matters in Xinjiang 1880–1949: Towards a Historical Anthropology of the Uyghur* (Leiden: Brill, 2008), 40.

2. The "imagined community of Christendom": Benedict Anderson, *Imagined Communities: Reflections on the Origin and Spread of Nationalism* (London: Verso, 1991), 42. Anderson sees the nation as one "*kind* of imagined community" (p. 25, emphasis original), which he elsewhere calls a "nationally imagined community (p. 42), and contrasts against the "sacred imagined community" (p. 41).

3. Even the exact form of the ethnonym is not fully standardized across Altishahr; many inhabitants of the Southern oases say "Urghuy" instead of "Uyghur."

4. Max Weber, *Economy and Society,* trans. Ephraim Fischof (Berkeley: University of California Press, 1978), 389.

5. This formulation comes from Fredrik Barth, "Enduring and Emerging Issues in the Analysis of Ethnicity," in *The Anthropology of Ethnicity: Beyond "Ethnic Groups and Boundaries,"* ed. Hans Vermeulen and Cora Govers (Amsterdam: Het Spinhuis, 1994), 11–32. In this essay Barth elaborates on his earlier view of ethnicity, giving equal weight to identity and alterity.

6. Anderson, *Imagined Communities,* 6.

7. Laura Newby, "'Us and Them' in Eighteenth and Nineteenth Century Xinjiang," in *Situating the Uyghurs between China and Central Asia,* ed. Ildikó Bellér-Hann et al. (Burlington: Ashgate, 2007); Bellér-Hann, *Community Matters in Xinjiang 1880–1949,* 69, 87.

8. O. F Akimushkin, ed., *Tārīkh-i Kāshgar: Anonimnaiā Tiurkskaiā khronika vladeteleĭ Vostochnogo Turkestana po konet͡s XVII veka: Faksimile Rukopisi Sankt-Peterburgskogo Filiala Instituta Vostokovedeniiā Akademii Nauk Rossii* (Sankt-Peterburg: T͡Sentr Peterburgskoe vostokovedenie, 2001), 100 (f. 98a).

9. Barth, "Enduring and Emerging Issues in the Analysis of Ethnicity," 11–32.

10. Manuscript of Mullah Ḥājī's *Tazkirat al-Bughrā-khān* in author's library, f. 201v.

11. However, another work, the so-called *Nasābnāmah* of Sayyid Qāsim Samarqandī, which was frequently bound alongside Mullah Ḥājī's work, presents the genealogy of the descendants of the Bughrā-khān's daughters, and even reports that the Sayyids of Tashkent, Kasan, and Samarqand (all in Western Turkestan) are descended from these daughters. The author's name suggests an origin in Western Turkestan. As it appears in Altishahri composite manuscripts, the work consists of the story of the virginal conception of 'Alī Arslān-khān, along with the genealogy just described. In some copies the genealogy is omitted or abbreviated, while the conception tale is always present, suggesting that the latter was the more universally compelling element of the work for Altishahris.

12. Saints with a Twelver genealogy include most of the imams of Khotan, Muhammad Sharīf (Yarkand), and Afaq Khoja (Kashgar).

13. Despite the claims of some Yarkandis, the historical Isḥāq Valī Khvāja was most likely buried near Samarqand, where his tomb remains an important site of worship.

14. Informants in Kashgar. For an Afaqi Khoja descendent as of 1993–1994, see Edmund Waite, "From Holy Man to National Villain: Popular Historical

Narratives about Apaq Khoja amongst Uyghurs in Contemporary Xinjiang," *Inner Asia* 8, no. 1 (2006): 19.

15. Gunnar Jarring, *Return to Kashgar: Central Asian Memoirs in the Present,* trans. Eva Claeson (Durham: Duke University Press, 1986), 194.

16. For example, Jarring Prov. 369.

17. Martin Hartmann, "Die Osttürkischen Handschriften der Sammlung Hartmann," *Mitteilungen des Seminars für Orientalische Sprachen an der königlichen Friedrich-Wilhelms-Universität zu Berlin* 7, no. 2 (1904): 1–21; G. Raquette, "Collection of Manuscripts from Eastern Turkestan. An Account of the Contents," in *Across Asia from West to East in 1906–1908,* ed. C. G. Mannerheim (Helsinki: Suomalais-Ugrilainen Seura, 1940), 3–15; Shinjang Uyghur aptonom rayonluq az sanliq millät qädimki äsärlirini toplash, rätläsh, näshir qilishni pilanlash rähbärlik guruppa ishkhanisi, *Uyghur, özbek, tatar qädimki äsärlär tizimliki* (Kashgar: Qäshqär uyghur näshriyati, 1989); Tursunmuhämmät Sawut, *Uyghur ādäbiyati tarikhi materiallar katalogi* (Ürümchi: Shinjang dashö til-ädäbiyat fakulteti, 1991); Gunnar Jarring, Handwritten Catalog of the Gunnar Jarring Collection of Manuscripts from Eastern Turkestan in the Lund University Library, 1997; Lĭudmila Vasil'evna Dmitrieva, *Katalog tĭurkskikh rukopiseĭ Instituta Vostokovedeniia Rossiĭskoĭ Akademii Nauk* (Moscow: Izdatel'skaia firma "Vostochnaia literatura," 2002).

18. I encountered four copies for sale between 2005 and 2010.

19. Rian Thum, "Untangling the Bughrā-Khān Manuscripts," in *Mazars: Studies on Islamic Sacred Sites in Central Eurasia,* ed. Jun Sugawara (Tokyo: Tokyo University of Foreign Studies Press, forthcoming).

20. Jarring Prov. 349, f. 70r.

21. Of course, Khiżr Bābā is likely a fiction, and the precise number used for his age was probably chosen for its mystical significance. The number forty-one appears, for example, as the number of saints' companions in two sections of the *Taẕkirah-i Uvaysīya* that were excerpted as individual tazkirahs: the sections on Sultan Satūq Bughrā-khān (e.g., Jarring Prov. 73, Prov. 148) and the section on 'Abd al-Raḥmān, (e.g., MZXY T70, Berkeley f4MS BP137 1800z). For numbers with mystical significance see Annemarie Schimmel, *The Mystery of Numbers* (New York: Oxford University Press, 1994).

22. The description of Khiżr Bābā's conception and birth make it clear that he is not to be understood as Khiżr the prophet. In general Khiżr Bābā's story is quite different from the stories of Khiżr the prophet that litter the literature, in which the prophet, who is always encountered suddenly and without companions, provides some guidance or a message to be transmitted, and then disappears. Patrick Franke, *Begegnung mit Khidr: Quellenstudien zum Imagindren im Traditionellen Islam* (Stuttgart: Franz Steiner Verlag, 2000); Anonymous, *Iskandarnamah: A Persian Medieval Alexander Romance,* trans. Minoo S. Southgate (New York: Columbia University Press, 1978).

23. Prov. 565.

24. Their shrine is actually located in the foothills of the Karakorum Mountains, southeast of the oasis proper, but they are nearer to Khotan than any other major oasis.

25. *The Tazkirah of Imam A'zam,* which is often found in tazkirah compilations, does not appear to have been an Altishahri text. It was also widely copied in Western Turkestan. While this tazkirah also stands out for not being limited to Altishahr, it cannot be ignored in the discussion of the Eastern Turki tazkirah tradition, because it was so frequently bound together with the local tazkirahs.

26. Engseng Ho, *The Graves of Tarim: Genealogy and Mobility across the Indian Ocean* (Berkeley: University of California Press, 2006), 3.

27. The last foreign saints to die in Altishahr arrived in the seventeenth century.

28. Ho, *The Graves of Tarim.*

29. *Tazkirah of Muhammad Sharif Khwājam.*

30. Or so the situation is represented in the tazkirahs. There were, of course, important Altishahris who left their homeland and gained renown abroad. For example, Mirza Haydar, author of the *Tarīkh-i Rashīdī,* who conquered Kashmir in service of the Mughal ruler Humayun.

31. M. Aurel Stein, *Sand-Buried Ruins of Khotan: Personal Narrative of a Journey of Archaeological and Geographical Exploration in Chinese Turkestan* (London: Hurst and Blackett, 1904), 244.

32. For example, Government of India, "Narrative of the Travels of Khwajah Shah Nukshbundee Syud Who Started from Cashmere on the 28th October, 1852, and Went through Yarkand, Kokan, Bohkara and Cabul, in Search of Mr. Wyburd," *Journal of the Asiatic Society* 4 (1856); Meer Izzut-Oollah, *Travels in Central Asia,* trans. P. D. Henderson (Calcutta: Foreign Department Press, 1872); Thomas Douglas Forsyth, *Report of a Mission to Yarkund in 1873* (Calcutta: Foreign Department Press, 1875).

33. Inscription on an interior wall of the Băysi Hekim Băg shrine, Altunluq cemetery, Yarkand (Uyghur: Yăkăn), photographed July 2007.

34. Dated early graffiti may exist inside the Iskăndăr Vang shrine, but I was only able to document graffiti visible through the gap in the locked doors.

35. C. G. Mannerheim, *Across Asia from West to East in 1906–1908* (Helsinki: Suomalais-Ugrilainen Seura, 1969), 101.

36. Even at Afaq Khoja's shrine, where signs warning against graffiti and careful maintenance have kept the walls of the main tomb building clean, pilgrims have scratched graffiti into the walls of some of the less conspicuous buildings in the complex. Examples of other shrines with extensive graffiti today include the shrines of Imam Ja'far Ṣādiq near Niya, the Four Imams near Khotan, and Ărshiddin in Kucha.

37. Stein, *Sand-Buried Ruins of Khotan,* 312. The full passage is reproduced in Chapter 3 of this book.

38. SP C551.

39. Prov. 73.

40. Prov. 349. The list of rulers is extremely unusual and probably unique to this manuscript.

41. Prov. 565.

42. For example, Mannerheim's copies of the *Tazkirah of the Four Sacrificed Imams* include only Khotan-related tazkirahs.

43. Examples include Prov. 102 and Prov. 565. Many, if not most, tazkirah compilations included material from outside the tazkirah tradition. However, such material nearly always makes up the lesser part of the manuscript and generally appears before the tazkirahs. The choices made by manuscript producers in linking the Altishahri tazkirahs to tales of early Islamic figures are worth a study in their own right. While tales of Muhammad, Fatima, Hasan and Husayn, and earlier prophets such as Moses are the most common, narratives of later figures, such as Abū Ḥanīfah and 'Abd al-Qādir al-Jīlānī, sometimes appear, as in Prov. 73.

44. A handful of such works were written but not widely copied. Only one of them, the Turki translation of Mirza Haydar's *Tārīkh-i Rashīdī,* comes anywhere close to the level of dissemination enjoyed by individual popular tazkirahs, but it omits discussion of nearly all the popular saints.

45. Jarring Prov. 73. The full contents are: the tazkirahs of Imam Muhammad al-Ghazālī (buried near Khotan), Abū al-Naṣr Sāmānī (Artush, near Kashgar), and Sultan Satūq Bughrā-khān (Artush, near Kashgar), Mullah Ḥājī's *Tazkirat al-Bughrā-khān* (saints buried between Kashgar and Yangihissar), and the tazkirahs of Imam A'zam (Abū Ḥanīfah) and Khvājah Muhammad Sharīf (Yarkand). Also included are two treatises on the virtues of 'Abd al-Qādir al-Jīlānī, one in Persian and one in Turki, and the book of secrets *(Rāznāmah)* of Moses.

46. Graffiti in Bǎysi Hekim Bǎg shrine.

47. Justin J. Rudelson, *Oasis Identities* (New York: Columbia University Press, 1998).

48. These identities, were, incidentally, noted by numerous scholars, beginning in the nineteenth century.

49. Dru C. Gladney, "The Ethnogenesis of the Uighur," *Central Asian Survey* 9, no. 1 (1990): 2; Rudelson, *Oasis Identities.*

50. Hodong Kim, *Holy War in China: The Muslim Rebellion and State in Chinese Central Asia, 1864–1877* (Stanford: Stanford University Press, 2004), 3; David John Brophy, "Tending to Unite?: The Origins of Uyghur Nationalism" (PhD dissertation, Harvard University, 2011), 31.

51. Ildiko Beller-Hann, *Community Matters in Xinjiang, 1880–1949: Towards a Historical Anthropology of the Uyghur* (Leiden: Brill, 2008), 51.

52. Joseph Fletcher, "The Heyday of the Ch'ing Order in Mongolia, Sinkiang and Tibet," in *The Cambridge History of China,* vol. 10, *Late Ch'ing, 1800–1911,* pt. 1, ed. John K. Fairbank (Cambridge: Cambridge University Press, 1978), 69.

53. Gunnar Jarring, *Materials to the Knowledge of Eastern Turki: Tales, Poetry, Proverbs, Riddles, Ethnological and Historical Texts from the Southern Parts of Eastern Turkestan,* vol. 4 (Lund: C. W. K. Gleerup, 1951), 162.

54. Ms. Ind. Inst. Turk 3. f. 50r.

55. The cultural, rather than religious, specificity of *Musulmān* is even more dramatically demonstrated in Mullah Bilāl's Ghazāt dar Mulk-i Chīn, wherein the author refers to the local Altishahri dialect of Turki as *Musulmāncha* (something like "Muslimese"), in contrast to the Chinese language spoken by the Dungans (Muslim Chinese). Nazym Bilal, "Kitāb-i Ghazāt Dar Mulk-i Chīn," in *Voina Musul'Man Protiv Kitaitsev: Tekst Nariechiia Taranchi,* ed. Nikolai Pantusov (Kazan: V Univ. Tip., 1880), 46. My thanks to David Brophy for bringing these passages in Bilāl's work and in the *Tazkirah-i ʿAzīzān* to my attention.

56. Jarring Prov. 349.

57. Jarring Prov. 73.

58. Anderson, *Imagined Communities,* 170–178.

59. Fletcher, "The Heyday of the Ch'ing Order in Mongolia, Sinkiang and Tibet," 79.

60. None of these begs nor their shrines entered the tazkirah tradition, however.

61. Mirza Haydar Dūghlāt, *Mirza Haydar Dughlat's Tarikh-i Rashidi: A History of the Khans of Moghulistan,* ed. W. M. Thackston (Cambridge, MA: Harvard University, Department of Near Eastern Languages and Civilizations, 1996); Shāh Maḥmūd Churās, *Khronika,* ed. O. F. Akimushkin (Moscow: Nauka, 1976).

62. Mirza Haydar Dūghlāt, for example, courted Abd al-Rashīd Khan's favor and perhaps hoped to regain his former status in the court at Yarkand by naming his history after the khan. Churās's history flatters the Black Mountain Naqshbandi faction that he patronized.

63. Joseph Fletcher, "Ch'ing Inner Asia c. 1800," in *The Cambridge History of China,* vol. 10, *Late Ch'ing, 1800–1911,* pt. 1, ed. John K. Fairbank (Cambridge: Cambridge University Press, 1978), 75.

64. Julie Meisami, *Persian Historiography to the End of the Twelfth Century* (Edinburgh: Edinburgh University Press, 1999), 146.

65. I count three works that fit this pattern. The only original work written squarely in the dynastic tradition is known from a single copy. This is the *Qiṣaṣ al-Gharāʾib* of Muhammad Niyāz, written at the behest of Muhammad ʿAzīz Wāng, hakim beg of Khotan in 1852. SP D102. See T. I. Sultanov, "Medieval Historiography in Manuscripts from East Turkestan," *Manuscripta Orientalia*

2, no. 1 (1996): 25–30. Despite its title, the *Tazkirah-i 'Azīzān,* a record of the Naqshbandi Khoja rulers down to the Qing conquest, should also be seen as a partial expression of this tradition. It follows the dynastic chronicle's interest in chronological continuity through the regular transfer of power from one individual to the next, and ends precisely with the Qing conquest. At the same time, the work was connected to the Black Mountain Naqshbandi Khojas, whose shrine was in Yarkand, and who continued to be venerated through the nineteenth and twentieth centuries. As such it surely benefitted from the tazkirah-shrine system, which may account for its relative popularity. The third work is the Turki translation of the *Tārīkh-i Rashīdī,* also by Muhammad Niyāz.

66. For lists of these works, see Kim, *Holy War in China,* 263–266.

67. Mullah Mūsá Sayrāmī, *Tārīkh-i Ḥamīdī,* Jarring Prov. 163, f. 1v.

68. Forsyth, *Report of a Mission to Yarkund in 1873,* 88.

69. Martin Hartmann, *Chinesisch-Turkestan: Geschichte, Verwaltung, Geistesleben und Wirtschaft* (Halle: Gebauer-Schwetschke Druckerei und Verlag, 1908), 44.

70. Manuel Castells, *The Power of Identity,* vol. 2 (Oxford: Blackwell, 1997), 8.

5. Saints of the Nation

1. Săypidin Ăzizi, *Sutuq Bughrakhan* (Beijing: Millătlăr năshriyati, 1987).

2. The title character is the same Satūq Bughrā-khan who was known in the manuscript age from his own tazkirah as well as a brief appearance in the most popular tazkirah, Mullah Ḥājī's *Tazkirat al-Bughrā-khān,* and the *Tazkirah-'i Khvājah Muhammad Sharīf.*

3. According to the publication information in the first edition, 13,000 copies were printed in September 1987. The second edition records that 15,500 additional copies were printed in July 1988. Second print runs are not entirely unusual in Xinjiang's publishing industry, but it is unusual for the second run to follow the first so quickly.

4. Sidiq Hăsăn and Ăskăr Hoshur, *Tarikhi yurt Aghu wă Aghuluqlar* (Ürümchi: Shinjang khălq năshriyati, 2002), 230.

5. By "nationalism," I mean here the historically specific complex of cultural, social, technological, and political systems that first arose in the West and spread to much of the world, in the sense described by Benedict Anderson, *Imagined Communities: Reflections on the Origin and Spread of Nationalism* (London: Verso, 1991), and to a lesser extent, Ernest Gellner, *Nations and Nationalism* (Ithaca, NY: Cornell University Press, 1983). At the same time, I recognize, following Partha Chatterjee (and also the Uyghur case), that, despite the early appearance of nationalism in the West, various forms of nationalism around the world have also been shaped by non-Western societies. Partha Chatterjee, "Whose Imagined Community?," *Millennium* 20, no. 3 (1991): 521–525.

6. Justin J. Rudelson, *Oasis Identities* (New York: Columbia University Press, 1998); Gardiner Bovingdon, "Contested Histories," in *Xinjiang: China's Muslim Borderland,* ed. S. Frederick Starr (Armonk, NY: M. E. Sharpe, 2004), 484.

7. Mullah Mūsá Sayrāmī, *Tārīkh-i Ḥamīdī,* Jarring Prov. 163, f. 1v.

8. E. Denison Ross, *Three Turki Manuscripts from Kashghar* (Lahore: Mufid-i-'Am Press, 1908).

9. Joseph Fletcher, "The Heyday of the Ch'ing Order in Mongolia, Sinkiang and Tibet," in *The Cambridge History of China,* vol. 10, *Late Ch'ing, 1800–1911,* pt. 1, ed. John K. Fairbank (Cambridge: Cambridge University Press, 1978), 366.

10. Muhămmătturdi Mirzi'ăkhmăt, ed., *Khotăn khălq nakhsha—küyliri* (Ürümchi: Shinjang khălq năshriyati, 2003).

11. Nazym Bilal, "Kitāb-i ghazāt dar mulk-i Chīn," in *Voĭna musul'man protiv' Kitaĭtsev: Tekst' narĭechiĭa taranchi,* ed. Nikolai Pantusov (Kazan: V Univ. Tip., 1880).

12. This translation from the *Tārīkh-i Amniyya* is based on the translation by Masami Hamada, "Supplement: Islamic Saints and Their Mausoleums," *Acta Asiatica,* no. 34 (1978): 79–105.

13. It is unclear where these manuscripts are now held. Mūsá Sayrāmī, *Tārīkh-i Ḥamīdī,* trans. Ănvăr Baytur (Beijing: Millătlăr năshriyati, 1986), 10.

14. Jarring Prov. 163 f. 2v.

15. Hodong Kim, *Holy War in China: The Muslim Rebellion and State in Chinese Central Asia, 1864–1877* (Stanford: Stanford University Press, 2004).

16. Nathan Light makes this case in detail through his comparison of "the adoption of the ideology of European modernity to the Turkic conversion to Islam," in Nathan Light, "Slippery Paths: The Performance and Canonization of Turkic Literature and Uyghur Muqam Song in Islam and Modernity" (PhD dissertation, Indiana University, 1998).

17. For detailed accounts of the political history of the period, see Andrew D. Forbes, *Warlords and Muslims in Chinese Central Asia: A Political History of Republican Sinkiang 1911–1949* (Cambridge: Cambridge University Press, 1986); Justin Matthew Jacobs, "Empire Besieged: The Preservation of Chinese Rule in Xinjiang, 1884–1971" (PhD dissertation, University of California, San Diego, 2011).

18. Adeeb Khalid, *The Politics of Muslim Cultural Reform: Jadidism in Central Asia* (Berkeley: University of California Press, 1998), 214.

19. My sketch of the émigrés' role in shaping the new Uyghur identity is based on the work of David Brophy, along with that of Sean Roberts. David Brophy, "Taranchis, Kashgaris, and the Uyghur Question in Soviet Central Asia," *Inner Asia* 7, no. 2 (2005): 163–184; David John Brophy, "Tending to Unite?: The Origins of Uyghur Nationalism" (PhD dissertation, Harvard University, 2011); Sean

R. Roberts, "Imagining Uyghurstan: Re-evaluating the Birth of the Modern Uyghur Nation," *Central Asian Survey* 28, no. 4 (2009): 361–381.

20. Khalid, *The Politics of Muslim Cultural Reform.*

21. Abliz Niyaz, "Parlaq Musapă—Shărăplik Ăslimă," in *Hüsăyniyă rohi—tăklimakandiki oyghinish,* ed. Ibrahim Alp Tekin (Ürümchi: Shinjang khălq năshriyati, 2000), 49. For the founding of the school, see Shirip Khushtar, "Musabayov vă uning soda karkhanisi," in *Hüsăyniyă rohi—tăklimakandiki oyghinish,* ed. Ibrahim Alp Tekin (Ürümchi: Shinjang khălq năshriyati, 2000), 37. The 1885 date is cited in many Uyghur-language secondary sources. The source of this date is not cited specifically, but Khushtar had access to archival materials from the Musabayovs' descendants. Shirip Khushtar, "Uyghur yengi ma'aripi vă tăntărbiyisini tarqatquchi aka—uka Musabaylar," in *Hüsăyniyă rohi—tăklimakandiki oyghinish* (Ürümchi: Shinjang khălq năshriyati, 2000), 230.

22. Abdurishit Khojăhmăt, "Qarghiliq nahiyisining 1926 yildin 1936 yilghichă bolghan 10 yilliq tarikhidin ăslimă," *Shinjang tarikhi materiyalliri* 12 (1983): 202, 245.

23. Khushtar, "Musabayov vă uning soda karkhanisi," 36.

24. Adeeb Khalid, "The Emergence of a Modern Central Asian Historical Consciousness," in *Historiography of Imperial Russia: The Profession and Writing of History in a Multinational State,* ed. Thomas Sanders (Armonk, NY: M. E. Sharpe, 1999), 173.

25. Ahmet Kemal, *Çīn Türkistān hatıraları* (Izmir: marifet matbaası, 1925), 35, 55.

26. Săypidin Ăzizi, "Tashkăntkă berip oqush," in *Tashkăntchilăr,* ed. Abdurakhman Abdulla (Ürümchi: Shinjang khălq năshriyati, 2002), 11.

27. Ăzizi, "Tashkăntkă berip oqush."

28. Brophy, "Taranchis, Kashgaris, and the Uyghur Question in Soviet Central Asia," 163–184.

29. This overview of Taranchi discourse is based on Brophy, "Tending to Unite?" It is of course possible that tazkirahs may be discovered for tombs in the Ili valley or Qumul, though is unlikely that they will be found in such numbers as to suggest an important place in the popular tradition.

30. "Uyghur Ne Dimakdur," *Yangī hayāt,* September 13, 1934.

31. Rudelson, *Oasis Identities.*

32. The only sustained study is Donald H. McMillen, *Chinese Communist Power and Policy in Xinjiang, 1949–1977* (Boulder: Westview Press, 1979).

33. Latin-, Cyrillic-, and Arabic-based alphabets were introduced at different periods, but the government eventually settled on a modified Arabic script. This script is different enough from the Perso-Arabic script that had been used before PRC rule that Uyghurs educated only in the new script cannot read manuscripts written in the Perso-Arabic form.

34. Gunnar Jarring, *Return to Kashgar: Central Asian Memoirs in the Present,* trans. Eva Claeson (Durham: Duke University Press, 1986), 105.

35. Hartmann indicates that he had some trouble locating his copy of the *Sacred Edict.* This text and the two practical treatises are cataloged in Martin Hartmann, "Das Buchwesen in Turkestan und die Türkischen Drucker der Sammlung Hartmann," *Mitteilungen des Seminars für Orientalisch Sprachen zu Berlin, Westasiatische Studien* 7 (1904): 100–102. For a more detailed history of the Qing press in Xinjiang, see Masami Hamada, "La Transmission du mouvement nationaliste au Turkestan Oriental (Xinjiang)," *Central Asian Survey* 9, no. 1 (1990): 29–48.

36. The following account of Nur Muhammad's printing projects is based on Hartmann's interview with the printer (whom he calls Nūr al-Dīn Ḥājjī), along with examination of surviving copies of his products.

37. Hartmann, "Das Buchwesen in Turkestan und die Türkischen Drucker der Sammlung Hartmann," 75.

38. Adeeb Khalid, "Printing, Publishing, and Reform in Tsarist Central Asia," *International Journal of Middle Eastern Studies* 26 (1994): 188.

39. The date of 1893–1894 is the date of the earliest surviving example of these editions, call numbers Zu 8393 and Zu 8394 in the Staatsbibliothek zu Berlin.

40. This work, known as *yuzhi quan shan yaoyan* (御製勸善要言) in Chinese and *han-i araha sain be hûwekiyebure oyonggo gisun* in Manchu, was originally published in 1655. Hamada, "La Transmission du mouvement nationaliste au Turkestan oriental (Xinjiang)," 33. According to the colophon of the Kashgar edition, the translation was overseen by the Dao Tai, or Circuit Intendant, of Kashgar.

41. It is represented by two copies in the Jarring collection (Lit. 54, Lit. 88) and five in the Hartmann collection (Zu 8390, Zu 8391, Zu 8392, Zu 8393, and Zu 8394).

42. Nur Muhammad, in an interview with Martin Hartmann, translated into German. Hartmann, "Das Buchwesen in Turkestan und die Türkischen Drucker der Sammlung Hartmann," 75.

43. See call numbers Zu 8393 and Zu 8394 in the Staatsbibliothek zu Berlin.

44. Given its limited audience and secret status, it is no surprise that specimens of this work have not yet materialized.

45. Tursunjan Abduljan and Ibrahim Alp Tekin, "Hüsăyniyă măktipi dăvridiki năshriyatchiliq, mătbă'ătchilik vă hösnkhătchilik," in *Hüsăyniyă rohi—taklamakandiki oyghinish* (Ürümchi: Shinjang khălq năshriyati, 2000), 172–173; Ghăyrătjan Osman, ed., *Uyghur klassik ădăbiyat tarikhi* (Ürümchi: Shinjang ma'arip năshriyati, 2002), 1192. Unfortunately, these authors do not cite sources for this information.

46. Hartmann, "Das Buchwesen in Turkestan und die Türkischen Drucker der Sammlung Hartmann," 75.

47. Only one edition of Tajallī's poems, a double divan, seems to exist. Its title page names the publisher as the Brilliant Rising Sun Press, announces a print run of 1000 copies, and gives the press's location as Kashgar. The author, double divan format, print run, and press location are identical to the project that Nur Muhammad described. I have traced three surviving copies: Princeton University Library, call number 2475.7457.314; Hartmann's copy in the Staatsbibliothek zu Berlin, call number Zv 1396; and a copy in the Xinjiang Academy of Social Sciences Historical and Ethnic Research Institute, listed as number 4201 in Tursunmuhǎmmǎt Sawut, *Uyghur ǎdǎbiyati tarikhi materiallar katalogi* (Ürümchi: Shinjang dashö til-ǎdǎbiyat fakulteti, 1991), 388.

48. It may be that the modern Uyghur claims of Musabayov patronage are incorrect, but the change in the name of the press (from the Press of Ḥājī Muhammad Nūr, as in Prov. Lit. 79, to The Brilliant Rising Sun Press in the Tajallī edition) would be a fitting reflection of a change to a joint venture.

49. Tajallī, *Barq-i Tajallī va sabq-i mujallī*, n.d.

50. I have only been able to trace copies of the *Ṣabāt al-ʿĀjizīn*, representing two editions: AH 1312 (1894–1895), Prov. Lit. 79 and AH 1316 (1898–1899), Prov. Lit. 67.

51. Jamāl al-Dīn Ibn al-Hājib, *Al-kāfiya bil-risāla* (Kashgar: Maṭbaʿ-i Ḥajjī Nūr Muhammad, 1900). Staatsbibliothek zu Berlin call number Zu 262452. The book is not listed in Hartmann's catalog, but markings in Hartmann's hand show this to be part of his collection. This text includes another work that Hartmann calls "Fawāʾidi Hefte," mentioned in the interview with Nur Muhammad as *pawajid*. Martin Hartmann, *Chinesisch-Turkestan: Geschichte, Verwaltung, Geistesleben und Wirtschaft* (Halle: Gebauer-Schwetschke Druckerei und Verlag, 1908), 48; Hartmann, "Das Buchwesen in Turkestan und die Türkischen Drucker der Sammlung Hartmann," 75.

52. Abduljan and Alp Tekin, "Hüsǎyniyǎ mǎktipi dǎvridiki nǎshriyatchiliq, mǎtbǎ'ǎtchilik vǎ hösnkhǎtchilik," 174.

53. Ahmet Kemal, *Çīn Türkistān hatıraları*, 43.

54. Tursun Zerdin, "Ilida gezitning barliqqa kelishi vǎ u besip ötkǎn musapǎ," *Ili dǎryasi* 2 (1995): 88.

55. Forbes, *Warlords and Muslims in Chinese Central Asia*, 39.

56. For examples, see MZXY lithographs T-46, T-77, U-20, a-4, a-62.

57. Jarring, *Return to Kashgar*, 78.

58. Anderson, *Imagined Communities*, 18, 39.

59. Ǎhmǎt Ziya'i, *Asari* (Kashgar: Shingjang gezita idarisi, 1948). Other literary works were published under the second East Turkestan Republic, based in Ili; two literary anthologies, *Almanax* (1947) and *Ǎdǎbiyat—sǎn'ǎt sǎhiri* (1948), are described in Liu Bin, ed., *Uyghur ǎdǎbiyat tarikhi*, vol. 3 (Beijing:

Millătlăr năshriyati, 2006), 473–475. I have been unable to locate specimens of these books.

60. Meitang Wang, "'Ili băykhua geziti' toghrisida," *Shinjang tarikhi materiyalliri* (1990): 375; Zerdin, "Ilida gezitning barliqqa kelishi vă u besip ötkăn musapă," 87, 88; Ălqăm Ăkhtăm and Ismayil Ăsqări, "Ili vilayitidă," *Shinjang tarikhi materiyalliri* 32 (1992): 151.

61. India Office Records, L/P&S/12/2342, P. 4839.1924, British Library, cited in Forbes, *Warlords and Muslims in Chinese Central Asia,* 19.

62. Officially, this date refers to Sheng Shicai's coup. It seems, however, that Uyghurs writing under PRC censorship often use the Uyghur phrase "changes of April" to avoid explicitly mentioning the establishment of the Republic of East Turkestan, a taboo subject. Zunun Qadir, *Khatirilăr* (Ürümchi: Shinjang khălq năshriyati, 1985), 74.

63. *Yangī hayāt,* September 24, 1936.

64. Qadir Măkit, "Azadliktin burunqi 'Aqsu geziti' hăqqidă," *Shinjang tarikhi materiyalliri* 42 (1999): 152.

65. Ismayil Ăsqări, "Azadliqtin ilgiri Shinjangning hărqaysi jaylirida năshir qilinghan gezit—zhurnallar hăqqidă ăslimlăr," *Shinjang tarikhi materiyalliri* 32 (1992).

66. Ibid.

67. G. W. Hunter, "The Chinese Moslems of Turkestan," *The Moslem World* 10 (1920): 168.

68. Among the exceptions to this trend are Islamic publications in Northern Nigeria, many of which are mechanically reproduced manuscripts that maintain the elaborate letter forms expected of sacred texts.

69. Somewhere around half of the surviving tazkirahs are copies produced in the period 1910–1930. See, for example, the examples in Gunnar Jarring, Handwritten Catalog of the Gunnar Jarring Collection of Manuscripts from Eastern Turkestan in the Lund University Library, 1997.

70. In 1927 a certain Ḥājī Ghulām Muhammad wrote a continuation of Sayrāmī's *Tārīkh-i Ḥamīdī.* Jarring Prov. 163 is the only known copy.

71. For an index of Yāvshev's historical pieces, see David Brophy, "Xinjiang in the Turco-Tatar Press: A Partial Bibliography," *Sinoturcica: Research Notes on Inner Asia,* n.d., http://www.sinoturcica.org/xinjiang-in-the-turco-tatar-press-a-partial-bibliography. The two translated works are the untitled, late seventeenth-century chronicle by Shāh Mahmūd Churās, published as *Khronika* by O. F. Akimushkin (Moscow: Nauka, 1976) and Mehmet Atıf's *Kaşgar tarihi ve bais-i hayret ahval-i gari-biyesi* (Istanbul: Mihran matbaası, 1882–1883).

72. Năzărghoja Abdusemătov, *Yoruq sahillar* (Almaty: Zhazushi, 1991).

73. Muhammad Amīn Bughrā, *Sharqī Turkistān tārīkhi* (Srinagar: Bruka Parlis Basmakhanesi, 1946).

74. As with so many of the pre-1949 printed works, I was unable to locate an original edition of Qadiri's history. Fortunately, a modern Turkish translation has appeared. In it, Qadiri describes his reliance on Bughrā's history. Polat Qadiri, *Baturlar: Doğu Türkistan Milli Mücadele Tarihi (1930–1949)* (Ankara: Berikan Yayınevi, 2009), xiii.

75. [Qūtlūgh Shawqī?], "Biznīng tārīkh," *Sharqī Tūrkistān ḥayati,* September 1933, p. 1. It remains possible that an earlier text will be discovered in the future.

76. Zerdin, "Ilida gezitning barliqqa kelishi vă u besip ötkăn musapă," 88.

77. In 1902 a mosque in Kashgar began promoting a fundamentalist agenda, based on literalist interpretation of the Quran and Sunna. Among other radical positions, they opposed shrine veneration and the celebration of Barat. Wang Jianping, "Islam in Kashgar in the 1950s," no date, unpublished article, 15. Wang's article, which is based on archival research, is summarized in more detail in James Millward, *Eurasian Crossroads: A History of Xinjiang* (New York: Columbia University Press, 2009), 247–251.

78. "Biznīng Tārīkh," *Sharqī Tūrkistān ḥayati,* September 1933, p. 1.

79. Sherip Khushtar, *Shinjang yeqinqi zaman tarikhidiki măshhur shăkhslăr* (Ürümchi: Shinjang khălq năshriyati, 2000), 357.

80. Ibid., 358.

81. Abdusemătov, *Yoruq sahillar,* 9.

82. 'Abd al-Ṣamad Oghli, Naẓar Khwāja, "Čïŋğïz sözi ḥaqqında," *Shūrā* 18 (September 15, 1912): 565–566. 'Abd al-Ṣamad Oghli contributed numerous historical essays to *Shūrā* in the 1910s. For a list see David Brophy, "Xinjiang in the Turco-Tatar Press: A Partial Bibliography."

83. Ellsworth Huntington, *The Pulse of Asia: A Journey in Central Asia Illustrating the Geographic Basis of History* (New York: Houghton, Mifflin Company, 1907), 199–200.

84. Wang Jianping, "Islam in Kashgar in the 1950s," no date, unpublished article, 21–22.

85. Millward, *Eurasian Crossroads: A History of Xinjiang,* 251.

86. Ibid., 275; James Millward, *Beyond the Pass: Economy, Ethnicity, and Empire in Qing Central Asia, 1759–1864* (Stanford: Stanford University Press, 1998).

87. Yusupbeg Mukhlisov, *Uyghur klassik ădibiyati qolyazmilirining katalogi* (Ürümchi: Shinjang yerlik muzeygha tăyarliq korush basqarmisi, 1957).

88. Eziz Atavulla Sartekin, *Uyghurchă năshr qilinghan tebbi—ădăbi ăsărlăr katalogi* (Ürümchi: Shinjang khălq săhiyă năshriyati, 2006), 36.

89. Zordun Sabir, *Izdinish* (Ürümchi: Shinjang khălq năshriyati, 1983); Qăyyum Turdi, *Süzük asman* (Beijing: Millătlăr năshriyati, 1985). Additional Cultural Revolution novels followed these.

90. Rudelson, *Oasis Identities;* Bovingdon, "Contested Histories," 484.

91. Ibid.

92. Molla Niyaz Khotăni, "Tot Imam tăzkirisi," *Bulaq* 11 (1984): 68–106.

93. Ibrahim Qurban, *Yăttă Qizlirim* (Kashgar: Qăshqăr Uyghur năshriyati, 1984), 119–120.

94. Molla Haji, *Bughrakhanlar tăzkirisi,* trans. Abdurehim Sabit (Kashgar: Qăshqăr uyghur năshriyati, 1988). The tazkirahs included in this work are the tazkirahs of Abū al-Naṣr Sāmānī and Sultan Satūq Bughrā-khān, both excerpts from the *Tazkirah-i Uvaysīya,* Mullah Ḥājī's *Tazkirat al-Bughrā-khān,* and the *Tazkirah of the Four Sacrificed Imams.* For an analysis of the printed work's relation to the manuscript, see Rian Thum, "Untangling the Bughrā-Khān Manuscripts," in *Mazars: Studies on Islamic Sacred Sites in Central Eurasia,* ed. Jun Sugawara (Tokyo: Tokyo University of Foreign Studies Press, forthcoming).

95. Jarring Prov. 576.

96. Shinjang Aptonom Rayonluq millătlăr til-yeziq khizmiti komiteti lughăt bölümi, *Uyghur tilining izahliq lughiti,* vol. 2 (Beijing: Millătlăr năshriyati, 1991), 138. The word can also indicate an oral utterance, according to Imin Tursun, "Ăllik sangha mubarăk," *Shinjang tăzkirichiliki,* no. 50 (2000): 3.

97. Mărhaba Shavudun, "Tăzkirichilikning bashqa pănlăr bilăn bulghan munasiviti," *Shinjang tăzkirichiliki,* no. 49 (1999): 1; David Nivison, *The Life and Thought of Chang Hsueh-ch'eng (1738–1801)* (Stanford: Stanford University Press, 1966), 192.

98. Uyghur Sayrani, "Zhurnilimizdin bir ümid," *Shinjang tăzkirichiliki,* no. 50 (2000): 1.

99. The term *bi'ografik roman* (biographical novel) appears in the editor's introduction to one of the most recent biographical novels, Ănvăr Tashtömür, *Qălb ărkisi—Năvbăti,* (Ürümchi: Shinjang khălq năshriyati, 2007).

100. Talip Abdulla, *Qaynam urkishi* ([Ürümchi]: Shinjang yashlar năshriyati, 1982); Ăzizi, *Sutuq Bughrakhan,* 1007; Khevir Tömür, *Baldur oyghanghan adăm* (Ürümchi: Shinjang khălq năshriyati, 1987), 375.

101. Walter J. Ong, *Orality and Literacy,* 2nd ed. (New York: Routledge, 2002), 69.

102. Jarring Prov. 413, f. 82r.

103. Ong, *Orality and Literacy,* 69.

104. Ăzizi, *Sutuq Bughrakhan,* 40.

105. The tazkirah of Abū al-Naṣr Sāmānī calls Sultan Satūq Bughrā-khān the son of the king of Kashghar. Gunnar Jarring, *Literary Texts from Kashghar* (Lund: C. W. K. Gleerup, 1980), 95. Sources closer to Satūq Bughrā-khān's own time depict him, instead, as a nomadic leader somewhere in Turkestan. Fernand Grenard, "La Légende de Satok Boghra Khân et l'histoire," *Journal Asiatique* 9, no. 15 (1900): 5–79.

106. For details of the translation and excerpting, see Thum, "Untangling the Bughrā-Khān Manuscripts."

107. The main sons in the tazkirah tradition are Hasan, Husayn, and 'Uṣmān Bughrā-khān. A very rare tazkirah, SP C584, also cites a son named Qilich Bughrā-khān.

108. A shortened form of "Haẓrat Sultānim," namely, "His Holiness, my sultan."

109. It is interesting here to see a participant's experience of the local-regional interface inherent in the tazkirah-shrine system. The shrine system preserves the local emphasis while linking people from across Altishahr. Ăzizi, *Sutuq Bughra-khan*, 1.

110. Ibid., 2.

111. Jarring, *Return to Kashgar,* 136.

112. Ibid.

113. Ăzizi, "Tashkăntkă berip oqush."

114. Săypidin Ăzizi, *Amannisakhan* (Beijing: Millătlăr năshriyati, 1980).

115. Abdulla Qadiri, *Ötkăn künlăr* (Ürümchi: Shinjang Khălq Năshriyati, 1998), 1.

116. Muhămmătturdi Mirzi'ăkhmăt, "Muhărrirdin," in *Năva'i,* Aybek (Ürümchi: Shinjang khălq năshriyati, 2003).

117. Although here the point is that the biographical novel, whatever its precise origins, provided a vehicle for the reemergence of a personage-centered approach to history, it would be interesting to compare the Uzbek and Uyghur biographical novel traditions for signs of both imitation and innovation. For a brief mention of fictionalized biography in Uzbek, see William Fierman, "Uzbek Feelings of Ethnicity: A Study of Attitudes Expressed in Recent Uzbek Literature," *Cahiers du monde russe et soviétique* (1981): 208.

118. Anderson, *Imagined Communities.*

119. Ăzizi, *Sutuq Bughrakhan,* 2.

120. Ibid.

121. Anderson, *Imagined Communities,* 27.

122. Părhat Jilan, *Măhmut Qăshqări* (Ürümchi: Shinjang yashlar-ösmürlăr năshriyati, 1994); Haji Mirzahid Kerimi, *Sultan Abdureshitkhan* (Ürümchi: Shinjang khălq năshriyati, 2000); Abduvăli Ăli, *Apaq Khoja* (Ürümchi: Shinjang khălq năshriyati, 2000).

123. At some point a connection was drawn between a saint called Haẓrat Mullām, who has a tazkirah and a shrine in the town of Opal, and Maḥmūd Kāshgharī. The shrine at Opal is now attributed to Maḥmūd Kāshgharī, but the connection is tentative at best. The tazkirah of Haẓrat Mullām does not suggest that the saint is Maḥmūd Kāshgharī.

124. Foreign-born characters in his books include Bădölăt (Ya'qub Beg), and Măkhdum Ăzăm, both born in the Ferghana Valley.

125. Prov. 563, f. 49v.

126. The textbook also contains a great deal of tendentious and propagandistic interpretation, and elides much factual material that challenges PRC legitimacy in Xinjiang. Shinjang Uighur Aptonom Rayonluq Maarip Komiteti Alii Măktăp Tarikh Dărslikini Tüzüsh Guruppisi, *Shinjangning yărlik tarikhi* (Ürümchi: Shinjang universiteti năshriyati, 1992).

127. He listed the following saints (given here in transcription from modern Uyghur): Amannisakhan, Sutuq Bughrakhan. Măhmut Qăshqări, Abdureshitkhan, Apaq Khoja and Musabay. The last, as far as I can tell, has not yet been the subject of a biographical novel, though he is very much regarded as a nationalist hero for his promotion of new-method education.

128. Anderson, *Imagined Communities,* 109, 113, 114.

129. Bovingdon, "Contested Histories."

130. Turghun Almas, *Uyghurlar* (Ürümchi: Shinjang năshriyati, 1990).

131. Clifford Geertz, *Islam Observed: Religious Development in Morocco and Indonesia* (Chicago: University of Chicago Press, 1971), 14.

6. The State

1. J. A. Millward, "A Uyghur Muslim in Qianlong's Court: The Meanings of the Fragrant Concubine," *The Journal of Asian Studies* 53, no. 02 (1994): 427–458; Thierry Zarcone, "Quand le saint légitime le politique: Le mausolée de Afaq Khwaja à Kashgar," *Central Asian Survey* 18, no. 2 (1999): 225–241; Graham E. Fuller and Jonathan N. Lipman, "Islam in Xinjiang," in *Xinjiang: China's Muslim Borderland,* ed. S. Frederick Starr, new edition (Armonk, NY: M. E. Sharpe, 2004), 320–352; Alexandre Papas, *Soufisme et politique entre Chine, Tibet et Turkestan: étude sur les Khwâjas Naqshbandîs du Turkestan oriental* (Paris: J. Maisonneuve, 2005); Edmund Waite, "From Holy Man to National Villain: Popular Historical Narratives about Apaq Khoja amongst Uyghurs in Contemporary Xinjiang," *Inner Asia* 8, no. 1 (2006): 5–28.

2. For the archival view, see Millward, "A Uyghur Muslim in Qianlong's Court."

3. Sign at the White Mountain Khoja tomb, erected by the Kashgar City Cultural Relics Protection and Management Bureau.

4. "Ethnic unity" promotions were particularly prominent in the months after the July 5, 2009 uprising. See, for example, a banner at the bottom of the *Wulumuqi wanbao* (August 11, 2009), which says, "Ethnic unity is the lifeline of Xinjiang's ethnic people." For a photograph of "ethnic unity" banners on military vehicles, see Rian Thum, "The Ethnicization of Discontent in Xinjiang," *The China Beat,* October 2, 2009, http://www.thechinabeat.org/?s=905.

5. Jarring Prov. 363.

6. Fuller and Lipman, "Islam in Xinjiang"; Waite, "From Holy Man to National Villain"; Millward, "A Uyghur Muslim in Qianlong's Court."

7. Justin J. Rudelson, *Oasis Identities* (New York: Columbia University Press, 1998); Gardner Bovingdon and Nabijan Tursun, "Contested Histories," in *Xinjiang: China's Muslim Borderland,* ed. S. Frederick Starr (Armonk, NY: M. E. Sharpe, 2004), 353–374.

8. In one version of the most popular biography of Afaq from the manuscript period, the saint is ridiculed by the children of Kashgar for being an outsider. He then asks his father, "Where did we come from?" His father answers, "Oh dear child, we came from Dahbid." Jarring Prov. 369, 26v.

9. Here I refer to the hereditary leadership of the *tariqāt* as opposed to purely spiritual succession. Around the same time, the significance of descent from prestigious figures, especially Chinggis Khan and the prophet Muhammad, also grew in significance. See Papas, *Soufisme et politique entre Chine, Tibet et Turkestan.*

10. Abduvăli Ăli, *Apaq Khoja* (Ürümchi: Shinjang khălq năshriyati, 2000); Bovingdon and Tursun, "Contested Histories," 371.

11. For example, Mawlānā Shaykh, *Maqāmāt-I Khvājah Aḥrār: Tazkirah-'i Khvājah Nāṣir Al-Dīn 'Ubayd Allāh Aḥrār (806 Tā 895 Q.)* (Tokyo: Institute for the Study of Languages and Cultures of Asia and Africa, 2004). Further examples are described in C. A. Storey, *Persian Literature: A Bio-Bibliographical Survey,* vol. 1, pt. 2, (London: Luzac and Company, 1972).

12. O. F Akimushkin, ed., *Tārīkh-i Kāshghar: Anonimnaĭa Tĭurkskaĭa khronika vladeteleĭ Vostochnogo Turkestana po koneĭs XVII veka: Faksimile Rukopisi Sankt-Peterburgskogo Filiala Instituta Vostokovedeniĭa Akademii Nauk Rossii* (Sankt-Peterburg: TSentr Peterburgskoe vostokovedenie, 2001); Shāh Maḥmūd Churās, *Khronika,* ed. O. F. Akimushkin (Moscow: Nauka, 1976); Mīr Khāl al-Dīn Yarkandī, *Hidāyatnāma,* 1730–1731, MS Or. 8162, British Library.

13. Shāh Maḥmūd Churās, *Anīs Al-Ṭālibīn,* 1695–1713, 84r–88r, MS Ind. Inst. Pers. 45, Bodleian Library.

14. Based on his 1929–1930 visit, Gunnar Jarring reported Chinese language flags at the shrine brought by Chinese Muslims. Gunnar Jarring, *Return to Kashgar: Central Asian Memoirs in the Present,* trans. Eva Claeson (Durham: Duke University Press, 1986), 193.

15. Akimushkin, *Tārīkh-i Kāshghar,* 7.

16. Ibid., ff. 101r–101v.

17. "falak ghidār u makkār" Bodleian MS Ind. Inst. Pers. 45, f. 105v.

18. As is discussed below, these views would fade from prominence in the face of the popular tazkirah tradition but later resurface in nationalist historiography.

19. The *Tazkirat al-Ḥidayāt,* also called *Manāqib-i tarjima-yi Hidāyat Allah Khvājam.* My dating is based mainly on the style, in combination with the fact that, like the *Hidāyatnāmah,* it was written in Persian, a language that was rarely used for original compositions in Altishahr after the mid-eighteenth century. The alternate title is cited by Papas, *Soufisme et politique entre Chine, Tibet et Turkestan,* 239. No investigation of the relationship between this work

and the *Hidāyatnāmah* has yet been published. An examination of Bodleian MS Ind. Inst. Pers. 122 *(Taẕkirat al-Hidāyat)* and British Museum (now in the British Library) Or. 8162 *(Hidāyatnāmah)* reveals many shared passages. I have been unable to examine the four copies in Tashkent: IVANRUz numbers 10051/2, 12501/2, 12666/1, 1156/6.

20. IVANRUz 12501/2 was copied in 1292, AH (1875–1876). A unique history of Hasan Khoja, written no earlier than the 1870s, was recently discovered in the Ferghana Valley (Kawahara 2006).

21. The find locations of manuscripts suggest readership in both Altishahr and Western Turkestan. For a list of manuscripts, see Rian Thum, "Beyond Resistance and Nationalism: Local History and the Case of Afaq Khoja," *Central Asian Survey* 31, no. 3 (2012): 307.

22. *Long Ahong* (Linxia: Gansu sheng Linxia shi Mingde Qingzhensi, 1996), 20–21; Joseph Trippner, "Islamische Gruppen und Gräberkult in Nordwest-China," *Die Welt des Islams* 7, no. 1/4 (1961): 143,148; Fuller and Lipman, "Islam in Xinjiang," 321; Papas, *Soufisme et politique entre Chine, Tibet et Turkestan.*

23. In the Chinese *Long Ahong* (1996), Afaq's reputation rests less on his miraculous powers and leadership of the *tariqat,* and more on his learning. He appears in the work mainly as a sought-after teacher.

24. Bancroft Library, University of California, Berkeley, call number 4MS BP189.7.N35.A23 1700z (misidentified as *Jāmiʻ al-Maqāmāt*) and a manuscript in China. For details see Thum, "Beyond Resistance and Nationalism," 307.

25. Jarring Prov. 369 and Prov. 48.

26. I will refer to Turki translation of the work by this name, though each known copy has a slightly different title. In addition to the popular translation, there is another Turki version known from a single manuscript, which includes material from the *Jāmiʻ al-Maqāmāt* regarding early Naqshbandi ancestors, followed by much of the material from the *Lives of the Loyal,* and then a history of the White Mountain Khojas through the first decades of the nineteenth century. The manuscript, entitled *Silsilat al-Ẕahāb,* is reproduced in Bahargül Hamut, *Silsilat aẕ-Ẕahab: Kommentierung einer čaġatai-uigurischen Handschrift zu den Aqtaġliq Ḫoǧilar, einer mystischen Gruppierung in Xinjiang im 16.–18. Jahrhundert* (Berlin: Klaus Schwarz Verlag, 2011).

27. This excludes the unique *Silsilat al-Ẕahāb,* which is an entirely different version. IOL MSS Turki 9: *Risālah-yi Tadhkīrat al-Hidāyat bil-Khayriyat;* Jarring Prov. 22: *Taẕkirah-i Ḥaẕrat Sayyid ʼĀfāq Khvājam;* National Library of India acc. no. 940: *Taẕkirah -i Sayyid ʼĀfāq Khvāja;* Jarring Prov. 363: *Ḥaẕrat Sayyid ʼĀfāq Khvājaning tasralar.* The word *tasra* is clearly a corruption of *tazkirah.*

28. Jarring Prov. 369.

29. ʻAbdallah Nidāʼī, "Shīrīn Shamāʼil," 1752, MS Aşir Efendi 411, Süleymaniye Library; Muhammad Zalīlī, *Zălili divani,* trans. Imin Tursun (Beijing: Millătlăr năshriyati, 1985).

30. Zalīlī, *Zălili divani*. For a summary of Zalīlī's travelog and itinerary, see Alexandre Papas, *Mystiques et vagabonds en Islam: Portraits de trois soufis qalandar* (Paris: Cerf, 2010).

31. IOL MSS Turki 9 calls it "Afaq Khoja's tomb." All European visitors also called it the shrine of Afaq, presumably following the local usage.

32. Clarmont Percival Skrine, *Chinese Central Asia* (New York: Houghton Mifflin, 1926), 184.

33. Ahmet Kemal, *Çīn Türkistān hatıraları* (Izmir: marifet matbaası, 1925), 94.

34. Ibid., 83, 85.

35. Jarring Prov. 48, Prov. 22. These were copied from now-lost specimens that do not otherwise appear in the archives, but they lack any marks of readership or deployment in indigenous contexts, which are often found on texts made for indigenous customers.

36. *ahl-i tā'rīkh* (literally, the people of history) Jarring Prov. 22, ff. 51r, 51v, 52r, 57r, 61v.

37. Hartmann 1316 and Jarring Prov. 369, respectively.

38. IOL MSS Turki 9, 129v.

39. The two manuscripts that contain this colophon are IOL MSS Turki 9 (1893) and IVANRUz 3426 (blundered date of 1100 AH). The hands are completely different, with the IVANRUz 3426 copyist's writing of much lower quality, eliminating the possibility that both manuscripts were copied by the same person. Another manuscript, to which I have not had access, is attributed in the catalog to Muhammad 'Alī Mirza, and may also contain a claim to copying at the tomb. Shinjang Uyghur aptonom rayonluq az sanliq millăt qădimki ăsărlirini toplash, rătlăsh, năshir qilishni pilanlash răhbărlik guruppa ishkhanisi, *Uyghur, özbek, tatar qădimki ăsărlăr tizimliki* (Kashgar: Qăshqăr Uyghur năshriyati, 1989), 196, MS XKQ 987.

40. Jarring Prov. 22, Hartmann 1316, and IOL MSS Turki 9.

41. Prov. 369 and Prov. 48.

42. Jarring Prov. 22, f. 62r.

43. However, he did promote veneration of his father's shrine, and he visited many holy sites during his preaching tours. Papas, 2005.

44. His tazkirah has his followers attending *ṣuḥbat* (discussion) focused on the *Maṣnavi* of Rumi on Fridays and Tuesdays.

45. Jarring Prov. 22, f. 62r.

46. Jarring, *Return to Kashgar*, 194.

47. Only one copy is bound with another text: Jarring Prov. 48 includes a *"Nūrnāma sharīf."*

48. For example, the Dzungar Mongols.

49. Bodleian MS Ind. Inst. Turk. 3, f. 20a–b; Hartmann MS Or. f. 3292. Cited and translated in Minoru Sawada, "Three Groups Tadhkira-i Khwājagān: Viewed from the Chapter on Khwāja Āfāq," in *Studies on Xinjiang Historical Sources in*

17–20th Centuries, ed. James A. Millward, Shinmen Yasushi, and Jun Sugawara (Tokyo: Toyo Bunko, 2010), 16. I have altered Sawada's translation slightly.

50. Admittedly the first two of these armies were at least Muslim, but as we have seen, religious identity was not a main theme for the nationalists.

51. Năzărghoja Abdusemătov, *Yoruq sahillar* (Almaty: Zhazushi, 1991), 17.

52. *Erkin Turkestan* November 15, 1933.

53. Muhammad Amīn Bughrā, *Sharqī Turkistān tārīkhi* (Srinagar: Bruka Parlis Basmakhanesi, 1946), 336.

54. Bughrā, *Doğu Türkistan: Tarihî, Coğrafî ve Şimdıki Duruku* (Istanbul: Güven Basimevi, 1952), 18.

55. Henry G Schwarz, *Chinese Policies towards Minorities: An Essay and Documents* (Bellingham, WA: Center for East Asian Studies, Western Washington Univ., 1971), 52–52.

56. Wang Jianping, "Islam in Kashgar in the 1950s," no date, unpublished article, 22.

57. Inscription on the wall of the shrine, 1956.

58. Between 1978 and 2007 domestic tourist income grew from 1.84 billion yuan to 777.1 billion yuan. Chris Ryan and Gu Huimin, eds., *Tourism in China: Destination, Cultures and Communities* (New York: Routledge, 2008).

59. These were gone by the time of Gunnar Jarring's 1978 visit. Jarring, *Return to Kashgar,* 194.

60. The opposite policy applies to the Ordam Padishah system, which has been scrupulously closed to visitors and pilgrims of all kinds since the late 1990s. Thierry Zarcone, "Le culte des saints au Xinjiang de 1949 à nos jours," *Journal of the History of Sufism* 3 (2001): 133–172, and author's field notes, summer 2005.

61. Hartmann papers, B192, Halle.

62. Millward, "A Uyghur Muslim in Qianlong's Court."

63. Sign at the Apaq Khoja shrine, photographed summer 2004. The exact same text is included in an anonymous photocopied book about Kashgar tourist sites, entitled *Daoyou Shouce (Handbook for Guides)* May 2005.

64. Xinjiang Association of International Cultural Exchange, *Kashi Luyou Tour in Kashgar* (Ürümchi: Xinjiang Meishu Sheying Chubanshe, 2001), no page numbers. The Chinese text is less far-fetched: *sucheng,* indicating a popular or colloquial name.

65. This was preceded by a play and film.

66. Edward W. Said, *Orientalism* (New York: Random House, 1979); Stevan Harrell, "Introduction," in *Cultural Encounters on China's Ethnic Frontiers,* ed. Stevan Harrell (Seattle: University of Washington Press, 1995), 3–36.

67. Xinjiang Weiwu'er Zizhiqu Jaioyu Ting and Xinjiang Lishi Jiaocai Bianxie Zu, *Xinjiang difang shi* (Ürümchi: Xinjiang Daxue chubanshe, 1991), 9. See also Jarring, *Return to Kashgar,* 29.

68. Waite, "From Holy Man to National Villain."

69. See ibid., 15 for a more detailed account of the shrine's role in the community of Hăzrăt, the neighborhood in which the shrine is situated.

70. Ăli, *Apaq Khoja.*

71. Contemporary understandings of Afaq Khoja are of course more varied than those presented in Ăli's novel, and even include interpretations directly at odds with Ăli's claims. Another historical novel, *Jallat Khenim,* which itself reflects much of Ăli's animosity toward Afaq Khoja, has also become quite influential: Yasinjan Sadiq Choghlan, *Jallat Khenim* (Ürümchi: Shinjang khălq năshriyati, 2003). Ăli's work also builds upon the writings of historians such as Ibrahim Niyaz, Ănwăr Batur, and Nizamidin Hüsăyin, all of whom published significant studies of Afaq Khoja beginning in the 1980s: Ănvăr Batur, "Apaq Khoja hăqqidă muhakimă," *Shinjang Sifăn Dashö ilmiy zhurnali* 3 (1987): 57–70; Nizamidin Hüsăyin, "Qabahăt 'ăqidă' yănă bir qetim Appaq Khoja toghrisida," *Shinjang mădăniyiti* 2, no. 3 (1989): 113–154; Ibrahim Niyaz, *Tarikhtin qiskichă bayanlar* (Kashgar: Qăshqăr uyghur năshriyati, 1989). Chinese and select Western views of Afaq's history have also entered Uyghur discourse through a study by Liu Zhengyin and Wei Liangtao that was published in Chinese in 1998 and in a Uyghur translation in 2006; Wei Liangtao and Liu Zhengyin, *Xiyu Hezhuo jiazu yanjiu* (Beijing: Zhongtuo shehui kexue chubanshe, 1998); Wei Liangtao and Liu Zhengyin, *Khojilar jămăti hăqqidă* (Beijing: Millătlăr năshriyati, 2006). Edmund Waite has documented another earlier negative view of Apaq as "spy," which differs from both Bughrā and Ăli's approaches. This vague narrative suggests a connection to Xiang Fei that is not significant in Ăli's novel or in the views of the urban youths I interviewed in 2000–2010. Waite, "From Holy Man to National Villain."

72. Waite, "From Holy Man to National Villain."

73. However, views inspired by Ăli's novel seem to be more prevalent among urban Uyghurs. Rural informants, particularly those from among the minority of Uyghurs who still participate in inter-oasis shrine pilgrimage, were more likely to view Afaq as a saint.

74. Choghlan, *Jallat Khenim.*

75. Ăli, *Apaq Khoja,* 1–2.

76. Batur, "Apaq Khoja hăqqidă muhakimă"; Hüsăyin, "Qabahăt 'ăqidă' yănă bir qetim Appaq Khoja toghrisida"; Niyaz, *Tarikhtin qiskichă bayanlar.* Some of these and other contemporary views are described in Waite, "From Holy Man to National Villain."

77. Ăli, *Apaq Khoja,* 74, 99, 150, 299.

78. Bovingdon and Tursun, "Contested Histories," 371.

79. Benedict Anderson, *Imagined Communities: Reflections on the Origin and Spread of Nationalism* (London: Verso, 1991), 29.

80. Robert Shaw and Ney Elias, "The History of the Khojas of Eastern-Turkistan," *Journal of the Asiatic Society of Bengal,* extra no. to LXVI, pt. 1

(1897): 39n19; Ăli, *Apaq Khoja,* 171. The *Tazkirah-i Azīzān* has more in common with the chronicle tradition than it does with the popular tazkirahs.

81. Ăli, *Apaq Khoja,* 169–170.

82. His son Hasan seemed to be on the way to such status, though his tazkirah is rare, and his burial place, said to be the White Mountain shrine in some traditions, has primarily been associated with Afaq.

83. Another interesting example can be found in the terminology regarding Afaq's father, Muhammad Yūsuf. In the popular tazkirah of Afaq, he is called Mazār Padshāhim (My King of the Shrine) after the tomb in which he is buried. The White Mountain tomb is, in turn, sometimes named after him, being called the "tomb of the king of the shrine."

84. Fuller and Lipman, "Islam in Xinjiang."

85. I have seen no manuscripts with copy dates between the late 1950s and the early 1980s. However, the tradition has since recovered.

86. Jonathan Z. Smith, *To Take Place: Toward Theory in Ritual* (Chicago: University of Chicago Press, 1987).

87. Just as there were exceptions to the rule of foreign birth in the tazkirah tradition, for example, Satuq Bughrā-khan and Afaq Khoja, there is an exception to the rule of local birth in the nationalist tradition: Yūsuf Khaṣṣ Ḥājib was from Balasaghun, in today's Kirghizstan. Outside Altishahr, he is better known as Yūsuf Balāsāghūnī. It is probably significant that Uyghurs have removed the geographical element from his name.

88. Waite, "From Holy Man to National Villain." Waite believed negative traditions regarding Afaq to be much more recent than the tradition outlined here, tracing them no further than the period of PRC rule, namely, after 1949, and seeing them as "a creative response to historical obfuscation and state propaganda surrounding the tomb."

89. In addition to nationalist discourse, historical habits that might best be described as elements of the Western academic tradition, with its focus on chronology, and Chinese historiography, with its dynastic emphasis, made inroads into Altishahri historical practice throughout the twentieth century.

90. Valerio Valeri, "Constitutive History: Genealogy and Narrative in the Legitimation of Hawaiian Kingship," in *Culture through Time: Anthropological Approaches,* ed. Emiko Ohnuki-Tierney (Stanford: Stanford University Press, 1990), 154–192.

Conclusion

1. Yusupbeg Mukhlisov, *Uyghur klassik ădibiyati qolyazmilirining katalogi* ([Ürümchi?]: Shinjang yerlik muzeygha tăyarliq korush basqarmisi, 1957), 29.

2. Rian Thum, "Untangling the Bughrā-khan Manuscripts," in *Studies on the Mazar Cultures of the Silk Road,* ed. Jun Sugawara, forthcoming.

3. Jan Vansina, *Oral Tradition as History* (Madison: University of Wisconsin Press, 1985).

4. Incredibly, the (largely oral) teaching of university history courses and the dominance of oral performance at academic conferences is often ignored as a part of historical practice.

5. Anthony Smith, *The Antiquity of Nations* (Cambridge: Polity, 2004), 186.

6. In its pure form, Qing indirect rule lasted from 1760 to 1864, but this period was also framed by other forms of loose outsider rule, namely, Dzungar overlordship ca. 1680 to 1760, and rather loose China-based rule from 1877 through the 1930s.

ACKNOWLEDGMENTS

This work would have been impossible to produce without the generous assistance of a great number of people. Most importantly, I want to express my deepest gratitude to the many Uyghur men and women who shared their knowledge and welcomed my investigations in their communities, sometimes at no small risk to their own interests. It is shameful that so many learned and generous contributors must remain anonymous. There are many whom I long to thank individually, but since I cannot, I thank them collectively for their shared characteristics: welcoming in even the most sacred and intimate matters, voracious in the study of history, generous with trade secrets, open to strange and disagreeable opinions, patient with linguistic weaknesses, and loyal in friendship.

My deepest gratitude goes to Mark Elliott, who, in addition to unfailing support in every aspect of my studies, devoted more time and thought to my project than could ever be expected. His insights and his shrewd but gentle critiques have been indispensable.

I am also very much indebted to Engseng Ho, who not only engaged my project carefully when I was his student but has continued to do so in the ensuing years. The influence of his work on this project is, I think, obvious. Thanks also to Cemal Kafadar, who was always willing to help at short notice.

Conversations with and comments from Magnus Fiskesjo, Steve Caton, James Millward, Devin DeWeese, and Oktor Skjaervo have been extremely useful. Jun Sugawara and David Brophy have been extraordinarily generous with their sources and deep knowledge of Altishahr's history. Jeff Eden, Joshua Freeman, and Eric Schluessel have also pointed me to critical sources on more than one occasion. Jonathan Lipman generously shared photocopies from the elusive *Long Ahong*. For comments on the final draft, I am indebted to the generosity and insight of Chris Washington and Paul Buehler. Michael Krautkraemer and Ava D'sa contributed valuable research assistance. For advice and inspiration, I thank Chris Victor-McCawley and Marcus Rautman.

Comments from the anonymous peer reviewers far exceeded my expectations, and strengthened the book immeasurably. Anonymous reader #1, drop me a line sometime.

Portions of Chapters 2, 3, and 4 are reprinted from Rian Thum, "Modular History: Identity Maintenance before Uyghur Nationalism," *Journal of Asian Studies,* vol. 71, no. 3 (August 2012): 627–653, © the Association for Asian Studies. Portions of Chapter 6 are reprinted from Rian Thum, "Beyond Resistance and Nationalism: Local History and the Case of Afaq Khoja," *Central Asian Survey,* vol. 31, no. 3 (September 2012): 293–310, © Southseries, Inc.

I wish to thank Loyola University New Orleans, which provided critical research leave time and travel funding, and the members of the History Department for warm, collegial support. Thanks are due also to Harvard's Inner Asian and Altaic Studies Committee, which provided the kind of flexible program necessary for the interdisciplinary study out of which this book grew.

The rare book room at Lund University Library stands out among archives for the staff's hospitality, professionalism, openness, and enthusiasm. Librarians at St. Petersburg's Institute of Oriental Studies were also extremely kind, and I am indebted to the librarian at the Nationalities University's Minzu Xueyuan Library for accommodating my rather last-minute request for a visit. I am grateful to Harvard University, the U.S. Department of Education's Foreign Language and Area Studies grant, the Sheldon Fellowship, and Loyola University New Orleans's Marquette Fellowship, all of which provided funding for this project. Thanks also to Gertrud Raquette for her warm hospitality. For generously providing one of her haunting images of Uyghur shrines for the cover, I am indebted to Lisa Ross, whose book of photographs, *Living Shrines of Uyghur China,* I strongly recommend.

Thanks go to my family members, especially Rick and LuAnn Thum, who have always provided moral support and unflagging optimism.

And thanks not least to my adventurous wife, Laura, for brilliant insights, sound advice, selfless support, and, more specifically, invaluable comments on drafts. Much of what is good in this study is attributable to her.

Errors and shortcomings are of course entirely my own.

INDEX

abbreviation of texts, 73–74
advice literature, 35–36
Afaq Khoja, 10; biography, 214–216; death, 216; histories, 217–219, 232, 241–244, 303n19, 308n83, 308n87; made local saint, 221–223; and nationalism, 228–232; and PRC, 232–234; proximity to present, 240; reputation, 212–213, 236–239, 240, 307n71, 307n73; transregional fame, 220–221, 304n23. *See also* White Mountain shrine
Afrāsiyāb, 25
Akhon, Abdu Vali, 115–116
Akhūnd, Ibn ʿAlī, Khvājah, 221, 223
Alexander romances, 34–35
Ăli, Abduvăli, 237–238, 244
Almas, Turghun, 194
alterity and identity formation, 135, 136, 150, 288n5
Altishahr, 3–4, 5–6, 124, 258n7
Altishahri, use of term, 6–7
Altunluq shrine complex, 235
Amannisakhan, 235, 306n65
Anderson, Benedict, 4, 135, 161, 183, 202, 208–209, 250, 287n2
anthologies: containing non-tazkirah material, 291n43; and development of tazkirah genre, 94; geographical consistency, 147; geographic networks, 133–134; and regional identity, 148–150, 291n44; selection

of contents, 90–92, 281n147, 290n25
Anwār-i Suhaylī, 35–36, 37
Apaq Khoja (Ăli, Abduvăli), 216, 237–238, 244
Arabic alphabet, 82, 172
archives, 28–29
Assmann, Jan, 2, 275n67
audible reading, 63–65, 273n40
authenticity/authority: of biographical novels, 206–207; despite plasticity of text, 89, 93–94; indicated by marginalia, 35; and origin of texts, 17–18, 25–26, 246; and place, 9, 22–23, 112–113; of printed texts, 88–89, 206–207; and relevancy, 54; of shrines, 106, 248–249, 284n35; of tazkirahs, 93–94, 168–169, 248–249, 284n35
authorship: absence of indicated, 51; collective, 275n63; and revisions, 69, 72–73; serial composition, 69; social, 275n63; source documentation, 65–69; stability in written texts, 247. *See also* community authorship
Awakening Land, The (Ötkür), 194
Ayni, Sadriddin, 62, 261n27
Ăzizi, Săypidin, 86, 110, 164–165, 199–203, 204, 205, 293nn2–3

Babur, 39
Barat devotions, 100–101, 108–109, 111, 223

313